D0846105

A BURNS COMPANION

A BURNS COMPANION

ALAN BOLD

St. Martin's Press   New York

RO122191762
HUMCA

HOUSTON PUBLIC LIBRARY

© Alan Bold 1991

All rights reserved. For information, write:
Scholarly and Reference Division,
St. Martin's Press, Inc., 175 Fifth Avenue,
New York, N.Y. 10010

First published in the United States of America in 1991

Printed in Hong Kong

ISBN 0–312–04500–X

Library of Congress Cataloging-in-Publication Data
Bold, Alan Norman, 1943–
A Burns companion / Alan Bold.
p.   cm.
Includes bibliographical references.
ISBN 0–312–04500–X
1. Burns, Robert, 1759–1796. 2. Poets, Scottish – 18th century –
Biography.   I. Title.
PR4331.B64   1991
821'.6 –dc20   89–70109
[B]   CIP

INDEXED IN ___MLA___

Contents

List of Plates

The author and publishers wish to acknowledge with thanks the following illustration sources, and to state that in cases where they may have failed to contact all copyright holders, they will be pleased to make the necessary arrangement at the first opportunity.

Preface

This Companion has been designed as a biographical and critical guide to Burns, indicating the personal outlines and social background of the personality; and assessing the most important poems and songs in some detail. It is in six parts.

Part I places Burns in context. The Chronology follows his career, 'The Burns Circle' describes his friends and enemies, and the Topography looks at those places that meant most to him as a man and a poet.

Part II explores significant Burnsian issues. Short essays on his use of language and technique frame discussions of his position with regard to religion, politics, philosophy, drink, drama and sex.

Part III is a more extended essay on Burns as a poetic phenomenon and, with its consideration of role-playing and reality, is intended to stimulate debate about the relevance of Burns to his time and ours.

The longest section of the book, Part IV: 'The Art of Burns', examines twenty-five poems, eighteen verse epistles and twenty-six songs. It also comments on his other writings: Election Ballads, Epigrams and Epitaphs, the Letters and the Common Place Books.

A Select Bibliography (Part V) and four Appendixes (Part VI) are followed by a Glossary of Scots words, a general index, and an index of poems.

The aim of the Companion is to inform and advise on the complex nature of this seemingly uncomplicated poet. This Companion is complete in itself in that biographical allusions and literary echoes in the poems discussed are elucidated and the poet's critical reputation is considered. Burns, of course, speaks for himself through the extensive quotations.

*　　　*　　　*

I would like to thank Oxford University Press for allowing me to make reference, throughout this Companion, to James Kinsley's monumental three-volume edition of *The Poems and Songs of Robert Burns* (1968); and the same editor's one-volume version of that edition, *Burns: Poems and Songs* (1969), available as an Oxford Paperback. I am similarly grateful to James A. Mackay for allowing me to make reference to his two editions, both authorised by the Burns Federation: *The Complete Works of Robert Burns* (1986) and *The Complete Letters of Robert Burns* (1987). Part III of the Companion, 'An Approach to Burns', adapts material from two sources: my essay 'Robert Burns: Superscot' from *The Art of Robert Burns*, edited by R. D. S. Jack and Andrew Noble and published by Vision Press (London) and Barnes and Noble (Totowa, New Jersey) in 1982; and my article 'Skulduggery with the Bard's Brains' in the *Observer Scotland* (22 January 1989).

I am indebted to two colleagues for professional advice and assistance: Sarah Roberts-West, my thoughtful editor at Macmillan Press; and Anthony Grahame, who edited the text of the Companion. Finally, I would like to thank two friends: Thomas Crawford, of Aberdeen University, who read the book in typescript and made useful comments; and Frank McAdams, of Strathclyde University, who kindly and expertly indexed the book.

A.B.

Abbreviations

Poems are cited with reference to two sources: the number assigned to them in James Kinsley's three-volume *The Poems and Songs of Robert Burns* (1968) and his one-volume *Burns: Poems and Songs* (1969), available as an Oxford Paperback; and the page numbers from James A. Mackay's one-volume *The Complete Works of Robert Burns* (1986), authorised by the Burns Federation. Thus 'Tam o Shanter' (321/CW, 410–15) indicates that the poem is numbered 321 by Kinsley and printed on pp. 410–15 of Mackay's edition.

For further details about the titles listed below, see the Select Bibliography.

AL   The Autobiographical Letter of 2 August 1787 from Burns
            to Dr John Moore (see Appendix C).

BE   Maurice Lindsay, *The Burns Encyclopedia* (3rd edn., 1980).

CB   Raymond Lamont Brown (ed.), *Robert Burns' Common
            Place Book* (1969).

CH   Donald A. Low (ed.), *Robert Burns: The Critical Heritage*
            (1974).

CL   James A. Mackay (ed.), *The Complete Letters of Robert
            Burns* (1987).

Crawford   Thomas Crawford, *Burns: A Study of the Poems and Songs*
            (1960).

Currie   James Currie, *The Works of Robert Burns* (1800; rept. 1815,
            ed. Alexander Peterkin)

CW   James A. Mackay (ed.), *The Complete Works of Robert Burns*
            (1986).

Fitzhugh   Robert T. Fitzhugh, *Robert Burns: The Man and the Poet* (1970).

GN   Gilbert's Narrative (see Appendix D).

Hecht   Hans Hecht, *Robert Burns: The Man and His Work* (1936; rept. 1971), containing Robert Heron's *Memoir* (1797).

Kinsley   James Kinsley (ed.), *The Poems and Songs of Robert Burns* (3 vols, 1968).

Snyder   Franklyn Bliss Snyder, *The Life of Robert Burns* (1932).

Part I:
Burns in Context

Part I:
Burns in Context

A Burns Chronology

1757   On 15 December, William Burnes (1721–84) marries Agnes Broun (1732–1820) and moves, with her, into the two-roomed clay thatched cottage he has built on land he has leased in Alloway.

1759   Robert Burns, the first of seven children, is born on 25 January in his parents' cottage, 'The auld clay biggin' ('The Vision'). One day after his birth he is baptised, in the Auld Kirk of Ayr, by the liberal Rev William Dalrymple, 'D'rymple mild' ('The Kirk's Alarm'). Ten days after his birth, a storm blows out the gable above the fireplace: 'Our monarch's hindmost year but ane/Was five-and-twenty days begun,/'Twas then a blast o Janwar win'/Blew hansel in on Robin' ('Rantin, Rovin Robin').

1760   On 28 September, Gilbert Burns is born. Other children are: Agnes (1762–1834), Annabella (1764–1832), William (1767–90), John (1769–85), Isabella (1771–1858).

1765   William Burnes and four neighbours hire, turn about, the services of an Alloway schoolmaster John Murdoch (1747–1824) who teaches Robert and Gilbert at the village school thereby established: 'Gilbert always appeared to me to possess a more lively imagination and to be more of the wit, than Robert' (Murdoch, cited by Snyder, 43).

1766   William Burnes rents, for £40 per year, the 70-acre hilltop farm of Mount Oliphant (two miles from the cottage) and stocks it on the strength of a £100 loan from his landlord, Provost William Fergusson of Ayr (who still employs Burnes as a gardener). Unfortunately the farm has 'the very poorest soil I know of in a state of cultivation' (GN).

1768   Murdoch leaves Alloway and William Burnes takes personal charge of his sons' education. 'He borrowed Salmon's *Geo-*

3

graphical Grammar for us, and endeavoured to make us acquainted with the situation and history of different countries in the world; while, from a book society in Ayr, he procured for us Durham's *Phisico and Astro-Theology*, and Ray's *Wisdom of God in Creation*, to give give us some idea of astronomy and natural history. Robert read all these books with an avidity and industry scarcely to be equalled' (GN).

1769   Provost William Fergusson, William Burnes's landlord, dies on 7 November. 'My father's generous Master died; [Mount Oliphant] farm proved a ruinous bargain; and, to clench the curse, we fell into the hands of a Factor who sat for the picture I have drawn for one in my Tale of two dogs' (AL).

1772   Robert and Gilbert attend Dalrymple parish school, week about, during the summer quarter. Gilbert recalls: 'a bookish acquaintance of my father's procured for us a reading of two volumes of Richardson's *Pamela*, which was the first novel we read' (GN). On Mount Oliphant farm, Robert 'at the age of thirteen, assisted in threshing the crop of corn' (GN). Murdoch, now teaching English at the burgh school in Ayr, sends Robert and Gilbert 'Pope's works, and some other poetry' (GN).

1773   With an interruption to help with the harvest at Mount Oliphant, Robert is sent to Ayr for three weeks to lodge with Murdoch and study grammar, French and a little Latin. Burns is considered 'a sort of prodigy' at French (GN).

1774   At Mount Oliphant, Burns 'at fifteen was the principal labourer on the farm, for we had no hired servant, male or female' (GN). In the autumn, after working at the Mount Oliphant harvest, Burns first commits 'the sin of RHYME' (AL), writing the song 'Handsome Nell' for Nelly Kilpatrick, a farmer's daughter: 'As bonie lassies I hae seen,/And monie full as braw,/But for a modest gracefu' mien/The like I never saw' ('Handsome Nell').

1775   In the summer Burns studies mathematics under Hugh Rodger at Kirkoswald: 'I made a pretty good progress. – But I made greater progress in the knowledge of mankind . . . learned to look unconcernedly on a large tavern-bill, and mix without fear in a drunken squabble' (AL). He is distracted from his studies by Peggy Thomson, celebrated as 'my lovely charmer' in the song 'Now Westlin Winds'. Burns reads Thomson and Shenstone.

1777   At Whitsun, William Burnes moves from Mount Oliphant to Lochlea farm, Tarbolton, renting 130 swampy acres for £130 per year (a pound an acre) from David McLure. 'For four years we lived comfortably here . . . I was, at the beginning of this period, perhaps the most ungainly, aukward being in the parish' (AL). Burns reads Shakespeare, Allan Ramsay and delights in *The Lark*, an anthology of Scots and English songs: 'The Collection of Songs was my vade mecum. – I pored over them, driving my cart or walking to labor, song by song, verse by verse' (AL).

1779   In the winter, Burns goes to a Tarbolton country dancing school against his father's wishes: 'from that instance of rebellion he took a kind of dislike to me, which, I believe was one cause of that dissipation which marked my future years' (AL). Around this time Burns reads Locke's *Essay Concerning Human Understanding*.

1780   Burns, his brother Gilbert, and six friends form the Tarbolton Bachelors' Club on 11 November. At the first meeting, in John Richmond's house, Burns is elected president for the night: one of the rules of the debating club specifies that 'Every man proper for a member of this Society . . . must be a professed lover of one or more of the female sex' (BE, 20).

1781   Burns makes romantic overtures to Alison Begbie, and is rejected: 'a belle-fille whom I adored and who had pledged her soul to meet me in the field of matrimony, jilted me with peculiar circumstances of mortification' (AL). William Burnes in dispute with McLure, his landlord. In Spring, Burns goes to seaport of Irvine to learn trade of flax-dressing. On 4 July, Burns is admitted as a freemason to St David's Lodge, No. 174, Tarbolton.

1782   On 1 January, the Irvine flax-dressing shop 'by the drunken carelessness of my Partner's wife, took fire and was burnt to ashes; and left me like a true Poet, not worth sixpence' (AL). Burns returns to Lochlea. Among his favourite books are Richardson's *Pamela*, Smollett's *The Adventures of Ferdinand Count Fathom*, Sterne's *Tristram Shandy*, Henry Mackenzie's *The Man of Feeling*.

The Second Edition of Fergusson's *Poems* is published and Burns buys a copy: 'Rhyme, except some religious pieces which are in print, I had given up; but meeting with Fergusson's Scotch Poems, I strung anew my wildly-sounding, rustic lyre with emulating vigour' (AL).

On 24 September the dispute between William Burnes and McLure is referred to arbiters.

1783 The *Glasgow Mercury* (16–23 January) notes that Burns won a prize of £3 for his linseed growing. In April he begins his first Common Place Book. On 17 May a warrant of sequestration is operated against William Burnes who, on 25 August, makes his first appeal to the Court of Session, Edinburgh. As a precaution against ruin, Robert and Gilbert Burns secretly arrange to rent, for £90 per year from Gavin Hamilton, the 180–acre upland farm of Mossgiel, about three miles from Lochlea, in Mauchline parish.

1784 On 27 January the Court of Session upholds William Burnes who is, however, physically and financially exhausted by the litigation. On 12 February, Burns's dog Luath is 'killed by the wanton cruelty of some person' (Gilbert Burns, cited by Kinsley, 1104). William Burnes dies on 13 February and, the following month, Burns and his family move into Mossgiel.

During the summer Burns almost succumbs to nervous breakdown and is treated by his brother mason, Dr John Mackenzie. On 27 July, Burns is elected Depute Master of St James's Lodge, Kilwinning, Tarbolton. Burns continues to see Elizabeth Paton, formerly a servant of his father, at her home in Largieside.

1785 In April, during Mauchline's Race Week, Burns meets Jean Armour – one of 'The Belles of Mauchline' – at a dance. On 22 May, 'Dear-bought Bess', his illegitimate daughter by Betty Paton, is born. Two days later the child is baptised and acknowledged by Burns as his daughter. He and Betty do public penance in Mauchline kirk, and he is fined a guinea: 'Before the Congregation wide,/I passed the muster fairly,/My handsome Betsy by my side,/We gat our ditty rarely' ('The Fornicator').

In September, Burns signs a paper attesting his marriage to Jean. In October Burns's youngest brother, John, dies and that month the poet completes his first Common Place Book.

1786 In March, Jean's father, master mason James Armour, faints when he hears of her pregnancy. Burns accepts a job as a plantation book-keeper in Port Antonio, Jamaica: 'As he had not sufficient money to pay for his passage [Gavin] Hamilton advised him to publish his poems . . . as a likely way of getting a little money' (GN). Burns plans publication of *Poems, Chiefly in the Scottish Dialect* and on 3 April sends Proposals for the book to the Kilmarnock printer, John

Wilson, who publishes the Proposals on 14 April: 'As the Author has not the most distant Mercenary view in Publishing, as soon as so many Subscribers appear as will defray the necessary Expence, the Work will be sent to the Press' (cited by Kinsley, 970).

On 14 April, James Armour has Burns's marriage attestation mutilated by Bob Aiken: 'old Mr Armour prevailed with [Aiken] to mutilate that unlucky paper . . . when he told me, the names were all cut out of the paper, my heart died within me, and he cut my very veins with the news' (CL, 66). Burns's outrage is indicated in 'The Lament': 'O! can she bear so base a heart,/So lost to honour, lost to truth,/As from the fondest lover part,/The plighted husband of her youth?' During April, Burns sees emigration to Jamaica as an opportunity to escape from pressing problems: 'Already the holy beagles, the houghmagandie pack, begin to snuff the scent; & I expect every moment to see them cast off, & hear them after me in full cry: but as I am an old fox, I shall give them dodging & doubling for it; & by & bye, I intend to earth among the mountains of Jamaica' (CL, 110).

Burns embarks on his affair with 'Highland' Mary Campbell and on 14 May the couple meet, at Failford, and plan to marry and emigrate together: 'we spent the day in taking a farewel, before she should embark for the West-Highlands, to arrange matters among her friends for our projected change of life' (cited by Kinsley, 1183).

On 10 June, Jean Armour confesses by letter to Mauchline Kirk Session that she is pregnant by Burns; on 12 June, the day before copy for the Kilmarnock Edition goes to the printer, Burns explains 'I have tryed often to forget [Jean]: I have run into all kinds of dissipation and riot, Mason-meetings, drinking matches, and other mischief, to drive her out of my head, but all in vain: and now for a grand cure, the Ship is on her way home that is to take me out to Jamaica, and then, farewel, dear old Scotland, and farewel dear, ungrateful Jean, for never, never will I see you more!' (CL, 111).

On 25 June, Burns agrees to stand three Sundays in kirk for rebuke in order to be obtain a certificate from Daddie Auld pronouncing him a free bachelor: 'Wi pinch I put a Sunday's face on,/An snoov'd awa before the Session/I made an open, fair confession' ('Reply to a Trimming Epistle'). Burns makes his first public penance for fornication on 9 July: 'I . . . was indulged in the liberty of standing in my own seat . . . . Jean and her friends insisted much that she should stand along with me in the kirk, but the minister would not allow it, which bred a great trouble' (CL, 112).

Knowing that Burns is to publish a volume of verse, James Armour persuades Jean to sign a complaint seeking security in a capital sum for the support of her offspring by the poet. To protect his assets from Armour, Burns (22 July) transfers his share in Mossgiel to Gilbert; conveys to Gilbert any profits that may arise from the Kilmarnock Edition; and gives Gilbert, as trustee for the child Elizabeth Paton, the copyright of the poems so he will be able to 'aliment clothe and educate [my natural daughter Elizabeth Paton] in a suitable manner as if she was his own' (cited by Snyder, 127). Burns is alarmed that 'Armour has got a warrant to throw me in jail till I find security for an enormous sum' (CL, 78): to escape service of the writ against him Burns, at the end of July, goes into hiding, 'sculking from covert to covert under all the terrors of a Jail' (AL). He writes to John Richmond on 30 July: 'My hour is now come. – You and I will never meet in Britain more. – I have orders within three weeks at farthest to repair aboard the Nancy, Captain Smith, from Clyde, to Jamaica, and to call at Antigua' (CL, 77–8).

The Kilmarnock Edition of *Poems, Chiefly in the Scottish Dialect* appears on 31 July in an edition of 612 copies, costing three shillings each, published by subscription, printed and issued by John Wilson. James Armour softens in his attitude to Burns, Jean regrets that her father pressurised her into signing the complaint, Burns feels safe enough to return to Mossgiel though 'The warrant is still in existence' (CL, 78). On 6 August, Burns and Jean Armour make their last public penitential appearance in kirk before Daddy Auld who formally rebukes them and warms them to 'Beware of returning to your sin as some of you have done, like the dog to his vomit, or like the sow that is washed to her wallowing in the mire' (cited by Snyder, 126).

Burns postpones his Jamaican voyage on 1 September, and on Sunday, 3 September, is at Mossgiel when he is told (by Jean's brother) that Jean has given birth to twins (Robert and Jean): 'poor Armour has repaid my amorous mortgages double' (CL, 87). On 4 September (in a letter that is passed to Burns) the blind poet and critic Thomas Blacklock praises the Kilmarnock Edition and suggests 'a second edition, more numerous than the former' (CH, 62). Burns is apparently overwhelmed by the praise: 'a letter from Dr Blacklock to a friend of mine overthrew all my schemes by rousing my poetic ambition' (AL). On 27 September he again postpones the Jamaican voyage as he plans a second edition of his poems. In October, Mary Campbell dies at Greenock, possibly in premature childbirth induced by typhus: the same month the *Edinburgh Magazine* carries the first of three extracts from the Kilmarnock Edition.

To Burns, the journey to Jamaica has become a pointless exercise and he considers other options (around 8 October): 'I have been feeling all the various rotations and movements within, respecting the excise. There are many things plead strongly against it . . . [Several] reasons urge me to go abroad; and to all these reasons I have only one answer – the feelings of a father' (CL, 93).

On 15 November, Burns begins his correspondence with Mrs Dunlop. Encouraged by the response to the Kilmarnock Edition, he decides to go to Edinburgh. On Monday morning, 27 November, Burns begins ride, on a borrowed pony, to the capital, arriving the next day (Kinsley, 979), with a hangover, to stay in John Richmond's room in Baxter's Close, Lawnmarket.

On 1 December, Elizabeth Paton accepts £20 as settlement of her financial claim on Burns. On 7 December, Burns writes to tell Gavin Hamilton that the Earl of Glencairn has persuaded the Caledonian Hunt to subscribe for 100 copies of a second edition. On 9 December, Henry Mackenzie's review of the Kilmarnock Edition appears in the *Lounger*: Burns is acclaimed as 'this Heaven-taught ploughman' (CH, 70). On 14 December, William Creech issues subscription bills for the First Edinburgh Edition of *Poems, Chiefly in the Scottish Dialect* (in all, 2876 copies are subscribed for).

1787   On 7 January, Burns writes to tell Gavin Hamilton he has met a pretty girl (believed by Snyder, 219, to be Margaret Chalmers), 'a Lothian farmer's daughter, whom I almost persuaded to accompany me to the west country, should I ever return to settle there' (CL, 67). On 14 January, Burns is considering a proposal from Patrick Miller to lease a farm near Dumfries: 'I dare say he means to favour me, yet he may give me, in his opinion, an advantageous bargain that may ruin me' (CL, 100).

On 1 February, the Canongate Kilwinning Lodge, Edinburgh's most influential masonic group, affiliates Burns as a member. Five days later Burns writes to the Bailies of the Canongate, requesting permission to erect a stone over Robert Fergusson's unmarked grave in the Canongate parish cemetery.

On 22 March Burns completes his corrections to the proofs of the First Edinburgh Edition of *Poems, Chiefly in the Scottish Dialect* which is published on 17 April; on 23 April he sells his copyright to Creech for one hundred guineas.

From 5 May to 1 June – during which time (22 May) the first volume of James Johnson's *Scots Musical Museum* is published – Burns makes the first of four vacation tours, his Border tour with Robert Ainslie. Burns, riding his recently purchased mare Jenny Geddes, arrives in Coldstream on Monday, 7 May, and crosses the Tweed into England: Ainslie records that, once in England, Burns 'prayed for and blessed Scotland most solemnly, by pronouncing aloud, in tones of the deepest devotion, the two concluding stanzas of the "Cotter's Saturday Night"' (cited by Snyder, 236, who thinks the anecdote apocryphal). Burns visits Jedburgh, Melrose, Selkirk, Ettrick, Duns, Berwick, Eyemouth (where, on 19 May, he is honoured by St Abb Masonic Lodge). On Sunday, 27 May, Burns crosses the Tweed for his second sojourn in England, riding as far south as Newcastle. On 2 June, Burns (then in Dumfries) receives May Cameron's appeal for help, having given birth to his child; Burns writes Ainslie to 'send for the wench and give her ten or twelve shillings, but don't for Heaven's sake meddle with her as a *Piece*' (CL, 332). While in Dumfries, Burns looks over Patrick Miller's vacant farm property on Dalswinton estate and, on 4 June, he is made an Honorary Burgess of Dumfries.

Returning to Mossgiel on 8 June, he makes his way to Mauchline village to see Jean: 'On my eclatant return to Mauchline, I was made very welcome to visit my girl [with the] usual consequences' (CL, 149).

Before the end of June, Burns tours the West Highlands as far as Inverary and Arrochar. A letter of 30 June explains how he fell from his horse, Jenny Geddes, in a drunken race by the side of Loch Lomond: 'Jenny Geddes trode over me with such cautious reverence, that matters were not so bad as might well have been expected; so I came off with a few cuts and bruises, and a thorough resolution to be a pattern of sobriety for the future' (CL, 120). Burns is made a Burgess of Dumbarton on 29 June.

On 8 August Burns returns (via Glasgow) to Edinburgh, initially staying at Richmond's room in Baxter's Close. A few days later he moves to William Nicol's home in Buccleuch Square. On 15 August he is discharged from May Cameron's writ demanding security for the support of her expected child.

From 25 August to 16 September, Burns tours Highlands with Nicol, travelling in a chaise: 'Nicol thinks it more comfortable than horse-back, to which I say, Amen: so Jenny Geddes goes home to Ayr-shire' (CL, 330). In a tour lasting twenty-two days and covering some 600 miles, Burns is irritated by Nicol and impressed by the sights (recorded in his Journal of a Tour in the Highlands, published in facsimile, 1927). On Sunday, 26 August, Burns visits Bannockburn and sees 'the hole where glorious Bruce set his standard' (cited by Snyder, 244); the next day he visits Gavin Hamilton's relatives at Harvieston (Margaret Chalmers is away on this occasion). On Thursday, 30 August, he visits the falls of Aberfeldy ('The braes ascend like lofty wa's,/The foamy stream deep-roaring fa's', he writes in 'The Birks of Aberfeldie'); next morning he hears Neil Gow play, then travels through the pass of Killiecrankie and spends night at Blair Castle, seat of the Duke of Athole, where he remains for two days and meets Robert Graham of Fintry. On Tuesday, 4 September, he visits 'Castle Cawdor – where Macbeth murdered King Duncan – Saw the bed in which King Duncan was stabbed' (cited by Snyder, 247); the next day he comes down Loch Ness to Foyers ('Among the healthy hills and ragged woods/The roaring Fyers pours his mossy floods', he writes in 'Lines on the Falls of Fyers'). On 6 September, Burns crosses Culloden Moor then passes through Kildrummie, Nairn, Brodie, Forres and Elgin, reaching Castle Gordon, at Fochabers, on Friday, 7 September. Two days later he is in Aberdeen and on 13 September in Montrose, home of his cousin James Burness. He and Nicol sail to Arbroath, then travel to Dundee, Perth, Kinross and – on Sunday, 16 September – cross the Firth of Forth to Queensferry, thence to Edinburgh.

Back in Edinburgh Burns attempts, unsuccessfully, to obtain the money Creech owes him; writes to Patrick Miller, confirming his interest in Ellisland farm; sees James Johnson to discuss the progress of the *Scots Musical Museum*.

From 4–20 October, Burns goes on a fourth vacation trip (his third Highland tour), touring Stirlingshire with Dr James Adair. Anxious to see Margaret Chalmers (the real love of the poet's life, according to Snyder, 25) he spends eight days at Harvieston, Clackmannanshire, where he proposes marriage and is rejected: in these eight days, during which he made excursions to the surrounding countryside, Burns 'lived more of a real life with [Margaret Chalmers] than I can do with almost any body I meet with in eight years' (CL, 237). Burns visits Dunfermline Abbey and returns to Edinburgh (20 October) with a miserable cold.

Back in Edinburgh, Burns hears of the death of his infant daughter Jean. At the end of October he accepts, from William Cruickshank, the offer of a room at 2 St James's Square. In November he begins serious work on Johnson's *Scots Musical Museum*, goes to Linlithgow where he is made a Burgess and Guild Brother of the Burgh, and meets Patrick Miller at Dalswinton to discuss the lease of Ellisland farm. Creech's London agents, Strahan and Cadell, bring out a third edition of Burns's poems during November.

December is the month that defines Burns's relationship with Mrs Agnes McLehose: he meets her on the 4th, dislocates his knee in a fall from a carriage on the 7th and, thus immobilised, on the 28th begins his celebrated correspondence with Mrs McLehose, the 'Clarinda' to his 'Sylvander'.

1788   Burns makes his first visit to Clarinda's home (General's Entry, Potterrow) on 4 January; three days later he writes asking Graham of Fintry to be his patron in the Excise. The second volume of the *Scots Musical Museum* is published on 14 February. On 18 February Burns leaves Edinburgh, arriving (via Glasgow, with two days at Dunlop House) in Mauchline five days later: he rents a room in the Backcauseway (in the house of Dr John Mackenzie) for himself and Jean, now in an advanced state of pregnancy. On 23 February he writes, from Mossgiel, to Mrs McLehose on the subject of Jean: 'I, this morning, as I came home, called for a certain woman. – I am disgusted with her; I cannot endure her! I, while my heart smote me for the prophanity, tried to compare her with my Clarinda: 'twas setting the expiring glimmer of a farthing taper beside the cloudless glory of the meridian sun . . . . I have done with her, and she with me' (CL, 399).

Before the end of the month he visits Ellisland and, when he returns to Mauchline, he writes to Ainslie (on 3 March, the day of Jean's confinement) 'I took the opportunity of some dry horse litter, and gave [Jean] such a thundering scalade that electrified the very marrow of her bones' (CL, 331): Jean gives birth to twin girls who die (on 10 and 22 March).

About a week after the birth of the twins, Burns returns to Edinburgh to settle with Creech, arrange for Excise instructions, sign the lease for Ellisland (on 18 March) and bid farewell to Mrs McLehose. On 20 March he leaves Edinburgh for Mauchline where he finds Jean in distress: 'I found a once much-loved and still much lov'd Female, literally & truly cast out to the mercy of the naked elements' (CL, 147–8). At the end of March, Burns marries Jean Armour: according to the Train manuscript, 'Jean Armour and Rob Burns were privately married in the writing office of Gavin

Hamilton, Mauchline' (BE, 52).

After a course of Excise instruction (April–May) at Mauchline and Tarbolton, Burns goes to Ellisland on 11 June but, no farmhouse being ready, stays alone in a hut near the tower of Isle, a mile down the river from Ellisland. Through Patrick Miller, he meets (in June) Captain Robert Riddell of Friars' Carse, a house and estate on the river Nith, near Ellisland. Riddell gives Burns a key to his grounds and the poet enjoys writing in the little summer-house, or hermitage, built by Riddell: on 28 June Burns writes his 'Verses in Friars' Carse Hermitage'.

An American reprint of the First Edinburgh Edition is published, on 7 July, in Philadelphia.

On 14 July, an Excise commission is issued to Burns. On 5 August, Rev Auld and the Mauchline Kirk Session recognise the authenticity of Burns's marriage to Jean. On 10 September Burns sends his 'Epistle to Robert Graham, Esq., of Fintry, Requesting a Favour'; as well as asking for an Excise apppointment, Burns explains 'If I were in the service, it would likewise favor my Poetic schemes. – I am thinking of something, in the rural way, of the Drama-kind' (CL, 426).

During September Burns commutes between Nithsdale and Mauchline; in November Jenny Clow bears him a son; and in December Jean joins her husband at the Isle, Nithsdale.

During December a reprint of the First Edinburgh Edition, with a selection of Fergusson's poems, is published in New York.

1789   Burns goes to Edinburgh (16 February) to settle accounts with Creech and deal with Jenny Clow's writ (settled 27 February). He does not visit Mrs McLehose on this visit: 'I would have called on you when I was in town, indeed I could not have resisted it, but [Robert Ainslie] told me that you were determined to avoid your windows while I was in town, lest even a glance of me should occur in the street' (CL, 406). He returns to Ellisland on 28 February, finding the farmhouse still unready.

By April Burns is acting as librarian and treasurer of the Monkland Friendly Society (organised by himself and Robert Riddell) and is considering which books to order for the circulating library; he is busy writing songs for the third volume of the *Scots Musical Museum*. In May he is reading Adam Smith's *Wealth of Nations*: 'I could not have given any mere *man*, credit for half the intelligence Mr Smith discovers in his book' (CL, 428).

Burns meets Captain Francis Grose at Friars' Carse in June or July, by which time Burns and Jean are living in the still unfinished Ellisland farmhouse where, on 18 August, Francis Wallace Burns is born. On 1 September the poet begins work as an Excise officer at a salary of £50 per year: 'But what d'ye think, my trusty fier?/I'm turn'd a gauger – Peace, be here!' ('Epistle to Dr Blacklock').

October finds Dumfries 'Election-mad' (CL, 179). Though more Whig than Tory, Burns dislikes the Tory candidate, Captain Patrick Miller (son of the poet's landlord), and detests his patron, the 4th Duke of Queensberry, as his Election Ballads indicate: 'The turn-coat Duke his king forsook,/When his back was at the wa', man' ('Election Ballad for Westerha'', second version).

On 16 October, Burns is present as a witness to the drinking-contest, for the prize of an ebony whistle, between Robert Riddell, Sir Robert Lawrie and Alexander Fergusson of Craigdarroch (who won by drinking upwards of five bottles of claret): 'I sing of a Whistle, a Whistle of worth,/I sing of a Whistle, the pride of the North' ('The Whistle').

Riding up to forty miles a day in all weathers, as an exciseman, affects Burns's health: on 13 December he complains 'For now near three weeks I have been so ill with a nervous head-ach, that I have been obliged to give up for a time my Excise-books, being scarce able to lift my head, much less to ride once a week over ten muir Parishes' (CL, 181).

Still, Burns (23 December) has 'some thoughts of the Drama' (CL, 499): he has become friendly with George Sutherland, manager of the Dumfries theatre, and is contemplating a Scottish play.

1790   Weary of working Ellisland farm, as well as discharging his Excise duties, Burns writes to his brother Gilbert on 11 January: 'This farm has undone my enjoyment of myself. – It is a ruinous affair on all hands . . . . If once I were clear of this accursed farm, I shall respire more at ease' (CL, 358).

On 27 January, Burns is listed as eligible for promotion to Examiner or Supervisor of Excise. He longs for promotion since, he writes on 2 February, he is depressed by the current demands of the Excise: 'I am a poor, damn'd, rascally Gager, condemned to gallop at least 200 miles every week to inspect dirty Ponds & yeasty barrels' (CL, 315).

In February he writes to Mrs McLehose: 'I have, indeed, been ill, Madam, this whole winter. An incessant headache, depression of spirits, and all the truly miserable consequences of a deranged nervous system, have made dreadful havoc of my health and peace' (CL, 406).

Burns is enthusiastic about the inaugural meeting of subscribers of the Dumfries theatre on 18 February: 'A new theatre is to be built by subscription . . . Three hundred guineas have been raised by thirty subscribers' (CL, 347).

On 9 July, Burns writes to Mrs Dunlop: 'I have just got a summons to attend with my men-servants armed as well as we can, on Monday at one o'clock in the *morning* to escort Captain Miller from Dalswinton in to Dumfries to be a Candidate for our Boroughs which chuse their Member that day' (CL, 189). In the election of 12 July, Captain Miller is victorious.

On 24 July, the month Burns is transferred to the Dumfries Third Division of Excise, his younger brother William dies in London. Burns completes 'Tam o Shanter' by 1 November and sends copy to Grose on 1 December.

1791   Towards the end of January Burns is injured in fall with horse. On 30 January the Earl of Glencairn dies: 'God knows what I have suffered, at the loss of my best Friend, my first and dearest Patron & Benefactor; the man to whom I owe all that I am & have!' (CL, 506). 'Tam o Shanter' first appears in print in the *Edinburgh Herald* of 18 March 1791.

Anna Park, the barmaid of the Globe Inn, Dumfries, gives birth (31 March) to Burns's daughter Elizabeth; just over a week later (9 April) Jean gives birth to the poet's son William Nicol Burns at Ellisland.

'Tam o Shanter' is published, in April, as a footnote in the second volume of Grose's *Antiquities of Scotland*. By 27 April Burns has completed the copying of the Glenriddell Manuscript, two calf-bound volumes, one containing fifty-two poems, the other containing twenty-seven of the poet's letters. In May, Burns sends thirteen songs to Johnson; from 19–22 June he returns to Ayrshire to attend Gilbert's wedding to Jean Breckenridge of Kilmarnock.

Burns's crops are auctioned at Ellisland on 25 August and on 10 September he formally renounces the Ellisland lease. Burns moves (11 November) to three-room apartment in Wee Vennel (now Bank Street), Dumfries.

Burns visits Edinburgh (29 November–11 December): on 6 December he meets Mrs McLehose for the last time, at Lamont's Land; on 27 December he sends her 'Ae Fond Kiss' from Dumfries.

1792   In February, Burns is promoted to the Dumfries Port Division of Excise, compact enough to be covered on foot: his salary rises to £70 a year with the possibility of an additional £20 in perquisites. On 29 February Burns, with other excisemen, captures the smuggling schooner *Rosamond* at Gretna (the story that he obtained four carronades and sent them to the French Convention to demonstrate his revolutionary sympathies has been disputed, notably by Snyder, 396: 'The whole thing would do full justice to Gilbert and Sullivan'; but see 'Burns and Politics').

On 10 April Burns is made an honorary member of the Royal Company of Archers; on 16 April he offers Creech new material for a new edition of his poems: 'A few Books which I very much want, are all the recompence I crave, together with as many copies of this new edition of my own works as Friendship or Gratitude shall prompt me to *present*' (CL, 306).

During the summer Burns is reading Tom Paine's *The Rights of Man* (1791–2) and endorsing his argument against Burke's romantic rhetoric in defence of the French aristocracy.

In August the fourth volume of *Scots Musical Museum* is published: 'Burns's most substantial contribution was made to this volume: over sixty songs newly made, or communicated with some revision, in a collection of one hundred' (Kinsley, 1380). On 16 September he agrees to contribute to George Thomson's *Select Scottish Airs*. In October he begins work on the fifth volume of *Scots Musical Museum*, writing to Johnson: 'give a copy of the Museum to my worthy friend, Mr Peter Hill, Bookseller, to bind for me interleaved with blank leaves, exactly as he did the laird of Glenriddell's, that I may insert every anecdote I can learn, together with my own criticisms and remarks on the songs. A copy of this kind I shall leave with you, the Editor, to publish at some after period, by way of making the Museum a book famous to the end of time, and you renowned for ever' (CL, 297).

On 3 November, Burns writes to Captain William Johnston, subscribing to his radical newspaper, the *Edinburgh Gazetteer*, launched that month: 'Go on, Sir! Lay bare, with undaunted heart & steady hand, that horrid mass of corruption called Politics & State-Craft! (CL, 681).

The poet's daughter, Elizabeth Riddell Burns (named after Robert Riddell's wife), is born on 21 November.

On 6 December, Burns writes to Mrs Dunlop about political unrest in Dumfries: 'in our Theatre here, "God save the king" has met with some groans & hisses, while Ça ira [the French revolutionary song] has been repeatedly called for' (CL, 202). About a week later Burns, accompanied by Dr Adair, makes a four- day visit to Dunlop House to see Mrs Dunlop. Before the end of the month an informer denounces Burns, to the Excise Board, as unpatriotic, as being 'head of a disaffected party' (CL, 436): on 31 December, John Mitchell, Collector of Excise, is instructed by his Board to investigate Burns's political conduct.

1793   On 5 January, Burns defends his political position in a letter to Robert Graham of Fintry, protesting that he honours the British Constitution and has become disillusioned with revolutionary France: 'I was her enthusiastic votary at the beginning of the business. – When she came to shew her old avidity for conquest, in annexing Savoy, &c. to her dominions, & invading the rights of Holland, I altered my sentiments' (CL, 437). Burns survives as an exciseman.

On 7 January, Burns tells George Thomson he wants to be closely involved with *Select Scottish Airs*: 'I would wish to give you my opinion on all the poetry you publish [as] it is my trade; & a man in the way of his trade may suggest useful hints that escape men of much superiour parts & endowments in other things' (CL, 622).

The Second Edinburgh Edition of *Poems, Chiefly in the Scottish Dialect* is published by William Creech on 16 February: this two-volume edition is 'greatly enlarged with New Poems', including 'Tam o Shanter'.

In March, Burns requests, and receives, burgess rights for the education of his children in the Dumfries schools. On 19 May, he moves into a fine red sandstone house in Mill Vennel (now Burns Street). In June, Thomson brings out the first part of *Select Scottish Airs*, containing the twenty-five songs promised by Burns who receives a copy and a five-pound note from the editor: 'I assure you, Sir, that you truly hurt me with your pecuniary parcel. – It degrades me in my own eyes' (CL, 631).

Burns tours Galloway, 30 July–2 August, with John Syme – 'I got Burns a grey Highland shelty to ride on' (Syme, cited by Kinsley, 1420) – and he visits Gatehouse and Kirkcudbright and on 1 August meets Pietro Urbani at St Mary's Isle.

On 30 August, the day Thomas Muir goes on trial for sedition in

Edinburgh, Burns sends 'Scots Wha Hae' to Thomson, and comments on 'that glorious struggle [at Bannockburn] for Freedom, associated with the glowing ideas of some other struggles of the same nature, *not quite so ancient*' (CL, 639).

In October, Burns meets the fiddler Nathaniel Gow in Dumfries and in December he lends his collection of bawdy ballads to John McMurdo of Drumlanrig: 'I could not conveniently spare them above five or six days . . . There is not another copy of the Collection in the world, & I should be sorry that any unfortunate negligence should deprive me of what has cost me a good deal of pains' (CL, 494).

Before the year ends, Burns makes the biggest social blunder of his Dumfries years while attending a party at Friars' Carse and simulating a rape scene with Elizabeth, wife of Robert Riddell 'who insisted on my drinking more than I chose' (CL, 697): the Sabine Rape incident leads to a break with the Riddells.

1794   At the beginning of the year Burns writes his anguished and apologetic 'letter from hell' to Elizabeth Riddell: 'Regret! Remorse! Shame! ye three hell-hounds that ever dog my steps and bay at my heels, spare me! spare me!' (CL, 698). On 12 January, Maria Riddell, keeping faith with the family, breaks with Burns. Despite his difficulties Burns sends forty-one songs to James Johnson in February. On 20 April, Robert Riddell dies; in June, Friars' Carse is put up for sale.

From 25–28 June, Burns and Syme make their second Galloway tour; on 12 August, James Glencairn Burns is born; in November, Burns begins his notes on Scots songs for Thomson.

On 22 December, Burns is promoted to Acting Supervisor of Excise, Dumfries. Before the end of the year Maria Riddell writes to him and Burns coldly acknowledges, in the third person, the gift of a book: 'Owing to Mr B[urns's] being at present acting as Supervisor of the Excise, a department that occupies his every hour of the day, he has not that time to spare which is necessary for any Belle Lettre pursuit' (CL, 608).

1795   At the beginning of the year Burns is in a revolutionary mood: early in January he sends George Thomson 'A Man's a Man for a That'; on 12 January he writes to Mrs Dunlop (who is outraged by the remark) describing the execution of Louis XVI and Marie Antoinette as 'the deserved fate of . . . a perjured Blockhead & an unprincipled Prostitute' (CL, 214).

Nevertheless, on 31 January Burns and some sixty leading citizens of Dumfries petition the War Office for authority to organise the Royal Dumfries Volunteers. (He is active in the Volunteers until the breakdown of his health at the end of the year.)

By February, Burns is again well disposed towards Maria Riddell and by March he is writing cordially to her.

In March, Burns writes three Election Ballads for Patrick Heron, Whig candidate in the Kirkcudbright parliamentary election: 'For a' that, and a' that,/Here's Heron yet for a' that!/The independent patriot,/The honest man, and a' that!' (First Heron Election Ballad).

In April, Alexander Reid paints his miniature of Burns, 'the most remarkable likeness of what I am at this moment, that I think ever was taken of any body' (CL, 674).

'Does Haughty Gaul Invasion Threat?', Burns's ostentatious patriotic response to a threatened French invasion, is published in the *Edinburgh Courant* on 4 May.

Smellie dies on 24 June. Elizabeth Riddell Burns, the poet's only legitimate daughter to survive infancy, dies at the age of three, in Mauchline, in September: 'I had scarcely began to recover from that shock, when became myself the victim of a most severe Rheumatic fever' (CL, 215).

1796　In January, Burns is seriously ill and psychologically distressed over his finances and the possible consequences of famine in Dumfries: 'here, we have actual famine . . . Many days my family & hundreds of other families, are absolutely without one grain of meal; as money cannot purchase it' (CL, 215). The 'Swinish Multitude' (CL, 215) react angrily, and there are Meal Riots in Dumfries from 12–14 March.

May–June: with Patrick Heron up for re-election as Whig MP, Burns writes a fourth Election Ballad for him.

Around 1 June, Burns writes his last letter to Johnson: 'Personal & domestic affliction have almost entirely banished that alacrity & life with which I used to woo the rural muse of Scotia . . . Your Work [*Scots Musical Museum*] is a great one [and] I will venture to prophesy, that to future ages your Publication will be the text book & standard of Scottish Song & Music' (CL, 303).

From 3–17 July, Burns is at Brow, a hamlet on the shores of the Solway Firth, seeking a cure for his condition in sea-bathing. On 7 July he writes, to Alexander Cunningham, 'Alas! my friend, I fear the voice of the Bard will soon be heard among you no more! . . . these last three months I have been tortured with an excruciating rheumatism, which has reduced me to nearly the last stage. – You actually would not know me if you saw me' (CL, 473).

On 12 July, he writes his last latter to Thomson, asking for five pounds to settle an account with a 'cruel scoundrel of a Haberdasher [who] has commenced a process & will infallibly put me into jail' (CL, 679). Thomson sends the money on 14 July.

On 18 July Burns returns to Dumfries where he dies, at home, on Thursday, 21 July. His funeral is conducted in military manner by the Dumfries Volunteers, the Cinque Port Cavalry and the Angusshire Fencibles on Monday, 25 July, when he is buried in the northeast corner of St Michael's churchyard, a quarter mile from his home. On the day of his funeral (25 July) his son Maxwell is born.

The Burns Circle

ADAIR, DR JAMES McKITTRICK (1765–1802). Son of an Ayr doctor and a relative of Mrs Dunlop, Adair studied medicine at Edinburgh University and was Burns's companion on the Highland tour of 4–20 October 1787. On 11 November 1789 Adair married Gavin Hamilton's half-sister Charlotte Hamilton to whom Burns addressed 'The Banks of the Devon'. Adair died in Harrogate, Charlotte survived him until 1806.

AIKEN, ROBERT (1739–1807). 'The Cotter's Saturday Night' is dedicated to Aiken, 'My lov'd, my honour'd, much respected friend!' The dedicatee was a solicitor and surveyor of taxes in Ayr where he met Burns around 1783. A skilled public speaker, 'Orator Bob' (as he is called in 'The Kirk's Alarm') was Burns's 'first, kind Patron' (CL, 99): he championed his friend's poetry and collected 145 names of subscribers to the Kilmarnock Edition, almost a quarter of the total. In the summer of 1785 the 'glib-tongued Aiken' ('Holy Willie's Prayer') successfully defended Gavin Hamilton before the Presbytery of Ayr against charges preferred by the Kirk Session of Mauchline.

Burns wrote many letters to Aiken though several were destroyed; one of the extant letters, dated about 8 October 1786 by DeLancey Ferguson, contains the first mention by Burns of the possibility of entering the Excise and also states 'Even in the hour of social mirth, my gaity is the madness of an intoxicated criminal under the hands of the executioner' (CL, 93). Burns briefly fell out with Aiken as the solicitor was probably responsible for mutilating Burns's promissory note to Jean Armour, but soon reestablished friendly relations with 'Aiken dear' ('The Farewell').

AINSLIE, ROBERT (1766–1838). Burns's companion on the first part of his Border tour of 5 May–1 June 1787, was born at Berrywell, near Duns, and was studying law in Edinburgh when he met the poet at a masonic meeting early in 1787. A convivial companion, Ainslie was with Burns in Eyemouth where they were both admitted to the local masonic lodge. Ainslie then returned to Edinburgh, while Burns continued his tour. On 29 May, Burns wrote to Ainslie from Newcastle: 'I dare not talk nonsense lest I lose all the little dignity I have among the sober sons of wisdom & discretion, and I have not had one hearty mouthful of laughter since that merry-melancholy moment we parted' (CL, 327).

On 2 June 1787 (Mackay's edition of the letters gives 1788) Burns wrote, from Dumfries, asking Ainslie to give 'ten or twelve shillings' to May Cameron, an Edinburgh girl who had given birth to the poet's child, then advised 'don't for Heaven's sake meddle with her as a *Piece*' (CL, 332).

Burns introduced his friend to Mrs McLehose and on 3 March 1788 sent Ainslie the infamous 'horse litter' letter from Mauchline, describing his intercourse with Jean Armour, then far advanced in pregnancy with twins: 'I took the opportunity of some dry horse-litter, and gave her such a thundering scalade that electrified the very marrow of her bones' (CL, 331). Ainslie is the 'Robin' of the song 'Robin Shure in Hairst' in which an elder's daughter laments: 'Robin promis'd me/A' my winter vittle:/Fient haet he had but three/Guse-feathers and a whittle!' He became a Writer to the Signet in 1789, married in 1798, and gradually became a pillar of Edinburgh society, serving as a kirk elder and writing two religious pamphlets.

ANDERSON, DR ROBERT (1750–1830). Ten when his father died, Anderson was educated in his native Carnwath and at Edinburgh University where he studied theology then switched to medicine. Settling as a married man in Edinburgh, he abandoned medicine for literature, compiling *A Complete Edition of the Poets of Great Britain* and editing *The Works of John Moore, M.D.* Anderson met Burns in Edinburgh and wrote a memoir of the poet as a letter (published in the *Burns Chronicle*, 1925): '[Burns] was eager to assert the dignity and importance of poetry, which he termed the gift of heaven, though he frequently debased and degraded it by the misapplication of his own great powers to mean and unworthy purposes' (BE, 10).

ARMOUR, JEAN (1767–1834). Jean Armour was one of 'The Belles of Mauchline' celebrated in Burns's poem of that title: 'Miss Miller is fine, Miss Markland's divine,/Miss Smith she has wit, and Miss Betty is braw,/There's beauty and fortune to get wi' Miss

Morton;/But Armour's the jewel for me o them a'.' Another poem, 'The Mauchline Lady', declares (in the second of two quatrains): 'But when I came roun' by Mauchline toun,/Not dreadin' anybody,/My heart was caught, before I thought,/And by a Mauchline lady.'

Jean was born in Mauchline on 27 February 1767, the daughter of master mason James Armour. She first met Burns, in April 1785, at a dance during Mauchline's Race Week. Tradition has it that the poet's rakish reputation made it difficult for him to persuade any of the girls to dance with him. Before leaving he sarcastically wished aloud for a girl to follow him as faithfully as the collie dog he had brought with him. It was this remark that Jean teased him with when they met, a few weeks later, on the village green: 'Have ye fa'n in wi' a lass yet to like you as weel as your dog?' The hint was well taken by Burns. He and Jean became intimate and, in September, he signed a piece of paper attesting her as his wife, a perfectly legal procedure in Scotland at that period.

In March 1786, shortly before Burns sent John Wilson proposals for the Kilmarnock Edition, Jean's father fainted on hearing of her pregnancy (she gave birth to twins on 3 September, the boy surviving, the girl dying in infancy). Like many other Mauchline fathers, James Armour disapproved of Burns's behaviour and lack of prospects, so he had the marriage attestation mutilated. As his poem 'The Lament' reveals, Burns was distressed by this development: 'O! can she bear so base a heart,/So lost to honour, lost to truth,/As from the fondest lover part,/The plighted husband of her youth?' He accepted a job as a plantation book-keeper in Jamaica and turned his bruised affections to another girl, 'Highland' Mary Campbell.

The success of the Kilmarnock Edition, and the death of Mary Campbell in October 1786, changed his mind. He was a literary celebrity when, in the summer of 1787, he saw Jean – with the 'usual consequences' (CL, 149). Appalled that his daughter was again pregnant, James Armour put her out of his house: on 3 March 1788 Burns wrote, to Robert Ainslie, 'Jean I found banished, like a martyr – forlorn destitute and friendless: All for the good old cause' (CL, 331). Jean gave birth to twin girls on 3 March (both died within the month) and at the end of March Burns married Jean in a private ceremony in Gavin Hamilton's office. On 5 August, Rev Auld and the Mauchline Kirk Session recognised the validity of the marriage.

All the extant evidence suggests that Jean Armour was a remarkably tolerant woman ('Our Robbie should have had twa wives', she
remarked after taking in his illegitimate daughter by Anna Park)
and a devoted wife. She had no great interest in books (apart from
the Bible) but enjoyed singing old songs and ballads. Burns wrote
fourteen songs related to Jean, including 'I Hae a Wife o My Ain'
and 'Of a' the airts the wind can blaw': 'Of a' the airts the wind can
blaw/I dearly like the west,/For there the bonie lassie lives,/The
lassie I lo'e best.'

AULD, REV WILLIAM (1709–91). Educated at the universities of
Edinburgh, Glasgow and Leyden, he was ordained Minister of
Mauchline in 1742. An Auld Licht ('old light' and rigidly Calvinist)
minister, he publicly rebuked Burns and Jean Armour for 'the sin of
fornication' in 1786. The poet explained, in a letter of 17 July 1786,
'I have already appeared publickly in Church, and . . . do this to
get a certificate as a batchelor, which Mr Auld has promised me'
(CL, 112). In another letter, of 1787 to Gavin Hamilton (who was
an egregious enemy of Auld), Burns referred to 'that Boanerges of
gospel powers, Father Auld' (CL, 70). Burns's satirical 'The Kirk's
Alarm' cites 'Daddie Auld'; 'The Twa Herds' sarcastically invokes
'great apostle Auld'; and the prefatory note to 'Holy Willie's Prayer'
mentions 'Father Auld'.

BALLANTINE, JOHN (1743–1812). A merchant and banker, John
Ballantine became Dean of Guild, in Ayr, in 1786; as such he
supported the building of the New Brig and was the dedicatee of
Burns's poem 'The Brigs of Ayr'. Ballantine offered to lend Burns
the money to pay for a second Kilmarnock Edition but also advised
him to try an Edinburgh publisher, which the poet duly did. In
1787 Ballantine became Provost of Ayr and was always ready to
advance Burns's interests. The poet kept in touch with the provost,
asking him, in 1788, to give to Gilbert some of the money raised in
subscriptions for the First Edinburgh Edition. Thirteen letters from
Burns to Ballantine survive, the last (25 October 1791) enclosing a
copy of 'Tam o Shanter'.

BEGBIE, ALISON. In his Autobiographical Letter, Burns refers to being
jilted by 'a belle-fille whom I adored and who had pledged
her soul to meet me in the field of matrimony' (AL). A farmer's daughter, Alison (or Ellison) was (according to the poet's
sister Isabella) the young lady who, in 1781, rejected Burns's

proposal of marriage; and to whom he sent five letters, making romantic overtures in painfully formal terms. The last letter, written from Lochlea in June 1781, reacts to Alison's rejection of his marriage proposal: 'It would be weak and unmanly to say that without you I never can be happy; but sure I am, that sharing life with you, would have given it a relish, that, wanting you I can never taste' (CL, 47). At the time of this letter, Alison was a servant working in a house near the river Cessnock and she is identified as the heroine of 'The Lass of Cessnock Banks' and 'And I'll kiss thee yet bonie Peggy Alison'. Alison is probably the Mary Morison of the celebrated song (see 'The Songs').

BLACKLOCK, DR THOMAS (1721–91). Blinded by smallpox in infancy, Dr Blacklock (a bricklayer's son from Annan, Dumfriesshire) was a retired minister with a reputation as a minor poet in Edinburgh. After receiving a copy of the Kilmarnock Edition, Blacklock wrote (4 September 1786) to Rev George Lawrie, minister of Loudon, who passed the letter, via Gavin Hamilton, to Burns. Professing himself astonished by the quality of the poems, Blacklock looked forward to a second, enlarged edition. According to Burns, it was Blacklock's letter that persuaded him to abandon his plans to emigrate to Jamaica and seek his poetic fortune in Edinburgh: 'The Doctor belonged to a set of critics for whose applause I had not even dared to hope' (AL).

BLAIR, REV DR HUGH (1718–1800). A kinsman of Robert Blair, author of *The Grave* (a poem well known to Burns), Hugh Blair was educated at Edinburgh University which, in 1762, appointed him Professor of Rhetoric and Belles Lettres, a position he combined with his work as senior minister of the High Kirk, St Giles. Blair was well placed to establish himself as one of Edinburgh's most influential intellects – encouraging James Macpherson in his Ossianic adventure, supporting the Scottish theatre and making friends with David Hume even though the philosopher was anathema to many members of the church. His *Lectures on Rhetoric and Belles Lettres* (1783) was much admired and his open admiration of Burns increased the poet's reputation in his Edinburgh period. On Blair's advice, Burns omitted 'The Jolly Beggars' (and another poem, 'The Prophet and God's Complaint', now lost) from the First Edinburgh Edition. Burns summed up the somewhat pompous minister in his second Common Place Book: 'In my opinion Dr Blair is merely an astonishing proof of what industry and application can do . . . . He has a heart not of the finest water, but far from being an ordinary one' (BE, 32).

BROUN, AGNES (1732–1820). The poet's mother was the eldest child of Gilbert Broun, tenant of Craigenton farm, Carrick. Ten when her mother died and twelve when her father remarried, she went to live with a grandmother at Maybole where, in 1756, she met William Burnes at the Maybole Fair (after breaking off an engagement to a ploughman, William Nelson). She married Burnes on 15 December 1757 and went to live with him in the 'auld clay biggin' ('The Vision'). In Burns's childhood Agnes sang old Scottish songs but, unlike her husband, had no appreciation of books. After her husband's death she lived mainly with the poet's brother (Robert having settled an annuity of £5 on her) and died at Gilbert's home, Grant's Brae, East Lothian. She was buried in the churhyard of Bolton.

BROWN, CAPTAIN RICHARD (1753–1833). Brown was born in Irvine where Burns met him in 1781 while learning the trade of flax-dressing. Burns, twenty-two at the time, was enormously impressed by the young seaman and describes his friendship with him at length in the Autobiographical Letter. Burns told Brown that it was his praise that 'encouraged me to endeavour at the character of a Poet' (CL, 418).

BURNES, WILLIAM (1721–84). The poet's father William Burnes (the 'e' was dropped after his death) was born at Clochnahill farm in the parish of Dunnottar, Kincardineshire, the third son of Robert Burnes and Isabella Keith. By the time William was twenty-four (in the year of the Jacobite Rising of 1745) his father had surrendered the lease of his farm, ruined by the combination of poor land and limited economic resources that was to become a family tradition. Burnes trained as a gardener and, in 1748, protected himself from his father's Jacobite reputation by obtaining a certificate of good character.

In Edinburgh he landscaped private gardens and worked on The Meadows, the city's recreation park. Then, in 1750, he accepted an offer of gardening in Ayrshire and earned enough to lease some seven acres of nurseryland at Alloway. He met Agnes Broun, a tenant-farmer's daughter, in 1756 and, with her in mind, spent the summer and autumn evenings of 1757 building – with his own hands on his own nurseryland – a clay thatched cottage of two rooms with adjoining stable and byre. By winter this but-and-ben was whitewashed and ready so, on 15 December 1757, he married Agnes and took her back to the 'auld clay biggin' ('The Vision'). Their son Robert (first of seven children) was born in the cottage on 25 January 1759. Ten days later a storm blew out the gable above the fireplace and Mrs Burns and her baby had to shelter in a neighbour's house. As Burns put it, in 'Rantin, Rovin Robin', 'Our monarch's hindmost year but ane/Was five-and-twenty days begun,/'Twas then a blast o Janwar win'/Blew hansel in on Robin.'

Burnes sent Robert and his brother Gilbert to a little school near the cottage and hired John Murdoch to educate his children. By 1766 Burnes had four children, too many for the 'auld clay biggin', so he rented the 70-acre hilltop farm of Mount Oliphant, two miles from the cottage, and stocked it on the strength of a £100 loan. The soil was poor, the work heart-breaking as well as back-breaking, yet Burnes used his evenings to instruct his boys from a collection of books on grammar and theology. In 1772 he sent Robert and Gilbert to study at the village school in Dalrymple and, the following summer, sent Robert to study with Murdoch at Ayr.

In 1769, on the death of the landlord, a factor took over the affairs of Mount Oliphant and hounded Burnes for payments. Unable to engage outside help Burnes had to rely on the efforts of his eldest son who, at fifteen, became the farm's principal labourer, driving a team of oxen over the rough ground of Mount Oliphant. Release from this misery came in 1777 when Burnes rented, for one pound per acre, the 130 swampy acres of Lochlea farm in Tarbolton parish. Robert was well pleased with the move and infuriated his rigidly Calvinist father by attending a dancing class in Tarbolton: 'from that instance of rebellion he took a kind of dislike to me, which, I believe was one cause of that dissipation which marked my future years' (AL).

Burns returned from Irvine in 1782 to find his father involved in a bitter dispute with his landlord McLure who, short of cash, demanded arrears of rent. Fearing the worst, Robert and Gilbert secretly arranged to lease Mossgiel farm. In January 1784 the Edinburgh Court of Session found in favour of Burnes but legal costs and the strain of litigation had taken their toll and he died, on 13 February, less than a month after the court decision.

According to Gilbert Burns, the pious and 'toil-worn Cotter' in 'The Cotter's Saturday Night' was an accurate portrait of the poet's father. William Burnes was buried in Alloway kirkyard and his original headstone was stolen, in bits and pieces, by souvenir hunters. Burns's 'Epitaph On My Honoured Father' praises 'The tender father, and the gen'rous friend'.

BURNESS, JAMES (1750–1837). First cousin of Burns, James Burness was a lawyer in Montrose. During his Highland tour with Nicol, Burns arranged to meet Burness in Stonehaven on Monday, 10 September 1787: 'I understand there is but one Inn at Stonhive [that is, Stonehaven] so you cannot miss me' (CL, 61). Burns kept in fairly regular touch with his cousin, telling him (9 February 1789) about his move to Ellisland and his marriage: 'My Wife is Jean, with whose story you are partly acquainted' (CL, 612). On 12 July 1796, the month he died, Burns wrote asking Burness for the loan of ten pounds, by return of post, to pay 'a rascal of a Haberdasher [who] will infallibly put my emaciated body into jail' (CL, 63). Burness sent the money and, after the poet's death, sent five pounds to Jean with an offer to accommodate and educate young Robert, an offer Jean politely refused.

BURNS, GILBERT (1760–1827). The poet's brother (born at the Alloway cottage on 28 September 1760), Gilbert shared Robert's upbringing and education, impressing John Murdoch as being the brightest of the two boys. With their father in difficulties over Lochlea farm, Robert and Gilbert arranged to become partners in Mossgiel farm which they moved into in March 1784. On 22 July 1786 Robert transferred his share of Mossgiel to Gilbert and enabled him to continue in the farm by lending him (towards the end of 1787) £180, about half the profits of the First Edinburgh Edition: compound interest was to be paid at five per cent per year and, out of interest, Gilbert was to deduct an annuity of £5 for the poet's mother and some £8 per year to support the poet's daughter Elizabeth (who was brought up by Gilbert).

Gilbert married Jean Breckenridge of Kilmarnock in 1791 (they had eleven children), left Mossgiel in 1798, and farmed for two years at Dinning, Nithsdale. In 1800 he became manager of Morham farm, West Mains, East Lothian; four years later he became factor on the East Lothian Estates of Lady Katherine Blantyre.

As well as supplying material to Currie, Gilbert commented on his brother in a long letter ('Gilbert's Narrative') to Mrs Dunlop. For preparing an eighth edition of Currie's *Works of Burns*, published in 1820, Gilbert was paid £250 on condition that he did not drastically differ from Currie's conclusions. Snyder felt that the diffident Gilbert missed an opportunity to set the record straight 'and the general impression that Burns was a confirmed alcoholic remained unshaken by Gilbert's timid denials' (Snyder, 488).

He died at his home – Grant's Braes, near Haddington – on 8 April 1827 and was buried in the churchyard of Bolton.

CAMERON, MAY. An Edinburgh servant girl who gave birth to a child by Burns. When he was in Dumfries, at the beginning of June 1787, he received a letter (dated 26 May and written for her) explaining May's position. Burns then wrote a letter asking Robert Ainslie to sort out the situation, which he duly did: 'but don't for Heaven's sake,' Burns warned Ainslie, 'meddle with her as a *Piece*' (CL, 332). May subsequently had a writ *in meditatione fugae* served on Burns but on 15 August 1787 he was freed from this writ.

CAMPBELL, MARY (1763–86). In 1786, with Jean Armour pregnant and Burns repudiated by her family, the poet contemplated emigrating to Jamaica after the publication of his poems. Meanwhile, he turned his attention to Mary Campbell, a Coilsfield dairymaid (born in Auchamore, by Dunoon, the daughter of a seaman) who had previously been a nursemaid in Gavin Hamilton's Mauchline house.

On the second Sunday of May, 1786, Burns and Mary met at Failford: over the Fail Water they clasped hands and made a matrimonial gesture by exchanging Bibles (the two-volume Bible Burns gave Mary is kept in the Alloway Burns Monument). The scene is recreated in the song 'Will Ye Go to the Indies, My Mary' which ends 'We hae plighted our troth, my Mary,/In mutual affection to join;/And curst be the cause that shall part us!/The hour and the moment o time!' Apparently Burns and Mary intended to marry and emigrate to Jamaica together.

Poems, Chiefly in the Scottish Dialect (published on 31 July 1786) was an immediate success and Burns planned to meet Mary at Greenock in September so they could both sail for Kingston. The voyage was postponed and, a month later, Mary died, possibly in premature childbirth: when Mary's grave, in Greenock's old West Highland Churchyard, was opened on 5 November 1920 the bottom board of an infant's coffin was found among the remains. (Fitzhugh, 106, says the child was that of one Agnes

Hendry.) Burns claimed that Mary died 'with a malignant fever' (BE, 64). In his song 'Highland Mary' Burns writes 'But O! fell Death's untimely frost,/That nipt my flower sae early!/Now green's the sod, and cauld's the clay,/That wraps my Highland Mary!' According to John Richmond, Mary was 'loose in the extreme' (BE, 66). Burns, however, mourned 'my lost, my ever dear MARY, whose bosom was fraught with Truth, Honour, Constancy & LOVE' (CL, 182).

CARMICHAEL, REBEKAH. On 19 March 1787 Burns gave his own copy of the Second Edition of Fergusson's *Poems* (1782) to Rebekah Carmichael, inscribed with his 'Apostrophe to Fergusson'. In 1790 he subscribed for two copies of Carmichael's *Poems*.

CHALMERS, MARGARET (1763–1843). According to Snyder, Margaret Chalmers was the most suitable woman Burns could have married, especially as he 'loved Margaret Chalmers' (Snyder, 250) with an intensity he never felt for Jean Armour. Burns probably first met Margaret Chalmers – whose mother was a sister of Gavin Hamilton's stepmother – at her father's farm, near Mauchline. He renewed his friendship in late 1786, at the Edinburgh home of Dr Blacklock for whom Peggy sang and played the piano. A letter of January 1787 declares 'your Piano and you together have play'd the deuce somehow, about my heart' (CL, 230). In October of that year, during his third Highland tour, Burns spent eight days at Harvieston in her company and she later told Thomas Campbell she had turned down a proposal of marriage from the poet. On 6 November, Burns sent her two love songs, 'My Peggy's Face' and 'Where, braving angry winter's storms', the first of these explaining: 'I love my Peggy's angel air,/Her face so truly heavenly fair,/Her native grace, so void of art:/But I adore my Peggy's heart.'

On 16 September 1788 Burns wrote from Ellisland to say he had married Jean Armour – 'not in consequence of the attachment of romance perhaps' (CL, 237) – and to clarify his feelings for Peggy:

> when I think . . . I have met with you, and have lived more of a real life with you in eight days, than I can do with almost any body I meet with in eight years – when I think on the improbability of meeting you in this world again – I could sit down and cry like a child! (CL, 237)

That December, Peggy married Lewis Hay, an Edinburgh banker, by whom she had three sons and three daughters. After the death of her husband she settled in Berne.

CLARK, SAMUEL (1769–1814). Born in Dumfries where, like his father, he worked as a solicitor, Samuel Clark, Jr. was a boozing crony of Burns who wrote him (in an undated letter): 'I recollect something of a drunken promise yesternight to breakfast with you this morning. – I am very sorry that it is impossible' (CL, 702).

One Saturday night in January 1794, Clark was present when Burns, during the war with revolutionary France, gave the toast: 'May our success in the present war be equal to the justice of our cause' (CL, 702). Outraged by the ambivalence of the toast, one Captain Dods insulted Burns who wrote a sorrowful letter to Clark on the subject the following morning asking him to intervene on his behalf: 'I request & beg that this morning you will wait on the parties present at the foolish dispute. – The least delay may be of unlucky consequence to me' (CL, 702). Two years after Burns died, Clark married Mary Wight who bore him fourteen children and saw him promoted to Conjunct Commissary Clerk and Clerk of the Peace for the County.

CLEGHORN, ROBERT (d.1789). Born in Corstorphine, then on the outskirts of Edinburgh, Cleghorn was a farmer (at Saughton Mills, where Burns often visited him when in Edinburgh) and a member of the Crochallan Fencibles, the convivial club that welcomed Burns to its company. To Cleghorn, who shared his interest in the subject, Burns sent some of the bawdy poems later collected in *The Merry Muses of Caledonia*.

CLOW, JENNY. While Burns was conducting his epistolary affair with Clarinda in Edinburgh, he had a sexual affair with Jenny who, in November 1788, bore him a son. It seems that, like May Cameron, Jenny served Burns with a writ: a letter of 6 January 1789 to Ainslie explains, 'I must again trouble you to find & secure for me a direction where to find Jenny Clow, for a main part of my business in Edinburgh is to settle that matter with her, & free her hand of the process' (CL, 337). In November 1791, Burns had a letter from Clarinda telling him that Jenny was apparently close to death; Burns asked her to get a porter to take her five shillings.

CREECH, WILLIAM (1745–1815). When Burns arrived in Edinburgh,

in 1786, the Earl of Glencairn introduced the poet to the parsimonious publisher-bookseller Creech who conducted his business
in his shop (which had been Allan Ramsay's) in the centre of
the High Street. The First Edinburgh Edition of *Poems, Chiefly
in the Scottish Dialect* – printed by William Smellie, published by
Creech, by subscription, for the poet – appeared on 17 April 1787.
On 23 April Creech bought the copyright on Burns's book for 100
guineas which meant he could issue new editions for his own
profit: a Second Edinburgh Edition was published by Creech, on
18 February 1793, in two volumes and 'greatly enlarged with New
Poems', one of which was 'Tam o Shanter'. Burns received only
twenty complimentary copies of this edition which was reissued
in 1794.

Notoriously mean, Creech was slow to pay Burns money due to
him on the First Edinburgh Edition and also delayed paying the
100 guineas he owed the poet. Burns had to travel to Edinburgh to
persuade Creech to part with the money. Before the quarrel, Burns
wrote affectionately of Creech in his 'Lament for the Absence of
William Creech, Publisher' which imagines literary Edinburgh lost
without the publisher (away in London on business): 'Nae mair we
see his levee door/Philosophers and Poets pour,/And toothy Critics
by the score,/In bloody raw:/The adjutant o a' the core,/Willie's
awa!' 'On William Creech', written after the quarrel, portrays the
publisher as offensively egotistical: 'A little upright, pert, tart,
tripping wight,/And still his precious self his dear delight;/Who
loves his own smart shadow in the streets/Better than e'er the fairest
She he meets.'

CRUICKSHANK, WILLIAM (d.1795). A graduate of Edinburgh Univer-
sity, Cruickshank became (in 1770) Rector of the High School in the
Canongate and (in 1772) Latin master at Edinburgh High School.
Introduced to Cruickshank by William Nicol, Burns lived with
the Cruickshank family in 2 St James's Square, Edinburgh, from
October 1787 to February 1788. Burns wrote two lyrics ('A Rose-Bud
By My Early Walk' and 'Beauteous Rosebud, young and gay') for
Cruickshank's twelve-year-old daughter Jean.

CUNNINGHAM, ALEXANDER (c.1763–1812). Eldest son of James Cunn-
ingham of Hyndhope and a nephew of the historian William
Robertson (appointed Principal of Edinburgh University in 1762)
Cunningham practised law in Edinburgh when Burns met him

(possibly at a meeting of the Crochallan Fencibles). Burns consoled Cunningham when he was jilted by Anne Stewart and wrote nineteen letters to him on such subjects as sex, marriage and religion. Through a financially advantageous marriage to Agnes Moir, Cunningham became a Writer to the Signet in 1798 and by 1806 he was in partnership with his uncle, the jeweller Patrick Robertson. He was the main fund-raiser for the poet's widow and orphans.

CUNNINGHAM, LADY ELIZABETH (c.1750–1804). Younger sister of Burns's patron, James, Earl of Glencairn, Lady Cunningham lived in Edinburgh with her mother, the Dowager Countess. Burns wrote to her about his poetic plans in January 1789; and sent her a copy of 'Lament for James, Earl of Glencairn' in September 1791, inscribing the gift in memory of Glencairn and 'in gratitude to your Ladyship for your goodness' (CL, 500).

CUNNINGHAM, JAMES, 14th EARL OF GLENCAIRN (1749–91). After the death of Glencairn (30 January 1791), Burns described him as 'the Patron from whom all my fame & good fortune took its rise' (CL, 262) and 'my best Friend, my first and dearest Patron & Benefactor; the man to whom I owe all that I am & have! (CL, 506). He also wrote a 'Lament for James, Earl of Glencairn' which ends: 'The mother may forget the child/That smiles sae sweetly on her knee;/But I'll remember thee, Glencairn,/And a' that thou has done for me!'

Ten years older than the poet, Glencairn was born at Finlayston, succeeded to the title in 1775, and married Lady Isabella Erskine in 1785. As patron of Kilmarnock parish the liberal Glencairn, in June 1785, presented the rigidly conservative Rev William Mackinlay for the vacant ministry and thus prompted Burns's satire 'The Ordination'.

Burns came to Edinburgh in 1786 with a letter of introduction from James Dalrymple of Orangefield (married to Lady Glencairn's sister) and was warmly welcomed by Glencairn who invited him to his home and introduced him to his friends, including the publisher William Creech. Glencairn and his mother subscribed for twenty-four copies of the First Edinburgh Edition of *Poems, Chiefly in the Scottish Dialect* and Glencairn encouraged the members of the Caledonian Hunt to subcribe for one hundred copies (the edition was dedicated to 'the Noblemen and Gentlemen of the Caledonian

Hunt'). When Burns decided to enter the Excise he approached Glencairn who used his influence on the poet's behalf. In honour of his friend, Burns named his fourth son (born 12 August 1794) James Glencairn Burns.

CURRIE, DR JAMES (1756–1805). The first editor of Burns, and the first author to give an extended account of the poet's life, Currie was born at Kirkpatrick Fleming, Dumfriesshire, and educated at Dumfries. From the money he made as a physician in Liverpool, he bought himself an estate in Dumfriesshire in 1792, the year of his only meeting with Burns. Somewhat reluctantly, since his previous writing had been confined to medical journals, he agreed to edit Burns's works and was astonished when John Syme sent him an unedited mass of materials on which he worked, without remuneration, for three years.

The Works of Robert Burns, with an Account of his Life appeared in the autumn of 1800, in four volumes, in an edition of 2000 copies, costing £1/11/6 per set: the £1200 profits from the sale of this edition went to the Trust Fund for Burns's family. Currie was concerned to protect the memory of the poet as sacred and so toned down expressions he found offensive. Ironically, Currie's own antipathy to alcohol (a reaction to overindulgence in his youth) overcame his desire to avoid controversial value judgements about Burns and he helped encourage the perception of the Scottish poet as self-destructive drinker and degenerate:

> Perpetually stimulated by alcohol in one or other of its various forms [Burns's] temper became more irritable and gloomy; he fled from himself into society, often of the lowest kind. And in such company, that part of the convivial scene, in which wine increases sensibility and excites benevolence, was hurried over, to reach the succeeding part, over which uncontrolled passion generally presided. He who suffers the pollution of inebriation, how shall he escape other pollution? But let us refrain from the mention of errors over which delicacy and humanity draw the veil. (Currie, I, 214)

The mention of 'other pollution' was interpreted as a reference to venereal disease and resented by generations of indignant Burnsians.

Currie died of heart failure, at Sidmouth, on 31 August 1805.

DALRYMPLE, REV WILLIAM (1723–1814). The day after his birth, Burns was baptised, in the Auld Kirk of Ayr, by the liberal parish minister, Rev Dalrymple. An uncle of Burns's friend Robert Aiken and a friend of the poet's father, Dalrymple had been preaching in Ayr as junior parish minister since 1746; in 1756 he was preferred to the first ministry. In 1779, St Andrews University conferred the degree of Doctor of Divinity on Dalrymple and in 1781 he was Moderator of the General Assembly of the Church of Scotland. Dalrymple is described as the 'fae' (foe) of the Auld Lichts in 'The Twa Herds'. In 'The Kirk's Alarm', Burns writes: 'D'rmple mild! D'rymple mild! tho your heart's like a child!/And your life like the new-driven snaw,/Yet that winna save ye, auld Satan, just have ye,/For preaching that three's ane an twa'.

DAVIDSON, BETTY. Widow of a cousin of Agnes Broun, Betty Davidson often stayed with the Burns family at Alloway and entertained the infant poet with her old wife's tales and songs about supernatural happenings: 'This cultivated the latent seeds of Poesy' (AL).

DAVIDSON, JOHN (1728–1806). Traditionally identified as the original of 'Souter Johnie' in 'Tam o Shanter', Davidson lived at Glenfoot of Ardlochan, near Douglas Graham's Shanter farm. A cobbler, he accompanied Davidson to Ayr on market days. Davidson moved into the thatched cottage now known as Souter Johnie's House, in Kirkoswald, in 1785, five years before Burns composed 'Tam o Shanter'. He married Anne Gillespie (who had worked for the poet's maternal grandfather Gilbert Broun) in 1763. Burns frequently visited Davidson.

DOUGLAS, DR PATRICK (d.1819). In 1773 Dr Patrick Douglas of Garallan (an estate two miles from Cumnock) was involved in the collapse of the Ayr-based bank of Douglas, Heron & Co. His Jamaican estate was managed by his brother Charles, and when Burns visited Dr Douglas in Ayr, in 1786, he was offered the position of book-keeper to Charles in Port Antonio. Dr Douglas remained an admirer of Burns, being present in 1801 at the first meeting in Burns Cottage to celebrate the birth of the poet.

DUNLOP, MRS FRANCES ANNA (1730–1815). In 1748 Frances Anna Wallace (eldest daughter of Sir Thomas Wallace of Craigie) married John Dunlop of Dunlop by whom she had thirteen children. In 1786, doubly distressed by the recent death of her husband and the financial problems of her son Thomas, she found solace in

'The Cotter's Saturday Night' (shown to her by a friend) and sent a messenger to Mossgiel requesting six copies of the Kilmarnock Edition and asking the author to visit Dunlop House. Burns sent her five copies, all he could spare, and visited Mrs Dunlop in June 1787, February 1788, May 1789, June 1791, and December 1792. During their long and stimulating correspondence she advised Burns to avoid impropriety in his poems and expressed strong disapproval of his political faith in the French Revolution. As she had put the poet in touch with Dr Moore, she was aghast when Burns wrote to her, on 1 January 1795, condemning the reactionary tone of Moore's *Journal during a Residence in France* (1793) and describing the execution of Louis XVI and Marie Antoinette as 'the deserved fate [of] a perjured Blockhead & an unprincipled Prostitute' (CL, 214). She ignored subsequent letters until Burns wrote to her on 10 July 1796, eleven days before his death:

> I have written you so often without receiving any answer, that I would not trouble you again but for the circumstances in which I am. – An illness which has long hung about me in all probability will speedily send me byond that bourne whence no traveller returns. – Your friendship with which for many years you honored me was a friendship dearest to my soul. – Your conversation & especially your correspondence were at once highly entertaining & instructive. – With what pleasure did I use to break up the seal! The remembrance yet adds one pulse more to my poor palpitating heart! Farewell!!! (CL, 215)

Mrs Dunlop replied to this in a letter which was one of the last things Burns read on his deathbed.

FERGUSSON, ALEXANDER (1746–96). The winner of the drinking-contest (the defeated contestants were Robert Riddell and Sir Robert Lawrie) described in Burns's mock-epic ballad 'The Whistle', Alexander Fergusson of Craigdarroch was a lawyer and Justice of the Peace for Dumfries. Apparently Fergusson won the little ebony whistle by drinking upwards of five bottles of claret: 'Next uprose our Bard, like a prophet in drink:–/"Craigdarroch, thou'lt soar when creation shall sink!/But if thou would flourish immortal in rhyme,/Come – one bottle more – and have at the sublime!"'

FISHER, WILLIAM (1737–1809). The original of Burns's Holy Willie was a farmer's son who, in July 1772, was ordained an elder in

Machline Parish Church where the Rev William Auld preached the virtues of Calvinism and condemned the vices of the villagers. Fisher, privately as much addicted to the pleasures of the flesh as Burns, was anxious to preserve theological appearances and was probably responsible for the Kirk Session's proceedings against Gavin Hamilton for failure to honour the Sabbath. Burns's response was to satirise Fisher as the hypocritical Holy Willie in 'Holy Willie's Prayer' and 'Epitaph on Holy Willie'.

In 'The Kirk's Alarm', of 1789, Burns accused Fisher of robbing the poor: 'Holy Will! Holy Will, there was wit i' your skull,/When ye pilfer'd the alms o the poor'. In a note, written for Glendriddel, on 'Holy Willie's Prayer' Burns observed: 'Holy Willie was a rather oldish bachelor elder in the parish of Mauchline, and much and justly famed for that polemical chattering which ends in tippling orthodoxy, and for the spiritualised bawdry which refines to liquorish devotion' (BE, 133). In 1790 Fisher was rebuked by Rev Auld for drunkenness. Years later, he was found dead in a ditch by the roadside near Mauchline.

FONTENELLE, LOUISA (1773–99). An actress who made her London debut on 6 November 1788 at Covent Garden and her Scottish debut on 17 October 1789 at the Theatre Royal, Edinburgh, Louisa Fontenelle was, in the winter seasons of 1792 and 1793, one of the players at the new Theatre Royal, Dumfries, managed by James Brown Williamson. Burns wrote a fan letter to Louisa on 22 November 1792, enclosing 'The Rights of Woman' as a prologue for her benefit night, 26 November 1792; and another 'Address' for her benefit night, 4 December 1793. Burns also wrote a poem, 'On Seeing Miss Fontenelle in a Favourite Character', in which he called her 'Simple, wild, enchanting elf' and (in a letter of December 1793) he praised her 'personal charms, amiable manner & gentle heart' (CL, 683). She married the actor-manager John Brown Williamson and the couple emigrated to America in 1796. She became a member of the South Carolina Company of Comedians at Charleston where she died of yellow fever.

FULLARTON, COLONEL WILLIAM (1754–1808). Son of an Ayrshire botanist, Fullarton was educated at Edinburgh University, made the Grand Tour of Europe as the ward of Patrick Brydone (Burns calls the Colonel 'Brydon's brave ward' in 'The Vision') and became a colonel, with the 98th Regiment, in the British Army. After he had visited Ellisland with a friend Burns wrote to him, on 3 October 1791, 'I am ambitious, covetously ambitious, of being known to a a gentleman [who was] a Leader of Armies as soon as he was a Soldier' (CL, 593). An agricultural improver, he published an *Account of Agriculture in Ayrshire* in 1793 and that same year, with the outbreak of war with revolutionary France, raised the 23rd Light Dragoons, known as Fullarton's Light Horse. Fullarton, whose wife was the elder daughter of the fifth Lord Reay, became Governor of Trinidad in 1802.

GLENCAIRN, EARL OF, *see* CUNNINGHAM, JAMES, 14th EARL OF GLENCAIRN.

GOW, NEIL (1727–1807). The celebrated fiddler and composer (whose tunes Burns used in his songwriting) was born at Inver, near Dunkeld. Burns met him on 31 August 1787 at Dunkeld: 'Breakfast . . . Neil Gow plays – a short, stout-built, honest highland figure . . . an interesting face marking strong sense, kind openheartedness mixed with unmistrusting simplicity' (cited by Kinsley, 1226). Gow's son Nathaniel, also a fiddler, met Burns in Dumfries in 1794.

GRAHAM, DOUGLAS (1738–1811). Usually identified as the original of 'Tam o Shanter', Graham rented the farm of Shanter (*seann tor* means old mound) in Carrick and had a boat, the 'Tam o Shanter' which he used for smuggling. As well as farming and smuggling, Graham was a dealer in malt so every market day he would go to Ayr (accompanied by John Davidson). These drunken visits were anathema to Graham's wife Helen (*née* McTaggart) who thus became a 'sulky sullen dame' (like Tam's wife Kate) in his absence. Burns met Graham, at Shanter farm, through his friendship with Davidson.

GRAHAM OF FINTRY, ROBERT (1749–1815). On 31 August 1787, during his Highland tour with William Nicol, Burns visited Athole House and met Robert Graham of Fintry, recently appointed a Commissioner of the Scottish Board of Excise. On 7 January 1788 the poet wrote to Graham asking him to use his influence to secure him a post with Excise. Graham obliged and Burns described his patron as 'one of the worthiest and most accomplished Gentlemen, not only of this Country, but I will dare to say it, of this Age' (CL, 151). When Burns's political opinions were investigated by the Excise Board in December 1792 he wrote (31 December) to Graham, asking him 'to save me from that misery which threatens to overwhelm me' (CL,

436). Again, Graham came to the poet's assistance. Burns wrote three verse epistles to Graham.

GROSE, CAPTAIN FRANCIS (1731–91). Born at Greenford, Middlesex, Grose studied art and served in the Surrey Militia, retiring with the rank of Captain. Having squandered a family fortune, he pursued his antiquarian interests with profit: his *Antiquities of England and Scotland* was published, in six volumes, from 1773–87. Burns met him, at Captain Robert Riddell's home, Friars' Carse, in July 1789, while Grose was in Scotland researching his *Antiquities of Scotland* (two vols, 1789 and 1791).

When Burns urged the corpulent antiquarian to include an illustration of Kirk Alloway in his work, Grose agreed on condition that the poet would provide a witch story to accompany the drawing. Burns obliged, in June 1790, with three witch stories, the second of which – beginning 'On a market day in the town of Ayr' (CL, 558) – was a prose version of the narrative of 'Tam o Shanter'. The poem itself was sent on 1 December 1790 and appeared in the second volume of Grose's *Antiquities of Scotland*.

Of the three poems Burns wrote on Grose, the finest is 'On the late Captain Grose's Perigrinations thro Scotland': 'Hear, Land o Cakes, and brither Scots/Frae Maidenkirk to Johnie Groatts,/If there's a hole in a' your coats,/I rede you tent it:/A chield's amang you takin notes,/And faith he'll prent it.//If in your bounds ye chance to light/Upon a fine, fat fodgel wight,/O stature short but genius bright/That's he, mark weel:/And wow! he has an unco sleight/O cauk and keel.'

Grose intended to produce another antiquarian work on Ireland but died, soon after arriving, of an apoplectic fit. He is buried near Dublin.

HAMILTON, CHARLOTTE (1763–1806). A half-sister of Gavin Hamilton, Charlotte lived at Harvieston (two miles west of Dollar, Clackmannanshire) on an estate by the banks of the river Devon. During his Highland tour with Nicol, Burns visited Harvieston on Monday, 27 August 1787, and wrote to Gavin Hamilton:

> Of Charlotte I cannot speak in common terms of admiration: she is not only beautiful; but lovely. – Her form is elegant; her features not regular but they have the smile of Sweetness and the settled complacency of good nature in the highest degree . . . (CL, 69)

Burns's second visit to Harvieston was in October, the same year, during his Highland tour with Dr James Adair: Burns went there to propose marriage to Charlotte's friend Peggy Chalmers (who rejected him); his companion Adair was similarly attracted to Charlotte who became his wife in 1789 (and mother of his five children). A visit to the Falls of Devon in Charlotte's company prompted 'The Banks of the Devon' (which appeared in the *Scots Musical Museum* in 1788). Burns's last song, 'Fairest Maid on Devon Banks', written nine days before his death, recalled the visit.

HAMILTON, GAVIN (1751-1805). Burns dedicated the Kilmarnock Edition to Gavin Hamilton in a series of affectionate couplets, including these: 'So, Sir, you see 'twas nae daft vapour;/But I maturely thought it proper,/When a' my works I did review,/To dedicate them, Sir, to you:/Because (ye need na tak it ill)/I thought them something like yoursel' ('A Dedication to Gavin Hamilton, Esq.'). A lawyer's son, Hamilton followed in his father's footsteps, first working in John Hamilton's office then setting up his own practice in Mauchline. Hamilton met Burns, a fellow freemason, in autumn 1783 and the poet and his brother Gilbert rented from Hamilton, for £90 per year, the 118-acre farm of Mossgiel.

As a liberal New Licht member of the kirk, Hamilton fell foul of Daddie Auld who, in 1785, persuaded the Kirk Session to accuse him of irregular attendence and failure to uphold family worship. Hamilton appealed to the Presbytery of Ayr who found in his favour; Auld then appealed to the Synod of Glasgow of Ayr which, again, exonerated Hamilton. The dispute is mentioned in 'Holy Willie's Prayer' and Hamilton is also cited in 'Epistle to John McMath' and 'The Farewell'. Burns wrote 'The Calf' after a wager with Hamilton and addressed his friend in 'Stanzas on Naething', 'To Gavin Hamilton, Esq., Mauchline' and 'Epitaph for Gavin Hamilton'. 'Nature's Law', composed after Jean Armour gave birth to twins on 3 September 1786, is 'humbly inscribed to Gavin Hamilton'.

According to the Train manuscript, when Burns married Jean Armour at the end of March, 1788, the private ceremony was held 'in the writing office of Gavin Hamilton, Machline' (BE, 52).

HERON, PATRICK (1736–1803). Towards the end of his life Burns wrote four Election Ballads on behalf of Patrick Heron who was a Whig candidate in the elections of 1795 and 1796. Heron was one of the founders (in 1769) of the Ayr-based bank Douglas, Heron

& Co which collapsed in 1773; though many of his depositors were ruined, he recovered through a financially advantageous marriage to the daughter of the Earl of Dundonald. Heron purchased the Galloway estate of Kerroughtree where Burns met him in June 1794.

In 1795 Heron defeated the Tory candidate Thomas Gordon of Balmaghie; and in 1796, after the dissolution of Parliament, he was re-elected, defeating Montgomery Stewart. He held his seat in the General Election of 1802 but was unseated the following year and his name was erased from the rolls by order of the House. He died at Grantham on his way home to Scotland.

HERON, ROBERT (1764–1807). The first biographer of Burns, Heron was born in Creehead, New Galloway; studied at Edinburgh University; became a licentiate of the Church in 1789; and earned his living as a writer (his *Journey through the Western Counties of Scotland* appeared in 1793). He met Burns (at Dr Blacklock's house) in Edinburgh and later visited him at Ellisland: Heron is cursed in the 'Epistle to Dr Blacklock' for failing to deliver a letter to Blacklock ('The Ill-Thief blaw the Heron south,/And never drink be near his drouth'). Heron's 'Original Memoirs of the Late Robert Burns' was serialised in the *Monthly Magazine and British Register* (January to June, 1797) and republished as *A Memoir of the Life of the Late Robert Burns* (1797). Heron acclaimed Burns as a poetic genius and, an assiduous gatherer of gossip from Dumfries, suggested that the poet gradually degenerated into a self-destructive drunk:

> In Dumfries his dissipation became still more deeply habitual. He was here exposed more than in the country, to be solicited to share the riot of the dissolute and the idle . . . . The morals of the town were, in consequence of its becoming so much the scene of public amusement, not a little corrupted: and, though a husband and a father, poor BURNS did not esape suffering by the general contamination, in a manner which I forbear to describe. In the intervals between his different fits of intemperance, he suffered still the keenest anguish of remorse and horribly afflictive foresight. (Hecht, 276–7)

Ironically, the writer who suggested that Burns drank himself to death himself suffered remorse, spending some of his final years as a debtor in Newgate Prison. He died at St Pancras Hospital, London.

HILL, PETER (1754–1837). In 1787, when Burns first met his 'liberal & much-respected Friend' (CL, 310), Peter Hill (born in Dysart, Fife) was a clerk in William Creech's bookshop. The following year he established his own bookselling business and counted Burns as one of his customers (though Elizabeth Lindsay, the woman Hill married in 1780, apparently disapproved of his friendship with the poet). Burns wrote to Hill ordering books for himself and (from 1789) for the Monkland Friendly Society though the correspondence went beyond business into a wide-ranging discussion.

In 1792 Burns sent Hill money to settle his account with the architect who erected the stone for 'poor Ferguson' (CL, 321). Accompanied by two friends – Cameron, a paper manufacturer; and Ramsay, printer of the *Edinburgh Evening Courant* – Hill visited Burns at Dumfries in 1794. Recalling the visit with relish, that October, Burns sent Hill 'a Kipperred Salmon' (CL, 323); by January 1796 the gift had become 'your *annual* KIPPER' (CL, 325). Hill became Edinburgh's City Treasurer and, in 1814, was appointed Collector of Cess.

JOHNSON, JAMES (c.1750–1811). Thought to have been a native of Ettrick, Johnson settled in Edinburgh, running an engraving shop in Bell's Wynd and a music shop in the Lawnmarket. On 22 May 1787 he published the first volume (containing a hundred songs) of his *Scots Musical Museum*, projected as an anthology of the words and music of all extant Scottish songs (he is credited with being the first person to use pewter plates for engraving music).

Burns met Johnson when the first volume was in the press and agreed to collaborate on subsequent volumes: three (each containing one hundred songs) were published during the poet's lifetime and a fifth was in production at the time of his death. Burns not only contributed around 200 songs to the *Museum* but 'was virtually the real editor' (BE, 190).

Johnson made little money from his work and eventually died in poverty (his widow dying destitute in a workhouse in 1819). However his innocent enthusiasm encouraged Burns to compose some of his finest lyrics and in his last letter to Johnson, June 1796, the poet ventured 'to prophesy, that to future ages your Publication will be the text book & standard of Scottish Song & Music' (CL, 303). The sixth and final volume of the *Museum* was published in 1803.

JOHNSTON, CAPTAIN WILLIAM. A radical reformist, Johnston founded the *Edinburgh Gazetteer* in November 1792, and Burns was quick to become a subscriber, writing to Johnston on the 13th of that month: 'Go on, Sir! Lay bare, with undaunted heart & steady hand, that horrid mass of corruption called Politics & State-Craft!' (CL, 681). Johnston was imprisoned for editing the newspaper, as was his successor. When Burns was being investigated by the Excise Board as 'head of a disaffected party' (CL, 436) he told Graham of Fintry (5 January 1793) that he had once met Johnston, subscribed to his newspaper and sent him two poems ('The Rights of Woman' and 'On Some Commemorations of Thomson'). That said, 'Of Johnston, the publisher of the Edinburgh Gazetteer, I know nothing . . . . If you think that I act improperly in allowing his paper to come addressed to me, I shall immediately countermand it' (CL, 437).

KILPATRICK, NELLY (*c.*1760–*c.*1820). The 'Handsome Nell' of Burns's first poem, composed in the autumn of 1774 'in a wild enthusiasm of passion' (first Common Place Book). Burns and Nelly (daughter of a farmer at Parclewan, Dalrymple) were gathering the harvest sheaves at Mount Oliphant when he experienced an amorous excitement in her presence. Consequently, he 'first committed the sin of RHYME' to celebrate this 'bonie, sweet, sonsie lass' (AL). Since Nelly's favourite Scotch reel was 'I am a man unmarried', Burns wrote his poem to fit the music. Two (of the seven) quatrains indicate the adolescent infatuation: 'A bonie lass, I will confess,/Is pleasant to the e'e;/But without some better qualities/She's no a lass for me.//But Nelly's looks are blythe and sweet,/And what is best of a',/Her reputation is complete,/And fair without a flaw' ('Handsome Nell').

Nelly, who became Mrs William Bone, is fondly remembered in the third stanza of 'To the Guidwife of Wauchope House' (1787): 'I see her yet, the sonsie quean/That lighted up my jingle,/Her witching smile, her pauky een/That gart my heart-strings tingle!/I fired, inspired,/At ev'ry kindling keek,/But, bashing and dashing,/I feared ay to speak.'

LAWRIE, SIR ROBERT (d.1804). Like Robert Riddell, Sir Robert Lawrie – MP for Dumfries from 1774–1804 – was defeated (by Alexander Fergusson) in the drinking-contest described in Burns's mock-epic ballad 'The Whistle'. The little ebony whistle was supposedly brought over to Scotland by a heavy-drinking Dane in the service of Anne, James VI's queen, and won in a drinking-contest by Sir

Robert Lawrie of Maxwelton, MP for Dumfriesshire, who then lost
it to a member of the Riddell family.

According to tradition, the whistle was placed on the table before
a drinking-contest and awarded to the man who could blow it when
his companions had collapsed. In 'The Whistle', Burns writes of Sir
Robert: 'The gallant Sir Robert fought hard to the end;/But who can
with Fate and quart bumpers contend?/Though Fate said, a hero
should perish in light;/So uprose bright Phoebus – and down fell
the knight.'

LORIMER, JEAN (1775–1831). Burns's 'Chloris' was born at Craigieburn, near Moffat; her father, William Lorimer, was a publican and
farmer at Kemmishall, near Dumfries. Burns was one of several
excisemen attracted to Jean and the poet wrote several songs for
her, including 'Craigieburn Wood', on behalf of his colleague John
Gillespie. To escape Gillespie's attentions, Jean eloped to Gretna
Green with a Moffat farmer called Whelpdale who quickly left her
to avoid his creditors (it was twenty-three years before she saw him
again, and then in the debtor's prison at Carlisle). She returned to
Kemmishall but, when her father lost his fortune and took to drink,
Jean moved to Dumfries where she frequently visited Burns. He
called her Chloris (for example, in the quatrain 'On Chloris') and, in
a letter of November 1794 to Thomson, described her as 'the lovely
goddess of my inspiration' (CL, 662). Burns insisted that Jean was
'a Mistress, or Friend . . . in the guileless simplicity of Platonic love'
(CL, 658) though James Hogg supposed that Burns had an affair
with her.

MACKENZIE, HENRY (1745–1831). Burns described Henry Mackenzie's
The Man of Feeling (1771) as 'a book I prize next to the Bible'
(CL, 55) and identified with the tearful Harley, soft-hearted hero
of the sentimental novel. The son of an Edinburgh physician,
Mackenzie studied law in Edinburgh and London and practised
in the Scottish Court of Exchequer. He was editor of the *Mirror*
(printed by William Creech) and (from 1785–7) the *Lounger*. Shown
a copy of the Kilmarnock Edition by Dugald Stewart, he wrote an
unsigned essay on the book in the *Lounger* of 9 December 1786,
acclaiming Burns as a genius and 'this Heaven-taught ploughman'
(CH, 70), a description that defined Burns for generations, despite
its inaccuracy (Burns being a tenant-farmer, not a ploughman). In
1787 Mackenzie advised Burns on his dealings with Creech.

MACKENZIE, DR JOHN (*c*.1755–1837). An Ayrshire man, Mackenzie studied medicine at Edinburgh University and, at the invitation of Sir John Whitefoord, established a practice in Mauchline where he married Helen Miller, one of 'The Belles of Mauchline'. Mackenzie met Burns at Lochlea, in spring 1783, when he attended the poet's ailing father. Burns's regard for Mackenzie is evident in 'The Holy Fair' where the doctor is personified as Common Sense who departs when confronted by an Auld Licht preacher: 'Common-sense has taen the road/An aff, an up the Cowgate'. In 1786 Mackenzie – as Depute Master of St James's Lodge, Tarbolton – received a verse epistle ('Friday first's the day appointed') – to attend 'our grand procession'; and (in September) a first draft of 'The Calf'.

It was Mackenzie who sent Dugald Stewart a copy of the Kilmarnock Edition and brought the poet and philosopher together. Mackenzie also eased Burns's entrance into Edinburgh society by sending off letters of recommendation to, for example, Sir John Whitefoord. When Burns returned to Mauchline in February 1788 he rented an upstairs room in Mackenzie's house for himself and Jean who there gave birth to a second set of twins. The house was purchased by the Burns Federation in 1917 and is preserved as a museum.

McLEHOSE, AGNES CRAIG (1759–1841). Burns's Clarinda, the daughter of a Glasgow surgeon, married John McLehose at the age of seventeen and bore him four children (one of whom died in infancy) in as many years. Before the birth of her fourth child she left the profligate McLehose and returned to her father who died in 1782 whereupon Agnes – Nancy to her friends – took a flat at General's Entry, Potterrow (house gone), living on an annuity supplied by her uncle, Lord Craig, a Court of Session Judge.

Her ambition to meet Burns, then the literary lion of Edinburgh, was realised on 4 December 1787 at a tea-party. If Burns's poems had excited her interest, this meeting in the flesh positively thrilled her and she invited the poet to take tea with her. Before he could accept he dislocated his knee in a fall from a coach. This enforced passivity led to the celebrated correspondence between 'Sylvander' and 'Clarinda', Arcadian names suggested by Nancy and welcomed by Burns (in a letter of 28 December 1787).

After exchanging formalities, Burns admitted to an emotional attraction which, Nancy felt, must be tempered by reason and religion. Burns was not put off and, while ostensibly flattering her insipid verses as 'good Poetry', slipped in a reference to the 'God of love' (CL, 372). Nancy reminded Burns she was a married woman and when he next mentioned love she countered with religion.

This epistolary courtship inflamed the poet: contemplating a month's correspondence with this attractive woman (who had, after all, instigated the relationship) he told a friend 'I am at this moment ready to hang myself for a young Edinburgh widow, who has wit and beauty more murderously fatal than the assassinating stiletto of the Sicilian Banditti' (CL, 419). Intent on physical conquest, Burns made six calls on Nancy in January 1788: on 24 January, Nancy accused Burns of indelicate behaviour and the poet apologised. Unsuited for a sustained period of Platonic love, Burns turned his attentions to the servant girl Jenny Clow and returned to Ayrshire to see Jean Armour.

On 23 February 1788 he wrote to Nancy, from Mossgiel, about his reunion with Jean, then in an advanced state of pregnancy: 'I am disgusted with her [and] tried to compare her with my Clarinda: 'twas setting the expiring glimmer of a farthing taper beside the cloudless glory of the meridian sun' (CL, 399). Nevertheless, he married Jean less than six weeks later, keeping in touch with Nancy by letter on such subjects as the misfortunes of Jenny Clow.

Learning that Nancy intended to rejoin her now prosperous husband in Jamaica, Burns made his last visit to Edinburgh and, on 6 December 1791 Clarinda and Sylvander met for the last time at Lamont's Land. On 27 December, Burns sent Nancy, from Dumfries, 'Ae Fond Kiss', the finest of the ten songs he wrote for her: 'I'll ne'er blame my partial fancy:/Naething could resist my Nancy!/But to see her was to love her,/Love but her, and love for ever.'

In January, Nancy sailed for Jamaica in the hope of a reconciliation with her husband but found, instead, that he had a black mistress and a daughter by her. Returning to Scotland, Nancy corresponded briefly with Burns and, in her *Journal* for 6 December 1831, noted 'This day I can never forget. Parted with Burns, in the year 1791, never more to meet in this world. Oh, may we meet in Heaven!'

McLURE, DAVID. A merchant in Ayr, he was William Burnes's landlord for Lochlea farm, Tarbolton, charging an annual rent of one pound per acre for 130 swampy acres. It was an oral agreement and eventually McLure, desperately short of cash, demanded arrears of rent. A warrant of sequestration was operated in May 1783 against William Burnes who took his case to the Edinburgh Court of Session which, in January 1784, upheld his case. William Burnes was ruined, having spent his savings in legal costs; less than a month after the court decision he died. McLure later became a merchant in Liverpool.

McMURDO, JOHN (1743–1803). Chamberlain to the 4th Duke of Queensberry (a man Burns detested), McMurdo lived at Drumlanrig Castle until he retired in 1797 and settled at Hardriggs, Dumfries. There is a reference to 'McMurdo and his lovely spouse' in the 'Election Ballad at Close of the Contest for Representing the Dumfries Burghs 1790' and Burns regarded McMurdo highly enough to send him, in February 1792, a copy of his manuscript collection of bawdy songs and poems (arguably the source of the 1800 edition of *The Merry Muses of Caledonia*): 'I think I once mentioned something to you of a Collection of Scots Songs I have for some years been making . . . When you are tired of them, please leave them with Mr Clint of the King's Arms. – There is not another copy of the Collection in the world . . . '(CL, 494). Burns wrote lines 'On John McMurdo, Esq' and 'To John McMurdo, Esq., of Drumlanrig'.

MAXWELL, DR WILLIAM (1760–1834). Both Jacobite and Jacobin in sympathies, Maxwell (son of James Maxwell of Kirconnell) was educated at the Jesuit College, Dinant, and studied medicine at Edinburgh University (1784–7). Drawn to France by his revolutionary views he joined the National Guard in which capacity, on 21 January 1793, he escorted Louis XVI to the scaffold. Returning to Scotland he settled, in 1794, in Dumfries and became friendly with Burns whom he treated during his final illness. Many Burnsians have blamed him for treating the poet by prescribing sea-bathing at Brow on the Solway coast. R. D. Thornton, in *William Maxwell to Robert Burns* (1979), argues that Burns prescribed the Brow treatment for himself, against the advice of Maxwell. The dying Burns greatly valued his friendship with his doctor: he presented Maxwell with a pair of Excise pistols; decided his unborn son should be called Maxwell, after the doctor; and called for help from Maxwell in his last moments. After the poet's death, Maxwell helped to raise money for a fund for Burns's family and served on the committee to erect a Burns Mausoleum.

MILLER, PATRICK (1731–1815). Burns's landlord at Ellisland was born in Glasgow. After working as a sailor he set up as a banker in Edinburgh, becoming a director of the Bank of Scotland in 1767. He purchased the estate of Dalswinton, in the Nith valley near

Dumfries, in 1785 and attempted to improve his run-down property through agricultural experiments (he also attempted innovations in steam navigation).

Discovering, in December 1786, that Miller was the giver of a gift of ten guineas, Burns met his admirer. On 14 January 1787 he cautiously considered Miller's offer to rent him a farm on Dalswinton estate, noting 'Mr Miller is no Judge of land; and though I dare say he means to favour me, yet he may give me, in his opinion, an advantageous bargain that may ruin me' (CL, 100). Burns eventually decided to strike a bargain with Miller in March 1788: he was to pay an annual rent of fifty pounds for the first three years, thereafter seventy pounds annually; Miller provided 300 pounds for the building of a farmhouse and the fencing of the fields.

Burns's doubts about the viability of Ellisland farm were confirmed by the first harvest and on 11 January 1790 he wrote to his brother Gilbert: 'This Farm has undone my enjoyment of myself. – It is a ruinous affair on all hands. – But let it go to hell! I'll fight it out and be off with it' (CL, 358). After some acerbic exchanges, Burns sold the lease of Ellisland to Miller whom the poet cursed for his 'meddling vanity' (CL, 320).

MILLER, PATRICK (1769–1845). The son of Burns's landlord (see above) and an army captain, Patrick Miller, Jun., was the successful Whig candidate in the election of 12 July 1790 for the Dumfriesshire Burghs: Burns, though more Whig than Tory (see 'Election Ballads'), distrusted young Miller 'a youth by no means above mediocrity in his abilities' (CL, 432); in Burns's ballad 'The Five Carlins' Miller is described as 'a Soger youth'. Captain Miller's friend, James Perry, owned the *Morning Chronicle* and offered Burns a literary post. The poet declined the offer, in a letter of March 1794, but agreed that the paper could publish 'Scots Wha Hae' anonymously:

> I dare not accept [the offer of a post on the *Morning Chronicle*]. You well know my Political sentiments; & were I an insular individual, unconnected with a wife & a family of children, with the most fervent enthusiasm I would have volunteered my services: I then could & would have despised all consequences that might have ensued. (CL, 699)

MITCHELL, JOHN (1731–1806). A farmer's son who first studied for the ministry, Mitchell became Collector of Excise at Dumfries in 1788. The following year Burns, armed with a letter of introduction from Robert Graham of Fintry, presented himself to Mitchell who, in August, indicated that Burns would be appointed to the Excise. In a letter of 9 December 1789 to Graham of Fintry, Burns acknowledged 'the generous friendship of Mr Mitchel my Collector' (CL, 431). When the poet's political opinions were investigated by the Excise Board in December 1792, Mitchell spoke up in Burns's favour. At the end of 1795 Burns sent an epistle 'To Collector Mitchell' asking for the loan of a guinea: 'I modestly fu fain wad hint it,/That One-pound-one, I sairly want it;/If wi the hizzie down ye sent it,/It would be kind;/And while my heart wi life-blood dunted,/I'd bear't in mind!' Mitchell became Collector at Haddington in 1802.

MOORE, DR JOHN (1729–1802). The man to whom Burns addressed his celebrated Autobiographical Letter of 2 August 1787 was born in Stirling, son of the Rev Charles Moore, and educated at Glasgow University where he studied medicine. From 1772 until 1778, when he established a practice in London, he was tutor and travelling companion to two successive Dukes of Hamilton. After publishing travel books he brought out, in 1786, a volume of Natural Sketches as well as the novel *Zeluco*. The same year his friend Mrs Dunlop sent him a copy of the Kilmarnock Edition. Impressed, he asked Mrs Dunlop to get Burns to write to him but the poet was, or said he was, intimidated by Moore's literary reputation. When Moore wrote directly to Burns, the response was (after a few letters of formal flattery) the Autobiographical Letter.

In 1792 Moore was in Paris when (10 August) the mob invaded the Tuileries and (13 August) imprisoned the royal family. His *Journal during a Residence in France* (1793) expressed his hostility to revolutionary developments and Burns condemned the book in a letter of January 1795 to Mrs Dunlop: 'Entre nous, you know my Politics; & I cannot approve of the honest Doctor's whining over the deserved fate of . . . a perjured Blockhead & an unprincipled Prostitute' (CL, 214). Mrs Dunlop was outraged at the reference to the executions of Louis XVI and Marie Antoinette, and Burns's association with Dr Moore was at an end.

MUIR, ROBERT (1758–8). Born in Kilmarnock, Muir became a wine merchant in his father's business. After meeting him in 1786 Burns became a firm friend of Muir who subscribed for seventy-two copies of the Kilmarnock Edition and forty copies of the First Edinburgh Edition. Burns wrote to Muir, on 8 September 1786, about the birth of Jean Armour's first twins; and on 7 March 1788 – shortly before Muir's death from consumption on 22 April – wrote to express the hope that 'the Spring will renew your shattered frame' (CL, 90). Writing to Mrs Dunlop (13 December 1789) Burns remembered Muir as 'the disinterested friend of my early life; the man who rejoiced to see me, because he loved me & could serve me' (CL, 181).

MURDOCH, JOHN (1747–1824). A powerful early influence on the poet, he was hired by William Burnes as tutor to his sons Robert and Gilbert. Born in Ayr, educated at the local burgh school and Edinburgh, Murdoch was engaged by Burnes (and four of his neighbours), in May 1765, to teach at the little Alloway school a few yards from Burnes's clay cottage.

Murdoch instructed Robert and Gilbert in reading and writing, using several standard texts: the Bible, A. Fisher's *New Grammar, with English Exercise*, Arthur Masson's *English Spelling Book* and Masson's *Collection of Prose and Verse* which contained verse by Shakespeare, Milton, Dryden, Addison, Thomson, Gray, Akenside, Shenstone as well as such prosaic models as Mrs Elizabeth Rowe's *Moral Letters*. ('The influence which [Masson's Collection] exerted on Burns can hardly be overstated. He memorized much of the poetry, and used Mrs Rowe's letters as models for many of his own "literary" attempts in prose' [Snyder, 44].) Murdoch wrote of this period:

> My pupil, Robert Burns, was then between six and seven years of age; his preceptor about eighteen . . . . In reading, dividing words into syllables by rule, spelling without book, parsing sentences, &c., Robert and Gilbert were generally at the upper end of the class, even when ranged with boys by far their seniors . . . . Gilbert always appeared to me to possess a more lively imagination and to be more of the wit, than Robert. I attempted to teach them a little church-music. Here they were left far behind by all the rest of the school. Robert's ear, in particular, was remarkably dull, and his voice untunable. It was long before I could get them to distinguish one tune from another. Robert's countenance was generally grave, and expressive of a serious, contemplative, and thoughtful mind . . . and certainly, if any person who knew the two boys, had been asked which

of them was most likely to court the muses, he would surely never have guessed that Robert had a propensity of that kind. (Murdoch, cited by Snyder, 42–3)

Murdoch left Alloway at the beginning of 1768 and in 1773, when he was teaching English at the burgh school in Ayr, Burns spent three weeks with him:

Robert Burns came to board and lodge with me, for the purpose of revising English grammar, etc., that he might be better qualified to instruct his brothers and sisters at home. He was now with me day and night, in school, at all meals, and in all my walks. At the end of one week I told him, that, as he was now pretty much master of the parts of speech, etc., I should like to teach him something of French pronunciation . . . Robert was glad to hear the proposal, and immediately we attacked the French with great courage. (Murdoch, cited by Snyder, 51–2)

For criticising Rev William Dalrymple, minister of the parish church (and the man who baptised Burns), Murdoch was (in 1776) dismissed from his teaching post in Ayr. He lived in London as a shopkeeper who supplemented his meagre income by teaching French.

NICOL, WILLIAM (1744–97). A tailor's son, born at Dumbretton in Annan parish, Nicol was educated at Annan Academy and Edinburgh University. In 1774 he became classical master in Edinburgh's High School: according to Lord Cockburn, who was one of his pupils, Nicol was an insensitive man and sadistic schoolteacher.

Burns was probably drawn to Nicol, in his Edinburgh period, by a common interest in drinking. Nicol accompanied Burns on his Highland tour of 25 August–16 September 1787 and often embarrassed the poet who described him as 'that obstinate Son of Latin Prose' (CL, 361) after one incident. Still, the two men remained friends despite Nicol's argumentative nature. In 1795 Nicol quarrelled with the Rector of the High School and left to form his own school which, appropriately enough, died when he did.

PATON, ELIZABETH. In the text of 'The Vision', as printed in the Kilmarnock Edition, Burns compares his muse, Coila, to a real woman: 'And such a leg! my Bess, I ween,/Could only peer it;/Sae straught, sae taper, tight and clean,/Nane else came near it.' Subsequent editions substituted 'my bonie Jean' (that is, Jean Armour) for 'my Bess, I ween'. Bess was Elizabeth Paton, a servant girl at Lochlea. After his father's death, in February 1784, Burns felt free to consummate his relationship with Bess when he moved to Mossgiel and she returned to her home at Largieside. Bess gave birth to the poet's first illegitimate child, Elizabeth, on 22 May 1785. Burns celebrated Bess in a bawdy poem included in his first Common Place Book ('My girl she's airy, she's buxom and gay'), referred to Bess's pregnancy in 'Epistle to John Rankine' and addressed his daughter in 'A Poet's Welcome to his Love-Begotten Daughter': 'Welcome my bonie, sweet, wee dochter!/Tho ye come here a wee unsought for'. The bawdy poem 'The Fornicator' suggest that Burns and Bess did public penance in Mauchline Kirk in 1785.

POOSIE NANSIE. Wife of George Gibson and owner of Poosie Nansie's Tavern, in the Cowgate (now Castle Street), Mauchline, Agnes Gibson knew Burns as a regular customer. Poosie Nansie's Tavern is the setting of 'The Jolly Beggars': 'Ae night at e'en a merry core/O randie, gangrel bodies,/In Poosie-Nansie's held the splore'. On account of her speed at running errands, Poosie Nansie's dimwitted daughter was known as 'Racer Jess' and is mentioned in 'The Holy Fair': 'There Racer Jess, and twa-three whores,/Are blinkin at the entry'.

RAMSAY, JOHN (1736–1814). During his eight-day stay in Harvieston, in October 1787, Burns twice visited John Ramsay of Ochtertyre, in the parish of Kincardine-in-Menteith, near Stirling. Ramsay, described by Burns as 'a man to whose worth I cannot do justice' (CL, 359), suggested that the poet should write a play, 'similar to *The Gentle Shepherd*' (BE, 294). Ramsay supplied Currie with material for his edition of Burns.

RICHMOND, JOHN (1765–1846). A lawyer's clerk in Gavin Hamilton's office, he was Burns's closest friend during his first year in Mauchline and, subsequently, the recipient of some of his most revealing letters. Richmond shared Burns's love of convivial and female company: he too was a fornicator disciplined by the Mauchline Kirk Session and appears in 'Libel Summons' (or

'Court of Equity') as 'Richmond the third, our trusty Clerk,/The minutes regular to mark'. Richmond moved to Edinburgh in 1785 and, at the close of the following year, Burns arrived in the city and stayed in the room his friend rented in Baxter's Close, Lawnmarket. In August 1787 Burns again stayed with Richmond (for two days) in Edinburgh. Richmond eventually went back to Mauchline and married Janet Surgeoner, with whom he had been cited by Mauchline Kirk Session.

RIDDELL, ELIZABETH KENNEDY (d.1801). Daughter of Walter Kennedy, Elizabeth married Robert Riddell of Glenriddell in 1784. Burns thought enough of her to name his daughter, born on 1 November 1792, Elizabeth Riddell Burns. Alas, he soon had cause to regret his friendship for it was almost certainly Elizabeth to whom Burns sent his notorious 'letter from hell'.

According to tradition, during the festive season of 1793 Burns attended a party at Friars' Carse, Elizabeth's home, and discussed the legendary Rape of the Sabine Women with the other men present, including Captain Robert Riddell. When the men joined the women in the drawing-room, an inebriated Burns playfully acted out the rape to Elizabeth who was horrified. Burns was ordered from the house and, next day, wrote to Elizabeth:

> I daresay this is the first epistle you ever received from this nether world. I write you from the regions of Hell, amid the horrors of the damned. The time and manner of my leaving your earth I do not exactly know, as I took my departure in the heat of a fever of intoxication, contracted at your too hospitable mansion . . . To the men of the company I will make no apology. – Your husband, who insisted on my drinking more than I chose, has no right to blame me, and the other gentlemen were partakers of my guilt. But to you, Madam, I have much to apologize. Your good opinion I valued as one of the greatest acquisitions I had made on earth, and I was truly a beast to forfeit it. (CL, 697)

Neither Elizabeth nor her husband forgave Burns.

RIDDELL, MARIA BANKS WOODLEY (1772–1808). Born and raised in England, in 1788 Maria went with her father (Governor of the Leeward Islands) to the West Indies where she met and (in 1790) married Walter Riddell – younger brother of Robert Riddell and a widower who had inherited his wife's sugar estates. In 1792 Walter put down a deposit on the estate of Goldielea, near Dumfries, and renamed it Woodley Park in honour of his wife.

Before she moved into Woodley Park, Maria asked Burns to introduce her to Smellie who was pleased to publish her *Voyages to the Madeira and Leeward and Caribbee Islands* (1792). She also wrote poems which Burns pronounced 'always correct, & often elegant [and] much beyond the common run of the Lady Poetesses of the day' (CL, 597).

Greatly attracted to Maria, Burns sent her effusive letters; when her husband returned to the West Indies, on business in 1793, he saw her in Dumfries and she was possibly present at Friars' Carse on the evening, in late 1793, he so outrageously offended Elizabeth Riddell with the Sabine Rape simulation. Maria felt bound to side with her sister-in-law and broke with Burns. Infuriated by what he saw as an injustice, Burns returned Maria's Common Place Book and composed some bitter lines about her: 'Here lies, now a prey to insulting neglect,/What once was a butterfly, gay in life's beam' ('Monody'); 'If you rattle along like your mistress's tongue,/Your speed will out-rival the dart;/But, a fly for your load, you'll break down on the road,/If your stuff be as rotten's her heart.' ('Pinned to Mrs Walter Riddell's Carriage.')

In 1795 Burns and Maria were reconciled. As her husband had been unable to complete the purchase of Woodley Park, she moved to Tinwald House (between Dumfries and Lochmaben) then to Halleaths (on the eastern side of Lochmaben). In 1796 she invited Burns to attend the Assembly to be held in honour of the King's birthday, but his last letter to her (1 June 1796) explained 'I am in such miserable health as to be utterly incapable of shewing my loyalty in any way' (CL, 611). When Burns was at Brow she sent a carriage to bring him, on 5 July 1796, to her lodgings (nearby, as she too was hoping to improve her health) and was horrified by his deathly appearance. After his death she wrote a fine tribute to him in the Dumfries *Weekly Journal* (August 1796).

Maria's husband died in Antigua in 1802. In 1807, a year before her death, she married a Welsh officer of Dragoons.

RIDDELL, CAPTAIN ROBERT (1735–94). Eldest son of Walter Riddell of Glenriddell (in Glencairn parish, Dumfriesshire) he was educated at Dumfries (James Currie was a fellow pupil) and at the universities of St Andrews and Edinburgh. Joining the Royal Scots, he was promoted to Captain in 1771. He retired in 1782 – settling in Friars'

Carse on the Glenriddell estate – and, two years later, married Elizabeth Kennedy. He sold Glenriddell estate, after inheriting it in 1788, and remained at Friars' Carse.

On moving into Ellisland in June 1788, Burns became friendly with his near-neighbour Riddell who gave him a key to the hermitage, a little summer-house on his estate: on 28 June, Burns produced the first version of 'Verses in Friars' Carse Hermitage'; in September, to celebrate Riddell's wedding anniversary, he wrote a poem ('The Day Returns') for Riddell's tune 'Seventh of November'. (Burns also used airs by Riddell in 'The Whistle', 'Nithsdale's Welcome Hame' and 'The Blue-eyed Lassie'.)

Together Burns and Riddell set up, in 1789, the Monkland Friendly Society, a communal library scheme for Dunscore parish, Nithsdale. On 16 October 1789, Riddell was (like Sir Robert Lawrie) defeated, by Alexander Fergusson, in the drinking-contest described in Burns's mock-epic ballad 'The Whistle'. The little ebony whistle (see entry on Sir Robert Lawrie) had passed to Riddell's family, but he was unable to drink as much claret as Fergusson: 'Then worthy Glenriddell, so cautious and sage,/No longer the warfare ungodly would wage:/A high Ruling Elder to wallow in wine!/He left the foul business to folks less divine.'

Riddell was active in establishing a permanent theatre, the Theatre Royal, in Dumfries (see 'Burns and the Theatre') and it was for Riddell that Burns prepared (in 1791) the Glenriddell Manuscript, two calf-bound volumes, one of verse, the other of letters. Only the volume of verse was given to Riddell for the two men fell out after Burns offended Riddell's wife Elizabeth, during the 'Sabine Rape' incident at Friars' Carse at the end of 1793 (see entry on Elizabeth Riddell). Elizabeth Riddell was unforgiving and Riddell died on 20 April 1794, a few months after the incident. Burns wrote a 'Sonnet on the Death of Robert Riddell' indicating his admiration for his lost friend: 'How can ye charm, ye flowers, with all your dyes?/Ye blow upon the sod that wraps my friend./How can I to the tuneful strain attend?/That strain flows round the untimely tomb where Riddell lies.' He also wrote to Riddell's sister Elinor, successfully requesting the return of his manuscript volume of verse.

RODGER, HUGH (1726–97). In the summer of 1775 Burns went to Kirkoswald to study mathematics under Hugh Rodger, the parish schoolteacher and local surveyor. By his own account he made 'pretty good progress' in his studies but 'made greater progress in the knowledge of mankind' (AL), learning to drink and falling in love with Peggy Thomson who lived next door to the school.

SMELLIE, WILLIAM (1740–95). Creech's partner and the printer of the Edinburgh editions of Burns's poems, 'old sinfull Smellie' (CL, 322), son of a stonemason, was born in Edinburgh and attended classes at the university while serving his apprenticeship as a printer. He became the first editor of the *Encyclopaedia Britannica* in 1771, co-founded the *Edinburgh Magazine* in 1773, and translated Buffon's *Natural History* (6 vols, 1780–1). He also founded the Crochallan Fencibles, a convivial club which met in Anchor Close (off the High Street) where Smellie's office was also located.

Smellie introduced Burns to the Crochallan Fencibles in 1787 and, as the poet's printer, entertained him in his office where Burns corrected his proofs on a stool which came to be known as Burns's Stool. Only one letter from Burns to Smellie survives, the others being destroyed as either obscene or abusive. Burns's 'William Smellie – A Sketch' salutes the man: 'His uncomb'd, hoary locks, wild-staring, thatch'd / A head for thought profound and clear unmatch'd;/Yet, tho his caustic wit was biting rude,/His heart was warm, benevolent, and good.'

SMITH, ADAM (1723–90). The great economist Adam Smith was a subscriber to the First Edinburgh Edition of *Poems, Chiefly in the Scottish Dialect*; and, as Commissioner of Customs in Edinburgh, felt Burns could be employed as one of his Salt Officers. Explaining this proposal to Burns, in a letter of 29 March 1787, Mrs Dunlop suggested the poet should call on Smith to discuss 'this Salt plan' (BE, 337). However, by the time Burns received Mrs Dunlop's letter of introduction, Smith (suffering from chronic obstruction of the bowel) had gone to London to see John Hunter, the Scots surgeon: 'Dr Smith was just gone to London the morning before I recieved your letter to him' (CL, 136) wrote Burns on 15 April 1787. The two men never met though each admired the other's work. Burns praises Smith's *Theory of Moral Sentiments* (1759) in his first Common Place Book; reading *The Wealth of Nations* (1776), in May 1789, he declared 'I could not have given any mere *man*, credit for half the intelligence Mr Smith discovers in his book' (CL, 428).

STEWART, PROFESSOR DUGALD (1753–1828). Professor of Moral Philosophy at Edinburgh University from 1785 until his retirement in 1810, Dugald Stewart was, for Burns, 'the most perfect character I ever saw' (cited by Snyder, 200). He first met Burns, on 23 October 1786, when the poet dined at his country house, Catrine Bank, near Mauchline. When Stewart returned to Edinburgh, for the university term, he took a copy of the Kilmarnock Edition to Henry Mackenzie who reviewed the volume enthusiastically in the *Lounger*. Stewart subsequently entertained and encouraged Burns in Edinburgh where he was a prominent advocate of Scottish Common Sense Philosophy. Stewart was more impressed by Burns's conversational powers than by his poetry: '[Burns's] predeliction for poetry, was rather the result of his own enthusiastic and impassioned temper, than of a genius exclusively adapted to that species of composition' (cited by Kinsley, 1534).

SUTHERLAND, GEORGE. On 11 January 1790 Burns wrote to his brother Gilbert about 'a set of very decent Players here just now' and enthusing about 'the Manager of the Company, a Mr Sutherland, who is indeed a man of genius and apparent worth' (CL, 358). Sutherland had been an actor in Edinburgh and, forming his own company, came to Dumfries in 1789, playing at the Old Asssembly Room in the George Hotel.

For the New Year's Evening of 1790 Burns wrote his 'Prologue Spoken at the Theatre of Dumfries' which Sutherland 'spouted to his Audience with great applause' (CL, 358). For the benefit night of Sutherland's wife, on 3 March 1790, Burns wrote his 'Scots Prologue for Mrs Sutherland'. That same year the actor canvassed support for the creation of a permanent theatre in the town and the Theatre Royal, Dumfries, was opened on 29 September 1792 with James Brown Williamson as actor-manager and Sutherland as assistant manager.

SYME, JOHN (1755–1831). After a spell in the Army, Syme became a Writer to the Signet in Dumfries. He inherited his father's Kirkcudbrightshire estate but, with the collapse of the Ayr Bank in 1773, had to leave the estate. In 1791, becoming Collector of Stamps for the District, he settled in Dumfries: Burns's three-room apartment in the Wee Vennell (now Bank Street) was located on the floor above Syme's office. Burns visited Syme at his villa at Ryedale, on the west side of the Nith, and the two men became close friends who twice toured Galloway together (30 July–2 August 1793 and 25–28 June 1794). Syme visited Burns at Brow on 15 July 1796 and was appalled at the poet's condition; after his friend's death Syme helped to organise his funeral and to raise funds for his family. Syme also encouraged Currie to make his edition. Burns addressed Syme in 'Inscription on a Goblett and 'To John Syme of Ryedale'.

THOMSON, GEORGE (1757–1851). Born at Limekilns, Dumfermline, Thomson was the son of the local schoolmaster. He studied law and, in 1780, was appointed clerk – subsequently Chief Clerk – to the Board of Trustees for the Encouragement of Art and Manufacture in Scotland. A skilled violinist, he pursued his musical passions as a performer (favouring the violin quartets of Pleyel) and as a collector of Scottish songs.

In September 1792 he wrote to Burns, asking him to write some twenty-five songs for melodies arranged by Pleyel. Burns replied from Dumfries on 16 September:

> As the request you make to me will positively add to my enjoyments in complying with it, I shall enter into your undertaking with all the small portion of abilities I have, strained to their utmost exertion by the impulse of Enthusiasm . . . . As to any remuneration, you may think my Songs either above, or *below* price; for they shall absolutely be the one or the other. – In the honest enthusiasm with which I embark in your undertaking, to talk of money, wages, fee, hire, &c. would be downright Sodomy of Soul! (CL, 617–8)

When the first part of *Select Scottish Airs* appeared in June 1793, with twenty-five songs by Burns, Thomson sent the poet a copy plus a five-pound note. Burns objected to this 'pecuniary parcel' (CL, 631) as an insult to his integrity and asked Thomson not to repeat the insult.

Delighted, however, by the quality of Thomson's production, Burns continued to supply songs – more than seventy in all – until shortly before his death (the other parts of *Select Scottish Airs* appeared after Burns's death, from 1798–1818). Sometimes Thomson altered songs without consulting the poet and in the case of 'Scots Wha Hae' he rejected Burns's preference for the air 'Hey, tutti, tatie' and substituted the tune 'Lewie Gordon'. Because of the disagreements between editor and poet, the long correspondence with Thomson gives a valuable insight into Burns's methods as a songwriter.

In his last letter to Thomson, of 12 July 1796, a desperate Burns asked for 'five pounds . . . by return of post' (CL, 679). Thomson promptly obliged, but in other ways he abused his association with the poet: he resented Burns's association with his rival Johnson; he attempted (unsuccessfully) to secure sole copyright of Burns's songs by falsifying the poet's Deed of Assignment; he altered Burns's letters when sending them to Currie. However he helped raise money for the Burns Memorial on Edinburgh's Calton Hill.

Thomson died in Leith and was buried in Kensal Green Cemetery. The inscription on his tombstone was written by Dickens, who married Thomson's grand-daughter Catherine Thomson Hogarth.

THOMSON, PEGGY. When Burns went to Kirkoswald, in 1775, to study mathematics under Hugh Rodger, he was distracted by a young woman: 'a charming Fillette who lived next door to the school overset my Trigonometry and set me off in a tangent from the sphere of my studies . . . . It was vain to think of doing any more good at school' (AL). Peggy Thomson, the 'charming Fillette', later married John Neilson of Monyfee and Burns (then intending to leave Scotland for the West Indies) presented her with a copy of the Kilmarnock Edition inscribed with his lines 'To an Old Sweetheart': 'Once fondly loved and still remember'd dear,/Sweet early object of my youthful vows,/Accept this mark of friendship, warm, sincere–/(Friendship! 'tis all cold duty now allows.)'

URBANI, PIETRO (1749–1861). After studying music in his native Milan, Urbani settled in Glasgow, in 1780, then in Edinburgh, in 1784. His *Selection of Scots Songs* (1792–4) was described, by his rival George Thomson, as 'a water-gruel collection' (BE, 366). Burns met Urbani in August 1793 at Lord Selkirk's estate at St Mary's Isle, and sent him 'A Red Red Rose' which first appeared in Urbani's *Scots Songs* in 1794. Burns fell out with Urbani at the end of 1793 when the Italian told Alexander Cunningham that he had persuaded the poet to become his collaborator: 'Urbani has told a damned falsehood – I made no engagements or connections with him whatever' (CL, 468). In 1795 Urbani and Liston (his partner) set up as music publishers at 10 Princes Street, Edinburgh; the company collapsed around 1809 and Urbani moved to Dublin where he died in poverty.

WHITEFOORD, SIR JOHN (1734–1803). Third Baronet of Blairquhan, Whitefoord was an Ayrshire laird and Master of St James's Lodge, Tarbolton: Burns first wrote to him, in November 1782, as a fellow

mason. After selling his Ballochmyle estate in 1785 he moved to
Edinburgh where, in December 1786, he received a letter from
Burns and replied, advising the poet to invest money raised on a
second edition of his poems 'in the stocking of a small farm' (CL,
51). Eventually Burns took this advice.

Whitefoord was friendly with the Earl of Glencairn and Burns
sent him his 'Lament for James, Earl of Glencairn' along with 'Lines
to Sir John Whiteford, Bart.': 'We'll mourn till we too go as he has
gone,/And tread the shadowy path to the dark world unknown.'

WILLIAMS, HELEN MARIA (1762–1827). Born in London and brought
up in Berwick, Williams was a friend, and sometime amanuensis, to
Dr John Moore. Through Moore she sent Burns a sonnet, honouring
him as a 'Heav'n taught' genius and in 1788 she published a
poem on *The Slave Trade* which Burns (August 1789) subjected
to considered criticism. In 1790, the year she published the novel
Julia, Williams went to France full of revolutionary fervour. Her
Girondist sympathies led to her being imprisoned until the death
of Robespierre and she later renounced her revolutionary beliefs,
turning to the Bourbon cause.

WILLIAMSON, DAVID (1766–1824). On 12 July 1796, nine days before
he died, Burns was frantic because he owed money, on a Dumfries
Volunteer uniform, to 'A Cruel scoundrel of a Haberdasher [who]
has commenced a process & will infallibly put me into jail' (CL, 679);
accordingly he wrote to his cousin James Burness for ten pounds,
and to George Thomson for five pounds. David Williamson, the
'scoundrel of a Haberdasher', married Jane Young who, inheriting
money from her uncle John Paul Jones, set up the Commercial Hotel
(now the County Hotel) in a High Street tenement where Bonnie
Prince Charlie had his headquarters in late 1745.

WILSON, JOHN (*c*.1751–1839). A parish schoolmaster in Tarbolton,
Wilson was the original of Burns's Dr Hornbook (a hornbook being
a sheet of paper, mounted on wood and covered with a protective
sheet of horn, displaying the alphabet, digits, the Lord's Prayer
and rules of spelling). To supplement his income, Wilson opened
a grocer's shop in which he sold medicines and dispensed medical
advice (relying on his reading of a few medical books). Burns heard
Wilson parade his medical opinions at Tarbolton Masonic Lodge, of
which Wilson was Secretary. In 1784 Wilson, as Kirk Session clerk,
signed the certificate of character which William Burnes's widow

took with her when moving from Tarbolton to Mauchline parish. The following year Burns wrote 'Death and Doctor Hornbook' in which Death complains of his rival: 'That's just a swatch o Hornbook's way;/Thus goes he on from day to day,/Thus does he poison, kill, an slay,/An's weel paid for't:/Yet stop me o my lawfu prey/Wi's damn'd dirt.' Having quarrelled with the Tarbolton minister, Wilson left the village in 1792. He became a schoolmaster in Glasgow and Session Clerk of Gorbals Parish.

A Burns Topography

Artistically one of the least parochial of poets, Burns nevertheless composed the verse in the Kilmarnock Edition without ever straying from his native Ayrshire. His early work is richly topographical as well as autobiographical, his later poems and songs often have geographical associations. The Topography indicates places that meant most to Burns as man and poet.

*   *   *

AYRSHIRE

Alloway

Two miles south of Ayr, the village where Burns was born on 25 January 1759 remains the main focus of attention for Burnsians. *Burns Cottage*, the 'auld clay biggin' ('The Vision'), adjoins the *Burns Cottage Museum* (open April–October) containing relics and 'the finest single collection of [poetical holographs] in the world' (Kinsley, 965). Half a mile south of Burns Cottage is the *Land o Burns Centre* with an audio-visual show and exhibition (open all year); this is the starting-point for the *Burns Heritage Trail* developed by the Scottish Tourist Board. Opposite the Centre is *Alloway Kirk* (where the poet's father is buried), scene of the witches' orgy in 'Tam o Shanter': 'Kirk-Alloway was drawing nigh,/Whare ghaists and houlets nightly cry.' The *Brig o Doon* (over which Tam and his grey mare Meg, minus tail, escaped from the witches) crosses the river near the *Burns Monument* (completed 1823, open April–Oct.)

which features some Burns characters as fashioned by local sculptor James Thom.

Ayr

The county town of Ayrshire, thirty miles south-west of Glasgow, is praised in a parenthesis in 'Tam o Shanter': '(Auld Ayr, whom ne'er a town surpasses,/For honest men and bonie lasses)'. The *Tam o Shanter Inn* (now a museum, open all year) was formerly a brewhouse supplied by Douglas Graham (the original of Tam). Outside the railway station is a *Statue* (1891) of Burns who, one day old, was baptised (by the moderate minister Rev William Dalrymple) in the *Auld Kirk* of Ayr (off the High Street, up Kirk Close). The *Auld Brig*, a fifteenth-century footbridge still in use, debates with the *New Brig* (designed by Robert Adam, completed 1788, rebuilt 1877) in 'The Brigs of Ayr', composed in the autumn of 1786 when the new bridge was being constructed. Burns writes: 'Auld Brig appear'd of ancient Pictish race,/The vera wrinkles Gothic in his face . . . New Brig was buskit in a braw new coat,/That he at Lon'on, frae ane Adams got.'

Failford

Two miles east of Mauchline, Failford – where the Water of Fail flows into the river Ayr – plays an important part in the story of Burns and his Highland Mary. A footbridge, in the centre of the village, leads to a grassy mound and *Memorial* supposed to mark the exact spot where Burns said farewell to Mary Campbell. On the second Sunday of May 1786 the poet met Mary in Failford: over the Fail Water they clasped hands and exchanged Bibles as a matrimonial gesture (the two-volume Bible Burns gave Mary is kept in the Alloway Burns Monument).

Irvine

Burns (to whom there is a bronze statue, by Pittendrigh MacGillivray, on *Irvine Moor*) spent seven months in Irvine (ten miles north of Ayr) from spring 1781. Determined to acquire a remunerative skill, he chose to learn flax-dressing in Irvine, lodging first at 4 *Glasgow Vennel* (the house and flex-dressing shop have been restored and are open all year). Disastrously his partner turned out to be 'a scoundrel of the first water, who made money by the mystery of thieving' (AL). Celebrating the New Year of 1782, the flax-dressing shop was accidentally burned down by the poet's partner's drunken wife. *Irvine Burns Club*, established in 1826 and one of the oldest in the world, is located in *Eglinton Street* and contains a museum open to the public on Saturday afternoons.

Kilmarnock

On the corner of Waterloo Street and King Street, in Starr Inn Close, stood *John Wilson's Printing Shop* (now gone, but site marked by a granite slab) which, on 31 July 1786, issued the first edition of Burns's *Poems, Chiefly in the Scottish Dialect*: the Kilmarnock Edition.

The book was published by subscription, the poet sending Wilson proposals in April 1786. It was stitched in blue paper, cost three shillings a copy and the edition of 612 was sold out in a month at a profit, to Burns, of around £50. Wilson refused to print a second, enlarged edition so Burns turned to William Smellie in Edinburgh.

There is a copy of the Kilmarnock Edition in the museum of the *Kay Park Monument* (built 1879).

Kirkoswald

A coastal Carrick village four miles south-west of Maybole, Kirkoswald delighted Burns in the summer of 1775 when he was sent there to study at Hugh Rodger's school: 'I spent my seventeenth summer on a smuggling coast a good distance from home at a noted school, to learn Mensuration, Surveying, Dialling, &c. in which I made a pretty good progress' (AL). By his own reckoning he made infinitely more progress in the study of humankind, drinking and becoming infatuated with the charming Peggy Thomson. The *Shanter Hotel*, on the site of Hugh Rodger's school, has a pewter tankard supposedly used by Burns. Douglas Graham, the original of Tam o Shanter, is buried in the *Old Graveyard* of Kirkoswald. Across the road from the graveyard is *Souter Johnie's House* (now owned by the National Trust for Scotland and open April–Sept.): John Davidson (Souter Johnie) moved into the thatched cottage in 1785 and the house contains period furniture and Burns relics including the poet's Masonic Badge. On the sward of Souter Johnie's kailyard are stone figures, by James Thom, showing Tam, Souter Johnie, and the innkeeper and his wife from 'Tam o Shanter'.

Leglen Wood

High above the banks of the river Ayr, Leglen Wood (about three miles from Auchenruivie) was identified as William Wallace's hiding-place in Blind Harry's poem *Wallace* (which Burns read in Hamilton of Gilbertfield's abridged version): 'Syne to the Leglen wood when it was late/To make a silent and a safe retreat'. In a letter of 15 November 1786 to Mrs Dunlop, Burns quotes Blind Harry's couplet then describes a youthful visit to the place: 'I chose a fine summer Sunday, the only day of the week in my power and walked half a dozen miles to pay my respects to the 'Leglen wood' [and] explored every den and dell where I could suppose my heroic Countryman to have sheltered' (CL, 131). A *cairn* was erected in the wood in 1929.

Lochlea

Burns lived in Lochlea farm (three miles north-west of Mauchline) from 1777 to 1784. The house in which he read Locke's *Essay Concerning Human Understanding* and composed such poems as 'The Ruined Farmer', 'Winter: A Dirge' and 'Mary Morrison' has been replaced by the present farmhouse.

The poet's father William Burnes left Mount Oliphant farm in 1777 and made an oral agreement with David McLure to rent the 130 swampy acres of Lochlea farm in the parish of Tarbolton. By 1781 Burnes was in dispute with his landlord who, finding himself short of cash, demanded arrears of rent. Ill from consumption and anguished by the prospect of prolonged litigation, Burnes nevertheless pursued his argument with McLure: in January 1784 the Edinburgh Court of Session upheld Burnes's case but the cost, in personal and legal terms, was high. Burnes died on 13 February 1784, less than a month after the court decision.

Mauchline

In the period when Burns lived at Lochlea, his father's farm, and himself farmed Mossgiel with his brother Gilbert, the poet was a frequent visitor to Mauchline (two miles from Lochlea, one mile from Mossgiel) which features in many of his poems: 'The Belles of Mauchline' celebrates Jean Armour who lived with her father, a master mason, at the foot of the Cowgate, at its junction with Howard Place. Burns probably met Jean in April 1784.

In February 1788 Burns first set up home with Jean by renting an upstairs room in Dr John Mackenzie's Mauchline house where, on 3 March, she gave birth to twins who both died that month. The doctor's house in the Backcauseway, now Castle Street, was purchased by the Burns Federation in 1917 and is preserved as a *Museum* (open all year). Around the end of March, Burns married Jean in *Gavin Hamilton's House* beside *Mauchline Castle Tower*.

Of the inns Burns enjoyed in Mauchline, three are still in evidence. *Poosie Nansie's Tavern*, once a lodging house in the Cowgate (now Castle Street) and still an inn, was the setting for 'The Jolly Beggars'. Near Poosie Nansie's is the site of the *Whitefoord Arms* (marked by a plaque on a later building) which was situated in the Cowgate opposite the parish church and which was the meeting place of 'The Court of Equity'. *Nanse Tinnock's*, almost opposite Dr Mackenzie's house, was the change-house in 'The Holy Fair' and is preserved as a museum.

In *Mauchline churchyard*, scene of 'The Holy Fair', are the graves of Gavin Hamilton, Rev William Auld, Holy Willie (William Fisher), Nanse Tinnock and – in the Armour family burial plot – the poet's in-laws and four of his children.

North of Mauchline, on the A76, is the *Burns Memorial Tower*.

Mossgiel

One mile north of Mauchline, on the Tarbolton road, Mossgiel farm was Burns's home from March 1784, a month after his father died, to July 1786 when the poet transferred his share of Mossgiel to his brother Gilbert. Some four months before the death of William Burnes, Robert and Gilbert had taken the precaution of renting, for £90 per annum, the 118-acre farm of Mossgiel from Gavin Hamilton. The single-storey but-and-ben of Burns's time has been replaced by the present farmhouse.

Burns hoped to make a success of farming but bought in bad seed which, confounded by a late harvest, deprived him of half his crops. As a poet, however, he began to assert himself, writing (at his table in the bedroom he shared with Gilbert in the stable loft) some of his finest poems, including 'The Vision', 'The Jolly Beggars', 'The Cotter's Saturday Night', 'Holy Willie's Prayer', 'Death and Dr Hornbook', 'Scotch Drink' and 'The Twa Dogs'.

Mount Oliphant

William Burnes rented, for £40 a year, the 70-acre hilltop farm of Mount Oliphant at Martinmas (11 November) 1765 and moved his family there, two miles from the 'auld clay biggin', at Whitsun 1766. Unfortunately the farm was in a poor state of cultivation and the family had to endure many difficulties. In 1769, on the death of the landlord, a factor took over the affairs of Mount Oliphant and hounded Burnes for payments, an experience Burns recreated in 'The Twa Dogs': 'Poor tenant bodies, scant o' cash,/How they maun thole a factor's snash:/He'll stamp an threaten, curse and swear/He'll apprehend them, poind their gear;/While they maun stan, wi aspect humble,/An hear it a', an fear an tremble!' The family moved to Lochlea farm in 1777.

While working at a Mount Oliphant harvest Burns, at the age of fifteen, fell in love with Nellie Kilpatrick and 'first committed the sin of RHYME' (AL) by writing a song ('Handsome Nell') for her.

Tarbolton

In 1777 Burns's father rented the 130 swampy acres of Lochlea farm in Tarbolton parish and the village of Tarbolton was much visited by the poet. During the first year he spent at Lochlea, Burns went to a country dancing school in Tarbolton: 'My father had an unaccountable antipathy against these meetings; and my going was, what to this hour I repent, in absolute defiance of his commands' (AL).

Burns, in 1780, helped found and became first president of the *Bachelors' Club*, a debating club which met in a two-storey seventeenth-century cottage, then an inn and now maintained by the National Trust for Scotland who restored it as a museum (open April–Sept.). On 4 July 1781 Burns became a freemason in St David's Lodge, No. 174, Tarbolton, which, like the monthly debating club, met in the upstairs room of the inn; a dispute later divided the

Tarbolton freemasons into two lodges, Burns moving to the St James's Lodge which met at *James Manson's inn* nearby (site marked by a stone).

To the east of Tarbolton is the signposted *Willie's Mill*, commemorated in Burns's mock epitaph on 'Wm Muir in Tarbolton Mill'. Willie, the miller, was one of the poet's closest friends: he took in Jean Armour when her father threw her out because of her association with Burns. Willie's Mill is the setting for 'Death and Dr Hornbook' – 'I was come round about the hill,/An todlin down on Willie's mill'.

EDINBURGH

Astonished by the success of the Kilmarnock Edition, Burns arrived in Edinburgh on 28 November 1786 to be met by his Mauchline friend John Richmond who accomodated him in his first-floor room in *Baxter's Close* overlooking *Lady Stair's House* where there is a museum (open June–Sept.) devoted to Burns, Scott and Stevenson. Though the Baxter's Close house has gone, there is a plaque over the Lawnmarket entrance to Lady Stair's House.

Burns was welcomed in Edinburgh as a social and cultural phenomenon: within ten days of his arrival in the capital, the Earl of Glencairn had persuaded the Caledonian Hunt to subscribe for 100 copies of the First Edinburgh Edition (duly dedicated to the Caledonian Hunt); on 9 December Henry Mackenzie's rhapsodic review of the Kilmarnock Edition appeared in the *Lounger*; on 1 February 1787 the Canongate Kilwinning Lodge, Edinburgh's most influential masonic group, affiliated him. He was welcomed by the Crochallan Fencibles, a convivial club founded by William Smellie (the printer of the First Edinburgh Edition) whose office was conveniently close in *Anchor Close* (gone).

While in Edinburgh, Burns was anxious to repay his poetic debts and, on 6 February 1787, wrote to the Bailies of the Canongate seeking permission (which was granted) to erect a memorial to Robert Fergusson in *Canongate churchyard*. The headstone, erected at Burns's expense, has an inscription by Burns: 'No sculptured Marble here, nor pompous lay,/No storied Urn nor animated Bust:/This simple stone directs pale Scotia's way,/To pour her sorrows o'er the Poet's dust.' The stone, with the inscription, was not ready until August 1789 and Burns did not pay the designer the fee of

£5.10s. until 5 February 1792 when he explained the delay to his friend Peter Hill: 'He [Robert Burn, the designer] was two years in erecting it, after I commissioned him for it; & I have been two years paying him, after he sent me his account; so he & I are quits. – He had the hardiesse to ask me interest on the sum; but considering that the money was due by one Poet, for putting a tomb-stone over another, he may, with grateful surprise, thank Heaven that ever he saw a farthing of it' (CL, 321).

The First Edinburgh Edition was published on 17 April 1787 and, after a tour of the West Highlands, Burns returned to Edinburgh on 8 August, staying in Richmond's room then moving to William Nicols's home in *Buccleuch Square*. After a Highland tour with Nicol and a tour of Stirlingshire, Burns returned to Edinburgh, moving (in late October) to a room in William Cruickshank's house on the south-west corner of *St James's Square*. On 4 December, the same year, Burns met Mrs Agnes McLehose (Nancy to her friends) at a tea-party in *Alison's Square*. Having dislocated his knee, the poet travelled in a sedan chair, on 5 January 1788, to visit Clarinda (Burns had agreed to be Sylvander to her Clarinda on 28 December 1787) at her house in General's Entry, *Potterrow* (house gone). Sylvander's romantic correspondence with Clarinda has passed into literary legend; in reality Burns tired of playing a Platonic game with Nancy. On 18 February 1788 he left Edinburgh for Ayrshire, returning only on visits.

In November 1791, Burns (now staying in Dumfries) heard from 'Clarinda' that Jenny Clow, a servant girl, was destitute in Edinburgh with a two-year-old son by the poet. In reply he claimed he had always been willing to look after the boy and asked Clarinda to give Jenny five shillings. Learning that Clarinda intended to join her now prosperous husband in Jamaica, Burns made his last visit to Edinburgh (29 November–11 December), staying at the *White Hart Inn*, on the north side of the Grassmarket, for eight days. On 6 December, Sylvander and Clarinda had their last meeting at Lamont's Land, Edinburgh. On his return to Dumfries, he sent her 'Ae Fond Kiss', the finest of his ten love songs to her.

Nancy later lived in 14 Calton Place where she died on 22 October 1841. In 1922 the Ninety Burns Club, Edinburgh, erected a *tablet* in Ravelstone stone on the east wall, containing a bronze head and bust and the word 'Clarinda'.

A *Burns Monument* was erected on the south side of Regent Road in 1830: the statue (by Flaxman) it once contained is in the Scottish

National Portrait Gallery; the relics are in Lady Stair's House. In 1985 a *Robert Burns Memorial Window* was installed in St Giles Cathedral.

DUMFRIESSHIRE

Brow

Outside the village of Ruthwell (nine miles south-east of Dumfries) a signpost indicates *Brow Well* which has the inscription 'The Brow Well visited by the poet Burns, July 1796'. Hoping, in vain, to restore his health Burns went, from 3–17 July 1796, to Brow, a hamlet on the shores of the Solway Firth, so he could drink the chalybeate waters from Brow Well and immerse himself up to his armpits in the Solway Firth. Maria Riddell saw the poet at this time and was aghast at his appearance. Burns was not only ill, but anguished. Receiving a tailor's demand for money for his Volunteer uniform, he wrote to George Thomson from Brow, on 12 July 1796, asking for £5 and enclosing the song 'Fairest Maid on Devon Banks'. He returned to Dumfries on 18 July and died three days later.

Craigieburn

Burns's first contribution to the fourth volume of Johnson's *Scots Musical Museum* (1792) was the first version of 'Craigieburn Wood': 'Sweet closes the ev'ning on Craigieburn Wood/And blythely awaukens the morrow;/But the pride o the spring on the Craigieburn Wood/Can yield me naught but sorrow.' This was one of twenty-four songs written to Jean Lorimer (Burns's 'Chloris) who was born at Craigieburn (near Moffat).

Drumlanrig Castle

The hereditary seat of the Dukes of Queensberry, and associated by Burns with William Douglas, 4th Duke of Queensberry (1724–1810), a man he attacked in 1790 as a political opportunist: 'All hail, Drumlanrig's haughty Grace,/Discarded remnant of a race/Once godlike' ('Election Ballad at Close of the Contest for Representing the Dumfries Burghs'). He was however, friendly with John McMurdo, the Duke's chamberlain. The present palace of local pink sandstone, built from 1679–90, is open to the public (mid April–mid August) and the grounds include a nature trail and an adventure woodland play area for children.

Dumfries

Burns lived in Dumfries from 11 November 1791 until his death. Tired of farming and determined to devote himself to the Excise he renounced the lease on Ellisland farm and moved into a three-room second-floor flat in the Wee Vennel, now *Bank Street* (where there is a plaque). Most of Burns's creative energy, during the Dumfries period, was concentrated on writing songs. Nevertheless, the songwriting exciseman could not avoid conflict and his enthusiasm for developments in revolutionary France – including his alleged participation in a call for the republican song 'Ç ira' at the the *Theatre Royal*, on 30 October 1792 – led to an Excise investigation at the end of 1793. Graham of Fintry saw to it that the poet kept his job but he was advised to hold his tongue in future.

On 19 May 1793 Burns moved into a fine red sandstone house in Mill Vennel – now a museum open to the public, in *Burns Street*. Here Burns wrote some of his finest songs, artistic evidence that he did not spend all his time in the *Globe Inn*, off the High Street, which still has the chair used by the bard (Burns had a daughter by the Globe's barmaid Anna Park). Because Burns was expansive in his cups, rumours still circulated about his revolutionary sympathies. As if to prove his loyalty he became a founder member of the Dumfries Volunteers on 31 January 1795 and, a few months later, wrote the patriotic song 'Does Haughty Gaul Invasion Threat?'

The poet's health deteriorated and, in the hope of a cure, he went to drink the waters at Brow and immerse himself in the Solway Firth. He died at home on 21 July 1796 and, on 25 July, his body was carried to *St Michael's churchyard* for burial in the north-east corner (Burns's pew in St Michael's Church is indicated by a tablet). In 1815 Burns's body was disinterred and moved to a vault in the *Mausoleum* erected to his memory and built by public subscription at a cost of around £1500. A sculptured group, by Turnerelli, depicts the Muse of Poetry finding Burns at the plough, an image used by the poet in the Dedication to the First Edinburgh Edition. Burns's widow was interred in the Mausoleum in 1834.

In 1986 the *Robert Burns Centre* (open all year), with audio-visual presentation of the the Dumfries Years, was established in Mill

Road, in the eighteenth-century water mill on the west bank of
the river Nith.

Ellisland Farm

Burns rented Ellisland Farm (some six miles north-west of Dumfries)
from 11 June 1788 to 10 September 1791, paying his landlord Patrick
Miller £50 a year. Although the farm's position on the west bank
of the river Nith was visually attractive, the poet was experienced
enough to suspect its agricultural viability. And he was soon to
find out that the soil was too exhausted to support his crops
profitably.

He was only a part-time farmer: having obtained his Excise commission on 14 July 1788, he was forced to divide his time between
two jobs; or, rather, three as he was active as a poet at Ellisland.
Burns is supposed to have composed 'Tam o Shanter', during one
day in 1790, while pacing the path at Ellisland overlooking the Nith
and visitors to the farm can follow the poet's footsteps on *Shanter
Walk*. At Ellisland he also wrote 'Of a' the airts the wind can blaw',
'O were I on Parnassus hill', 'I hae a wife o' my ain' and 'Willie
brewed a peck o' maut'.

By 1790 Burns was referring to 'this accursed farm' (CL, 358);
on 25 August 1791 his crops were auctioned at Ellisland and
on 10 September, that year, he formally renounced the lease on
the farm.

Ellisland was farmed until 1921, then purchased by George
Williamson, a former President of Edinburgh Burns Club. It was
gifted it to the nation in 1929 and it is preserved as a working farm,
open all year to the public.

OTHER LOCATIONS

Aberdeen

Burns visited Aberdeen, on Sunday, 9 September 1787, during
his Highland tour with William Nicol. Aberdeen's *Burns Statue*,
unveiled on 15 September 1892, is by local sculptor Henry Bain
Smith.

Aberfeldy

A signposted footpath leads to the Falls of Moness (one mile south-west of the Perthshire village of Aberfeldy) where (as the poet himself noted) Burns wrote 'The Birks of Aberfeldie' on 30 August 1787: 'Now simmer blinks on flow'ry braes,/And o'er the crystal streamlets plays,/Come let us spend the lightsome days/In the birks of Aberfeldie.'

Bannockburn

One mile south of Stirling, Bannockburn is the site of the battle of 24 June 1314 in which Robert the Bruce's army defeated a much larger army headed by Edward II. At the beginning of his Highland tour with Nicol, Burns visited Bannockburn on Sunday, 26 August 1787. In his Journal he mentioned 'the hole where glorious Bruce set his standard'; and, in a letter written the day of his visit, said 'two hours ago, I said a fervent prayer for old Caledonia over the hole in a blue whin-stone where Robert de Bruce fixed his royal Standard on the banks of Bannockburn' (CL, 89). Burns celebrated Bruce's victory in 'Scots Wha Hae', written in 1793. The site, maintained by the National Trust for Scotland, contains an Information Centre (with audio-visual display), and C. D'O Pilkington Jackson's bronze equestrian statue of Bruce (unveiled in 1964 by the Queen).

Cawdor Castle

Cawdor Castle, Nairnshire (five miles south-west of Nairn) is a structure (central tower of 1372, fortified 1454, remodelled seventeenth-century) supposedly standing on the site of the castle where Macbeth murdered Duncan in 1040. On his Highland tour with Nicol, Burns visited the castle on Sunday, 4 September 1787, noting in his Journal: 'Castle Cawdor – where Macbeth murdered King Duncan – Saw the bed in which King Duncan was stabbed.'

Culloden

Culloden battlefield (on Drummossie Moor, on the border of Nairnshire and Inverness-shire), maintained by the National Trust for Scotland, was the scene of the defeat of the Scottish clans (led by Bonnie Prince Charlie) by 'Butcher' Cumberland on 16 April 1746.

On his Highland tour with William Nicol, Burns crossed Culloden on Thursday, 6 September 1787, and noted in his Journal 'Came over Culloden Muir – reflections on the field of battle'. Burns's 'The Chevalier's Lament', completed in 1793, is cast as a monologue spoken by Bonnie Prince Charlie after Culloden. In this sentimental song the Young Pretender tells the clansmen: 'But 'tis not my suff'rings, thus wretched, forlorn,/My brave, gallant, friends, 'tis your ruin I mourn.'

Dunoon

A holiday resort in Argyllshire on the west shore of the Firth of Clyde, Dunoon has, at the foot of Castle Hill, a *Statue* to Burns's Highland Mary who was born, in 1763, on the site of Auchamore farm, behind the town.

Gatehouse of Fleet

In this little village at the head of Fleet Bay, Kircudbrightshire, Burns is supposed to have written 'Scots Wha Hae' in 1793. A room in the *Murray Arms Hotel* is pointed out as the place where he sat and completed his manuscript. Burns did visit Gatehouse around 31 July 1793; his companion John Syme recalled 'We got utterly wet, and to revenge ourselves Burns insisted at Gatehouse, on our getting utterly drunk' (cited by Kinsley, 1420). However a letter of 30 August 1793 to George Thomson suggests that the poem was composed in Dumfries and inspired in part by current political events: on 30 August, the radical lawyer Thomas Muir went on trial for sedition in Edinburgh, which is why Burns mentions, to Thomson, 'that glorious struggle for Freedom, associated with the glowing ideas of some other struggles of the same nature, *not quite so ancient*' (CL, 639). Thus the verbal assault, in the song, on 'Oppression's woes and pains' had, for Burns, a contemporary relevance.

Greenock

Planning to emigrate to Jamaica with Mary Campbell, Burns arranged to meet her in Greenock in September 1786 but the voyage was postponed and Burns went to Mauchline where (3 September) Jean Armour gave birth to twins. In October that year, Burns heard that Mary had died at Greenock, possibly in premature childbirth induced by typhus. Suddenly the journey to Jamaica seemed pointless and Burns headed, instead, for Edinburgh and literary celebrity. Mary was buried in the West Churyard and when, due to industrial expansion, her grave was opened on 5 November 1920, the bottom board of an infant's coffin was found among the remains, renewing speculation about death by premature childbirth. Mary was reinterred in the new cemetery in Nelson Street West where there is a monument.

Kirkcudbright

Burns and John Syme visited Kirkcudbright (county town of Kirkcudbrightshire) on 1 August 1793. In the *Selkirk Arms Hotel* (so tradition insists) Burns wrote the 'Selkirk Grace': 'Some have meat and cannot eat./Some cannot eat that want it:/But we have meat and we can eat,/Sae let the Lord be thankit.'

Stirling Castle

Standing on a 250-foot rock, Stirling Castle (remodelled in the fifteenth and sixteenth centuries) was recaptured from the English by Wallace in 1297, captured by the English (under Edward I) in 1304, and again recaptured from the English after Bruce's victory at Bannockburn, 1314. James II was born in the castle, Mary Queen of Scots and James VI both stayed in it. Burns first visited Stirling Castle on Sunday, 26 August 1787, after visiting Bannockburn with Nicol. A letter, written that day, explains: 'Just now from Stirling castle I have seen by the setting-sun the glorious prospect of the windings of Forth through the rich carse of Falkirk' (CL, 89). Burns revisted the Castle in October, in the company of Adair. In 1914 a *Burns Statue*, by Albert H. Hodge, was set up in Stirling.

Part II:
Aspects of Burns

Part II:
Aspects of Burns

Dialect and Diction in Burns

In a book generally dismissive of Scots as a literary language, Edwin Muir suggested that when he 'wished to express his real judgement [Burns] turned to English' (Edwin Muir, *Scott and Scotland*, 1936; rept. Edinburgh, 1982, p. 12). Muir's supposition that, for Burns, Scots was 'a language for sentiment but not for thought' (*op. cit.*, p. 13) simply ignores the evidence of Burns's poetry in pursuit of the argument that, since the sixteenth and early seventeenth centuries, the Scottish people had felt in Scots and thought in English. Muir's patronising remarks about Burns's Scots verse are as crass as those the poet had to put up with in his lifetime, as an anecdote illustrates.

On 1 February 1787 the 11th Earl of Buchan, David Erskine, wrote to Burns about the Kilmarnock Edition, praising 'These little doric pieces of yours in our provincial dialect' (CL, 266). As usual, Burns was not above 'kissing the arse of a peer' (as he accused the Douglas brothers of doing in his 'Ballad Second: The Election'), and replied in the humble role he had assumed: 'I must return to my rustic station, and, in my wonted way, woo my rustic Muse at the Ploughtail' (CL, 267). In August 1791 Lord Buchan again wrote to Burns, inviting him to travel to Ednam (seventy-five miles from Ellisland), the birthplace of James Thomson, to attend 'the coronation of the bust of Thomson, on Ednam Hill, on the 22d of September; for which day perhaps [Mr Burns's] muse may inspire an ode suited to the occasion' (cited by Kinsley, 1370).

In his reply (29 August 1791), Burns declined the invitation, on account of the harvest, but thanked 'your Lordship for the honour, the very great honour, you have done me, in inviting me to the coronation of the bust of Thomson' (CL, 267). As for an ode, Burns declared himself unequal to the task of emulating Collins's 'Ode Occasioned by the Death of Mr Thomson' but he enclosed an 'Address to the Shade of Thomson, on Crowning his Bust at Ednam, Roxburghshire, with Bays'. Collins's ode begins:

> In yonder grave a Druid lies,
>   Where slowly winds the stealing wave!
> The year's best sweets shall duteous rise
>   To deck its poet's sylvan grave!

Burns's address ends:

> So long, sweet Poet of the year!
>   Shall bloom that wreath thou well has won;
> While Scotia, with exulting tear,
>   Proclaims that Thomson is her son.
>
> (331/CW, 421)

There is not much to choose qualitatively between the two quatrains, Burns simply going through the metrical motions in honour of a poet he genuinely admired.

Burns need not have bothered with his occasional ode for the ceremonial occasion was a farce. As the bust of Thomson had been broken – 'in a midnight frolic during [September] race week' (Buchan, cited by Kinsley, 1370) – Lord Buchan laid a laurel wreath on a copy of Thomson's *The Seasons*. Burns commented on this in his quatrains 'On Some Commemorations of Thomson'. This time he broke into Scots, after the first line, and gave his honest opinion of the likes of Lord Buchan:

> Dost thou not rise, indignant Shade,
>   And smile wi spurning scorn,
> When they wha wad hae starved thy life
>   Thy senseless turf adorn?
>
> They wha about thee mak sic fuss
>   Now thou art but a name,
> Wad seen thee damn'd ere they had spar'd
>   Ae plack to fill thy wame.
>
> (332/CW, 421–2)

That, reminiscent of his attack on the Edinburgh gentry who wasted money on cards while Fergusson starved ('Epistle to

William Simson'), represents Burns's honest opinion of poets and aristocratic patrons. And when he was most honest as a poet, he was most Scottish.

Writing to George Thomson on 19 October 1794, Burns confessed:

> These English Songs gravel me to death. – I have not that command of the language that I have of my native tongue. – In fact, I think that my ideas are more barren in English than in Scottish. (CL, 660)

By that time Burns had seen three editions of his poems published and must have reflected, on reading them, that his English efforts were pastiches of favourites like Pope, Thomson, Shenstone and Gray whereas his poems 'chiefly in the Scottish dialect' were masterful. He had no longer any need for the diffidence he showed in January 1787 when writing to Dr John Moore:

> For my part, my first ambition was, and still my strongest wish is, to please my Compeers, the rustic Inmates of the Hamlet . . . I know very well, the novelty of my character has by far the greatest share in the learned and polite notice I have lately got; and in a language where Pope and Churchill have raised the laugh, and Shenstone and Gray drawn the tear; where Thomson and Beattie have painted the landskip, and Littleton and Collins described the heart; I am not vain enough to hope for distinguished Poetic fame. (CL, 246–7)

Using the language of Pope, Shenstone and Gray, he was destined to come off second best.

Quoting some lines from Burns's 'On the Death of Lord President Dundas', Matthew Arnold ('The Study of Poetry', *Essays in Criticism*, Second Series, 1888) remarked 'By his English poetry Burns in general belongs to the eighteenth century, and has little importance for us. Evidently ['On the Death of Lord President Dundas'] is not the real Burns, or his name and fame would have disappeared long ago.' This judgement of one poet by another is just. Burns became internationally celebrated through his Scots poems, not his English pastiches. Remarkably, Burns achieved such recognition by casting his finest work in a national language in a state of atrophy though his linguistic efforts were not always appreciated by his contemporaries. Several of his admirers, including Dr John Moore, urged the poet to write in English rather than Scots. On 23 May 1787 Moore gave the poet some gratuitous advice: 'you already possess a great variety of expression and command of the English language; you ought, therefore, to deal more sparingly, for the future, in the provincial dialect' (cited by Snyder, 218).

Similarly, various early reviewers regretted the language of his verse. James Anderson, discussing the Kilmarnock Edition in the *Monthly Review* of December 1786, felt that Burns was badly limited by his language:

> We much regret that these poems are written in some measure in an unknown tongue, which must deprive most of our Readers of the pleasure they would otherwise naturally create; being composed in the Scottish dialect, which contains many words that are altogether unknown to an English reader . . . (CH, 72)

John Logan, writing in the *English Review*, February 1787, regretted that 'his provincial dialect confines his beauties to one half of the island' (CH, 78). An unsigned notice in the *General Magazine and Impartial Review* (1787), worried over the linguistic resources of Burns:

> It is greatly to be lamented that these poems are 'chiefly in the Scottish dialect', as it must necessarily confine their beauties to a small circle of readers, and as the author has given good specimens of his skill in the English . . . (CH, 89)

All the collections of Burns's verse published in the poet's lifetime – the Kilmarnock Edition of 1786 and the Edinburgh editions of 1787 and 1793 – are entitled *Poems, Chiefly in the Scottish Dialect*. In the Preface to the Kilmarnock Edition, Burns introduces himself as a poetic primitive who 'sings the sentiments and manners, he felt and saw in himself and his rustic compeers around him, in his and their native language'. Two stanzas from separate verse-epistles in the Kilmarnock Edition reinforce this proclamation of faith in the natural, though not naive, use of a native language:

> Gie me ae spark o Nature's fire,
> That's a' the learning I desire;
> Then, tho' I drudge thro dub an mire
>   At pleugh or cart,
> My Muse, tho hamely in attire,
>   May touch the heart.
>   (57/CW, 102)

> In days when mankind were but callans
> At grammar, logic, an sic talents,
> They took nae pains their speech to balance,
> Or rules to gie;
> But spak their thoughts in plain, braid Lallans,
> Like you or me.
>
> (59/CW, 110)

The implication is obvious: Burns's muse is to make an emotional appeal through the use of the familiar language of Lallans (Lowland Scots); what he also (in 'The Brigs of Ayr') called 'braid Scots' (broad Scots). Linguistically, the situation was not so simple as Burns suggests.

Scots, like English a dialect of Anglo-Saxon, had developed as an indigenous and eloquently expressive language in Scotland and, by the first half of the sixteenth century, had acquired 'its full status as a national speech adequate for all the demands laid on it, for poetry, for literary and official prose, public records and the ordinary business transactions of life' (David Murison, *The Guid Scots Tongue*, Edinburgh, 1977, p. 5). However, Scots began to be undermined by the triumph of the Protestant Reformation in 1560. In the absence of a Scots translation of the Bible, the Reformers adopted a translation completed in 1560 by English refugees in Geneva. This had profound linguistic implications. The word of God, the sacred logos, was given in English. Scots began to be perceived as an inferior language, suitable for everyday conversation and comic verse but lacking the scriptural authority of English.

In 1603 the Scottish and English crowns were both conferred on James VI and I and with the Union of Crowns the Scottish court followed the king to London. The king himself began to write poetry in English and other Scottish poets followed the royal example. Consecrated by the Geneva Bible and commended by the court, the king's English was twice-blessed. With the parliamentary Act of Union, 1 May 1707, English became the official language of Scotland (North Britain) as well as England.

Born into a nation reduced to provincial status, Burns looked back in anger and indignation at the 'parcel of rogues' (the thirty-one Scottish commissioners) who sold Scotland 'for English gold'. The first stanza of his patriotic lament 'Such a Parcel of Rogues in a Nation' (1792) conveys his feelings, ironically enough, in a Scots-accented English.

> Fareweel to a' our Scottish fame,
> Fareweel our ancient glory!
> Fareweel ev'n to the Scottish name,
> Sae famed in martial story!
> Now Sark rins o'er the Solways sands,
> An Tweed rins to the ocean,
> To mark where England's province stands –
> Such a parcel of rogues in a nation!
>   (375/CW, 460)

'England's province' set about accomodating the English in style. Scottish expressions – 'Scotticisms' – became, for the intellectuals, synonymous with vulgarisms. David Hume used Scottish words in convivial conversation but scrupulously avoided them in his philosophical writing. In 1761 Edinburgh's Select Society, of which Hume was a founder-member, employed an actor (ironically, an Irishman, Thomas Sheridan, father of Richard Brinsley Sheridan) to coach its members in the southern pronunciation of English. In 1779 James Beattie, a man Burns admired both as poet and (Common Sense) philosopher, published his *Scotticisms, Arranged in Alphabetical Order, Designed to Correct Improprieties of Speech and Writing*. According to Dugald Stewart, Burns avoided Scots expressions in conversation:

> Nothing, perhaps, was more remarkable among his various attainments, than the fluency, and precision, and originality of his language, when he spoke in company; more particularly as he aimed at purity in his turn of expression, and avoided more successfully than most Scotchmen the peculiarities of Scottish phraseology. (cited by Snyder, 200)

Burns, however, would have been anxious to impress a university philosopher like Stewart with his command of the English language. In other circumstances he may well have used a Scots as rich as that in his letter of 1 June 1787 to William Nicol (see section on 'The Letters').

It was not only Burns's rural upbringing in Ayr that gave him a more creative attitude to Scots than his urban contemporaries. If he spoke Scots at home, he also knew that Scots had an artistic dimension beyond everyday conversation for, as a child, he heard songs and ballads of the oral tradition from his mother and his mother's friend Betty Davidson. Though he was educated as 'an excellent

English scholar' (AL) these songs and ballads (some of which he adapted, like 'John Barleycorn', some of which he preserved, like 'Tam Lin') became an inescapable part of his poetic inheritance. Still, it took a decidedly literary movement to give him poetic motion and the confidence to generate his own artistic energy.

If Scots was deplored as a conversational medium in polite urban society, Scottish poets were not willing to abandon the rich literary resources of Scots. Initiating a revival in the 1720s Allan Ramsay used Scots in his most successful poems and, following this precedent, Robert Fergusson found his own voice in Scots, writing vigorously vernacular poems about the urban vitality of his native Edinburgh. Burns studied Ramsay's work and, in 1782, bought a copy of the Second Edition of Fergusson's *Poems*. It was, as Burns repeatedly acknowledged, the Scots revivalist verse of Ramsay and Fergusson that prompted him to apply himself to the art of poetry. In the Preface to the Kilmarnock Edition, he confessed himself unequal to 'the genius of a Ramsay, or the glorious dawnings of the poor, unfortunate Fergusson'; in the 'Epistle to J. Lapraik' he hoped for 'a spunk o Allan's glee/Or Fergusson's, the bauld an slee'. In his Inscription for Fergusson's headstone (erected at his expense) he directed Scotland to 'the Poet's Dust'; in his 'Apostrophe to Fergusson' (1787) he lamented 'my elder brother in misfortune,/By far my elder brother in the Muse'; in 'Lines on Fergusson, the Poet' he acclaimed the 'Heaven-taught Fergusson'; and in his Autobiographical Letter to Dr John Moore he said he had abandoned rhyme 'but meeting with Fergusson's Scotch poems [in 1782], I strung anew my wildly-sounding, rustic lyre with emulating vigour' (AL).

As the Kilmarnock and First Edinburgh Editions demonstrated, Burns used Scots not only for emotional outbursts and descriptive 'manners-painting' ('The Vision') but for ecclesiastical satire ('The Holy Fair', for example), social comment ('The Twa Dogs'), political evaluation ('A Dream'), philosophical reflection ('To a Mouse'), graveyard humour ('Death and Doctor Hornbook') and matters of morality ('Address to the Unco Guid'). For all his role-playing as a poetic ploughman, Burns took his Scots work extremely seriously, denying that the use of dialect alone automatically produced poetry. Writing to Mrs Dunlop in 1789 he complained 'my success has encouraged such a shoal of ill-spawned monsters to crawl into public notice under the title of Scots Poets, that the very term, Scots Poetry, borders on the burlesque' (CL, 169). The Scots-writing Scottish poet had to use the language poetically and not rest passively on the linguistic laurels of the past.

Burns was enough of a product of his period to assume English affectations: his professed admiration for Shenstone, his elegant epistolary style, his ability to hold his own as a conversationalist in polite company (Scott, who heard Burns speak, thought his conversation 'expressed perfect self-confidence, without the slightest presumption', CH, 262). As a poet, however, he transcended his period by renewing the Scots tradition in a startling way, applying his art to a bewildering variety of subjects. Writing in Scots he managed, by great artistry, to simulate a conversational tone that sounded anything but artificial. Not so in English. All poetic language is, by definition, artificial but, for Burns, English was excruciatingly artificial – indeed alien – as a poetic medium.

Burns's poems in English are, by general consent, his weakest artistic efforts. The Kilmarnock Edition has poems that alternate Augustan English with Scots, most effectively in 'The Cotter's Saturday Night' where the first English stanza is in deliberate contrast to the Scots stanzas that follow. In 'Epistle to Davie', however, the use of English in the ninth and tenth stanzas vitiates the overall impact of the verse, as Burns awkwardly imitates the insipid English diction of favourite poets like Shenstone. Ending 'A Solemn Meditation' Shenstone writes:

> O life! how soon of ev'ry bliss forlorn!
> We start false joys, and urge the devious race:
> A tender prey, that cheers our youthful morn,
> Then sinks untimely, and defrauds the chase.

Beginning 'The Lament' Burns similarly expresses world-weariness in an inflated English full of affectation:

> O Thou pale Orb, that silent shines,
> While care-untroubled mortals sleep!
> Thou seest a *wretch*, who inly pines,
> And wanders here to wail and weep!
> (93/CW, 204)

A poet had to achieve other effects than pining and wandering and wailing and weeping in English.

Shortly after he arrived in Edinburgh, Burns composed an 'Address to Edinburgh' which duly appeared in the First Edinburgh Edition. Here Burns might have risen racily to the occasion. After all, he was worldly enough to observe what went on in the capital with 'bucks strutting, ladies flaring, blackguards sculking, whores leering' (CL, 81) and he knew 'Auld Reikie' by his favourite Scots poet, Fergusson:

> Auld Reikie, wale o ilka town
> That Scotland kens beneath the moon;
> Where couthy chiels at e'ening meet
> Their bizzing craigs and mous to weet;
> And blythly gar auld care gae bye
> Wi blinkit and wi bleering eye . . .

Alas, Burns was unable to emulate Fergusson on this occasion, beginning his poem by apostrophising 'Edina! Scotia's darling seat!'

Whereas his Scots poems had vividly explored the landscape of Ayrshire in unforgettably energetic language, this English poem praises the capital through a catalogue of unconvincing personifications:

> Here Wealth still swells the golden tide,
>   As busy Trade his labour plies;
> There Architecture's noble pride
>   Bids elegance and splendour rise:
> Here Justice, from her native skies,
>   High wields her balance and her rod;
> There Learning, with his eagle eyes,
>   Seeks Science in her coy abode.
>
>   (135/CW, 262)

The poem is constructed around clichés – 'noble pride', 'native skies', 'eagle eyes' – and comprises a sustained cliché which makes it typical of Burns's English poems.

Burns's poems in Scots were inspirational, his poems in English were occasional. The English Pindaric ode that appears, framed by Scots, in 'A Winter Night' was occasional in that the occasion was a set-piece, an exercise in a particular form and little more than that: 'my first attempt in that irregular kind of measure in which many of our finest Odes are wrote' (CL, 98). To please the likes of Robert Riddell Burns wrote occasional poems for particular places. 'Verses in Friars' Carse Hermitage' – with clichés such as 'russet weed', 'silken stole', 'idle dream' – may have gratified one man but never reached out to an international audience the way the great Scots poems did, and do.

The most celebrated English passage in Burns is that in 'Tam o Shanter' beginning 'But pleasures are like poppies spread' which has some of the delicacy of the Milton of 'L'Allegro' ('There on beds of violet blue,/And fresh-blown roses washt in dew') and is an advance on 'Address to Edinburgh'. It does not, however, support Muir's argument, in *Scott and Scotland*, about the intellectual superiority of English to Scots (see the discussion of 'Tam o Shanter') and it functions poetically because its languid diction interrupts the narrative and allows Burns to put an urgent stress on the Scots dialect that immediately follows it: 'Nae man can tether time or tide,/The hour approaches Tam maun ride'. Had the succeeding lines been in Burns's best Augustan English, it is a safe bet to say the poem would have plodded along, not galloped along the way it does.

English poetic diction was alien to Burns's artistic talent and temperament. He could imitate English poets as witness his 'From Esopus to Maria' which is a parody of Pope's 'Eliosa to Abelard': 'In these deep solitudes and awful cells,/Where heavenly pensive contemplation dwells' (Pope); 'From these drear solitudes and frowsy cells/Where Infamy with sad Repentance dwells' (Burns). He could echo Shenstone and Thomson and Gray. Such derivative pieces, though, make no advance on the originals and are remarkable only as a contrast with Burns's Scots poems. For when he was not imitating Pope and others, Burns was emulating Fergusson – and surpassing him because he imaginatively raised the Scots dialect to an international poetic language.

Not all Burns's poems in an English diction are atrocious, of course; some snatches of song, some epitaphs and epigrams, and the English passage in 'Tam o Shanter' show he was not always insipid when writing in English, but these are brief bursts, odd exceptions to the rule. Similarly, not all Burns's poems 'chiefly in the Scottish dialect' are masterpieces but enough of them are to show that for Burns (as for few other poets) Scots was a poetic language capable of expressing any feeling – or thought – that excited him.

Burns and Religion

According to the Westminster Confession (accepted by the Scottish parliament in 1643, and again in 1690, as the doctrine of the Church of Scotland) only 'the Elect', as chosen by God, are redeemed by Christ: theoretically, therefore, good works are irrelevant since all children of the sinner Adam are depraved from birth. Scottish theologians of the eighteenth century constantly reiterated this claim. For example, Thomas Boston's *Human Nature in its Fourfold State* (1720) asserted that 'even the new-born babe [is] a child of hell' (cited by David Daiches, *God and the Poets*, Oxford, 1984, p. 134). Burns, an avid reader of theological works, described Boston's book as 'stupid' (CL, 260) and 'trash' (CL, 318). The absurd antinomianism of Boston and likeminded ministers (Boston had preached in Ettrick) was not lost on Burns.

Saturated in biblical imagery, the work of Burns distinguishes between the teaching of Christ and the preaching of certain self-styled Christians. 'Christ,' Burns wrote to Mrs McLehose, 'will bring us all, through various ways and by various means, to bliss at last' (CL, 379). A letter to Mrs Dunlop, approved 'the sublimity, excellence, and purity of [Christ's] doctrine . . . though *to appearance*, he himself was the obscurest and most illiterate of our species' (CL, 174). Another letter to Mrs Dunlop, nevertheless expressed some doubts:

> Jesus Christ, thou amiablest of characters, I trust thou art no imposter, & that thy revelation of blissful scenes of existence beyond death and the grave, is not one of the many impositions which time after time have been palmed on credulous mankind. (CL, 182)

Burns did not want to be crucified, as a poet, by such credulity.

A long way from Christ, Burns placed the 'Orthodox! orthodox! wha believe in John Knox' ('The Kirk's Alarm'). Years before Burns had the relative luxury of corresponding with cultivated women like Mrs Dunlop and Mrs McLehose, he had to contend with the antics of the kirk in rural Scotland. 'The first of my poetic offspring that saw the light', Burns told Dr John Moore, 'was a burlesque lamentation on a quarrel between two reverend Calvinists' (AL). This poem, 'The Twa Herds: or, The Holy Tulzie', was omitted from the Kilmarnock Edition since to print it 'would have been to compromise [Burns's] friends, and needlessly to exasperate his – and their – opponents' (Snyder, 160). Written at the end of 1784, the poem satirises a squabble over parish boundaries between Rev Alexander Moodie of Riccarton and Rev John Russell of Kilmarnock. Transforming the ministers to shepherds, Burns writes of the two antagonists:

> Moodie, man, an wordy Russell,
> How could you raise so vile a bustle?
> Ye'll see how New-Light herds will whistle,
>   An think it fine!
> The Lord's cause gat na sic a twissle
>   Sin I hae min'.
>   (52/CW, 90)

Although the two ministers, or herds, are in dispute, they are theologically at one (which, of course, makes the squabble even more amusing). Burns writes of Moodie's congregation:

> What flock wi Moodie's flock could rank
> Sae hale an hearty every shank?
> Nae poison'd, soor Arminian stank
>   He loot them taste;
> Frae Calvin's fountain-head they drank, –
>   O, sic a feast!
>   (52/CW, 90)

'New-Light', 'Arminian', 'Calvin's fountain-head': Burns knew the friends he showed the poem would be familiar with his references though they are not so recognizable to modern readers.

Calvin of course, then as now, was celebrated as the founder of a theological system with an emphasis (as he explains in his *Institutes*) on predestination: 'the eternal decree of God by which He has determined with Himself what He would have to come of every man [since] eternal life is foreordained for some and eternal damnation for others' (cited by Kinsley, 1049). Arminian: as Arminius of

Leyden (d.1609) had opposed Calvin, Scots critical of Calvinism were disparagingly termed Arminians. As for 'New-Light', this was an issue that illuminated Burns's ecclesiastical poems.

Far from representing a unified House of God, the Presbyterian kirk of Burns's day was a house divided – and subdivided. The Patronage Act of 1712, giving lay patrons the right to present ministers to vacant parishes, was held to violate the Act of Security (1707) and eventually led to a secession, in 1732, when an Act of Assembly gave the power of election to heritors and elders whenever the patron did not exercise his right. A further secession occurred in 1747 over the Burgher's Oath (requiring holders of public office to affirm the Presbyterian religion) and the Anti-Burghers established synods independent from those of the Burghers. Yet another secession resulted from the issue of civil compulsion in religious affairs: the minority, holding the Solemn League and Covenant as a sacred obligation, comprised the Original Burghers, or Auld Lichts (old lights); the majority, wishing to modify Presbyterian commitment to the Covenant, comprised the 'New Lichts'.

As Kinsley (or the Rev James Kinsley, to acknowledge his ecclesiastical title) points out:

> Below differences in attitude to the establishment, these terms represent a deeper distinction of theology and temperament. The 'Auld Lichts' were 'orthodox', Calvinist – with traditional emphasis on the doctrines of original sin, election, and predestination – stern in their discipline, evangelical and rhetorical in their preaching. The 'New Lichts' were 'Arminian', 'Moderate', liberal in their theology and moralistic in their preaching. (Kinsley, 1045–6)

Burns spent a great deal of energy in Ayrshire, where the Auld Licht burned brightly, querying 'Calvinism with so much heat and indiscretion that I raised a hue and cry of heresy against me' (CL, 250). His attitude led him to embrace a body of thought formed by the notion of love. When he rejoiced in religion, he qualified his feelings: 'We can no more live without Religion, than we can live without air; but give me the Religion of Sentiment and Reason' (CL, 191). In theory as well as practice Burns was inclined to value natural and artistic creation more than arid doctrinaire opinions.

His father – who watched the one-day-old Burns being baptised by the liberal minister of Ayr, Rev William Dalrymple – would have found his advocacy of 'Sentiment and Reason' provocative in its anti-authoritarian implications but would certainly have understood the logic behind the preference for delight over dogma. William Burnes was relatively liberal in his approach to religion and certainly did not confine his sons to the repressive Calvinist doctrines of the Auld Licht of Ayrshire. He is credited, by Currie and Gilbert Burns, as the author of the *Manual of Religious Belief in the Form of a Dialogue between Father and Son* (published in Kilmarnock in 1875). Apparently the original manuscript was written not by Burnes but by the man he employed to tutor his children: John Murdoch. Whether the work is as Burnes composed it or as Murdoch 'improved' and/or interpreted it, it is a seminal source of the poet's theological suppositions.

Commentators agree that the *Manual* amounts to a liberal critique of Calvinist orthodoxy: it is 'definitely not Calvinistic' (Snyder, 53) and 'not of the extreme Calvinist or Auld Licht variety' (Crawford, 40). Certainly the *Manual* accepts, and encourages, the pursuit of physical pleasure. It advises against 'setting nature at variance with herself, by placing the animal part before the rational' but does not dismiss the animal appetite:

> On the contrary, setting the rational part above the animal, though it promote a war in the human frame, every conflict and victory affords us grateful reflection, and tends to compose the mind more and more, not to the utter destruction of the animal part, but to the real and true enjoyment of [it], by placing Nature in the order that its Creator designed it, which in the natural consequences of the thing, promotes spiritual life, and renders us more and more fit for Christ's spiritual kingdom; and not only so, but gives animal life pleasure and joy, that we never could have had without it. (cited by Crawford, 40–1)

Burns's poetry frequently dwells on the relationship of the individual to the natural environment and, in a letter of 1788, he refers to 'a great unknown Being who could have no other end in giving [man] existence but to make him happy' (CL, 90).

As well as expressing his own views on religion William Burnes made sure his children were well versed in the Bible and acutely aware of its significance. The young Burns read such works as John Ray's *The Wisdom of God Manifested in the Works of the Creation* (1691); William Derham's *Astro-Theology, or, a Demonstration of the Being and Attributes of God* (1714); and Thomas Stackhouse's *A New History of the Holy Bible* (1737, reprinted in Edinburgh in 1765), a re-telling of the Bible in eighteenth-century prose. Outside his home and away from his books, however, Burns was exposed to the theological climate of his period, to the Scottish Calvinism imposed on the country by those who thought they were being loyal to John Knox's successful Reformation of 1560. The poet had practical, and painful, experience of parochial Scottish Calvinism in action, especially during his Mossgiel period.

It will not do to blame Knox alone for Scotland's subsequent theological problems though this is the approach taken by modern Scottish writers – such as Edwin Muir who claimed, in his *John Knox* (London, 1929, p. 309), 'What Knox really did was to rob Scotland of all the benefits of the Renaissance'; or Fion Mac Colla who (*At the Sign of the Clenched Fist*, Edinburgh, 1967, p. 201) held Knox responsible for Scotland's adherance to 'an anti-human ideology'. Knox was, first and foremost, a reformer who fought against an oppressive institution, the Roman Catholic church of his time. Like Burns, Knox was a man of enormous intellectual energy and, also like Burns, was (as the son of a peasant) born into poverty. As Burns did with his poetry, Knox used his preaching to assert that a common man could be the equal those who claimed to be his superiors. His First Book of Discipline, presented to the Scottish parliament on 15 January 1561, allowed congregations to elect their own pastors, divided Scotland into parishes and proposed educational reforms that created mass literacy in Scotland.

If Knox had lived in Burns's period, argued A. Burns Jamieson (*Burns and Religion*, Cambridge, 1931, p. 114) 'he would have been the poet's stoutest supporter in his fight against the hypocrisy and cant of the Auld Lights'. It is a plausible contention, one that would have appealed to Thomas Carlyle who admired both Knox ('The one Scotchman to whom of all others, his country and the world owe a debt') and Burns. Knox was, if anything, more defiant than Burns: when in 1563 Mary Queen of Scots, smarting at his criticism of her consideration of a marriage to Don Carlos of Catholic Spain, asked the preacher 'What have you to do with my marriage? Or what are you in this commonwealth?' Knox replied with dignity 'A subject born within the same.' It took a great deal of courage to put a queen in her place and Burns must have pondered the story as told in Knox's *History of the Reformation in Scotland*, a book he ordered for the Monkland Friendly Society on 2 March 1790 (CL, 316). A few months later, on 6 June 1970, he sent Mrs Dunlop his 'Lament of Mary Queen of Scots', in which the imprisoned queen anticipates her death:

> The meanest hind in fair Scotland
>   May rove their sweets amang;
> But I, the Queen o a' Scotland,
>   Maun lie in prison strang.
>
> (316/CW, 401)

Burns's view of Mary was sentimental, but his rebellious outlook on life put him firmly in the radical Scottish tradition of Knox, if not the Knoxists.

After Knox's death, in 1572, Scottish Calvinism evolved in response to political developments. A Solemn League and Covenant (1643) offered aid to the English parliament against Charles I on condition that England would adopt a Presbyterian church system. Burns acknowledged the historic importance of the Solemn League and Covenant and the heroism of the Covenanters:

> The Solemn League and Covenant
>   Now brings a smile, now brings a tear,
> But sacred Freedom, too, was theirs:
>   If thou'rt a slave, indulge thy sneer.
>
> (512/CW, 560)

As a fulfilment of the Solemn League and the Covenant, the Westminster Assembly of English Presbyterians, with six Scots as assistants, met in 1643 to frame a Confession of Faith which was accepted by the Scottish parliament. Reaffirmed by the Scottish parliament on 25 April 1690 as the doctrine of the Church of Scotland, the Westminster Confession declared 'Neither are any other redeemed by Christ, effectually Called, Justified, Adopted, Sanctified and Saved, but the Elect only' (cited by Daiches, *op. cit.*, p. 134). This Calvinistic concept of predestination was holy writ to the Auld Lichts but intellectually irksome to the liberal New Lichts. In Mauchline, the Auld Licht was not put out by the opposition.

The Mauchline Burns knew was dominated by kirk politics and disputed by the evangelical Auld Lichts and the tolerant New Lichts. Rigidly Calvinistic, and faithful to the Westminster Confession, the Auld Lichts believed in preordained damnation or salvation so worshipped a God who punished sinners in a blazing hellfire, 'A vast, unbottom'd, boundless pit,/Fill'd fou o lowin brunstane' ('The Holy Fair'); a vindictively selective God who 'Sends ane to Heaven, an ten to Hell' ('Holy Willie's Prayer'). The moderate New Lichts tempered religion with 'carnal wit and sense' ('The Holy Fair') and held that a merciful God would reward good deeds, thus modifying the deterministic doctrine of the elect.

Burns, like his friend Gavin Hamilton, was temperamentally drawn to the New Lichts, partly as a result of his father's critical reading of Calvinist fundamentalism and partly as a result of observation and experience. He particularly deplored the power of the Kirk Session, a council of parish elders presided over by the minister. In Mauchline the Kirk Session, presided over by the minister Rev William Auld ('Daddie Auld' of 'The Kirk's Alarm'), publicly rebuked Burns for fornication and insinuated that Gavin Hamilton was failing to keep the Presbyterian faith. Burns's great ecclesiastical satires ('Holy Willie's Prayer', 'The Holy Fair', 'Address to the Deil') make his position clear: he detested the hypocrisy of Calvinism and regarded the Auld Lichts as inimical to the concept of a benign God.

Since Burns twice fell foul of the kirk's way with sexual offenders, it is worth recalling the punitive power of the Kirk Session. For dealing with fornicators it retained the 'cutty-stool', the stool of repentance, as described in R. H. Cromek's *Remains of Nithsdale and Galloway Song* (1810):

> This stool of terror was fashioned like an arm-chair, and was raised on a pedestal, nearly two foot higher than the other seats, directly fronting the pulpit. [Arrayed 'in the black sack-cloth gown of fornication', the culprit] stood three Sundays successively, his face uncovererd, and the awful scourge of unpardoning divinity hung over him. The women stood here in the same accoutrements, and were denied the privilege of a veil. (cited by Kinsley, 1038)

As a result of his affair with Elizabeth Paton, Burns sat on the cutty-stool in 1785: 'Before the congregation wide,/I passed the muster fairly' ('The Fornicator').

The following year, as a result of his affair with Jean Armour, he had to make three penitential appearances in Mauchline Kirk though (he wrote to John Richmond on 9 July 1786) 'I am indulged so far as to appear in my own seat' (CL, 77). On 6 August 1786, after their third penitential appearance, Burns and Jean had to listen as Daddie Auld publicly condemned them for their sins:

> You appear there to be rebuked, and at the same time making profession of repentence for the sin of fornication. The frequency

of this sin is just matter of lamentation among Christians, and
affords just ground of deep humilation to the guilty persons
themselves . . . . Beware of returning to your sin as some of you
have done, like the dog to its vomit, or like the sow that is washed
to her wallowing in the mire. (cited by Snyder, 126)

Burns had good reason to remember the quotation (2 Peter 2:22)
with which Auld ended his rebuke and it turns up, incongruously
in relation to his failure as a farmer, in his Autobiographal Letter: 'I
returned "Like the dog to his vomit, and the sow that was washed
to her wallowing in the mire"' (AL).

As a student of religion Burns knew that the Auld Lichts adhered
to a dogma that owed more to Calvin than the Bible. He had read
John Taylor's *The Scripture Doctrine of Original Sin* (1740) which
denied that the doctrine of original sin was sanctioned by the
Bible. Taylor argued that the sacrificial Christ had recreated man
in a merciful manner, blessing the individual with 'privileges and
advantages . . . abundantly beyond the reversing of any evils we
are subject to in consequence of Adam's sin' (cited by Crawford,
49). John Goldie, a Kilmarnock wine-merchant, supported Taylor's
humane reading of scripture in his *Essays on various Important
Subjects, Moral and Divine* (1780) and when a second edition of
this appeared in 1785 Burns sent the author (in August of that
year) his 'Epistle to John Goldie, in Kilmarnock'. The poem ridiculed
the 'Poor gapin, glowerin Supersition' of the Auld Lichts and
humorously paired Taylor and Goldie as dangerous opponents of
Orthodoxy: "Tis you an Taylor are the chief/To blame for a' this
black mischief'.

Sending a copy of 'Holy Willie's Prayer' to the New Licht minister
Rev John McMath, in 17 September 1785, Burns condemned (in his
'Epistle to the Rev John McMath') the Auld Lichts with 'Their
three-mile prayers, and hauf-mile graces', accusing them of using
religion as an instrument of torture to be applied sadistically to the
most vulnerable:

> They take Religion in their mouth,
> They talk o Mercy, Grace an Truth:
> For what? to gie their malice skouth
>   On some puir wight;
> An hunt him down, o'er right an ruth,
>   To ruin streight.
>
> (68/CW, 130)

Two stanzas earlier, in the same poem, Burns said:

> God knows, I'm no the thing I should be,
> Nor am I even the thing I could be,
> But twenty times I rather would be
>   An atheist clean,
> Than under gospel colors hid be
>   Just for a screen.
>
> (68/CW, 130)

He would rather be an atheist than a canting hypocrite (Burns may have had David Hume in mind, in referring to 'An atheist clean' since Hume was synonymous with atheism in Scotland). Ideally, however, he wanted to be worthy of the 'candid lib'ral band' who embraced religion as a life-enhancing experience. If there was an afterlife, Burns reasoned in a letter of 1789, 'it must be only for the just, the amiable & the humane' (CL, 181).

Under the influence of Enlightenment ideals and his reading of unorthodox works – Locke's *Essay Concerning Human Understanding* (1690) which undermines dogmatic faith, John Taylor's *Scripture Doctrine of Original Sin* (1740) which questions the biblical basis of original sin – Burns developed as a Deist, believing he had a personal, rather than an institutional, relationship with a benign Being (Snyder, 53, refers to 'the Deistic belief of his more mature life'). Locke argued, in his celebrated *Essay*, in favour of 'some knowing intelligent Being in the world . . . which, whether any one will please to call God, it matters not'; Burns was twenty-five when, in his first Common Place Book, he declared 'the grand end of human life is to cultivate an intercourse with that Being to whom we owe life' (CB, 22). Two years before that he named as one of his favourite novels – one of his 'bosom favourites' (AL) – Sterne's *Tristram Shandy*, a novel whose sceptical tone is heavily influenced by Locke's *Essay*. Burns, however, did not wish to make a dogma of Deism, observing 'I hate a Man that wishes to be a Deist, but I fear, every fair, unprejudiced Enquirer must in some degree be a Sceptic' (cited by Fitzhugh, 15–16).

In letters to Mrs Dunlop he expounded his position. On New Year's Day 1789:

> I own myself partial to those proofs of those aweful & impor-
> tant realities, a God that made all things, man's immaterial &

immortal nature, & a World of weal or woe beyond death & the grave, these proofs that we diduct by dint of our own powers & observation. (CL, 164)

On 22 June 1789 (emulating the logical tone of Locke):

That there is an incomprehensibly Great Being, to whom I owe my existence, and that he must be intimately acquainted with the operations and progress of the internal machinery, and consequent outward deportment of this creature which he has made; these are, I think, self-evident propositions . . . . I will go further, and affirm, that from the sublimity, excellence, and purity of his doctrine and precepts un-paralleled by all the aggregated wisdom and learning of many preceding ages, though *to appearance*, he himself was the obscurest and most illiterate of our species; therefore Jesus Christ was from God. (CL, 174)

On 1 January 1795:

I have nothing to say to any body, as, to which Sect they belong, or what Creed they believe; but I look on the Man who is firmly persuaded of Infinite Wisdom & Goodness superintending & directing every circumstance that can happen in his lot – I felicitate such a man as having a solid foundation for his mental enjoyment; a firm prop & sure stay, in the hour of difficulty, trouble & distress; & a never-failing anchor of hope, when he looks beyond the grave. (CL, 213)

The concept of religion as a domestic comfort for poor people was strong in Burns who 'continued a churgoer and sermon critic [and] led family worship at Mossgiel and Ellisland' (Fitzhugh, 16).

Like the Common Sense philosophers of his period (he was friendly, of course, with Dugald Stewart) Burns affected a moderate and humane Presbyterianism in his domestic life, appreciating that religion had a solid social function. Critical of the negativity of the kirk and the vicious behaviour of 'Calvin's sons! Calvin's sons!' ('The Kirk's Alarm'), he held back from the sceptical atheism of Hume, supposing 'an unshaken faith in the doctrines of Christianity is not only necessary by making us better men, but also by making us happier men' (CL, 199). Nevertheless, he actively disliked irrational dogma and life-denying doctrine as he made clear in a letter, of 10 September 1792, to Alexander Cunningham. Contrasting School Divinity with 'Common Sense' he wrote:

But of all Nonsense, Religious Nonsense is the most nonsensical;
so enough, & more than enough of it – Only, by the bye, will you,
or can you tell me, my dear Cunningham, why a religioso turn
of mind has always had a tendency to narrow & illberalize the
heart? They are orderly; they may be just; nay, I have known
them merciful: but still your children of Sanctity move among
their fellow creatures with a nostril snuffing putrescence, & a
foot spurning filth, in short, with that conceited dignity which
your titled Douglases, Hamiltons, Gordons, or any other of your
Scots Lordlings of seven centuries standing, display when they
accidentally mix among the many-aproned Sons of Mechanical
life. (CL, 466)

There Burns's hatred of religious hypocrisy becomes a social issue.

Brought up on a demanding land and in a socially divided land,
as well as by the Bible, Burns drew on his own experience, as well
as on ideas currently in philosophical fashion, when he associated
himself with 'the Religion of God & Nature; the Religion that exalts,
that ennobles man' (CL, 208). The most compelling evidence for
his Deism, understood as a natural religion devoid of doctrinal
supersition, is in his art. His fine 'Elegy on Captain Matthew
Henderson', for example, sends the subject not to some theological
heaven but to a universal infinity among the 'twinkling starnies',
a vision of a wonderfully complex cosmos beyond dogma and
doctrine.

Burns and Politics

In a letter of 28 February 1793 to his publisher William Creech, Burns drew a distinction between 'Great Folks whom I respect [and] Little Folks whom I love' (CL, 307). In fact there were very few aristocratic Great Folks he genuinely admired (with obvious exceptions like the Earl of Glencairn); for example, he described the 4th Duke of Queensberry ironically as a 'Great Man' and accurately as 'a flaming Zealot [with] a character of which one cannot speak with patience' (CL, 432). In the same letter (of 9 December 1789 to Graham of Fintry) he described himself as 'too little a man to have any political attachments' (CL, 432). Contemporary party politics, indeed, he saw as a game played by the great at the expense of the poor (as his Election Ballads indicate). His political opinions sought wider horizons than those displayed in Ayrshire or Dumfriesshire.

Gilbert Burns supposed his brother had 'a particular jealousy of people who were richer than himself, or who had more consequence in life' (GN). 'Jealousy' is a misleading word here. Burns resented the rich, despised them for the way they exploited the poor as he makes clear in 'The Twa Dogs' and other poems. Though on occasion he was obliged to treat his self-styled social superiors obsequiously, he believed profoundly, as letters as well as poems demonstrate, that an impoverished tenant-farmer was as worthy as any aristocrat up to and including a king. His egalitarian ideas were hardly original, but he prized them as the most encouraging part of the political options of his time.

In *Common Sense* Tom Paine had written 'Of more worth is one honest man to society and in the sight of God, than all the crowned ruffians that ever lived' (Thomas Paine, *Common Sense*, 1776; rept. Harmondsworth, 1976, p. 81). In 'A Man's a Man for a' That' (1795) Burns wrote 'The honest man, tho e'er sae poor,/Is king o men for a' that'. Though he had, periodically, to conceal his opinions and compromise for the sake of his career, his revolutionary faith in the common people was consistent. His vision of an international republic presumed an informed majority, not 'a rabble' (CL, 436), an 'uninformed mob' (CL, 691), a 'Swinish Multitude' (CL, 215); what Milton, one of his favourite poets, called 'A miscellaneous rabble, who extol/Things vulgar' (*Paradise Regained*, III.ll.50–1). The honest man in whom Burns believed was made in the image of his father – and himself.

Growing up in a period when egalitarian ideals were being applied internationally, he was seventeen when, on 4 July 1776, the Continental Congress carried the American Declaration of Independence. Jefferson's prose (Franklin substituted 'self-evident' for Jefferson's 'sacred and undeniable') sharply focused a vision that Burns shared:

We hold these truths to be self-evident, that all men are created equal; that they are endowed by their Creator with certain unalienable rights; that among these are life, liberty, and the pursuit of happiness. That, to secure these rights, governments are instituted among men, deriving their just powers from the consent of the governed; that, whenever any form of government becomes destructive of these ends, it is the right of the people to alter or to abolish it, and to institute a new government, laying its foundation on such principles, and organizing its powers in such form, as to them shall seem most likely to effect their safety and happiness.

This doctrine of natural rights, encouraging the pursuit of happiness and recognising the supremacy of 'the people', informs Burns's poetry and prose. For him, as for the American revolutionaries, a meaningful life was synonymous with liberty: 'Liberty's a glorious feast' Burns sang in 'The Jolly Beggars'.

Burns's enthusiasm for the American Revolution is seen in such works as 'When Guildford good' (1784), 'Address of Beelzebub' (1786) and the Pindaric 'Ode for General Washington's Birthday' (1794), sent to Mrs Dunlop with the explanation 'The Subject is, LIBERTY; you know . . . how dear the theme is to me' (CL, 210). The poem moves from Washington alive in an independent America to Wallace dead in a Scotland lacking the independence for which Wallace fought and died:

> But come, ye sons of Liberty,
> Columbia's offspring, brave as free,

In danger's hour still flaming in the van,
Ye know, and dare maintain the Royalty of Man! . . .
Thee, Caledonia, thy wild heaths among,
Fam'd for the martial deed, the heaven-taught song,
To thee I turn with swimming eyes!
Where is that soul of Freedom fled?
Immingled with the mighty dead!
Beneath the hallow'd turf where Wallace lies!
Hear it not, Wallace, in thy bed of death!
(451/CW, 515–6)

A resurrection of the spirit of Wallace, Burns implies, would be modern Scotland's inspirational equivalent of Washington's struggle for independence.

In terms of domestic politics, Burns was a Scottish patriot who bitterly regretted the loss of Scottish independence that resulted from the parliamentary union of 1707: 'what are all the boasted advantages which my Country reaps from a certain union, that can counterbalance the annihilation of her Independance, & even her very Name!' (CL, 185). The notion of Scotland reduced to the regional status of North Britain disturbed him as he made clear by describing the Scottish commissioners, who sold out Scotland in 1707, as 'a parcel of rogues in a nation!' ('Such a Parcel of Rogues in a Nation'). Looking back, he found his heroes in Wallace and Bruce, the great Scots of the Wars of Independence (1296–1328) he celebrated in 'Scots Wha Hae':

Scots, wha hae wi Wallace bled,
Scots, wham Bruce has aften led,
Welcome to your gory bed
Or to victorie!
(425/CW, 500)

However, Burns was not being merely nostalgic in that song which was, partly, the expression of his interest in revolutionary politics.

His most colourful gesture of support for revolutionary France occured in 1792: in February he and other excisemen captured the smuggling brig *Rosamond*, in the Solway estuary below Dumfries; then, at a sale of the seized vessel, he purchased four carronades which he despatched to the French Assembly (according to Sir Walter Scott the corronades were intercepted by the Customs at Dover). Snyder was inclined to think this story entirely fictional and that 'the brig *Rosamond* affair should be absolutely deleted from any account of Burns's life' (Snyder, 397). However, documents in the National Library of Scotland have convinced a more recent biographer that the story is substantially true (see Fitzhugh, 217–20). If so Burns was openly friendly to France which was not yet the official enemy of his country.

Internal events in 'North Britain', however, were worrying the government. In July 1792 the Friends of the People was established in Scotland as a radical reformist movement largely organised by a young lawyer, Thomas Muir of Huntershill, who had close contacts with revolutionary France. That summer Burns was reading Tom Paine's *The Rights of Man* (1791–2) and accepting its argument against Burke's romantic rhetoric in favour of the French aristocracy. Some passages in Paine must have delighted Burns by reinforcing observations of his own:

> The aristocracy are not the farmers who work the land, and raise the produce, but are the mere consumers of the rent; and when compared with the active world are the drones . . . who neither collect the honey nor form the hive, but exist only for lazy enjoyment. (Thomas Paine, *The Rights of Man*, 1791–2; rept. Harmondsworth, 1969, p. 249)

It was subversive stuff (so much so that one of the charges later hurled at Thomas Muir was that he had used his premises for passing *The Rights of Man* to his friends).

On 22 September 1792 the French National Convention declared France a republic and the British government's hatred of native radicals and foreign revolutionaries reached hysterical proportions. Captain William Johnston, a radical reformist, founded the *Edinburgh Gazetteer* in November 1792 and was subsequently imprisoned for editing the newspaper (as was his editorial successor). Burns, who had met Johnston in Edinburgh, subscribed to the *Edinburgh Gazetteer* on 13 November 1792, encouraging Johnston to 'Lay bare, with undaunted heart & steady hand, that horrid mass of corruption called Politics & State-Craft!' (CL, 681).

The reactionary Tory government of Pitt had reason to be nervous of developments in Scotland. Even in Dumfries there was an upswell of revolutionary unrest, as Burns explained to Mrs Dunlop on 6 December: 'in our Theatre here, "God save the king" has meet with some groans & hisses, while Ça ira [the French revolutionary song] has been repeatedly called for' (CL, 202). Before the month was out, an informer had told the Excise Board that Burns was the 'head of a disaffected party' (CL, 436) in Dumfries and he was 'accused to the Board of Excise of being a Republican' (CL, 689). John Mitchell, Collector of Excise, was instructed by the Board to investigate the poet's political position.

Himself hysterical with worry over the economic implications and political repercussions of the investigation, Burns wrote for help to his influential friend Robert Graham of Fintry, a Commissioner of the Scottish Board of Excise, on 5 January 1793. The letter was an apostatic statement, a diplomatic retreat from principles Burns held dear:

> I know of no [disaffected] party in this place, either Republican or Reform . . . I was in the playhouse one night, when Ça ira was called for [but] neither knew of the Plot, nor joined in the Plot; nor ever opened my lips to hiss, or huzza, that, or any other Political tune whatever . . . . . I never uttered any invectives against the king [and] always revered, & ever will, with the soundest loyalty, revere, the Monarch of Great-britain, as, to speak in Masonic, the sacred KEYSTONE OF OUR ROYAL ARCH CONSTITUTION . . . . I look upon the British Constitution, as settled at the Revolution, to be the most glorious Constitution on earth . . . Of Johnston, the publisher of the Edinburgh Gazetteer, I know nothing [and if] you think that I act improperly in allowing his Paper to come addressed to me, I shall immediately countermand it . . . . As to France, I was her enthusiastic votary in the beginning of the business. – When she came to shew her old avidity for conquest, in annexing Savoy, &c. to her dominions, & invading the rights of Holland, I altered my sentiments. (CL, 436–7)

This from the man who had ended a letter (to Creech in late 1792) with the revolutionary slogan 'Ça ira!' (CL, 307); who had ridiculed George III as a usurper in 'A Dream' in the Kilmarnock Edition; who had urged William Johnston to expose 'that horrid mass of corruption called Politics & State-Craft'; who had recently made a gesture of support for revolutionary France and had enjoyed reading Tom Paine.

If Burns did not join in the chant of 'Ça ira' it was not because of his politics but because of his official position as an exciseman; as he told Mrs Dunlop he was 'a *Placeman* . . . so much so as to gag me from joining in the cry. – What my private sentiments are, you will find out without an Interpreter' (CL, 202). In writing to Graham of Fintry, Burns – the suspected radical friend of France – may not have been pleading for his life, but he was certainly pleading for his livelihood and his statement should be read as such. As a skilled piece of special pleading – complete with the emotional blackmail of a masonic bond – it succeeded in convincing Graham of Fintry of Burns's political innocence, not to say naivety.

On 1 February 1793, the French Republic declared war on Britain and the government increased its attempts to suppress the Friends of the People. Thomas Muir was arrested and it was on, or around, 30 August 1793 – the date fixed for Muir's trial – that Burns sent 'Scots Wha Hae' to George Thomson. In a postscript he referred, pointedly, to 'that glorious struggle for Freedom, associated with the glowing ideas of some other struggles of the same nature, *not quite so ancient'* (CL, 639). In that context, Burns undoubtedly regarded his song as having contemporary radical relevance as well as celebrating Bruce's victory at Bannockburn:

> By Oppression's woes and pains,
> By your sons in servile chains,
> We will drain your dearest veins,
> But they shall be free!
>
> Lay the proud usurpers low!
> Tyrants fall in every foe!
> Liberty's in every blow! –
> Let us do, or die!
>
> (425/CW, 500)

Muir was sentenced to fourteen years' transportation for seditiously inciting the Scottish people to rise up and oppose the government. In his speech from the dock (a speech subsequently included in the curriculum in schoolrooms in the American republic) Muir declared: 'Gentlemen, from my infancy to this moment I have devoted myself to the cause of the people. It is a good cause – it shall ultimately prevail – it shall finally triumph' (cited in P. Berresford Ellis and Seamus Mac a' Ghobhainn, *The Scottish Insurrection of 1820*, London, 1970, p. 64). Clearly, Muir was a man after Burns's heart.

One month later another Scottish radical, Thomas Palmer – accused of writing and printing seditious literature – was sentenced to seven years' transportation. To openly declare radical and republican principles, in that climate, would have been suicidally stupid and Burns was never that. He was mindful of the fate of the two radicals, as witness the lines in the epistle 'From Esopus to Maria', written in the winter of 1794-5 but not published in the poet's lifetime (the 'Woolwich hulks' are transportation ships):

> The shrinking Bard adown the alley skulks,
> And dreads a meeting worse than Woolwich hulks,
> Though here, his heresies in Church and State
> Might well award him Muir and Palmer's fate.
>
> (486/CL, 540)

That fate was no fantasy in a North Britain ruled by a London government determined to suppress 'the Reform, or . . . Republican spirit' (CL, 202), as Burns well knew.

Conditioned to be cautious in public and in print, Burns turned to close friends when he wanted to discuss revolutionary politics. In September 1794 he described Dr William Maxwell as 'my most intimate friend, & one of the first characters I ever met with' (CL, 211). Maxwell was a man with an impeccably revolutionary past. His efforts on behalf of the French Republicans incurred the wrath of the *Sun* (8 October 1792) which condemned him as a dangerous English Jacobin; and the fury of Edmund Burke who, pursuing the *Sun*'s line in a parliamentary speech of 28 December 1792, accused him of collecting daggers for the French. On 21 December 1793 Maxwell – a Jesuit-trained son of a famous Catholic family – had been a member of the National Guard who escorted Louis XVI to the scaffold.

The poet's own opinion of the executions of Louis XVI and Marie Antoinette was expressed in a letter of 12 January 1795 to Mrs Dunlop. Commenting on the reactionary tone of Dr John Moore's *Journal during a Residence in France* (1793) Burns wrote:

> Entre nous, you know my Politics: & I cannot approve of the honest Doctor's whining over the deserved fate of a certain pair of Personages. – What is there in the delivering over a perjured Blockhead & an unprincipled Prostitute into the hands of the hangman, that it should arrest for a moment, attention, in an eventful hour, when, as my friend Roscoe in Liverpool gloriously expresses it – 'When the welfare of Millions is hung in the scale And the balance yet trembles with fate!' (CL, 214)

Not only did this offend Mrs Dunlop and, indirectly, end Dr Moore's friendship but it has continued to irk Burnsians. Maurice Lindsay, for example, moralised:

> At the time his letter was written, Burns's remarks offended the recipient; since then, they have saddened those upholders of the liberal values who are admirers of Burns's work. For words like these, justifying political murder, have become all too familiar in recent years. (BE, 244)

Probably Lindsay was thinking of the revolutionary rhetorical question in Hugh MacDiarmid's poem 'First Hymn to Lenin': 'What maitters 't wha we kill/To lessen that foulest murder that deprives/Maist men o' real lives?'

On 31 January 1795 Burns became a founder member of the Dumfries Volunteers and, a few months later, wrote the ostentatiously patriotic song 'Does Haughty Gaul Invasion Threat?' which was first published in the *Edinburgh Courant* on 4 May 1795. To Snyder, this song is proof positive that Burns 'was heartily on the side of King and Country' (Snyder, 372). The evidence suggests otherwise. At the beginning of the year, as stated, Burns had expressed a hostile opinion of the late French royal family in his letter to Mrs Dunlop. The same month as that letter, January, he had sent George Thomson his most revolutionary song, 'A Man's a Man for a That', unequivocally expressing his republican faith and ridiculing the pretensions of the aristocracy (see discussion of the song).

'Does Haughty Gaul Invasion Threat?' does oppose the imposition of the will of one country on another but its moral message amounts to no more than an insistence on providing British answers for British problems: 'For never but by British hands/Maun British wrangs be righted!' Moreover, the last stanza is open to ironic interpretation and can be read as a criticism of the tyrant and the throne, rather than the two wretches. Note also that Burns does not say that the radical *should* hang, but that he 'Shall hang' and that he ends subversively by giving the last word to the common people:

> The wretch that would a tyrant own,
>   And the wretch, his true-sworn brother,
> Who would set the mob above the throne,
>   May they be damn'd together!
> Who will not sing *God Save the King*

> Shall hang as high's the steeple;
> But while we sing *God Save the King,*
> We'll ne'er forget the people!
>
> (484/CW, 538)

Having been in trouble with the Excise on account of his political sympathies, Burns had sound pragmatic reasons for making gestures of loyalty in a period of hysterical outrage at the possibility of a French invasion. Hugh MacDiarmid suggested (in the *Glasgow Herald* of 14 March 1967) that Burns joined the Dumfires Volunteers as part of a republican plan to infiltrate the ranks of the soldiery. Given Burns's political principles, it is not an absurd idea; given his official position and desire to protect himself and his family, it is highly improbable.

Two years before the French Revolution, Burns told Mrs Dunlop 'I set as little by kings, lords, clergy, critics, &c. as all these respectable Gentry do by my Bardship' (CL, 136). Unfortunately, for the public assertion of his principles, he lived during a turbulent time when occasionally he had to assume a sycophantic role in order to escape the most vicious attentions of 'these respectable Gentry'. Politically he was a child of the American Revolution – devoted to 'life, liberty, and the pursuit of happiness' – who matured in a country where it was not always politic to affirm that similar ideals animated the French Revolution. The 'glorious feast' of liberty was not something a poetic exciseman could openly enjoy in North Britain.

Burns and Philosophy

As a result of the obsequious Preface to the Kilmarnock Edition and Henry Mackenzie's influential description of the poet as a 'Heaven-taught ploughman' (CH, 70) Burns was regarded, by his early readers, as an ignorant man able, by some miracle, to produce poetry. An unsigned notice in the *General Magazine and Impartial Review* (1787) summed up the position: 'By general report we learn, that R. B. is a plough-boy, of small education' (CH, 88). In fact, by the time the Kilmarnock Edition was published, Burns had read not only the poetry of Pope and Shenstone, not only the fiction of Richardson and Fielding, but the philosophy of John Locke and Adam Smith. Before he left Lochlea in 1784, Burns had read Locke's *An Essay Concerning Human Understanding* (1690), a work regarded as the foundation of British empiricism.

The impact of Locke's *Essay* on Burns must have been profound, stimulating his insights into human nature and reinforcing his critical attitude to the kirk (religious dogmatists were disturbed by Locke's implication that reasonable discourse depended on 'determined ideas', not obscurantist religious dogma). Briefly, the *Essay* is an assault on dogmatic beliefs, a book that showed Locke to be preeminent among those David Hume described (in his Introduction to *A Treatise of Human Nature*) as 'philosophers in England, who have . . . put the science of man on a new footing, and . . . excited the curiosity of the public'. In Book I, Locke dismisses the doctrine of an innate knowledge of moral and speculative truths; in Book II he argues that experience accounts for ideas, both ideas of sensation derived from the outer senses, and ideas of reflection induced by introspection; in Book III he discusses the subjective limitations of language; in Book IV he undermines Cartesian assumptions about general truths.

Burns mentions Locke's *Essay* in his Autobiographical Letter and, writing to Mrs McLehose in January 1788, refers to 'the Great and likewise Good Mr Locke, Author of the famous essay on the human understanding' (CL, 386). Burns would have delighted in Locke's appeals to individual observation, taking this as an encouragement to remain open to natural experience rather than relying on dogma. Locke argued that the mind knows nothing but what it receives from without; so knowledge is founded on observation which the mind rearranges ('Nothing can be in the intellect which was not first in the senses'). Endorsing empirical science (in particular the achievement of 'the incomparable Mr Newton'), with its basis in observation and experiment, Locke rejected the arrogant appeal to innate ideas (of God or anything else). Reacting against scholastic essentialism, Locke drew a distinction between the real (and unknown) essence of an object and its 'nominal essence', accessible to observation. It was a philosophy attractive to a poet of Burns's inquisitive outlook. Indeed, Locke (in 'The Epistle to the Reader') encouraged the individual to regard his own intellectual quest as an end in itself:

> For the understanding, like the eye, judging of objects only by its own sight, cannot but be pleased with what it discovers, having less regret for what has escaped it, because it is unknown. Thus he who has raised himself above the alms-basket, and not content to live lazily on scraps of begged opinions, sets his own thoughts on work, to find and follow truth, will (whatever he lights on) not miss the hunter's satisfaction; every moment of his pursuit will reward his pains with some delight, and he will have reason to think his time not ill spent, even when he cannot much boast of any great acquisition.

That reference to 'scraps of begged opinions' must have been relished by Burns as putting the self-righteous in their place.

Burns was never a systematic student of philosophy but, in the course of his short life, showed a shrewd appreciation of those philosophers who confirmed what he concluded through observation and experience. By turns radical, reformist and revolutionary in politics, he was liberal in philosophy; as well as gaining an understanding of Lockean liberalism he was able, in the early summer of 1789, to enthuse over Adam Smith's *Wealth of Nations* with its emphasis on natural liberty and its insistence that productivity should take priority over pedigree, thus putting the gentry in *their* place. The Scottish intellectual climate of his time was enlightened and Burns, though raised in a farming community, expanded his intellect through reading and embraced the body of thought that stood for the Enlightenment.

In his first Common Place Book (completed by October 1785), Burns praises Adam Smith's *The Theory of Moral Sentiments* (1759), a collection of lectures influenced by the empiricist Francis Hutcheson who had taught Smith at Glasgow University and whose *Inquiry Into the Origins of Our Ideas of Beauty and Virtue* (1725) associated moral judgement with an intuitive apprehension of virtue as a pleasure. Smith considered that happiness was quantitative and endorsed Hutcheson's sentimental view of morality. Burns wrote: 'I entirely agree with that judicious philosopher Mr Smith in his excellent Theory of Moral Sentiments, that Remorse is the most painful sentiment that can embitter the human bosom' (CB, 7).

Elsewhere in the first Common Place Book, Burns expressed a Deism that was implicit in Locke's *Essay* (with its reference to 'some knowing intelligent Being . . . which whether any one will please to call God, it matters not') and current among Scottish Common Sense philosophers. Burns declared 'the grand end of human life is to cultivate an intercourse with that Being to whom we owe life' (CB, 22), a teleology that informs a letter of 1788 where he refers to 'a great unknown Being who could have no other end in giving [man] existence but to make him happy' (CL, 90). The Common Sense philosophers, suspicious of rigid Calvinism but reluctant to abandon this 'great unknown Being', were willing to defend the moderate, liberal Presbyterian tradition against the atheistic onslaughts of Hume. One of them, John Gregory, wrote to James Beattie in 1767:

> Atheism and materialism are the present fashion. If one speaks with warmth of an infinitely wise and good Being, who sustains and directs the frame of nature, or expresses his steady belief of a future state of existence, he gets hints of his having either a very weak understanding, or of being a very great hypocrite. (William Forbes, *An Account of the Life and Writings of James Beattie*, New York, 1807, p. 73)

Beattie was not only a prominent Common Sense philosopher and Professor of Moral Philosophy at Aberdeeen University; he was also a poet. Burns admired Beattie in both capacities. Beattie had, in his *Essay on the Nature and Immutability of Truth* (1770), attempted to refute Hume's scepticism; his poem *The Minstrel: or, The Progress of Genius* (1771–4) was a greatly popular work in its time. Burns

praised Beattie in 'The Vision' (1785) for his verse and for his attack
on Hume:

> Hence, sweet, harmonious Beattie sung
> His *Minstrel* lays;
> Or tore, with noble ardour stung,
> The sceptic's bays.
>
> (62/CW, 118)

In a letter of 1788 Burns saluted Beattie as 'the immortal Author of
the *Minstrel*' (CL, 364).

Burns's satire 'The Holy Fair' (1785), pointedly depicts Common
Sense distancing itself from the dogmas of an Auld Licht minister.
As soon as the minister gets up to preach, Common Sense departs:

> See, up he's got the word o God,
> An meek an mim has view'd it,
> While Common-sense has taen the road
> An aff, an up the Cowgate
> Fast, fast that day.
>
> (70/CW, 137)

On a parochial level, Burns personifies Common Sense as a tribute
to his humane friend Dr John Mackenzie of Mauchline. However, the
poem transcends the parochial level and Common Sense is regarded
as the natural enemy of life-denying reactionary religion. Again, in
'The Ordination' (1786), Burns invokes 'Curst Common-sense, that
imp o Hell' as the enemy of the Auld Licht minister Mackinlay:

> And Common-sense is gaun, she says,
> To mak to Jamie Beattie
> Her plaint this day.
>
> (85/CW, 194)

And in 'The Brigs of Ayr' (1786) the New Brig (the liberal voice of
progression) contrasts 'common-sense' with 'Plain, dull stupidity'.

In the 'Epistle to James Tennant of Glenconner' (1786), Burns
praises both Adam Smith and Thomas Reid, the most prominent
Common Sense philosopher but, humorously, suggests that Reid's
philosophy only elaborates on the sagacity of the common people:

> Smith, wi his sympathetic feeling,
> An Reid, to common sense appealing.
> Philosophers have fought and wrangled,

An meikle Greek and Latin mangled,
Till, wi their logic-jargon tir'd
As in the depth of science mir'd,
To common sense they now appeal –
What wives and wabsters see and feel!
(90/CW, 200)

From personal experience and observation, as well as philosophical inclination, Burns allied himself with a sturdy commonsense and with the Scottish Common Sense philosophers. Coincidentally, Tom Paine's republican treatise of 1776, a book Burns would certainly have known about as a potent influence on the American revolution, was called *Common Sense*, thus giving the term a revolutionary connotation.

One Common Sense philosopher was personally well known to Burns. Dugald Stewart, whom Burns considered 'The most perfect character I ever saw' (cited by Snyder, 200), met the poet before he went to Edinburgh then went on walks with him in the capital. Professor of Moral Philosophy at Edinburgh University from 1785 until his retirement in 1810, Stewart was an admirer (and biographer) of the Common Sense philosopher Thomas Reid who oppposed Hume's concept of mind-dependent entities and argued in favour of a commonsense contact with mind-independent realities. Stewart's introduction to his *Outlines of Moral Philosophy* (1793) gives some indication of his approach:

> The ultimate object of philosophical inquiry is the same which every man of plain understanding proposes to himself, when he remarks the events which fall under his observation with a view to the future regulation of his conduct. The more knowledge of this kind we acquire, the better can we accommodate our plans to the established order of things, and avail ourselves of natural Powers and Agents for accomplishing our purposes. (*The Collected Works of Dugald Stewart*, ed. Sir William Hamilton, Edinburgh, 1854–60, vol. II, p. 6)

If, as is likely, Stewart expressed such ideas in conversation with Burns, the impact would have been positive for Burns also aspired to articulate the insights of 'every man of plain understanding'.

Gilbert Burns suggested that, in his Mount Oliphant period, Burns 'remained unacquainted . . . with Hume' (GN), thus implying that he subsequently read Scotland's greatest philosopher though in his capacity as a historian (since Gilbert links Hume with William Robertson). As noted above, there is a reference to Hume as 'the sceptic' in 'The Vision' and in the 'Prologue Spoken by Mr Woods' (on the actor's benefit night, 16 April 1787) there is, Kinsley supposes in annotating a passage on Edinburgh's cultural reputation, a 'tribute to the philosophers Hume, Dugald Stewart, and Adam Smith . . . and to Hume and Robertson as historians' (Kinsley, 1232):

> Philosophy, no idle pedant dream,
> Here holds her search by heaven-taught Reason's beam:
> Here History paints with elegance and force
> The tide of Empire's fluctuating course . . .
>   (151/CW, 275)

The second line of the quotation pays no tribute to Hume who had no faith in heaven and who insisted, in *A Treatise of Human Nature*, 'Reason is, and ought only to be, the slave of the passions.' Produced for declamation in public, the phrase about 'heaven-taught Reason' sounds suspiciously like a specific disavowal of Hume the philosopher, though Hume the historian is given due credit.

Before Burns left Edinburgh and its 'heaven-taught Reason', he sent an 'Address to William Tytler', Tytler (1711–92) being the author of *A Historical and Critical Enquiry into the Evidence against Mary Queen of Scots* (1760), an attempt to refute the Stuart volumes (1754, 1757) of Hume's *History of England*. On reading the *Enquiry* Hume described Tytler as 'a Scots Jacobite, who maintains the innocence of Queen Mary [and is] beyond the reach of argument or reason' (cited by Kinsley, 1233). Burns, however, described Tytler as

> Revered defender of beauteous Stuart,
>   Of Stuart! – a name once respected,
> A name which to love was once mark of a true heart,
>   But now 'tis despis'd and neglected!
>   (152/CW, 276)

Burns advised Tytler to burn this poem as 'rather heretical' (CL, 291). Though he disapproved of Hume's treatment of Mary Queen of Scots, Burns was proud to list – in a letter of 1791 written for publication in the *Statistical Account of Scotland* – 'Hume's History of the Stewarts' (CL, 587) among the books in the library of the Monkland Friendly Society.

Burns could be devious when it suited his strategy and was cautious about condemning Hume the historian in public. Hume the philosopher required different tactics: the implied rebuke of the 'Prologue Spoken by Mr Woods' and a diplomatic silence. Though Hume had been dead for a decade when Burns arrived in Edinburgh, the sceptical philosopher was still a dangerous figure to discuss, still widely regarded as the atheistic scourge of God-fearing folk. Yet the work of Burns is in accord with Hume's naturalism and his affirmative attitude. In his Conclusion to Book I of *A Treatise of Human Nature* (which fell 'dead-born from the press' when published in 1739) Hume declared 'Human Nature is the only science of man; and yet has been hitherto the most neglected.' In Section I, Part IV of Book I of the *Treatise*, Hume said:

> Nature, by an absolute and uncontrollable necessity, has determined us to judge as well as to breathe and feel; nor can we any more forbear viewing certain objects in a stronger and fuller light, upon account of their customary connection with a present impression, than we can hinder ourselves from thinking, as long as we are awake, or seeing the surrounding bodies, when we turn our eyes towards them in broad sunshine . . . . It is happy, therefore, that nature breaks the force of all sceptical arguments in time, and keeps them from having any considerable influence on the understanding.

This appeal to nature is as compelling as that of Rousseau, Hume's hostile friend. Hume may have felt that poets were 'liars by profession' but, as a man who valued passion above reason, would surely have approved of Burns. And it is difficult to believe that Burns, sometimes a liar through discretion, did not approve of Hume – the enemy of dogma, the empirical successor to Locke, the admirer of nature, the friend of Adam Smith and Dr Blacklock (to whom Hume transferred his salary as librarian of the Advocates' Library) – even though direct evidence is elusive.

Burns and Booze

At the age of sixteen, Burns went to Kirkoswald, ostensibly to study at Hugh Rodger's school, but found he made 'greater progress in the knowledge of mankind'. What this knowledge amounted to, Burns gladly specified: 'scenes of swaggering riot and roaring dissipation were as yet new to me . . . I learned to look unconcernedly on a large tavern-bill, and mix without fear in a drunken squabble' (AL). As a teenager, by his own admission, he enjoyed drink and tavern life. Not a surprising confession, really, from the man who, fifteen years after the Kirkoswald episode, glorified the social pleasures of drinking in 'Tam o Shanter':

> While we sit bousing at the nappy,
> An getting fou and unco happy . . .
> Fast by an ingle, bleezing finely,
> Wi reaming swats, that drank divinely . . .
>   (321/CW, 410–11)

These lines were the result of serious research in the field, that is the tavern.

On Monday, 10 September 1787, during his Highland tour with Nicol, Burns arranged to meet his cousin James Burness in Stonehaven: 'there is but one Inn at [Stonehaven] so you cannot miss me' (CL, 61). Writing to Burness again, on 9 February 1789, Burns explained that he had now moved to Ellisland and had married Jean Armour. He also admitted 'After I parted from you, for many months, my life was one continued scene of dissipation' (CL, 62). This suggests that he was regularly intoxicated during the period he confirmed his interest in Ellisland, proposed marriage to Margaret Chalmers (October 1787), and embarked on his infatuation with Mrs McLehose (December 1787). Nothing odd about that, the reader might reasonably observe.

An anecdote takes us a little further. Samuel Clark was a

116

Dumfries lawyer and drinking friend of Burns. On Saturday night in January 1794, Clark was present when Burns, during the war with revolutionary France, gave the toast: 'May our success in the present war be equal to the justice of our cause' (CL, 702). Outraged by the the ambiguity of the toast, one Captain Dods insulted Burns who wrote a sorrowful letter to Clark on the subject the following morning:

> I was, I know, drunk last night, but I am sober this morning. – From the expressions Captain Dods made use of to me, had I nobody's welfare to care for but my own, we should certainly have come, according to the manners of the world, to the necessity of murdering one another about the business. – The words were such as generally, I believe, end in a brace of pistols; but I am still pleased to think that I did not ruin the peace [and] welfare of a wife & a family of children in a drunken squabble. (CL, 702)

A 'drunken squabble' in Ayrshire at sixteen, a prolonged period of 'dissipation' in and out of Edinburgh in 1787, another 'drunken squabble' in Dumfries. The epistolary evidence is clear: Burns was, to put it mildly, no stranger to drink and drunkenness – which would not matter except that the issue has been a crucial one for Burns scholarship.

'I am miserably fou' (CL, 309) Burns wrote to Peter Hill on 17 May 1787; 'occasional hard drinking is the devil to me' (CL, 203) he wrote to Mrs Dunlop on 31 December 1792. These two statements, from the poet's own parched lips as it were, speak volumes for a drinking problem that has been distorted by dogma since the death of Burns. Burns was haunted by hangovers and given to sporadic, rather than regular, drinking. However, commentators have rarely been willing to leave the matter there though his friends took his boozing in their stride. Writing to Currie about the Galloway tour he made with Burns in July–August 1793, John Syme recalled 'We got utterly wet, and to revenge ourselves Burns insisted at Gatehouse, on our getting utterly drunk' (cited by Kinsley, 1420). Had he known of his posthumous reputation as a tippler, Burns might have extended the session, insisting that he and Syme (like Tam o Shanter and Souter Johnie) got 'fou for weeks thegither'.

Every year, on 25 January, the birthday of Burns is celebrated, in Scotland and internationally, with Burns Suppers at which haggis and whisky are consumed in large quantities. The haggis, of course, honours Burns's enthusiastic 'Address to a Haggis'.

The whisky, equally obviously, endorses the sentiments Burns expressed in 'Scotch Drink' (a poem, modelled on Fergusson's 'Caller Water' and strategically placed second in the Kilmarnock Edition though Snyder, 170, dismisses it as 'a relatively trivial piece of Bacchanalianism'):

> Whisky! soul o plays an pranks!
> Accept a Bardie's gratefu thanks!
> When wanting thee, what tuneless cranks
>   Are my poor verses!
> Thou comes – they rattle i' their ranks,
>   At ither's arses!
>
> (77/CW, 167)

Because of songs like 'The Silver Tassie' ('Go fetch to me a pint o wine') and poems like 'Scotch Drink', 'The Author's Earnest Cry and Prayer' ('Freedom and whisky gang thegither') and 'Tam o Shanter' Burns is generally associated with boozing. T. W. H. Crosland, in his hostile account of *The Unspeakable Scot* (London, 1902, p. 105) declared 'Burns was undoubtedly the poet of licence and alcoholism'.

The assumption that Burns was an alcoholic was aired in Robert Heron's *Memoir* (1797), the earliest biography, in which the poet was accused of being, on more than one occasion, 'dead drunk' (Hecht, 277) in Dumfries. Gilbert Burns, in his long letter to Mrs Dunlop (written in 1797, the year Heron's memoir was serialised in the *Monthly Magazine and British Register*, January–June 1797) defended his brother, claiming disingenuously, in an obviously strained piece of special pleading, that the poet was not 'given to drinking' (GN). James Currie's influential edition of *The Works of Robert Burns, with an Account of his Life* (1800) gave as gospel the liquid legend of Burns the alcoholic for the poet was portrayed as 'Perpetually stimulated by alcohol in one or other of its various forms' (Currie, I, 214).

It seems a familiar enough poetic failing, and one that does not normally trouble readers of poetry unduly. Admirers of the Welsh poet Dylan Thomas or the American poet John Berryman do not expend energy in denying that their hero got drunk or was an alcoholic. Burns, however, is Scottish and so a moral issue. Currie's censorious remarks were those of a Scottish doctor who had overindulged in his youth and it is not astonishing that he should feel free to make moralistic remarks. It is, however, surprising that modern Burnsians should be every bit as moralistic as Currie in attempting to refute his argument. The Heron–Currie thesis of the alcoholic poet has been replaced by the dogma of the moderate drinker.

Despite the epistolary and (often reliable) anecdotal evidence to the contrary, Franklyn Bliss Snyder asserted, in his much-admired *The Life of Robert Burns* (1932), that Burns 'was never a drunkard' (Snyder, 435). Maurice Lindsay, following the same source as Synder, rejoiced that 'In 1926 . . . the legend of Burns the drunkard, was, at long last, finally nailed to the mast by one of the most eminent men of his day, Sir James Crichton-Browne' (BE, 102). Lindsay also confidentaly declared 'Burns, in an age when excessive drinking was common, was not himself a heavy drinker' (BE, 129). An earlier Burnsian, Robert Chambers (*The Life and Works of Robert Burns*, Edinburgh 1851–2, rept. 1891, p. 184), had paved the way for such statements by claiming that Burns 'was no lover of drink'.

So anxious was Snyder to seize any opportunity to clear Burns from the contamination of alcoholism that he (and Lindsay after him) accepted as absolutely authoritative Crichton-Browne's opinion, first given in a series of five articles in the *Glasgow Herald* (4, 5, 7, 8, 9 December 1925) then reissued, the following year, as a book. Crichton-Browne's *Burns from a New Point of View* (London, 1926) asserted 'Burns died of endocarditis, a disease of the substance and lining membrane of the heart' (p. 61) and 'It will not, I think, be disputed that Burns died of rheumatic endocarditis' (p. 85).

After Crichton-Browne's book appeared, the dogma of the rheumatic heart replaced the doctrine of alcoholism, both opinions relying on faith rather than fact. The American Burnsian, Robert Fitzhugh, regarded the matter as settled by the opinions of four doctors (Crichton-Browne and three others) whose interpretation of the epistolary evidence is itself open to interpretation since all four 'speak of rheumatic fever and endocarditis, and they all agree that Burns showed no sign of alcoholism' (Fitzhugh, 204). Robert D. Thornton's *William Maxwell to Robert Burns* (Edinburgh, 1979, p. 187) refused to endorse the Synder line, perceiving Burns as 'an habitual drinker whose drinking became more and more detrimental to his health'. Richard Hindle Fowler, in *Robert Burns* (London, 1988) was more specific in disputing Crichton-Browne's claim that Burns died of rheumatic endocarditis.

Fowler pointed out that Crichton-Browne was far from being infallible on the subject of Burns's health since he specialised in psychiatric – not clinical – medicine, holding the post of Lord

Chancellor's Visitor in Lunacy until his retirement in 1922. On the basis of epistolary and anecdotal evidence, Fowler put a new interpretation on the condition that killed Burns. In his view, Burns contracted brucellosis, a disease (common in the eighteenth century) transmitted to humans by animals, specifically cattle. Moreoover, he exacerbated his condition by habitually drinking excessive quantities of wine which, in his time, was adulterated with lead. Fowler's conclusions about brucellosis and alcoholically induced lead poisoning give new life to the much-maligned Heron–Currie thesis about the alcoholic poet.

Oddly, devoted Burnsians seem unable to accept that their hero might have been as susceptible as many other Scots to alcoholism. Introducing his edition of the poet's letters, J. A. Mackay writes 'The letters ought to dispel . . . any lingering notion of Burns's last years being clouded by dissipation' (CL, 212) and later refers to 'the *canard* about Burns being a heavy drinker' (CL, 538). Bardolators are not only reluctant to connect Burns with booze but seem as convinced as Currie that drinking is a sin. Burns himself was more philosophical about drink. His Autobiographical Letter to Moore speaks of a dispute with his father leading to 'that dissipation which marked my future years' (AL). Writing to Samuel Clark he saw no contradiction between drinking and decency though, on this occasion, he was too hungover to tell the whole truth about his own condition:

> I recollect something of a drunken promise yesternight to break-
> fast with you this morning. – I am sorry that it is impos-
> sible . . . . Some of our folks about the Excise Office, Edinburgh,
> had and perhaps still have conceived a prejudice against me as
> being a drunken dissipated character. – I might be all this, you
> know, & yet be an honest fellow, but you know that I am an honest
> fellow and am nothing of this. (CL, 702)

The 'drunken promise' is typical of the heavy tippler.

Still, there is no evidence to suggest that Burns was habitually drunk from morning to night on a daily basis. Josiah Walker spent two days with Burns in November 1795 and recalled a visit to the Globe Inn:

> When it began to grow late, he shewed no disposition to retire, but
> called for fresh supplies of liquor, with a freedom which might
> be excusable, as we were in an inn, and no condition had been

distinctly made, though it might easily have been inferred, had the inference been welcome, that he was to consider himself as our guest; nor was it till he saw us worn out, that he departed, about three in the morning . . . He, on this occasion, drank freely without being intoxicated, a circumstance from which I concluded, not only that his constitution was still unbroken, but that he was not addicted to solitary cordials; for if he had tasted liquor in the morning, he must have easily yielded to the excess of the evening. (cited by Fitzhugh, 360–1)

Drunken nights in the Globe Inn and drunken promises: it fits a definite pattern.

Burns does conform to the behavioural pattern of the bout-alcoholic who can do without drink for sustained periods and then depend on it for days on end. Dugald Stewart, who went on walks with Burns in Edinburgh, found him a sober companion: 'I should have concluded in favour of his habits of sobriety, from all of him that ever fell under my own observation' (cited by Snyder, 201). As it is undeniable that Burns was extremely drunk on other occasions, this can be taken as an example of the bout- alcoholic between bouts and Burns would have taken care to be on his best behaviour with Stewart, a university professor and 'The most perfect character I ever saw' (cited by Snyder, 200).

Burns certainly suffered from the guilt-edged insecurity of the bout-alcoholic, as his letters make clear. Towards the end of 1791 he wrote to Bob Ainslie about 'the horrors of penitence, regret, remorse, head-ache, nausea, and all the rest of the damned hounds of hell, that beset a poor wretch, who has been guilty of the sin of drunkenness' (CL, 339). In March 1793 he apologised for his behaviour the night before in a letter to John McMurdo:

I believe last night that my old enemy, the Devil, taking the advantage of my being in drink (he well knows he has no chance with me in my sober hours) tempted me to be a little turbulent. – You have too much humanity to heed the maniac ravings of a poor wretch whom the powers of Hell, & the potency of Port, beset at the same time. (CL, 494)

His notorious 'letter from hell', apologising to Elizabeth Riddell (for the Sabine Rape incident, see her entry in 'The Burns Circle') at the beginning of 1794, expresses alarm at the behavioural changes wrought by drink:

To all the other ladies please present my humblest contrition for my conduct, and my petition for their gracious pardon. O, all ye powers of decency and decorum! whisper to them that my errors, though great, were involuntary – that an intoxicated man is the vilest of beasts – that it was not in my nature to be brutal to any one – that to be rude to a woman, when in my senses, was impossible with me – but – Regret! Remorse! Shame! ye three hell-hounds that ever dog my steps and bay at my heels, spare me! spare me! (CL, 698)

Bout-alcoholism, with its euphoric self-indulgence dissolving into remorse as the bout shakily ends, is often associated with manic-depressive behaviour which, in turn, is often found in highly creative individuals. Poets, with their bouts of intense creativity and their bouts of despair, are understandably prone to bout-alcoholism and Burns was definitely a bout-writer producing the great poems of the Kilmarnock Edition in a short period of time (the *annus mirabilis* of 1784–5), writing songs for Johnson and Thomson in bursts. Burns's remark that 'occasional hard drinking is the devil to me' (CL, 203) is a classic confession of bout-alcoholism.

Heron's much-criticised memoir of 1797 actually rings true if we accept that Burns was a bout-alcoholic: 'In the intervals between his different fits of intemperance, he suffered still the keenest anguish of remorse and horribly afflictive foresight' (Hecht, 277). All that can be said with certainty is that Burns drank often from the age of sixteen onwards and drank enough, in bouts over a long period, to damage his health. Maria Riddell, who knew Burns well, acknowledged his heavy drinking and refused to 'undertake to be the apologist of the irregularities even of a man of genius' (BE, 308). Almost two centuries after the death of Burns it is even less necessary to apologise for a poet who, in 'Scotch Drink', made his position clear:

> May gravels round his blather wrench,
> An gouts torment him, inch by inch,
> What twists his gruntle, wi a glunch,
>   O sour disdain,
> Out owre a glass o whisky-punch
>   Wi honest men!
>
>   (77/CW, 167)

Burns and the Theatre

With the overestimated exception of the Rev John Home's *Douglas* (1756) – received with hysterical rapture at its premier, acclaimed by David Hume, admired by Sarah Siddons who played the role of Lady Randolph when she returned to the stage in 1819 – Scottish drama in the eighteenth century was virtually non-existent. To the extremists of the Scottish kirk, the stage was an alien territory, the actor a rival to the preacher. John Knox himself had gone to plays (in St Andrews he watched a drama anticipating the execution of Mary Queen of Scots) but, after his death, the Church of Scotland associated drama with the work of the devil.

Allan Ramsay founded Scotland's first organised theatre in 1736 in the hope of building a new tradition on the basis of his pastoral ballad-opera *The Gentle Shepherd* (published in 1725 and first performed in 1729 as Scotland's answer to John Gay's *The Beggar's Opera* of 1728) but the Licensing Act of 1737 closed Ramsay's theatre. On the opening night of Home's *Douglas* in Edinburgh's Canongate Theatre, on 14 December 1756, a member of the first-night audience shouted, 'Whaur's yer Wully Shakespeare noo?' It was the popularity of this pseudo-Shakespearean tragedy that alarmed the Church of Scotland which worried that its worshippers might transfer their allegiance from the pulpit to the stage.

Home, after all, was minister of Athelstaneford and it was considered he was setting an atrocious example. As a public gesture of disapproval of Home's play, the Edinburgh Presbytery issued, on 5 January 1757, an Admonition and Exhortation, reported in the *Edinburgh Courant* two days later:

> The Presbytery taking into serious consideration the declining state of religion, the open profanation of the Lord's Day, the contempt of public worship, the growing luxury and levity of the present age . . . judged it their indispensable duty to express

123

in the most open and solemn manner, the deep concern they feel on this occasion. The opinion which the Christian Church has always entertained of stage plays and players as prejudicial to the interest of religion and morality is well known, and the fatal influence which they commonly have on the far greater part of mankind, particularly the younger sort, is too obvious to be called into question.

Home resigned his ministry and became private secretary to the Earl of Bute; his subsequent plays, written for the London stage, have been forgotten. The success of *Douglas*, however, renewed the hostility of the kirk to the stage, and demonstrated that Scottish audiences were desperate for an indigenous dramatist. Burns, who liked to quote Douglas's play in his letters, had more than a passing interest in being that dramatist.

Some of Burns's dramatic monologues – 'Address of Beelzebub', 'Holy Willie's Prayer' – show a brilliant ability to inhabit a character, a gift that might have been translated into dramatic terms given the right opportunity and environment. From an early age Burns was interested in drama. A well-known anecdote, recorded by his brother Gilbert, describes the impact of Shakespeare on the nine-year-old Burns when John Murdoch was about to leave Alloway in 1768:

> Murdoch came to spend the night [and] brought us a present and memorial of him, a small compendium of English Grammar, and the tragedy of *Titus Andronicus*, and by way of passing the evening, he began to read the play aloud. We were all attention for some time, till presently the whole party was dissolved in tears. A female in the play (I have but a confused recollection of it) had her hands chopt off, and her tongue cut out, and then was insultingly desired to call for water to wash her hands. At this, in an agony of distress, we with one voice desired that he would read no more. My father observed, that if we would not hear it out, it would be needless to leave the play with us. Robert replied that if it was left he would burn it. (GN)

Around 1777, at Mount Oliphant, Burns composed a tragic fragment of his own, later transcribed in his first Common Place Book (entry for March 1784) as 'A pentitential thought in the hour of Remorse, Intended for a tragedy'. This dramatic monologue, using iambic pentameter with what is clearly intended to be Shakespearean flexibility, was prompted by William Burnes's humiliations at the hands of the Factor who handled the affairs of Mount Oliphant farm when the landlord, Provost William Fergusson, died (Burns also expresses his indignation at the Factor in 'The Twa Dogs'):

> Still my heart melts at human wretchedness;
> And with sincere, though unavailing sighs
> I view the helpless children of distress.
> With tears indignant I behold th'Oppressor
> Rejoicing in the honest man's destruction
> Whose unsubmitting heart was all his crime.
>
> (5/CW, 46)

One of the most stimulating friends Burns made in Edinburgh was William Woods (1751–1802), an English actor who had known Robert Fergusson well and given Burns's 'elder brother in the Muse' ('Apostrophe to Fergusson') free seats at the Haymarket Theatre. A member of the Edinburgh Company of players for thirty-one years, Woods had a benefit night on 16 April 1787 and Burns obliged the actor with a 'Prologue' to be spoken before the production of *The Merry Wives of Windsor*. The 'Prologue' shows Burns's familiarity with the reputation of Sarah Siddons, with the fame of John Home's *Douglas*, and with 'the actor's lot' (hardly surprisingly since he expertly acted a role of the poetic primitive for his own Edinburgh audience):

> When by a generous Public's kind acclaim
> That dearest need is granted – honest fame;
> Where here your favour is the actor's lot,
> Nor even the man in private life forgot;
> What breast so dead to heavenly Virtue's glow
> But heaves impassion'd with the grateful throe?
>
> Poor is the task to please a barb'rous throng:
> It needs no Siddons' powers in Southern song.
> But here an ancient nation, fam'd afar
> For genius, learning high, as great in war.
> Hail, Caledonia! name for ever dear!
> Before whose sons I'm honor'd to appear! . . .
> Here *Douglas* forms wild Shakespeare into plan,
> And Harley rouses all the God in man.
>
> (151/CW, 275)

Apart from the obligatory reference to Harley, the hero of Henry Mackenzie's sentimental novel *The Man of Feeling*, the passage shows appreciation of the art of acting and resentment that a great cultural capital should have to import its drama (with the exception of *Douglas*).

Burns's admirers felt he might attempt a pastoral drama along the lines of Ramsay's *The Gentle Shepherd*. Henry Mackenzie recalled,

> I suggested to Burns the idea of his writing a pastoral after the manner of *The Gentle Shepherd*, and he seemed to relish the idea much. Yet . . . it is questionable if he could have constructed a drama consisting of a combination of characters, woven into a well-arranged plot and carried on to a natural conclusion. He was the poet of impulse and was always unwilling to study for excellence. (cited by Kinsley, 1539)

During his eight-day stay in Harvieston, in October 1787, Burns met John Ramsay of Ochtertyre who likewise advised him to follow the pastoral path of *The Gentle Shepherd*

> What beautiful landscape of rural life and manner might not have been expected from a pencil so faithful and forcible as his, which could have exhibited scenes as familiar and interesting as those in *The Gentle Shepherd* which everyone who knows our swains in their unadulterated state instantly recognises as true to nature! But to have executed [such a drama], steadiness and abstraction from company were wanting, not talents! (BE, 295)

Ramsay of Ochtertyre's assumption that Burns was temperamentally equipped to write a pastoral drama was misplaced: 'The Jolly Beggars' (1785) – which Ramsay had not read – was more Burns's style, being earthy and realistic.

However, Burns did not immediately discard John Ramsay's advice as unsuitable. Requesting the favour of an Excise appointment, in a letter of 10 September 1788 to Robert Graham of Fintry, he explained: 'If I were in the Service, it would likewise favor my Poetical schemes. – I am thinking of something, in the rural way, of the Drama-kind' (CL, 426). That reference to a rural drama suggests he was indeed thinking about a pastoral play. On 23 December 1789, writing from Ellisland to Lady Elizabeth Cunningham, Burns was more forceful, enlarging on his ambition to write indigenous Scottish plays:

I have some thoughts of the Drama. – Considering the favorite things of the day, the two and three act pieces of Okeefe [John O'Keefe, author of *The Highland Reel*], Mrs [Elizabeth Simpson] Inchbald, &c. does not your Ladyship think that a Scottish Audience would be better pleased with the Affectation, Whim & Folly of their own native growth, than with manners which to by far the greatest of them can be only second hand? – No man knows what Nature has fitted him for until he try; and if after a preparatory course of some years' study of Men and Books, I should find myself unequal to the task, there is no great harm done – Virtue and Study are their own reward. – I have got Shakespeare, and begun with him; and I shall stretch a point & make myself master of all the Dramatic Authors of any repute, in both English and French, the only languages which I know. (CL, 499)

According to Ramsay of Ochtertyre (cited by Kinsley, 1534), Burns had decided on a plot for a play to be entitled *Rob Mac Quechan's Elshon*, about the cobbler who (so tradition tells) drove his awl into the foot of Robert the Bruce while repairing a shoe damaged in battle. Burns might have made much of a play featuring Robert the Bruce and, significantly, his plan had a practical potential in Dumfries.

As Ellisland was only some six miles from Dumfries, Burns was able to keep in contact with the theatre since a 'well-supported theatre added a definitely metropolitan touch to the life of Dumfries, and gave an opportunity for its residents to enjoy a sort of diversion available in few provincial centres' (Snyder, 358). The poet became friendly with George Sutherland whose company performed at the old Assembly Rooms in the George Hotel, Dumfries. For the New Year's Evening of 1790 Burns wrote, for Sutherland, a 'Prologue Spoken at the Theatre of Dumfries', beginning with an appeal for a sympathetic approach to theatrical enterprises in Scotland:

> No song nor dance I bring from yon great city
> That queens it o'er our taste – the more's the pity!
> Tho, by-the-bye, abroad why will you roam?
> Good sense and taste are natives here at home.
>   (396/CW, 376)

Sending the poem to his brother Gilbert from Ellisland ('this accursed farm') on 11 January 1790, Burns enthused:

We have gotten a set of very decent Players here just now. I have seen them an evening or two. – David Campbell in Ayr wrote me by the Manager of the Company, a Mr Sutherland, who is indeed a man of genius and apparent worth. – On Newyearday evening I gave him [my] Prologue which he spouted to his Audience with great applause. (CL, 358)

With dramatic ideas in his mind, Burns was obviously delighted to have access to a competent theatrical company.

Sutherland may not have been 'a man of genius', as Burns claimed, but he was ambitious and keen to establish a permanent playhouse in Dumfries. Writing to William Nicol from Ellisland, on 9 February 1790, Burns declared:

> There is little new in this country. Our theatrical company, of which you must have heard, leave us in a week. Their merit and character are indeed very great, both on the stage, and in private life; not a worthless creature among them; and their encouragement has been accordingly. Their usual run is from eighteen to twenty-five pounds a night; seldom less than the one, and the house will hold no more than the other. There have been repeated instances of sending away six, and eight, and ten pounds in a night for want of room. A new theatre is to be built by subscription; the first stone is to be laid on Friday first to come. Three hundred guineas have been raised by thirty subscribers, and thirty more might have been got if wanted. The manager, Mr Sutherland, was introduced to me by a friend from Ayr; and a worthier or cleverer fellow I have rarely met with. Some of our clergy have slipt in by stealth now and then; but they have got up a farce of their own. (CL, 347)

On 18 February 1790 Sutherland attended the inaugural meeting of subscribers of the Dumfries theatre, a project whose progress largely depended on the influence and position of the poet's friend Robert Riddell who was granted ground on the Barnraws to build (as a Founding Deed put it) 'a house intended for a Theatre or Playhouse' (cited in BE, 392). Burns was elated at the dramatic possibilities that could, before long, be at his disposal. For the benefit night of Sutherland's wife, on 3 March 1790, he wrote his 'Scots Prologue for Mrs Sutherland' which indicates his own ambition:

> What needs this din about the town o Lon'on,
> How this new play an that new sang is comin?
> Why is outlandish stuff sae meikle courted?
> Does nonsense mend, like brandy – when imported?

Is there nae poet, burning keen for fame,
Will bauldly try to gie us plays at hame?
For Comedy abroad he need na toil:
A knave and fool are plants of every soil.
Nor need he hunt as far as Rome or Greece
To gather matter for a serious piece:
There's themes enow in Caledonian story
Would show the tragic Muse in a' her glory.

Is there no daring Bard will rise and tell
How glorious Wallace stood, how hapless fell?
Where are the Muses fled that could produce
A drama worthy o the name o Bruce?
How here, even here, he first unsheath'd the sword
'Gainst mighty England and her guilty lord
And after monie a bloody, deathless doing,
Wrench'd his dear country from the jaws of Ruin!
O, for a Shakespeare, or an Otway scene
To paint the lovely, hapless Scottish Queen!

(315/CW, 399)

That is magnificently said and suggests how 'burning keen' Burns was to try his hand at tragedy, and a drama on Bruce or Wallace at that. A copy of the Scots Prologue was sent to Mrs Dunlop with an explanation:

> I have made a very considerable acquisition in the acquaintance of a Mr Sutherland, Manager of a company of Comedians at present in Dumfries. – The [enclosed poem] is a Prologue I made for his wife, Mrs Sutherland's benefit-night. – You are to understand that he is getting a new Theatre built here, by subscription; & among his Subcribers are all the first Names in the country. (CL, 185)

Even when he got rid of his 'accursed farm' and settled in Dumfries, on 11 November 1791, Burns was still burdened by his Excise work and involved with songwriting so had little time to spare for sustained work on a Scottish drama. Instead he had to be content with writing fragments for declamation in the theatre which, as planned, became a permanent fixture in Dumfries: on 29 September 1792 the Theatre Royal was opened in the Barnraws, optimistically renamed Shakespeare Street. The actor-manager of the new theatre was James Brown Williamson, Sutherland acting as assistant manager. For the winter seasons of 1792 and 1793 the company was joined by Louisa Fontenelle, a young London actress. For Louisa, nineteen when she arrived in Dumfries, Burns wrote two prologues for performance: 'The Rights of Woman' as an address for her benefit night, 26 November 1792 and an 'Address' for her benefit night, 4 December 1793. 'The Rights of Woman' was sent to Louisa on 22 November 1792 with a fan letter:

> To you, Madam, on our humble Dumfries boards, I have been more indebted for entertainment, than ever I was in prouder Theatres. – Your charms as a woman would insure applause to the most indifferent Actress, & your theatrical talents would secure admiration to the plainest figure. (CL, 682)

Provocatively, 'The Rights of Woman' ended with a reference to 'Ça ira', the French revolutionary song:

> But truce with kings, and truce with Constitutions,
> With bloody armaments, and Revolutions;
> Let Majesty your first attention summon,
> Ah, ça ira! THE MAJESTY OF WOMAN!!!
> (390/CW, 472)

Sending a fair copy of 'The Rights of Woman' to Mrs Dunlop, on 6 December 1792, Burns mentioned the republican unrest in Dumfries: 'we are a good deal in commotion ourselves, & in our Theatre here, "God save the king" has met with some groans & hisses, while Ça ira has been repeatedly called for' (CL, 202). That month Burns the exciseman was accused of revolutionary rabble-rousing in Dumfries and subsequently defended himself in a letter of 5 January 1793 to Graham of Fintry:

> I was in the playhouse one night, when Ça ira was called for. – I was in the middle of the pit, & from the Pit the clamour arose. – One or two individuals with whom I occasionally associate were of the party, but I neither knew of the Plot, nor joined in the Plot; nor ever opened my lips to hiss, or huzza, that, or any other Political tune whatever. – I looked on myself as far too obscure a man to have any weight in quelling a Riot; at the same time, as a character of higher respectability, than to yell in the howlings of a rabble. (CL, 436)

The explanation is not only understandably apologetic, it is disingenuous. Burns not only inserted a reference to Ça ira in 'The Rights of Woman' but ended a letter (of late 1792 to William Creech) with the slogan 'Ça ira!' (CL, 307). However he was now convinced that the playhouse was a dangerous place: Sutherland had thought his Scots Prologue subversive in tone (Kinsley, 1341) and his job had been put in jeopardy as a result of a night at the theatre. In the political climate of the 1790s the stage was obviously an unsafe place for a poet with revolutionary opinions.

At the end of 1794 Williamson, manager of the Theatre Royal (and soon to become the husband of Louisa Fontenelle) applied for leave for the Dumfries players to perform at Whitehaven, Cumberland, but the Earl of Lonsdale had the company charged with vagrancy and imprisoned in the house of correction at Penrith. This incident prompted Burns's epistle 'From Esopus to Maria' – a parody of Pope's 'Eloisa to Abelard' – where Esopus (a tragic actor in Cicero's Rome) is Williamson and Maria is Maria Riddell, at that time the object of Burns's hatred (since she had fallen out with him over the Sabine Rape incident). Before he directs his scorn at Maria, Burns has some fun with the concepts of reality and role-playing:

> 'Alas! I feel I am no actor here!'
> 'Tis real hangmen real scourges bear! . . . .
> The hero of the mimic scene, no more
> I start in Hamlet, in Othello roar;
> Or, haughty Chieftain, 'mid the din of arms,
> In Highland bonnet woo Malvina's charms:
> Whiles sans-culottes stoop up the mountain high,
> And steal me from Maria's prying eye.
>   (486/CL, 539)

Burns, a consummate role-player as the poet of the Kilmarnock Edition, had good reason to avoid offending political opponents with 'real' power to inflict 'real' tragedy on him.

Though he admired actors and took a great interest in the theatre, then, Burns never adequately advanced his dramatic ambitions because of political and artistic obstacles. Politically, he had cause to keep a dramatic silence. Artistically, there was no ready example to inspire him to dramatic heights, no Fergusson of the theatre, only the unlikely precedent of *The Gentle Shepherd*. The one authentic classic of Scottish drama, Sir David Lyndsay's *Ane Pleasant Satyre of the Thrie Estaitis* (1540), was a distant period piece by Burns's time. Home's *Douglas* was a self-consciously sophisticated piece a long way from the ballad of 'Gil Morice' that suggested the plot. A poet of genius but no innovator, Burns produced his best work when prompted by precedent and there was nothing apposite around. What Burns might have done by applying his gifts to dramatic composition is one of the imponderables of Scottish culture. He showed, in 'The Jolly Beggars' and his dramatic monologues, that he could create convincing characters but, alas, he was never able to test this talent in a play. He asked 'Is there no daring Bard will rise and tell/How glorious Wallace stood, how hapless fell?' The role of the dramatically daring bard was one he was prepared to rehearse but not to risk in public.

The Bawdy Burns

A sexual athlete who fathered both legitimate and illegitimate children (see 'A Burns Chronology' for details), Burns was uninhibited on the subject of sex in private, believing it to be a natural blessing, a rare pleasure for the poor. A letter to Alexander Cunningham enthusiastically sums up his general position:

> I myself can affirm, both from bachelor and wedlock experience, that Love is the Alpha and Omega of human enjoyment. – All the pleasures, all the happiness of my humble Compeers, flow immediately and directly from this delicious source. – It is that spark of celestial fire which lights up the wintry hut of Poverty, and makes the chearless mansion, warm, comfortable and gay. – It is the emanation of Divinity that preserves the Sons and Daughters of rustic labour from degenerating into the brutes with which they daily hold converse. – Without it, life to the poor inmates of the Cottage would be a damning gift. (CL, 456)

He doubtless had one poor cotter in mind, namely his father William Burnes whose *Manual of Religious Belief* (see 'Burns and Religion') acknowledged the natural impulse which gives 'animal life pleasure and joy'.

Significantly, Burns's notorious 'horse litter' letter to Bob Ainslie heaps religious references on the penis:

> It is . . . the solemn league and covenant, the plenipotentiary, the Aaron's rod, the Jacob's staff, the prophet Elisha's pot of oil, the Ahasuerus' Sceptre, the sword of mercy, the philsopher's stone, the Horn of Plenty, and Tree of Life between Man and Woman. (CL, 331–2)

In his public role as a poet, however, Burns was comparatively restrained. 'The Holy Fair', with its celebration of the sexual energy of the common people, has frankly amorous passages that diplomatically stop short of being outrageous. 'Epistle to John Rankine' so cleverly presents an erotic adventure in a sexual allegory that Hugh Blair 'took it literally, and the indecency did not strike me' (CH, 81). That Burns wanted the Kilmarnock Edition to be acceptable in society is indicated by a stanza, in 'Address to the Deil', he altered prior to publication in the interests of blunting the point of a joke about an erect penis (see section on 'Address to the Deil'). Elsewhere in the Kilmarnock Edition the poet, speaking personally, locates passion in the heart rather than in the penis:

> But the latest throb that leaves my heart,
> While Death stands victor by,
> That throb, Eliza, is thy part,
> And thine that latest sigh!
>
> (9/CW, 50)

How very different that is from a poem Burns wrote in 1788 – 'its simple energy, as well as the form of a woman's monologue, are characteristic of him' (Kinsley, 1298) – but kept from public view:

> The carlin clew her wanton tail,
>   Her wanton tail sae ready –
> I learn'd a sang in Annandale,
>   Nine inch will please a lady –
>
> But for a koontrie cunt like mine,
>   In sooth, we're nae sae gentle;
> We'll tak tway thumb-bread to the nine,
>   And that's a sonsy pintle.
>
> (252/CW, 348)

Clearly that could never have been openly published as the work of Burns, not when he was alive and able to control the contents of his volumes of verse. Burns thought of including 'The Jolly Beggars' in the First Edinburgh Edition but was easily persuaded to omit the poem when Hugh Blair judged it 'much too licentious' (CH, 82). Away from the likes of Blair, Burns enjoyed verse much more licentious than 'The Jolly Beggars'. He judged, for example, that George Thomson would not be shocked by bawdry. Complaining, in a letter of January 1795 to Thomson, about the predictability of songs about Spring, Burns mentioned that 'Some years ago, when I was young, & by no means the saint I am now' (CL, 669) a friend bet him that it was impossible to write an original song on the subject. Burns accepted the wager:

> I accepted it; & pledged myself to bring in the verdant fields, – the budding flowers, – the chrystal streams, – the melody of the groves – & a love-story into the bargain, & yet be original. (CL, 669)

Burns's 'Ode to Spring' (to the tune 'The tither morn') begins with an image of hares and birds copulating:

> When maukin bucks, at early fucks,
> In dewy glens are seen, Sir,
> And birds, on boughs, take off their mows,
> Amang the leaves sae green, Sir
> > (481/CW, 535)

After some fun with mythological figures, Burns ends with Damon attempting to synchronise his love-making with that of the birds:

> First wi the thrush, his thrust and push
> Had compass large and long, Sir:
> The blackbird next, his tuneful text,
> Was bolder, clear and strong, Sir:
> The linnet's lay came then in play,
> And the lark that soar'd aboon, Sir;
> Till Damon, fierce, mistim'd his arse,
> And fuck'd quite out o tune, Sir.
> > (481/CW, 535)

This is a fairly sophisticated piece of bawdry, deriving its humour from a knowledge of conventional song, pastoral tradition and classical myth. Burns could be much more direct than that.

He was determined, he said in his second Common Place Book, to preserve 'Poems and fragments that must never see the light' (cited by Kinsley, 1224) and, in February 1792, he wrote from Dumfries to John McMurdo about his private anthology of bawdry:

> I think I once mentioned something to you of a Collection of Scots Songs I have for some years been making: I send you a perusal of what I have gathered. – I could not conveniently spare them above five or six days, & five or six glances of them will probably more

than suffice you . . . . There is not another copy of the Collection
in the world, & I should be sorry that any unfortunate negligence
should deprive me of what has cost me a good deal of pains.
(CL, 494)

This letter was altered by Burns's biographer James Currie, who
added the sentence, 'A very few of them are my own'. Actually,
more than a dozen of the bawdy pieces were by Burns but he had no
intention of allowing the collection to be printed as it would damage
his public reputation as a poet. Still, he prized his own bawdy verse
enough to preserve it in a manuscript he was pleased to circulate to
close and like-minded friends, like McMurdo and the members of
the Crochallan Fencibles, the convivial club Burns associated with
in Edinburgh.

Around 1800 (some of the paper is watermarked 1800, some
1799) the first edition of *The Merry Muses of Caledonia* appeared.
The publisher and place of publication were unspecified though
the title-page claimed the contents were 'Selected for use of the
Crochallan Fencibles'. Despite the fact that the book was not credited
to Burns, Burnsians speculated that it was printed in Dumfries and
based on the manuscript sent to McMurdo. J. DeLancey Ferguson,
a respected Burns scholar, pointed out that this manuscript almost
certainly passed to Currie in 1797 and that in 1800 the manuscript
was still in Currie's hands and could not, therefore, be the source
of the 1800 edition since the prudish Currie would not have become
involved with such a publication. Ferguson concluded:

[At Currie's death in 1805] the [Burns] papers were not
returned . . . . Some may have been lost or destroyed . . . Hence,
if *The Merry Muses* was really printed at Dumfries about 1800,
it was printed from some other source than Burns's holograph
collection . . . . If [the first edition of] *The Merry Muses* was
printed in Dumfries or, more likely, Edinburgh in 1800, it
could not have been taken from a holograph in Dr Currie's
home in Liverpool. Even if it was printed else where, at another
date, it still could not have been taken from the holograph, for
the texts are both inaccurate and incomplete. The obvious –
and only – alternative is that the *Muses* was compiled from
versions set down from memory, or from hasty transcriptions
by hands other than the poet's. Plenty of cronies, in Dumfries
and elsewhere, could have brought together the collection on
those terms, but it is easier to say who probably did not do

it than to say who probably did . . . . In sum, then, the '1800' edition ceases to have any unique authority. Whatever the source of its contents, it was [not] printed from Burns's own manuscript collection of bawdy verse. (J. DeLancey Ferguson, 'Sources and Texts of the Suppressed Poems', in *The Merry Muses of Caledonia*, ed. James Barke and Sydney Goodsir Smith, 1965; rept. London 1966, pp. 15–20)

Of such stuff is Burnsian speculation made, for the egregious flaw in Ferguson's argument is that Burns is known to have circulated his manuscript among his friends (such as McMurdo) who could – would – have made copies of such a curiosity. If they did, the 1800 edition would have, albeit indirectly, the authority of Burns's manuscript. At any rate, Kinsley reached the 'tentative conclusion that *The Merry Muses* [of 1800] was printed at least partly from Burns's papers, and probably in Edinburgh' (Kinsley, 993).

Collections printed after the 1800 edition confidently attributed the work to Burns. An anthology, *The Giblet Pie* (1806), claimed to be based on original manuscripts of Burns and an edition of *The Merry Muses* (dated 1827 but actually 1872) claimed (unreliably) to be 'A Choice Collection of favourite Songs gathered from many sources. – By Robert Burns.' In 1911 a limited edition of *The Merry Muses* was published by the Burns Federation. Duncan McNaught, the editor, declared – misleadingly as it transpired – that he had meticulously reproduced his text from Lord Rosebery's copy of the 1800 edition (one of two known, the other belonging to G. Ross Roy). As McNaught's bogus edition was inaccessible to the general public Synder, in 1932, could still mention 'Burns's connection with a collection of more or less unprintable songs known as *The Merry Muses of Caledonia*' (Snyder, 424).

A private edition of *The Merry Muses of Caledonia*, edited by novelist James Barke and poet Sydney Goodsir Smith, was issued in 1959 for the Auk Society. Introducing this, Smith stressed the authority of the 1800 edition:

Professor [J. DeLancey] Ferguson has provided texts from authentic holograph manuscripts of the Bard [but] the bulk of the rest of the book is taken from [Lord Rosebery's copy] of the original [1800] *Muses* . . . This present edition is the first to reproduce the 1800 texts *verbatim et literatim* [so is] an 'ideal' *Merry Muses* – what might or conceivably could be found if Burns's notebook were discovered. To make room for sixteen new items we have jettisoned ten songs from the 1800 edition which are available in the ordinary editions . . . The new songs are taken either from Burns's own MSS or from printed sources such as the 1827 [that is, 1872] edition of the *Muses*, *The Giblet Pye* (*c*.1806) and David Herd's collections [of *The Ancient and Modern Scots Songs*, 1769, 1776, 1791]. They are all connected with Burns; either his own work or ascribed to him or songs from which he rewrote polite versions. ('Merry Muses Introductory', in *The Merry Muses of Caledonia*, ed. Barke and Smith, pp. 35–7)

After the successful publication of D. H. Lawrence's *Lady Chatterley's Lover*, by Penguin Books in 1960, the cultural climate changed and the Barke-Smith edition was openly published in 1965, with a paperback reprint the following year. Burns was at last revealed, to the public at large, as a connoisseur of erotica and as the author of bawdy poems and songs.

Some of the traditional bawdy songs were magnificent, for example 'John Anderson, My Jo', the source for Burns's sentimental song of the same name. Consider two of the six stanzas from the traditional 'John Anderson, My Jo' which had survived in the oral tradition until printed in the 1800 *Merry Muses*:

> John Anderson, my jo, John,
>   When first that ye began,
> Ye had as good a tail-tree,
>   As ony ither man;
> But now it's waxen wan, John,
>   And wrinkles to and fro;
> I've twa gae-ups for ae gae-down,
>   John Anderson, my jo.
>
> I'm backit like a salmon,
>   I'm breastit like a swan;
> My wame it is a down-cod,
>   My middle ye may span:
> Frae my tap-knot to my tae, John,
>   I'm like the new-fa'n snow;
> And it's a' for your convenience,
>   John Anderson, my jo.

Burns turns this gloriously erotic monologue of a sexually active woman into the admittedly poignant song of an old woman uxoriously linked to her ancient and enfeebled companion:

John Anderson, my jo, John,
    We clamb the hill thegither,
And monie a cantie day, John,
    We've had wi ane anither;
Now we maun totter down, John,
    And hand in hand we'll go,
And sleep thegither at the foot,
    John Anderson, my jo!

                        (302/CW, 391)

Kinsley thought Burns's version an improvement, since the poet 'alters the tone from licentious complaint to affection, and over the same air he makes a new song for old age in which passion has turned to gentle companionship' (Kinsley, 1335). However, Evelyn Waugh thought the sentiments of Burns's old and faithful wife amusing enough to cite in *The Loved One* (1948). Located in the Wee Kirk o' Auld Lang Syne (dedicated to Burns and Harry Lauder), Waugh places a double throne of rough-hewn granite, separated by a slab pierced by a heart-shaped aperture. Behind this Lover's Seat is an inscription promising that lovers who plight their troth 'shall have many a canty day with ane anither and maun totter down hand in hand like the immortal Anderson couple'.

Another bawdy song included in the 1800 *Merry Muses* begins:

O gin a body meet a body,
    Comin thro the rye:
Gin a body fuck a body,
    Need a body cry.

Burns, sending a variant to the *Scots Musical Museum*, coyly substituted 'kiss' for 'fuck'. If Burns's versions of extant bawdy songs were cast in a romantic mould, they were so shaped to conform to a polite standard he did not observe in the company of convivial companions. His own bawdy creations were far from subtle, expressing a combative attitude to sex, a fundamentally physical relish of intercourse. 'Gie The Lass Her Fairin' – 'almost certainly his work' (Kinsley, 1526) – has the lusty refrain 'The mair she bangs the less the squeels/An hey for houghmagandie.' 'My Girl She's Airy' (included in the original manuscript of the first Common Place Book) evokes the sexual charms of Elizabeth Paton:

Her slender neck, her handsome waist,

Her hair well buckled, her stays well lac'd,
    Her taper white leg with an et, and a, c,
For her a, b, e, d, and her c, u, n, t,
And oh, for the joys of a long winter night.
                                                (46/CW, 82)

'The Patriarch' (a holograph of which was sold at Sotheby's on 4 December 1873) makes comic play of the complaint of a sexually unsatisfied wife:

'How lang' she says, 'ye fumblin wretch,
    Will ye be fuckin at it?
My eldest wean might die of age,
    Before that ye could get it.

Ye pegh, and grane, and groazle there,
    And mak an unco splutter,
And I maun ly and thole you here,
    And fient a hair the better.'
                                                (609/CW, 603)

The bawdy verse composed by Burns, then, is basic, a matter of resolving tension through the humorous naming of sexual parts. It has none of the seductive eroticism of Donne's 'To His Mistress Going to Bed', none of the provocative delicacy of Marvell's 'To his Coy Mistress', none of anatomical ingenuity of Sheridan's 'The Geranium'. Its linguistic frankness links it to the Earl of Rochester's bawdy verse, but there is an important difference between the English aristocrat and the Scottish farmer. Rochester's 'A Ramble in St James's Park' displays disgust at sexual habits:

Full gorged at another time
With a vast meal of nasty slime
Which your devouring cunt had drawn
From porters' backs and footmen's brawn . . .

Burns, likewise using couplets in 'Libel Summons' (recalling Kirk Session tribunals on fornication), finds only fun in the spectacle of the sexually active woman, ridiculing the reluctant male who cheats her of orgasm:

He who when at a lass's by-job,
Defrauds her wi a frig or dry-bob;

> The coof that stands on clishmaclavers
> When women haflins offer favors . . .
>   (109/CW, 227)

Burns had a healthier animal appetite for sex than most poets with
a penchant for bawdy verse.

By common consent, one of Burns's finest and most characteristic
songs is 'Green Grow the Rashes, O', entered in the first Common
Place Book, August 1784, and built around the following chorus:

> Green grow the rashes, O,
> Green grow the rashes, O,
> The sweetest hours that e'er I spend,
> Are spent amang the lasses, O.
>   (45/CW, 81)

On 3 September 1786, he wrote to tell John Richmond that Jean had
given birth to twins, and quoted a bawdy version of the chorus:

> Green grow the rashes, O,
> Green grow the rashes, O,
> A feather bed is no sae saft,
> As the bosoms o the lasses, O.
>   (CL, 79)

A fuller fragment of the song (also sent to Richmond on 3 September
1786) has a more explicit chorus:

> Green grow the rashes O,
> Green grow the rashes O,
> The lasses they hae wimble bores,
> The widows they hae gashes O.
>   (124)

And this is complemented by an equally explicit resolution of the
poet's encounter with one of 'the lasses':

> I dought na speak – ye was na fley'd –
> My heart play'd duntie, duntie, O
> An ceremony laid aside,
> I fairly fun' her cuntie, O.
>   (124)

That song is 'almost certainly Burns's own work [displaying his]
compactness and energy' (Kinsley, 1210).

The three variants of the chorus show Burns being successively romantic, lecherous and crude – three aspects of his attitude towards women. The bawdy Burns shows but one part of his complex personality, a part he loved to exercise in private but was understandably reluctant to show in public in his role as Scotia's bard.

A Technical Note

The best-known works of Burns – 'To a Mouse', the verse epistles, the songs, 'Tam o Shanter' – give an impression of a poet who, however revolutionary in politics, was conservative in technique. These poems suggest that Burns was content with the Standard Habbie stanza, the quatrain and the octosyllabic couplet. The impression of metrical caution is misleading, based on an inadequate knowledge the poetry. Ridiculing Bardolators in *A Drunk Man Looks at the Thistle* (1926) Hugh MacDiarmid scoffed 'No' wan in fifty kens a wurd Burns wrote' and he was partially right. In a later poem, *To Circumjack Cencrastus* (1930), MacDiarmid described Burns as 'That Langfellow in a' but leid' (that Longfellow in all but song) and he was completely wrong.

Certainly there are ploddingly pedestrian passages in the English poems but Burns, at his best, was a technically accomplished and adventurous poet. For example, while many of his couplets are self-contained (like those of Pope, one of his favourite poets) and many of his rhymes end a line with the finality of a full-stop, he could use enjambement imaginatively, as in 'The Twa Dogs':

> Hech man! dear sirs! is that the gate
> They waste sae monie a braw estate!
> Are we sae foughten an' harass'd
> For gear ta gang that gate at last?
> (71/CW, 145)

In the same poem there is a pararhyme as effective as anything in Wilfred Owen:

> I see how folk live that hae riches;
> But surely poor-folk maun be wretches!
> (71/CW, 142)

143

Burns was also energetically adept at using internal rhymes to pace his satirical poems:

> Poet Burns! Poet Burns, wi your priest-skelpin turns,
>   Why desert ye your auld native shire?
> Your Muse is a gipsy, yet were she e'en tipsy,
>   She could ca' us nae waur than we are –
>   (264/CW, 361)

That Poet Burns thought carefully about technique is evident in his comments, in the first Common Place Book, on the metrical irregularity of Scottish songs (see 'The Songs'). He grew up listening to his mother, and his mother's friend Betty Davidson, sing songs – and ballads. One of the hallmarks of his genius is his ability to use metrical forms with a conversational tone and a musical fluency, just as the great ballad-singers of the oral tradition did. Burns combined a literary tradition (or traditions, since he enjoyed Augustan English verse as well as Scots revivalist poetry) with the oral tradition. He grew up on the popular ballads that scholars like Child later collected. Dugald Stewart, the philosopher, wrote of Burns:

> His memory was uncommonly retentive, at least for poetry, of which he recited to me frequently long compositions with the most minute accuracy. They were chiefly ballads, and other pieces in our Scottish dialect; great part of them (he told me) he had learned in his childhood, from his mother, who delighted in such recitations, and whose poetical taste, rude as it probably was, gave, it is presumable, the first direction to her son's genius. (cited by Kinsley, 1535)

Before he could read, then, Burns was aware of Scottish ballads. These narrative songs were crucial to his poetic development.

Burns collected ballads and (like Sir Walter Scott after him) tinkered with the texts he had transcribed. 'John Barleycorn', included in the First Edinburgh Edition, appeared with a note acknowledging 'This is partly composed on the plan of an old song known by the same name.' Burns's theme – 'the wide-spread myth of the corn spirit' (Kinsley, 1016) – is solemnly announced, in the ballad manner and measure, in the splendid opening quatrains:

There was three kings into the east,
Three kings both great and high,
And they hae sworn a solemn oath
John Barleycorn should die.

They took a plough and plough'd him down,
Put clods upon his head,
And they hae sworn a solemn oath
John Barleycorn was dead.

(23/CW, 60)

'Tam Lin' (Child's text 39A), a ballad communicated by Burns to the *Scottish Musical Museum*, was 'improved' by Burns who (according to Kinsley, 1500) recast the following quatrain from Tam's transformation sequence:

And last they'll turn me, in your arms,
Into the burning lead;
Then throw me into well-water,
O throw me in wi' speed.

(558/CW, 575)

If retouched by Burns then it shows the touch of a man intimately aware of ballad techniques and those techniques inform even the most subjective of his songs.

For his Scots poems, Burns experimented with various options available to him. His use of the Christis Kirk stanza (in, for example, 'The Holy Fair', 'The Ordination', the seventh recitativo of 'The Jolly Beggars') was influenced by Allan Ramsay who, in his *Poems* (1721) added two cantos to the poem 'Christis Kirk on the Green' (then attributed to James I) and used the stanzaic pattern *ababababc*, that is two quatrains with an abbreviated last line. Like Fergusson, Burns took poetic liberties with the stanzaic pattern. Again through Ramsay, Burns learned the tricks of the Cherrie and the Slae stanza. Alexander Montgomerie's poem 'The Cherrie and the Slae' (1597) was included in James Watson's *Choice Collection of Comic and Serious Scots Poems* (1706–11) and in Ramsay's *Ever Green* (1724). Burns used the fourteen-line stanza imaginatively in the first recitativo of 'The Jolly Beggars', in 'Epistle to Davie, a Brother Poet', in 'To the Guidewife of Wauchope House'. The Gilliecrankie stanza (used in 'When Guildford good' and 'The Tree of Liberty', assuming the latter to be by Burns) was a popular measure in Jacobite songs.

As for the six-line Standard Habbie stanza, which deserves to be renamed the Standard Rabbie stanza since Burns used it so brilliantly and so frequently, Burns got the measure of this from several items in Watson's *Choice Collection*, including the eponymous 'The Life and Death of Habbie Simpson' by Robert Sempill of Beltrees (*c.*1595–*c.*1668). Burns seems to have first used it in 'Poor Mailie's Elegy' (1785) and done so to fine comic effect:

> Lament in rhyme, lament in prose,
> Wi' saut tears trickling down your nose;
> Our Bardie's fate is at a close,
>   Past a' remead!
> The last, sad cape-stane of his woes;
>   Poor Mailie's dead.
>
> (25/CW, 64)

In 'To a Mouse' Burns used the stanza philosophically, in 'Holy Willie's Prayer' satirically, in 'Elegy on Captain Matthew Henderson' poignantly. As Burns used it the stanza could be sublime or ridiculous or both, so great was his skill with the form.

In English poems Burns used the heroic couplet (for example, 'From Esopus to Maria', a parody of Pope's 'Eloisa to Abelard'), the Pindaric Ode ('A Winter Night'), the sonnet ('Sonnet on the Death of Robert Riddell'); in 'The Cotter's Saturday Night', a mixture of Scots and English, he used the Spenserian stanza (as did Fergusson in 'The Farmer's Ingle', the model for Burns's poem). None of the English poems, however, is much more than a literary pastiche, a period piece.

As a product of a literary period, Burns was inordinately fond of personification, a device he uses in both Scots and English. At the beginning of 'The Holy Fair', Burns meets Fun, Supersitition and Hypocrsity. In 'The Ordination' there are appearances by Patronage, Orthodoxy, Learning and Morality. In 'A Winter Tale' he sees Oppression, Ambition, 'Woe, Want, and Murder', Luxury, Flattery, Property, Love, Honour, Pity, Misery, Guilt, Misfortune, Fortune and Afflication. In 'The Brigs of Ayr' he ends with a parade of personifications, the allegorical figures of Beauty, Spring, Rural Joy, Summer, Plenty, Autumn, Winter, Hospitality, Courage, Benevolence, Learning, Worth, Peace, Agriculture.

A more telling technique is the use of the cumulative catalogue to overwhelm the reader with evidence – think of the catalogue of Scots worthies in 'The Vision', the catalogue of ministers in 'The Holy

Fair', the catalogue of diabolic relics in 'Tam o Shanter' ('Five toma-hawks, wi bluid red-rusted,/Five scymitars, wi murder crusted' and so on). This goes back to the medieval catalogue poem, a tradition that was poignantly renewed in Dunbar's 'Lament for the Makars', a poem Burns knew from Ramsay's *Ever Green* (where it has the title 'On the Uncertainty of Life and Fear of Death, or a Lament for the Loss of the Poets'). Dunbar, ballads from the oral tradition, the Scots revivalist poems of Ramsay and Fergusson: from such sources Burns evolved his own distinctively conversational-cum-confidential tone, simulating the sound of a man talking – singing – to those in tune with that tradition.

Part III:
An Approach to Burns

An Approach to Burns

Robert Burns was born a farmer's son in 1759, the year before George III was crowned king of Great Britain. He was fifteen when he wrote his first poem (typically, a love lyric), seventeen when the Continental Congress carried the American Declaration of Independence, twenty-seven when he published his first volume of verse, thirty when Parisians sacked the Bastille and set the French Revolution in motion. His poetry and personality are intimately connected with the politics of his period; though controversial and complex as a poet and person he has come close to deification. Thirty-seven when he died as exciseman in Dumfries, Burns has become probably the best-known poet in the world: statues have been raised to Burns not only in Scotland but in London, Albany, Barre, Chicago, Denver, Milwaukee, San Francisco, Fredericton, Toronto, Adelaide, Ballarat, Melbourne, Sydney and Dunedin. American Presidents sing 'Auld Lang Syne', Soviet schoolchildren chant 'A Man's a Man for a' That'. His verse has been translated into all the major languages of the world; a recent paperback of Chinese translations of his poems went into a first edition of 100,000.

Burns's birthday is celebrated internationally and in his native land the celebrations can rival those of New Year in terms of an intoxicating evening. Indeed, in Scotland Burns is revered as an institution rather than an individual, his face used as a marketable icon on all sorts of goods from whisky to shortbread. Despite the bitter lines the poet wrote on a Bank of Scotland one-guinea note in 1786 ('Wae worth thy power, thy cursed leaf!') Burns's face is still featured on a banknote, the Clydesdale Bank fiver. Amidst all this adulation, the creative work of Burns is neglected. 'No' wan in fifty kens a wurd Burns wrote', said Hugh MacDiarmid, of the Burns Suppers, in 1926. And those who claim to know Burns best cannot agree about his art and his personality. He remains an issue.

For sentimentalists, Burns is a soft-hearted lady's man; for chauvinists he is a hard-drinking man's man. For socialists, he is the revolutionary poet of the people; for nationalists he is the patriotic poet of the Scottish people. Almost every statement made about Burns has been questioned so scholars squabble over his alleged alcoholism, his apparently ambivalent attitude to democracy, his views on sexual and romantic love. So open to interpretation is Burns that writers can easily use his name as a peg on which to hang personal opinions. Introducing his *Burns Encyclopedia*, Maurice Lindsay acclaimed Burns as 'Scotland's greatest poet' (BE, viii) though Dunbar and MacDiarmid are equally worthy candidates for that honour. A compilation book revealingly entitled *The Intimate Sex Lives of Famous People* (London, 1981, p. 59) saw Burns as 'Scotland's national poet' – and foremost fornicator.

Burns was, if not all things to all men, at least many things to his admirers. Those disturbed by the womanising Burns could always recall that the poet was a freemason, a member of masonic lodges from 1781 until his death (he was admitted to St David's Lodge, Tarbolton, on 4 July 1781; in Edinburgh, on 1 February 1787, he was made a member of the Canongate Kilwinning Lodge; in Dumfries, he was a member of St Andrews Lodge, becoming Senior Warden in 1792). Those hostile to the Jacobin Burns could take comfort in the fact that Burns was a Jacobite long after that cause was lost, producing songs and poems inspired by unfortunate Stuarts like Mary Queen of Scots ('Lament of Mary Queen of Scots', 'Address to William Tytler') and Bonnie Prince Charlie ('The Chevalier's Lament', 'Charlie, he's my darling', 'The Bonnie Lass of Albanie').

In his poetic address to William Tytler, author of a *An Historical and Critical Enquiry into the Evidence against Mary Queen of Scots* (1760), Burns laments that 'something like moisture conglobes in my eye' which is not simply a heartfelt sentiment but the pose of someone accustomed to acting the part of Harley, the moist-eyed hero of Henry Mackenzie's sentimental novel *The Man of Feeling* (1771) which Burns described (in 1783) as 'a book I prize next to the Bible' (CL, 55). The plural personality, the role-playing, the appeal to sacred texts; all are significant to a study of Burns.

Since it first materialized in print, before the public, on 31 July 1786 the Kilmarnock Edition of Burns's *Poems, Chiefly in the Scottish Dialect* has remained to haunt Scotland like a ghost that brings out the reassuring best and frightening worst in generations of Scotsmen (though not Scotswomen as Burns, to his admirers, is the apotheosis of the man's man). It is a sheer coincidence that Burns's name alliterates with the Bible but the connection between the great bard and the good book is more than accidental. Scotsmen – and David Hume's essays in empiricism made a philosophy out of this national characteristic – are habitually cautious, immune to the charms of novelty, stolidly prone to shut the mind on a subject once it has been tested then sealed up in a closed book. To Scotsmen the Bible (not the practice of Christ) is religion pure and simple; it is a convenient package that can be kept on the shelves and delved into as the need arises with births, marriages and deaths. In much the same way Burns is poetry pure and simple. He is a revered figure who remains above criticism, God-like in his acts of creation, Christ-like in appearance (by courtesy of Nasmyth, Buego, Skirving and Reid).

Burns and the Bible not only coexist in the Scottish consciousness as the twin pillars supporting a decent life; the twain frequently meet in a memorable way that is admired, if not imitated, in the ideal Scottish household:

> The chearfu supper done, wi serious face,
> They, round the ingle, form a circle wide;
> The sire turns o'er, wi patriarchal grace,
> The big ha'-Bible, ance his father's pride.
> His bonnet rev'rently is laid aside,
> His lyart haffets wearing thin and bare;
> Those strains that once did sweet in Zion glide,
> He wales a portion with judicious care;
> 'And let us worship God!' he says with solemn air.
> (72/CW, 149)

The fact that we could substitute the name of Burns for that of God in the last line of that stanza says much about Scotland's attitude to the national bard. Burns depicts the Scot as a rough diamond whose cutting edge may be conversationally blunt but who ultimately treasures domestic life. The supreme quality isolated is honesty – which can cover a multitude of sins. In a letter of early 1794 to Samuel Clark, Burns articulates the matter:

> Some of our folks . . . have conceived a prejudice against me as being a drunken dissipated character. – I might be all this, you know, & yet be an honest fellow; but you know that I am an honest fellow and am nothing of this. (CL, 702)

His poetry is full of eulogies to honesty. It is, to Burns, the virtue of virtues. So the Scot can be objectionable, boorish, irascible, cruel so long as he brings honesty to bear on his delivery. It is a credo that has the same visceral appeal as Burns's poetry. Burns, as the vernacular prophet of honesty, is transformed into Burns the patron-saint of honesty. In fact he was martyred by his inability to live with this impossible, almost solipsistic, notion, for he was also obliged to live with other people and to be acceptable to them.

Burns certainly suffered for his sanctity. His whole life was an astonishing exercise in role-playing, and he was so good at adopting attitudes that he became all things to all men. When the company demanded it he could turn on whatever charm would most enchant. He was, by turns, agnostic, religious; royalist, republican; Jacobite, Jacobin; narrow nationalist, citizen of the world; 'sexploiter', chaste lover; humble, arrogant; tender, cynical. His perennial capacity to elicit fanatical support all over the world is startling proof of his expertise at mass communication. Burns first advertised himself as a rustic bard because he knew this was the image the back-to-nature eighteenth-century public wanted. Although he had a great – and justified – opinion of his own abilities, he managed, by a posture of modesty, to make all his claims seem inconsequential. When we examine the product he was selling – for the sake of fame, not monetary reward – there is more cunning than cringing. A letter sent from Edinburgh in January 1787 to the Earl of Eglinton testifies to his skills as a salesman:

> There is scarcely anything to which I am so feelingly alive as the honor and welfare of old Scotia; and as a Poet, I have no higher enjoyment than singing her Sons and Daughters. – Fate had cast my station in the veriest shades of Life, but never did a heart pant more ardently than mine to be distinguished; tho' till very lately I looked on every side for a ray of light in vain. (CL, 271)

Burns *used* his humble birth to implant a sense of guilt in others who could expiate their sins by bestowing patronage on the unfortunate poet. In this letter there is, superficially, the sound of submission; on a deeper level, though, the authentic voice is authoritative. This is not so much a missive as a piece of advertising copy sent to a brother-mason who could help the poet. The epistolary mastery disguises the appeal in an attractively servile cosmetic wrapping. Burns is ostensibly addressing the aristocrat as his social superior,

but in saying that he has 'no higher enjoyment' than to be Scotland's
national poet (for that is what the ambition amounts to), he is playing
on the credulity of an earl – and we know what he really thought of
titled gentlemen:

> A prince can mak a belted knight,
> A marquis, duke, and a' that;
> But an honest man's aboon his might,
> Gude faith he mauna fa' that!
>
> (482/CW, 536)

Burns had to resort to role-playing to escape from the provincial
pressure of Ayrshire. Although his pose as the poetic primitive was
often irksome it suited his purpose and, by his own admission,
explained the phenomenal interest in his personality: 'I know very
well,' he wrote Dr John Moore in January 1787, 'the novelty of my
character has by far the greatest share in the learned and polite
notice I have lately got' (CL, 246). Robert Anderson, a doctor and
minor man of letters who edited *The Works of John Moore*, met Burns
when he was the literary lion of Edinburgh and (in a letter to
Currie, published in the *Burns Chronicle* of 1925) commented on
the self-conscious role-playing of the poet:

> It was, I know, part of the machinery, as he called it, of his poetical
> character to pass for an illiterate ploughman who wrote from pure
> inspiration. When I pointed out some evident traces of poetical
> imitation in his verses, privately, he readily acknowledged his
> obligations and even admitted the advantages he enjoyed in
> poetical composition from the *copia verborum*, the command of
> phraseology, which the knowledge and use of the English and
> Scottish dialects afforded him; but in company he did not suffer
> his pretensions to pure inspiration to be challenged, and it was
> seldom done where it might be supposed to affect the success of
> the subscription for his *Poems*. (cited by Kinsley, 1537–8)

Had he not chosen the page for his profession, he might well
have chosen the stage (see 'Burns and the Theatre') for he was,
as Anderson realised, a consummate actor.

In 'The Vision' Burns is content to be a 'rustic bard' blessed by
a local muse; in 'The Author's Earnest Cry and Prayer' he is the
'humble Bardie'. These are poetic poses, affectations of inadequacy
from a man who was not always honest in his self-assessments for he
pitched his performance to the expectations of his audience. When he

was not 'kissing the arse of a peer' (Second Heron Election Ballad) –
putting on airs but putting off graces for the Earl of Glencairn and
Lord Buchan and the Duke of Queensberry – he was assertive,
assuring John McMurdo (the Duke of Queensberry's chamberlain)
that his poetic gifts were 'the presents of Genius' (CL, 495). Still, his
diffident strategy was ostensibly successful; through his supposedly
humble bardship he escaped from Ayrshire and thanks to his
influential admirers he surmounted the political obstacles put in
his way by those who suspected he was a political threat.

It is as a poet that he commands international attention but, to the
Scottish people, Burns is, and always has been, more than a poet. He
is regarded as the rhythmic heart of the nation forever supplying
warm sustaining blood to the otherwise cold body of Scotland. He
keeps the country alive and the citizens gratefully respond every
year by paying tribute to this restorative power among them.
Without Burns, Scotland would be a poorer place, a country devoid
of a nationally symbolic lifeforce; without the uncritical adulation
of Burns, Scotland would be a richer place. Every attack on Burns
shakes Scotland like a heart-attack; he is loved, protected, cherished,
nursed, jealously guarded. Hugh MacDiarmid, in his magnificent *A
Drunk Man Looks at the Thistle* (1926), could say:

> No' wan in fifty kens a wurd Burns wrote
> But misapplied is a'body's property,
> And gin there was his like alive the day
> They'd be the last a kennin' haund to gi'e . . .

Yet enough of Burns has been orally absorbed by the Scottish people
for them to draw out of the memory-bank an apt phrase or two to
give a warm internal glow and a simulation of received wisdom.
From 'To a Mouse':

> The best-laid schemes o mice an men
> Gang aft agley
>   (69/CW, 133)

And from 'Epistle to Dr Blacklock':

> To make a happy fireside clime
> To weans and wife,
> That's the true pathos and sublime
> Of human life.
>   (273/CW, 372)

Burns, with the knack of turning platitudes into poetry, is seen as the Scottish Everyman. This extraordinary status accorded to a poet in a country not especially known for its love of poetry is as much due to perfect timing as to undeniable poetic genius. Dunbar, after all, wrote many quotable lines without making a lasting impression on the Scottish public; so did John Barbour before him and Robert Fergusson after him. Fergusson, indeed, might have filled the role taken up so successfully by Burns, but his death in an Edinburgh madhouse at the age of twenty-four made him, unfairly, an ignominious figure of failure. What Scotland wanted was a man the public could identify with, a man common enough to be an ideal friend, but uncommon enough to command respect outside Scotland. A *Superscot*. If he had the usual human faults, then these could be excused on the grounds of Scottishness, take it or leave it. If his behaviour offended public morality, then his image could be retouched, his icon restored, by a communal exercise in wishful thinking. Scotland was waiting and Burns turned up. So he became the Honest Man, the Superscot. An archetype for every other Scot to aspire to.

Yes, Burns – coming only a few years after the fall of Bonnie Prince Charlie – appeared at just the right historical moment to be treated as the saviour of his country. Scotland had a massive spiritual hangover prompted by the toxic taste of successive defeats and retained by a long folk memory of loss. In 1513 the flowers of the forest had fallen at Flodden; in 1603 the crown had gone, with James VI and I, to London; in 1707 the Scottish parliament had been destroyed in the process of English empire-building; in 1715 the Old Pretender staged an unseemly farce in Scotland; in 1746 the clans had their catastrophe at Culloden, and the clan system was subsequently obliterated by genocidal legislation. Scotland was at a loss as to its own identity in the contemporary world: it existed in a limbo as North Britain, a mere appendage to the Auld Enemy. All this was hard to swallow and the bitterness shaped the Scottish character into a creature of violent moods whose flag-waving arrogance alternated with a melancholy submission. A modern American scholar formulated this quintessential Scottishness:

There operates . . . in Scotland (as elsewhere), a most important sociological law . . . And that is *the petrifying but protective influence of great military defeats on those nations which have nevertheless managed to survive these defeats*. As the Scots themselves are

the first to recognize, the whole cultural and political life of
Scotland is still attuned, basically, to no later historical period
than the mid- or late eighteenth century . . . Cultured Scotsmen
today still brood over their defeat by England – under the
flattering pretence of 'Union' of the two kingdoms – in the early
and mid-eighteenth century . . . (G. Legman, *The Horn Book*, New
York, 1964, p. 365)

Into the defeatist cultural atmosphere of eighteenth-century
Scotland came a fully fledged national poet, a man who could
hold his own in any company – rooted in the Scottish soil but still
cerebral enough to sustain impressive flights of fancy. A credit to
Scotland. A success to compensate for the failure of Bonnie Prince
Charlie. John Wilson of Kilmarnock published only 612 copies of
Poems, Chiefly in the Scottish Dialect but the book was greeted by
a storm of applause. Not only was the author obviously talented,
he was determined to draw attention to his nationality at every
opportunity, as witness these lines from 'The Cotter's Saturday
Night':

> From scenes like these, old Scotia's grandeur springs,
>   That makes her lov'd at home, rever'd abroad . . .
>
>   O Scotia! my dear, my native soil!
>   For whom my warmest wish to Heaven is sent!
>
>   O Thou! who pour'd the patriotic tide,
>   That stream'd thro Wallace's undaunted heart . . .
>   O never, never Scotia's realm desert
>   (71/CW, 150–1)

Never mind the rumours that this particular patriot-bard was seriously considering deserting Scotia's realm by emigrating to Jamaica.
Here was a poet to be proud of, an independent voice for Scotland.
There were folk all over Scotland who had waited for years to hear
the sort of thing Burns encapsulated into ringing phrases.

The early critics who responded to the Kilmarnock Edition have
been vilified for turning the well-educated son of a tenant-farmer
into an ignorant ploughman. Yet they were not so much patronizing
the poet as gladly celebrating a phenomenon that so decisively
demonstrated Scottish greatness. Furthermore, this bard was not
contaminated by a foreign education in England. He was the genuine article, a native genius, and – like the earth he ploughed –

Scottish through and through. Burns himself cultivated the ignorant-ploughman syndrome and the critics simply acquiesced. His Preface to the Kilmarnock Edition refers to 'the toils and fatigues of a laborious life' and asks readers to make 'every allowance for education and circumstances of life'. If that did not hammer the message home, then the 'Epistle to J. Lapraik' put the matter in a metrical nutshell:

> I am nae poet, in a sense;
> But just a rhymer, like by chance,
> An hae to learning nae pretence;
> Yet, what the matter?
> Whene'er my Muse does on me glance,
> I jingle at her.
>
> (57/CW, 102)

Given such autobiographical crumbs of discomfort the critics swallowed the myth whole, then regurgitated it so frequently that it reached legendary proportions.

Far from reducing Burns to the level of poetic amateur, the first critics praised Burns as the embodiment on earth of the spirit of Scotland. In 1786 the *Edinburgh Magazine* commented:

> The author is indeed a striking example of native genius bursting through the obscurity of poverty and the obstructions of a laborious life. (CH, 64)

Henry Mackenzie, The Man of Feeling, felt even more strongly on the subject. In the *Lounger* (9 December 1786), as well as pinning the label of 'Heaven-taught ploughman' to Burns, he made the point that the poet

> has been obliged to form the resolution of leaving his native land, to seek under a West Indian clime that shelter and support which Scotland has denied him. But I trust means may be found to prevent this resolution from taking place; and that I do my country no more than justice, when I suppose her ready to stretch out her hand to cherish and retain this native poet. (CH, 70/1)

In other words, Burns was too precious a Scottish commodity to export to the West Indies. He had to be kept in Scotland, and so the reception of the Kilmarnock Edition continued. The early critics may have raised objections to Burns's use of the vernacular – and throughout his life he was urged to write in English by colleagues as cute as Mackenzie and creatures as crass as the Clarinda on whom Burns so magnanimously bestowed 'Ae Fond Kiss' – but their motive was not unpatriotic. If Burns wrote in English, they reasoned, then his superiority to the indigenous English poets would cut the Auld Enemy down to size.

The Kilmarnock Edition remodelled the face of Scotland in the features so cleverly presented to his readers by Burns. Burns became a Scottish hero whose heroics – like drinking and wenching – were within the imaginative reach of every Scot who thought he had a touch of the poet in him. Burns became, too, a convenient justification for every Scottish foible. Almost every Scotsman thinks of himself as a reincarnation of Rabbie, so if he is condemned for being typically Scottish – with all that implies – then he can retort that he is simply being like Burns. And Burns was a genius, *ergo* there is a bit of the genius in every Scot. To cite MacDiarmid's garrulous drunk man again:

> As Kirks wi' Christianity ha'e dune,
> Burns' Clubs wi' Burns – wi' a'thing it's the same,
> The core o' ocht is only for the few,
> Scorned by the mony, thrang wi'ts empty name.

The seeds of the Burns cult were carefully planted by his contemporaries. To them Burns was a great Scotsman for whom poetry was a peripheral activity. Mrs Maria Riddell's *Memoir Concerning Burns* (published in the *Dumfries Journal*, August 1796, and Currie's first edition of 1800) was explicit:

> for the fact is, even allowing his great and original genius its due tribute of admiration, that poetry (I appeal to all who have had the advantage of being personally acquainted with him) was actually not his *forte*. Many others perhaps may have ascended to prouder heights in the region of Parnassus, but none certainly ever outshone Burns in the charms – the sorcery I would almost call it, of fascinating conversation, the spontaneous eloquence of social argument, or the unstudied poignancy of brilliant repartee. (CH, 102)

Dr Robert Anderson, in his letter to Dr Currie, endorsed this opinion:

> No words can do justice to the captivating charms of his conversation. It was even more fascinating than his poetry. He was truly a great orator. (cited by Kinsley, 1536)

James Currie himself, whose moralistic approach to the poet did so much mischief, wrote in a preface to his 1800 edition of Burns:

> in the summer of 1792, I had [in Dumfries] an opportunity of seeing and of conversing with Burns . . . who in the course of a single interview, communicated to me so strong an impression of the force and versatility of his talents. After this I read the poems then published with greater interest and attention, and with a full conviction that, extraordinary as they are, they afford but an inadequate proof of the powers of their unfortunate author. (Currie, I, xix)

Dugald Stewart, too, was in agreement:

> The idea which [Burns's] conversation conveyed of the powers of his mind, exceeded, if possible, that which is suggested by his writings . . . his predilection for poetry, was [not that] of a genius exclusively adapted to that species of composition. (cited by Kinsley, 1534)

All four writers reveal as much about themselves as they do about Burns. First, they attempt to show that Scotland did not produce only a great poet in Burns but a man (English take note) who could have conquered the world with his eloquence; second, they display a low opinion of poetry as a pursuit for a man of genius. After all, the saviour of Scotland was expected to do more than write verses for the entertainment of others. Burns's contemporaries regretted that he had (unlike Wilde) put his genius into his art and only his talent into his life. Burns, through his relish for role-playing and in response to the social pressures of the period, went along with this perception of himself when he succumbed to superficiality. He could not admit, to those who undervalued poetry, that being a poet was his ultimate ambition, his sole (and soul) purpose in life. Instead – when introducing his volumes of verse, when keeping the company of his supposed social superiors, when projecting himself as 'nae poet . . . But just a rhymer like by chance' – he affected an indifference to his destiny. Being a poet, he implied, was not an end in itself but a marvellous escape from obscurity. It was the calling card of an impoverished Honest Man seeking social security.

In his first Common Place Book, written in the period 1783–5, Burns described his debut as a poet:

For my own part I never had the least thought or inclination of turning Poet till I got once heartily in Love, and then Rhyme and Song were, in a manner, the spontaneous language of my heart. (CB, 3)

The role became a reality. Burns never attempted a major philosophical poem, totally eschewed the epic, displayed only a limited interest in metrical innovations. Though he used the Spenserian, Christis Kirk, Cherrie and the Slae, and Gilliecrankie stanzas he preferred the couplet, the quatrain and, of course, the Standard Habbie measure which he handled with superlative conversational ease. His thematic and stylistic repertoire was largely restricted: to impressions of love, for his fellow man as well as for women; and expressions of hate, partly political, partly a result of what his brother called 'a particular jealousy of people who were richer than himself' (GN). His poetry was like a small rich vein he worked with such vigour that he invariably (in Scots anyway) struck gold. Astonishingly, too, the poems of the Kilmarnock Edition were conceived and executed before he had set a foot outside his native Ayrshire and related to particular localities. That in itself is enough to give the usually pejorative epithet 'parochial' a more positive connotation.

Once the Kilmarnock Edition had established Burns as the darling bard of the Scottish nation (the man whose work reasserted the nationhood that was obscured by the notion of North Britain) Burns was not encouraged to add to his Scots stature: unfortunately he wasted precious creative time composing derivative English verse; fortunately he reasserted himself by devoting artistic energy to revealing to the world Scotland's rich heritage of folksong. Thus Burns's poetic works, with the glorious exception of 'Tam o Shanter', were fairly complete in 1786 when the poet was twenty-seven. The First Edinburgh Edition of 17 April 1787 expanded the canon with the atrocious 'Address to Edinburgh' and the amusing 'Address to a Haggis' (the first of his poems to be published in periodicals, and written after his arrival in Edinburgh) but the hitherto-unpublished 'Death and Doctor Hornbook' and 'The Ordination' were completed before he left Ayrshire. Other important Ayrshire poems, such as 'Holy Willie's Prayer' and 'The Jolly Beggars', were too provocative too print openly (the anonymous chapbook printing of 'Holy Willie's Prayer' in 1789 was not authorised by Burns). The bulk of Burns's best-known poems 'belong to the period from January 1785 till June 1786' (Hecht, 74).

After that, if we distinguish between his verse and his work on folksong, Burns added little to that great burst of poetic composition in Ayrshire. His contributions to *The Merry Muses of Caledonia* increased his rakish reputation but not his poetic stature and few of the Dumfriesshire poems have the interest of his earlier work, the exceptions being 'The Kirk's Alarm', 'Elegy on Captain Matthew Henderson' and 'Tam o Shanter' – which was specifically written for Francis Grose's *Antiquities of Scotland* (1791). So, Burns opened his poetic account with 'Handsome Nell', written in 1774 when he was fifteen, virtually closed it after coming to Edinburgh then drew on it triumphantly with 'Tam o Shanter', written in 1790 when he was thirty-one. During the last decade of his life his imaginative powers were almost exclusively concerned with the restoration of Scottish folksong, and he contributed some 200 songs to Johnson's *Scots Musical Museum* and more than seventy songs to Thomson's *Select Scottish Airs*.

Although Burns's output is impressive it is insignificant in terms of sustained poetic effort when compared to that of a national poet like Pushkin (who died at thirty-eight, only one year older than Burns was when he died). Burns had played the part of the ploughman-poet and found it difficult to take pleasure in it when the role became the reality for those he respected. After the daft days of celebrity in Edinburgh, no one wished him to keep in touch with his visionary vernacular muse. He needed an audience so contemplated writing plays and concentrated on songs that tapped his authentic source of inspiration. When he wrote his 'Scots Prologue for Mrs Sutherland' (1790) he appealed to Scottish poets to be true to their talents, to be heroic in theme and audacious in approach:

> Is there nae poet, burning keen for fame,
> Will bauldly try to gie us plays at hame? . . .
> There's themes enow in Caledonian story
> Would show the tragic Muse in a' her glory.
>
> Is there no daring Bard will rise and tell
> How glorious Wallace stood, how hapless fell?
> Where are the Muses fled that could produce
> A drama worthy o the name o Bruce?
>   (315/CW, 399)

Where are the Muses fled? In Burns's case they had taken flight in Scottish song.

There is no poet with a reputation comparable to that of Burns who has achieved so much with the one book (plus 'Tam o Shanter') – the songs, as Burns himself knew, are a separate issue. The Kilmarnock Edition was Burns's passport to territory normally forbidden to an inquisitive farmer's boy. More than most poets he used verse to bring attention to himself, and he has become firmly established as an ordinary bloke who possessed extraordinary gifts. The two most popular portrayals of Burns produced this century treat him as a Scottish Messiah (and if he had blemishes, well then so had Christ). James Barke's five-part novel sequence *Immortal Memory* (1946–54) gives a full-scale portrait of the artist as a splendid young man in pursuit of willing young women, a devil-may-care Superscot. Barke himself acknowledged in his prefatory note to the final part of the cycle the extent of his idolatry:

> Above all, in Dumfries he came to final terms with man in relation to human society: his philosophy ripened to full maturity. He knew all there was to know: saw everything there was to see . . . My portrait of Robert Burns is unashamedly romantic and idealistic . . . (James Barke *The Well of the Silent Harp*, Glasgow, 1954, pp. i–ii)

In claiming that Burns 'knew all there was to know' (which is a claim far in excess of Keats's 'all ye need to know'), Barke is telling the public, particularly the Scottish public, a lie to bolster up the myth of Burns's infallibility. It is to make a paragon out of a person.

The second significant popular portrayal of Burns was the actor John Cairney's finely realised, witty and elegant reconstruction of the poet's life. Cairney wore the britches of the bard on stage and television and also put his version of the poet on record. His theatrically cultured voice evoked the icon of Burns the sentimental Superscot. Like Barke before him, Cairney was in the business of hero worship as witness his words about 'the immortal part of Robert Burns – The flame still burning from a brief bright spark which lit up a grey Scotland so long ago' (sleevenote to *John Cairney Tells the Robert Burns Story*, 2 records, Edinburgh, 1976). Thus Burns is an auld licht (though not an Auld Licht) illuminating Scotland, a voice from the past miraculously whispering to the present, an immortal memory of auld lang syne.

What convinced Bardolaters tend to gloss over is the evidence of the poet's hypersensitivity. Every role played resulted in an agony of remorse, every false step was retraced in his Calvinistic conscience.

The continuous effort of playing out the roles he had created for himself enervated him and this, as much as his legendary rheumatic heart, darkened his final days. It has long been recognized that Scotland is a country that has built a national culture on contradiction. Burns, as Superscot, demonstrated the internal psychological schism more than most. On the one hand, he was the gentle, lovable, caring Scotsman; on the other, the coarse, earthy, ranting Scotch git – the stage Scotsman. He could woo the members of the Caledonian Hunt with fulsome words of dedication just as persuasively as he could supply members of the Crochallan Fencibles with examples of bawdry. He constantly worried about this split in his personality, but was so caught in the grip of his own publicity that he was reduced to a spectator watching his own public image taking on a life of its own.

Stevenson's division of the Scotsman – and though *Dr Jekyll and Mr Hyde* is set in London, it could hardly have been produced by anyone but a Scotsman – into rational professional and monstrous amateur is perhaps the most profound clinical analysis Scotland has been treated to. The Scotsman's attempts at rationality cost him the suppression of emotions, and the occasional instability that breaks out can resemble insanity. As his letters show, Burns was constantly aware of the appalling effect of his own tendency to break out. His guilt tormented him and he wrote to his cousin James Burness on 12 July 1796 to say that 'my Physician assures me that melancholy & low spirits are half my disease' (CL, 64).

According to Currie, irresponsibility and high spirits supplied the other half. Currie's infamous questionmark on Burns – 'He who suffers the pollution of inebriation, how shall he escape other pollution?' (Currie, I, 214) – so outraged modern scholars that they have gone to the other extreme in virtually canonising Burns then finding the latter-day saint not guilty of sexual and alcoholic sins: Burns 'was never a drunkard, and he did not throw away his health in brothels' (Snyder, 435); 'Burns . . . was not himself a heavy drinker' (Maurice Lindsay, BE, 129). Denying that Burns was a drinker (possibly a bout alcoholic, see 'Burns and Booze') requires considerable convenient amnesia about the evidence in the letters and the poems.

It was Burns himself who said (in a letter) 'occasional hard drinking is the devil to me' (CL, 203); it was Burns himself who rejoiced that whisky 'cheers the heart o drooping Care' ('Scotch Drink'), Burns who declared 'Freedom and whisky gang thegither'

('The Author's Earnest Cry and Prayer'). It was Burns who projected himself as a careless genius who could knock back a power of drink and knock out an immortal poem. It was not Currie who instigated the myth of Burns the boozer; it was the bard himself.

It is unlikely that Burns – the industrious farmer, the energetic exciseman, the prolific songwriter – was ever the epic drinker he was supposed to be by Heron, Currie, Lockhart and others. He had enough experience of drunken squabbles and 'scenes like these' and horrendous hangovers to regret 'the fever of intoxication', the appallingly subjective thought that 'an intoxicated man is the vilest of beasts' (CL, 698). Yet the role-playing part of him led him to eulogise boozing in poems and the adoring public have taken him at his word to such an extent that he has become synonymous with Scotch drink. What other poet is celebrated every year in an orgy of alcoholic self-indulgence? What other poet has had a type of beer and a brand of whisky named after him? What other poet is freely quoted (or misquoted) and discussed in pubs?

It will not do, however, to deny the drinking of Burns and turn the oft-plastered poet into a plaster saint as some scholarly Bardolaters do. Their determination to keep the icon of Burns spotlessly clean is as absurd as earlier efforts to tarnish the image. Burns's poetry is honest and revealing yet its candour is not enough for those who want to get inside the man's skull, or remake him in their own image. It is the perception of Burns as a Superscot, as a shining example to others, that causes problems and has done so for decades. What other poet, for example, has been resurrected?

When the pseudo-science of phrenology was established at the end of the eighteenth-century it was inevitable that it would eventually be accepted in Scotland and there applied to the national bard. According to Dr Franz Joseph Gall (1758–1828), founder of phrenology, the character of an individual was revealed by the physical formation of the skull. From 1802 lectures on phrenology were banned in Gall's native Vienna, but in Scotland phrenology flourished, with a Phrenological Society in Edinburgh. What the Scottish phrenologists wanted was an opportunity to examine the head of Burns, to touch the skull of the poetic saviour.

Originally buried in an ordinary grave in St Michael's churchyard, Dumfries, Burns's body was disinterred in 1815 and moved to a vault in the Mausoleum erected to his memory. In 1834, when the Mausoleum was opened for the interment of the poet's widow some phrenological enthusiasts in Dumfries received permission to disturb the poet's remains for a second time. During the night of 31 March 1834, therefore, the skull of Burns was taken from his grave so a cast could be made of it (all is revealed in a volume erroneously entitled *The Complete Works of Robert Burns*, 1890). One A. Blacklock, a surgeon present during the removal of the skull, reported excitedly:

> Nothing could exceed the high state of preservation in which we found the bones of the cranium, or offer a fairer opportunity of supplying what has so long been desiderated by phrenologists – a correct model of our immortal poet's head.

Given that Burns was revered as 'immortal' it makes a curious kind of sense.

After washing it, plaster of Paris was applied to the skull and a cast was sent to the Phrenological Society in Edinburgh which published a report by George Combe. Burns's skull, with a circumference of 22 inches, was larger than the average Scottish head. On a scale assessing the development of the organs at 2 for idiotcy and 20 for 'very large', the bard scored highest marks for Philoprogenitiveness, Adhesiveness, Combativeness, Love of Approbation and Benevolence (all marked 20 and 'very large'). He had a 'large' rating for Secretiveness and Self-Esteem, a 'full' rating for Order and Tune, and 'uncertain' rating for Language. Had the resurrectionists taken the poetry, instead of the legend, as their priority they would have abandoned their efforts on account of that uncertain linguistic rating. Alas, the legend was all.

'No phrenologist can look upon this head,' Combe lamented, 'and consider the circumstances in which Burns was placed, without vivid feelings of regret.' Burns was a poor man whose humble circumstances were at variance with his sense of self-esteem. 'If,' Combe concluded,

> he had been placed from infancy in the higher ranks of life, liberally educated, and employed in pursuits corresponding to his powers, the inferior portion of his nature would have lost part of its energy, while his better qualities would have assumed a decided and permanent superiority.

A fellow phrenologist of Combe's, Robert Cox, suggested that Burns's character suffered because his poverty frustrated his 'rather large' organ of Acquisitiveness.

The conclusions of Combe and Cox say more about their own

mentality than the personality of Burns; and the same can be said for some scholarly Bardolaters. For the phrenologists, poverty was a social disgrace; for the scholarly Bardolaters drunkenness is a social disgrace. Bardolaters invariably go to the bard (are called to the bard) in order to reinforce their own preconceptions. Burns's poetry has suffered because of the treatment of the bard as some things to some men. In his lifetime, as in the time of Combe and Cox, Burns was regarded more as a social phenomenon, a flawed saviour, than as a serious poet. This is still the case and the cause is that Burns himself went along with the mythopoetic process. It was his expertise in performing the role of the 'Heaven-taught ploughman' that led to the legend of Burns. Scotland, as much as the rest of the world, wanted a saviour and Burns was able to act the part.

Here was a poor man's son come to save a chosen people through their neglected language, a poetic Christ to be worshipped rather than understood. 'Whaur's yer Wullie Shakespeare noo?' an excited onlooker had shouted at the opening night of Home's *Douglas*. Ten years after Home's Norval strutted on the Edinburgh stage, Burns arrived in Edinburgh to be royally received by an adoring audience. The reception was eloquently implicit. Whaur's yer Wullie Shakespeare noo? Whaur's yer English parliament noo? Where's yer German king o England noo? On Burns were focused an abundance of vague perceptions. On Burns could be projected images of what might have been and what yet might be. This is why Burns has survived as a sacred figure, this is why scholars squabble about his moral status, this is why there is such a holy tulzie about his personality. The reverence for Burns is a religious affair.

He is, after all, an odd kind of saviour. A master of the Scots language, he made a fuss about his lack of a classical education. As a young man he felt he could not 'make verses like printed ones, composed by men who had Greek and Latin' (AL), and in the Preface to the Kilmarnock Edition he regretted he could not read 'Theocrites or Virgil . . . in their original languages'. Yet when he was writing poems as brilliant as his 'Epistle to J. Lapraik' he knew he had the measure of those who 'think to climb Parnassus/By dint o Greek!'. It is not classical learning or philosophy this poet offers, it is the spectacle of himself:

> Now Robin lies in his last lair,
> He'll gabble rhyme, nor sing nae mair;

> Cauld poverty wi hungry stare,
> Nae mair shall fear him;
> Nor anxious fear, nor cankert care,
> E'er mair come near him.
>
> (141/CW, 268)

It is a characteristically Scottish paradox that the ideal of the Honest Man was advanced by a man who had to survive by the exercise of his native cunning.

With all his shifts of opinion and his necessity to conceal his political beliefs, Burns never evolved a systematic philosophy, nor would we expect it of him. That does not, however, prevent the Scottish public regarding him as the fount of all wisdom. If Burns's cogitations could be paraphrased into a bundle of related ideas – and that would be a difficult task given his circumstances and habits of thought – then we might peel off layers of prejudice before getting to the central insight. This was his conviction that the potential of each individual should be realized without the unfair burden of a hostile environment. Not an original thought in eighteenth-century Europe with the likes of Thomas Paine and Jean Jacques Rousseau about, but one that he expressed in his own particular way. Nor was he a political romantic; he did not advise the poor to accept their poverty while they waited for the promised land. The revolution was 'comin yet' but meanwhile, if the poor had nothing else, they had themselves:

> And why shouldna poor folk mowe, mowe, mowe.
> And why shouldna poor folk mowe:
> The great folk hae siller, and houses and lands,
> Poor bodies hae naething but mowe.
>
> (395/CW, 476)

Burns left no recognised successors; the Scottish public ensured that he was a one-off phenomenon. They simply were not greatly interested in any poetry that did not have the label Burns on it as a guarantee of excellence. It was a matter of – beware of imitations! Two outstanding Scottish poets of the twentieth century came to the conclusion that Burns had little to do with the appreciation of poetry. His star shone brightly over all and sundry, but it did not guide the public to other poets. Edwin Muir, a deeply introspective poet opposed to the calculated popularization of poetry, saw Burns clearly as the creation of the public:

> For a Scotsman to see Burns simply as a poet is well-nigh an impossibility . . . . He is more a personage to us than a poet, more a figurehead than a personage, and more a myth than a figurehead . . . . He is a myth evolved by the popular imagination, a communal poetic creation . . . a great man who by some felicitous miracle has been transformed into an ordinary man, and is the greater because of it . . . . He became legendary because he was uniquely ordinary. He was the ordinary man for whom Scotland had been looking as it might have looked for a king; and it discovered him with greater surprise and delight than if it had found a king; for kings are more common. (Edwin Muir, 'Burns and Popular Poetry', *Uncollected Scottish Criticism*, London, 1981, p. 193)

Hugh MacDiarmid, who wanted to restore a sense of intellectual perspective to Scottish literature, deplored the tendency of post-Burnsian Scottish writers to sink into a swamp of sentimentality and complacency:

> Burns led directly to this sorry pass through his anti-intellectualism and his xenophobia. It is nonsense to say that he embodies all the great elements of the Scottish tradition when in these two main respects he in fact completely betrayed it . . . . All that Burns wanted, however, was 'ae spark o Nature's fire/That's a' the learning I desire'. Well, it is not enough and less so today than ever. It is a betrayal of Dunbar and Gavin Douglas and the other great *makars* to whom Burns owed so much, and it has been largely responsible for landing the Scottish Muse in the horrible mess it has occupied since. (Hugh MacDiarmid, *Burns Today and Tomorrow*, Edinburgh, 1959, p. 23)

Muir sees Burns as 'uniquely ordinary', MacDiarmid blames Burns for his egregious affectation of ignorance. Neither poet is entirely happy with his distinguished predecessor.

What Muir and MacDiarmid objected to was that the ominous shadow of Burns's reputation hung over the creative efforts of all subsequent writers in Scotland. With its penchant for having a subject settled for once and for all, the Scottish public equated Burns with an entire national literature. For that, Burns is hardly to blame. He may have been a victim of his own role-playing, but he did draw attention to the great oral tradition of Scotland and to 'Ramsay and famous Fergusson' ('Epistle to William Simson') and to the daring bards he hoped would shape the future. He saw himself as a man renewing a great tradition so that tradition could continue but the Dugald Stewarts and the Maria Riddells preferred his conversational presence to his artfully conversational poetry. Modern readers, who treat Burns as a sacred figure and then ignore his appeal to the poetic past and potentially poetic future, simply take his name in vain. Such is the fate of poets who become plaster saints.

It is essential to return to Burns's poetry; to rediscover the source that somehow swelled into the flood of trivia in which the Burns industry is submerged. His art is more meaningful than his immortal memory. An American scholar has spoken wisely on the subject of Burns:

> His appeal to Scotsmen has served to foster the notion that he is but a local or national poet, and persistent fascination with his personality and his dramatic career, and with his all too human frailties, continues to shift interest from his having been a poet at all. (Fitzhugh, 388)

That is what the Scottish Society for the Prevention of Cruelty to Burns has achieved. Burns was shaped by Scottish tradition and by revolutionary political developments in America and France, but Bardolaters have faithfully honoured the role-playing of the poetic primitive rather than appreciating the reality of the man of literary genius who was most fully alive in the act of poetic creation. It is important to demythologise Burns; to acknowledge the man who read Ramsay and Fergusson and Locke and Tom Paine as well as the man who fell in love with several women. A female writer on the supposedly determinedly masculine Burns has commented:

> Scotland, ever since Burns, has become more and more the country of 'The Cotter' and of the political songs and of 'Auld Lang Syne'. The master has stamped himself on the imagination of the people so that they see in each other – and to that extent reproduce in each other – the qualities he ascribes to them. (Christina Keith, *The Russet Coat*, London, 1956, p. 218)

That sounds like an example of nature copying art, but it is actually an instance of fantasists rehearsing roles Burns created. It is the art that ultimately matters, not the role-playing.

In deifying Burns, Bardolaters do a disservice to themselves and to the bard. Hard literary labour was required to achieve the fame and it came with no fortune. Hazlitt, lecturing on Burns at the Surrey

Institution in 1818, realised this when he described 'how a poet, not born to wealth or title, was kept in a constant state of feverish anxiety with respect to his fame and the means of a precarious livelihood' (CH, 300). Behind the role-playing was an artistic integrity that should be respected more than it is. His poems and his songs were his gift to his country, and to the world, and he knew it. Jean Armour could be toyed with, Highland Mary could be kept hanging on at Greenock, Clarinda could be teased in an epistolary courtship. But the poems and songs he made about men and women were the reality that made his life more than a series of roles. In moments when he reflected on the contrast between artistic reality and social roles he became understandably depressed, lamenting how 'Personal & domestic affliction have almost entirely banished that alacrity & life with which I used to woo the rural Muse of Scotia' (CL, 303). If he had substituted 'personal and poetic affectation' for 'Personal & domestic affliction' – and 'visionary' for 'rural' – he would have told a rare truth about his career after the Kilmarnock Edition.

Ultimately he valued the artistic reality above the social role-playing. His last letter to James Johnson, editor of the *Scots Musical Museum*, pays a compliment that is actually intended for himself: 'Your work is a great one . . . the text book & standard of Scottish Song & Music' (CL, 303). His last letter to George Thomson, editor of *Select Scottish Airs*, promises (nine days before his death) further examples of his 'song genius' (CL, 679). Earlier he had told Thomson that accepting payment for his songs would be 'downright Sodomy of Soul' (CL, 618). Admirers of Burns's poems and songs owe him credit on his creative work which should be approached with the utmost attention for he was a conscious artist.

A distinguished Burnsian has written of the bard: 'He saved Scotland; himself he could not save . . . his worshippers are ashamed of the best part of his nature and his work. And nobody else reads him.' (J. DeLancey Ferguson, *Pride and Passion: Robert Burns*, New York, 1939, pp. 306–8) That, of course, is as much an exaggeration as MacDiarmid's dismissive comment on Bardolaters, 'No' wan in fifty kens a wurd Burns wrote.' It is the kind of exaggerated comment Burns's romantic reputation prompts. Critics are confused by the emotional power of Burns's poetry, Bardolaters forget that the Honest Man paved his way to Edinburgh with useful introductions and masonic contacts.

Artistically, Burns stood head and shoulders above his immediate predecessors Ramsay and Fergusson: though he was not always as technically resourceful as they were he did have a remarkably direct communication with his audience and a powerful enough persona to supply his work with a heroic dimension. Personally, he was a remarkable man who could rationalise even his inconsistencies. If he went astray, for example, then he could assume he had a divine right to do so, for his muse Coila tells him in 'The Vision':

> I saw thy pulse's maddening play,
> Wild-send thee Pleasure's devious way,
> Misled by Fancy's meteor-ray,
>   By passion driven;
> But yet the light that led astray
>   Was light from heaven.
>   (62/CW, 120)

Burns was the last man to want this heavenly light to encircle his head forever like a halo. Playing the part of the poetic saviour was one thing, becoming an eternal object of religious reverence quite another. Burns, after all, was a man who endorsed the Common Sense philosophy.

It is typical of Burns's complex of contradictions that he became interested in creative armorial bearings for himself to prove (as if it needed proving) that he was as honest as the next man. For his motto he took the phrase 'Better a wee bush than nae bield'. Bield, for those who know their Scots, is shelter. For more than two centuries Burns's reputation has sheltered under the protective care of Bardolaters. It is time to remove the cover and reveal the poet. With unusual percipience Burns anticipated the problem of his artistic immortality. In a letter of 15 January 1787 he told Dr John Moore:

> That I have some merit, I do not deny, is my own opinion; but I see, with frequent wringings of heart, that the novelty of my character, and the honest, national prejudice of Scotchmen (a prejudice which do Thou, O God, ever kindle ardent in their breasts!) have borne me to a height altogether untenable to my abilities. (CL, 247)

In deference to these words from the poet's own pen, Burns should be approached as a living poetic presence not as an artificially preserved corpse entitled to undying allegiance.

The poetic art of Burns was a serious business, the public career of Burns a skilful performance: the one brought him fame, the other misfortune. He created a role for himself and came to regret that role when he found his formally educated audience did not share his genuine passion for poetry but expected him to act the part of the Scottish saviour. When he was alive Burns had to endure the patronising tone of those who wanted their saviour to do as he was told (produce English verse, manufacture pastoral dramas); he was required to be a diffident saviour without the passion. Almost two centuries after his death the approach to Burns has hardly changed. He is still neglected as a poet, still used as a convenient peg on which to hang any old opinion, still set up as a screen on which to project a handy prejudice. It is time to reverse the roles and see Burns as a poet first and last; a serious poet and not a 'humble Bardie' or Honest Man diminished by an exclusively poetic destiny. 'My Muse, tho hamely in attire,/May touch the heart', said Burns. The only way to understand that emotion is to touch his art. That is the only honest approach to Burns.

Part IV:
The Art of Burns

Poems

THE DEATH AND DYING WORDS OF POOR MAILIE, THE AUTHOR'S ONLY PET YOWE

Text   24/CW, 62–4

Composition   Written at Lochlea, possibly late 1782 since Burns associates it with his 'twenty-third year' (AL); subsequently entered in the first Common Place Book, June 1785. It is 'Burns's first significant essay in Scots' (Kinsley, 1018).

Publication   First published in the Kilmarnock Edition (31 July 1786).

Reception   Josiah Walker (*Account of the Life and Character of Robert Burns*, 1811) thought the poem a good example of Burns's command of 'that description of humour which exalts insignificant things to a ludicrous dignity . . . . His *Ewe* is a sagacious and affectionate matron' (CH, 230).

Snyder felt the two Mailie poems lacked human interest and that 'to enjoy them to the full one must be familiar with the tradition which established the mock-elegy as a legitimate type of vernacular literature' (Snyder, 170). Hecht, however, admired 'The Death and Dying Words' as 'this humorous masterpiece of animal characterisation' (Hecht, 34) and Crawford praised the poem as 'a delightfully comic treatment of many of the themes expressed elsewhere by Burns in mournful and elegiac numbers, but here objectified as animal attitudes and character types' (Crawford, 77).

*   *   *

According to the poet's brother, Gilbert, Burns wrote the poem almost immediately after a diverting incident at Lochlea. Burns had bought a ewe and two lambs from a neighbour. The ewe Mailie (a

pet name for Mary) was tethered in a field adjoining the farmhouse.
Writing to Currie in April 1798, Gilbert explained:

> He and I were going out with our teams, and our two younger
> brothers to drive for us, at mid-day, when Hugh Wilson, a
> curious-looking, awkward boy, clad in plaiding, came to us with
> much anxiety in his face, with the information that the ewe had
> entangled herself in the tether, and was lying in the ditch. Robert
> was much tickled with Hughoc's appearance and posture on the
> occasion. Poor Mailie was set to rights and when we returned
> from the plough in the evening, he repeated to me her 'Death and
> Dying Words' pretty much in the way they now stand. (BE, 225)

The first six lines of the poem confirm this anecdotal account:

> As Mailie, an her lambs thegither,
> Was ae day nibblin on the tether,
> Upon her cloot she coost a hitch,
> An owre she warsl'd in the ditch:
> There, groanin, dying, she did lie,
> When Hughoc he cam doytin by.

Burns's apparently spontaneous production, however, was tempered by tradition. The mode of the mock elegy ostensibly uttered
by a Scots-speaking animal dates back to 1706 and the publication
of 'The Last Dying Words of Bonnie Heck, a Famous Grey-hound
in the Shire of Fife' by William Hamilton of Gilbertfield (whose
modernised version of Blind Harry's *Wallace* was an inspiration to
Burns). Hamilton's poem uses the Standard Habbie stanza, Burns
(surprisingly given the precedent and his subsequent expertise with
the Standard Habbie) uses couplets, mainly in iambic tetrameter.
The relaxed conversational Scots of Mailie's monologue comes not
only from Hamilton of Gilbertfield for this poem was written in
the year (or the year after) Burns acquired the second edition of
Fergusson's *Poems* and 'strung anew my wildly-sounding rustic lyre
with emulating vigour' (AL). Frequently, Burns's couplets have a
Fergussonian ring; compare 'As Mailie, an her lambs thegither,/Was
ae day nibblin on the tether' with Fergusson's 'In sun-shine, and in
weety weather,/Our thrawart lot we bure thegither' (Fergusson,
'Mutual Complaint of Plainstanes and Causey').

As given in the Kilmarnock Edition, the full title of the poem is

'The Death and Dying Words of Poor Mailie, the Author's Only Pet Yowe, An Unco Mournfu' Tale'. This prepares the reader for a comical poem, as do the introductory lines. Mailie addresses 'Hughoc' Wilson, whose appearance and apprehension establish him as a figure of fun; indeed the first line of Mailie's monologue refers to Hughoc's 'lamentable face'. Burns, however, intends the comedy to encourage thought as well as laughter for what Mailie advocates is that liberty the poet celebrated in so many of his poems. Mailie instructs Hughoc to tell Burns to release his sheep from restraint:

> O, bid him never tie them mair,
> Wi wicked strings o hemp or hair!
> But ca' them out to park or hill,
> An let them wander at their will . . .

Moving from the general to the particular, Mailie speaks for her kind by seeking salvation from dogs and foxes 'and butcher's knives', the human enemy listed last as the most deadly. There is humour in this special pleading by a sheep, but Burns turns the joke against the reader, capable of devouring Mailie's 'helpless lambs'.

Having spoken on the subject of freedom from restraint and attack, Mailie paradoxically acknowledges the importance of moral restrictions. Burns is to restrain Mailie's son ('My poor toop-lamb, my son and heir') by confining him to home and the company of his kind; similarly, Burns is to protect Mailie's daughter ('my yowie, silly thing') but not tether her. Mailie's sentiments hark back to the biblical reference to a protective God who 'shall gather the lambs with his arm, and carry them in his bosom, and shall gently lead those that are with young' (Isaiah 41:11). Mailie saves her 'last breath' for a warning to her young – 'An when you think upo your mither,/Mind to be kind to ane anither' – then dies.

This was not, however, the poet's last word on Mailie. While he was arranging the contents of the Kilmarnock Edition in 1785–6 he wrote a comic elegy, in the Standard Habbie stanza (thus following the measured steps of Hamilton of Gilbertfield's 'Bonnie Heck') to accompany 'The Death and Dying Words of Poor Mailie'. 'Poor Mailie's Elegy' (25/CW, 64–5) encourages a thoughtful reading of the companion poem by describing Mailie as an exceptional animal:

> I wat she was a sheep o sense,

> An could behave hersel wi mense:
> I'll say't, she never brak a fence,
>   Thro thievish greed.
> Our Bardie, lanely, keeps the spence
>   Sin' Mailie's dead.

So though Burns uses the tradition of the mock elegy he does so with
a farmer's perception of the companionship of an animal. Characteristically, he ends the elegy with a stanza that is simultaneously
preposterous and poignant:

> O, a' ye Bards on bonie Doon!
> An wha on Aire your chanters tune!
> Come, join the melancholious croon
>   O Robin's reed!
> His heart will never get aboon!
>   His Mailie's dead!

As later poems confirm, Burns could enthusiastically savage his
fellow man, but was at his most sentimental in his treatment of
animals be they mice or ewes.

HOLY WILLIE'S PRAYER

Text   53/CW, 93–5.

Composition   Written early in 1785, after a judgement of January
1785 by the Presbytery of Ayr (see below).

Publication   Burns considered the poem too provocative to
include in any collection of his. 'Holy Willie's Prayer' was first
published anonymously, as 'The Prayer of Holy Willie, A Canting,
Hypocritical, Kirk Elder', in an eight-page pamphlet of 1789 (there
are no details of author, publisher or place of publication on the
title page). Ten years later it was attributed to Burns in a pamphlet
published in Glasgow, but it was not included in Currie's edition
of 1800, being (as Sir Walter Scott said) 'cast in a form too daringly
profane to be received into Dr Currie's Collection' (CH, 198). It
appeared in Thomas Stewart's edition of *Poems ascribed to Robert
Burns, the Ayrshire Bard* (1801) and in Josiah Walker's *Poems by Robert
Burns* (1811).

Reception   In *The Lives of the Scottish Poets* (1804), David Irving found the poem 'reprehensible for the extreme indecency which it occasionally exhibits' (CH, 166). Walter Scott (writing in the first issue of the *Quarterly Review*, February 1809) called it 'a piece of satire more exquisitely severe than any which Burns afterwards wrote' (CH, 198).

Snyder ecstatically affirms 'this poem alone would have admitted Burns to the fellowship of Swift and Aristophanes . . . one is hard put to find anywhere in literature another hundred lines of satiric verse which can rank with it' (Snyder, 160–1). Other modern critics concur, seeing the poem as 'one of the finest satires of all time' (Crawford, 52), 'one of the world's great and final satires' (Fitzhugh, 64). For Kinsley, the satire is 'both personal and general [exposing] the hyporcrisy, viciousness, and uncharitableness of Willie Fisher, and beyond these, the corruption of the old attitudes and beliefs of Presbyterian orthodoxy' (Kinsley, 1048).

*   *   *

Burns's own note on 'Holy Willie's Prayer', in the Glenriddell Manuscript, reads:

> Holy Willie was a rather oldish bachelor elder in the parish of Mauchlilne, and much and justly famed for that polemical chattering which ends in tippling orthodoxy, and for that spiritu-alized bawdry which refines to liquorish devotion. In a sessional process with a gentlemen in Mauchline – a Mr Gavin Hamilton – Holy Willie and his priest, Father Auld, after full hearing in the presbytery of Ayr, came off but second best; owing partly to the oratorical powers of Mr Robert Aiken, Mr Hamilton's counsel, but chiefly to Mr Hamilton's being one of the most irreproachable and truly respectable characters in the country. On losing his process, the Muse overheard him at his devotions.

William Fisher (1737–1809), Burns's 'Holy Willie', was neither par-ticularly old nor a bachelor, being forty-eight in 1785 and married to Jean Hewatson, so the poet's note is misleading in that respect. Otherwise it records a story that, but for Burns, would have disap-peared.

Fisher was an elder of Mauchline Kirk and a member of the Kirk Session presided over by the minister William Auld, an Auld Licht by nature as well as Auld by name (and in fact – he was seventy-six when the dispute ended). It was apparently at Fisher's instigation that the Kirk Session took action against the poet's enlightened friend Gavin Hamilton, accusing him of absences from the kirk 'two Sabbaths in Dec[ember 1784] and three Sabbaths in Jan[uary]' and 'Habitual, if not total, neglect of family worship' (cited by Snyder, 110). Hamilton appealed to the Presbytery of Ayr which, in January 1785, found in his favour (as did the Synod of Glasgow when the Mauchline Kirk Session appealed against the Presbytery's decision). For Burns this was a welcome triumph of the liberal New Lichts over the Auld Lichts of Mauchline. Burns circulated the poem in Mauchline with mixed results: 'Holy Willie's Prayer next made its appearance, and alarmed the kirk-Session so much that they held three several meetings to look over their holy artillery, if any of it was pointed against profane Rhymers' (AL).

Technically a dramatic monologue in the Standard Habbie stanza, the poem begins with a statement of the Calvinist doctrine of pre-ordained damnation and salvation, addressing a God who 'Sends ane to Heaven, an ten to Hell'. Smugly, Holy Willie assumes he is one of the elect who will be sent to heaven. The concept of an innate fall from God's grace is cleverly developed by linking biblical with obstetric imagery. Holy Willie recalls the original fall of man through 'Adam's cause', which is then juxtaposed with the physical fall of the child from the womb. By evoking the notion of a new-born infant (with its gums and tears) in a nightmarish hell, Holy Willie subcribes to the sadistic excesses of Calvinism (as expounded in such theologial works as Thomas Boston's *Human Nature in its Four-fold State*, 1720, with its assurance that 'even the new-born babe [is] a child of hell'):

> When from my mither's womb I fell,
> Thou might hae plung'd me deep in hell,
> To gnash my gooms, and weep and wail,
>   In burning lakes,
> Whare damned devils roar and yell,
>   Chain'd to their stakes.

For the next stanza the mood abruptly changes from the infernal to the self-congratulatory as Holy Willie, blissfully unconscious of the irony involved, thanks the Calvinistic God for choosing such a man as himself as living proof of the wisdom of his ways:

> Yet I am here a chosen sample,

> To show Thy grace is great and ample:
> I'm here a pillar o Thy temple,
> > Strong as a rock,
> A guide, a buckler, and example,
> > To a' Thy flock!

Willie's insistence on his own presence ('I am here', 'I'm here') reveals the monstrous egotism of his creed: 'Vile self gets in' he acknowledges in the following stanza. By simply existing as one of the elect he embodies what he recognises as the goodness of God. In that context, the confession that follows sabotages his theological certainty for if he represents God-given grace his God is egregiously flawed in his judgement. Willie holds himself up as an 'example' and damns himself in doing so.

Gossiping, rather than communing, with God he admits he is 'fash'd wi fleshly lust' and, with the same relish he previously reserved for hell, catalogues his sexual and alcoholic adventures:

> O Lord! yestreen, Thou kens, wi Meg –
> Thy pardon I sincerely beg –
> O, may't ne'er be a livin plague
> > To my dishonour!
> An I'll ne'er lift a lawless leg
> > Again upon her.

> Besides, I farther maun avow,
> Wi Leezie's lass, three times I trow –
> But, Lord, that Friday I was fou,
> > When I cam near her,
> Or else, Thou kens, Thy servant true
> > Wad never steer her.

Willie takes it for granted that God has a special interest in his indiscretions. The extent of his conceit, hilarious in its ironical implications, encourages the reader to go along with Willie's assumption that Mauchline is (for the duration of the poem anyway) central to the divine design.

Burns now prods Holy Willie into directly revealing the arrogance of his ignorance. Willie speculates that God may permit sexual temptation to come his way in order to remind him of his exalted position: one 'sae gifted' has to endure such gifts nobly. Every time Willie strives for humility, however, he condemns himself by his own words. This self-destructive rage emerges clearly within the confines of one stanza which has Willie, a member of a new chosen race, cursing the neighbours he is supposed to love ('Thou shalt love thy neighbour as thyself', according to Leviticus 19:18 and Matthew 19:19):

> Lord, bless Thy chosen in this place,
> For here Thou has a chosen race!
> But God confound their stubborn face,
>   An blast their name,
> Wha bring Thy elders to disgrace
>   An open shame.

The four stanzas that follow this curse invite God's wrath on Gavin Hamilton (who 'drinks, an swears, an plays at cartes'); the Presbytery of Ayr that supported him; and Robert Aiken ('that glib-tongu'd Aiken') who defended him. Here the logic that began the poem is reversed: in the beginning Willie regarded himself as made in God's image; towards the end he attempts to make God in his own spiteful image. The God he worships is thus revealed as a creation of Calvinism, not as a wise creator.

Finally, Willie reasserts the egotism that is essential to his creed. Hamilton and his friends are to be tried by a vengeful God in a divine reversal of the verdict of the Presbytery of Ayr (in constantly bringing God down to earth in Ayrshire Willie displays his parochial mentality while Burns triumphantly uses this device to lift this insignificant kirk elder into the sphere of humanity at large). Willie is to be rewarded on earth as well as heaven:

> But, Lord, remember me and mine
> Wi mercies temporal and divine,
> That I for grace an gear may shine,
>   Excell'd by nane,
> And a' the glory shall be Thine –
>   Amen, Amen!

The closing stanza perfectly illustrates Burns's strategy of juxtaposition in this poem. Willie is not, after all, content to be one of the chosen for the afterlife is not enough. He wants material proof of God's wisdom, wants to be rewarded on earth with both 'grace and gear'. The enduring appeal of the poem is its juxtaposition of the ridiculous and the sublime. In treating God as an extension of his conversational self, in clarifying his Calvinist creed, Willie is a preposterous figure of fun. In revealing his own vulnerability, however, Willie is a figure with a certain pathos, a victim of his time and temperament.

Burns's choice of the dramatic monologue as the means to condemn Holy Willie is triumphant. A frontal attack on the man (such as Burns delivers in 'Epitaph on Holy Willie' and 'The Kirk's Alarm') would have revealed the poet's indignation and little more. By presenting Holy Willie as speaking for himself, Burns not only damns the hypocrite but profoundly imparts the psychology of the self-deceiver, the kind of character still at large and as large as life.

DEATH AND DOCTOR HORNBOOK

Text   55/CW, 96–100.

Composition   Written at Mossgiel, 'early in the year 1785' (Gilbert Burns, cited by Kinsley, 1053). According to Allan Cunningham's *The Works of Robert Burns with his Life* (1834) Burns wrote the poem immediately after hearing a pedantic speech, at Tarbolton Masonic Club, by John Wilson (see below).

> On his way home he seated himself on the parapet of the bridge near 'Willie's Mill', and in the moonlight began to reflect on what had passed . . . . He composed the poem on his perilous seat, and when he had done, fell asleep; he was awakened by the rising sun, and, on going home, committed it to paper. (CH, 405)

According to Snyder, however, Cunningham's biography is 'absolutely unreliable as regards specific facts' (Snyder, 489). Lockhart, as romantic a biographer as Cunningham, claimed that the satire had forced Wilson out of business but this has no foundation in fact, and Wilson remained in Tarbolton until 1792.

Publication   Omitted from the Kilmarnock Edition because 'it would have constituted an unnecessary offence to a neighbour' (Snyder, 159), it first appeared in the First Edinburgh Edition (17 April 1787).

Reception   Burns himself considered the poem 'too trifling and prolix to publish' (CL, 97) but Hugh Blair, advising the poet on the contents of the First Edinburgh Edition, approved of it: 'Of the proposed additions to the New Edition . . . The best are – "John

Barleycorn" – "Death & Dr Hornbook" – "The Winter Night"'
(CH, 82). Wordsworth (*A Letter to a Friend of Robert Burns*, 1816)
was impressed by the poem:

> His brother can set me right if I am mistaken when I express a
> belief, that at the time when he wrote his story of 'Death and Dr
> Hornbook', he had very rarely been intoxicated, or perhaps even
> much exhilarated by liquor. Yet how happily does he lead his
> reader into that track of sensation! and with what lively humour
> does he describe the disorder of his senses and the confusion of
> his understanding, put to test by a deliberate attempt to count the
> horns of the moon! (CH, 286–7)

Crawford calls it 'the best of all his purely local poems' (Crawford,
117).

*   *   *

The origin of the poem is anecdotal (as the subtitle, 'A True Story',
suggests). John Wilson (*c*.1751–1839), a Tarbolton schoolteacher,
supplemented his income through his grocer's shop in which he
sold medicines and dispensed medical advice. During a speech at
Tarbolton Masonic Lodge, of which he was Secretary from 1782–7,
Wilson gave a pedantic speech full of Latin phrases and pharmaceu-
tical allusions. Burns heard the speech and subsequently satirised
Wilson as Dr Hornbook: since a hornbook was a pedagogic aid (a
sheet of paper, mounted on wood and covered with a protective
sheet of horn, displaying the alphabet, digits, the Lord's Prayer and
rules of spelling) a human hornbook was a pedant.

Burns drew on poetic precedent in his presentation of Death
and in his verbal portrait of Dr Hornbook. The medieval *danse
macabre*, with Death as a skeletal figure, was refined in Dunbar's
'Lament for the Makars' (included in Allan Ramsay's anthology
Ever Green, 1724) where Death is 'That strang unmercifull tyrand'.
Spenser (whose work Burns revered) depicted 'Death with most
grim and griesly visage serene' in *The Faerie Queene* (VII.vii.46).
It has been suggested, by A. H. MacLaine in the *Burns Chronicle*
(1955), that Burns may have followed the satirical example of Paul
Whitehead's 'Death and the Doctor' which appeared in January
1775 in the *Scots Magazine*, back numbers of which would have
been available in Ayrshire. Death, in Burns's poem, finds his dart
blunted by Hornbook's medical art; Death, in Whitehead's poem

'aimed his keenest dart' but missed 'the vital part' (cited by Kinsley, 1056). Like Whitehead, Burns produced a satirical variation on a traditional theme.

Cast in the Standard Habbie stanza, the poem begins by humorously insisting on its own veracity. 'Some books are lies frae end to end', Burns declares in his first line then, in the second stanza, ironically vouches for this tale which 'Is just as true's the Deil's in Hell/Or Dublin city'. The ironical treatment of the concept of truth is underlined by the poet's condition, given in the characteristically swaggering style of the drinker who boasts that his alcoholic intake has hardly incapacitated him.

> The clachan yill had made me canty,
> I was na fou, but just had plenty:
> I stacher'd whyles, but yet took tent ay
>   To free the ditches;
> An hillocks, stanes, an bushes, kend ay
>   Frae ghaists and witches.

So this 'true story' expresses the truth of a staggering drunk, a man (so the fourth stanza explains) incapable of counting the horns on the rising moon. This deft self-portrait of the poet as a toper sets the scene for the odd encounter.

Lurching past Willie Muir's mill, Burns focuses on 'Something' which puts him in a panic. His description identifies the figure before it names itself as Death: it has a scythe across one shoulder and a skeletal figure ('The picture was probably familiar to Burns . . . from chap-book woodcuts', Kinsley, 1054). After hearing Death speak its name, Burns attempts to defend himself with a knife. However, Death has not come to claim him so the poet shakes its hand and sits down to hear what gossip Death can offer. The remainder of the poem, apart from a conversational intervention from the poet and the final stanza, comprises Death's monologue – a morbid monologue within a drunken monologue.

Death begins by recalling his career and complaining of an obstacle to the progress of his trade. Dr Hornbook has cheated Death by the application of tricks of the medical trade he has lifted from such books as William Buchan's *Domestic Medicine* (1769). Faced with such competition, Death has lost the use of the tools of his own trade:

> 'See, here's a scythe, an there's a dart,

> They hae pierc'd monie a gallant heart,
> But Doctor Hornbook wi his art
>   An cursed skill,
> Has made them baith no worth a fart,
>   Damn'd haet they'll kill!'

The crudity of Death's diction informs a further grievance against
Dr Hornbook:

> 'Ev'n them he canna get attended,
> Altho their face he ne'er had kend it,
> Just shite in a kail-blade, an send it,
>   As soon's he smells 't,
> Baith their disease, and what will mend it,
>   At once he tells 't.'

Death gives a list of Dr Hornbook's cures – the Latin names emphasise the charlatanism of the doctor – which prompts the poet to
remark that Hornbook will do the gravedigger, as well as Death,
out of a job ('They'll ruin Johnie', he says, referring to Johnie Ged the
parish gravedigger). This intervention allows Death to get the last
laugh on Dr Hornbook ('The creature grain'd an eldrich laugh').

Hornbook, Death exults, eventually kills those he intends to cure
so the apparent enemy of Death is actually a rival doing Death's
work. Death gives some examples of Hornbook's fatal incompetence
then promises to visit the doctor:

> 'But hark! I'll tell you of a plot,
> Tho dinna ye be speakin o't!
> I'll nail the self-conceited sot,
>   As dead's a herrin;
> Neist time we meet, I'll wad a groat,
>   He gets his fairin!'

At this point the kirk bell strikes, the poet realises it is well past
midnight, and the poem ends abruptly on the word Death.

Burns has created a nightmare-poem, albeit with comical connotations, that is more compelling than some of the dream-poems of
tradition. One one level the encounter with death is a drunken
hallucination (that leads forward to 'Tam o Shanter'); on another
it is sober reflection on the notion that death is the ultimate end of

life. Only superficially is it a satire on an actual individual for the real Wilson (who was apparently flattered by his part in the poem) is dead while Dr Hornbook lives on in Burns's poem. A Tarbolton anecdote has been elevated to an enduring work of art.

THE HOLY FAIR

Text   70/CW, 133–9.

Composition   A note by Burns on the manuscript of the poem in the Kilmarnock Monument Museum reads 'Composed in 1785'. It is likely that the poem was written during, or shortly after, August 1785 since the Mauchline Communion was held annually on the second Sunday in August.

Publication   First published in the Kilmarnock Edition (31 July 1786).

Reception   David Irving, in *The Lives of the Scottish Poets* (1804), thought the poem 'entitled to every praise except that of scrupulous decency' (CH, 166); Josiah Walker's *Account of the Life and Character of Robert Burns* (1811), described it as 'a caricature of exquisite humour' (CH, 221). The moralistic approach of Irving was continued by Thomas Campbell who, in *Specimens of the British Poets* (1819), wrote: 'It is enough, however, to mention the humour of this production, without recommending its subject. Burns, indeed, only laughs at the abuses of a sacred institution; but the theme was of unsafe approach, and he ought to have avoided it' (CH, 323).

Modern critics have been more generous in their praise, Snyder, for example, finding it 'a flawless piece of personal and social satire' (Snyder, 177) and Christina Keith (*The Russet Coat*, London 1956, p. 43) praising it as 'the most subtly constructed of all Burns's poems'. Crawford regards it as a poetic triumph of the Life Force, technically adroit in showing 'complete mastery of traditional poetic skills' (Crawford, 75). Kinsley relates the poem to the (originally medieval) tradition of the peasant 'brawl' which Burns was familiar with through Fergusson ('Hallow-Fair', 'Leith Races') and chapbook tales:

'The Holy Fair' lifts the 'brawl' to a new level of complexity, satiric art, and social significance. Burns sets the life of nature (ll. 1–9) and natural man (ll. 37–63, 73–81, 91–9, 163–80, 226–43) against the artifices of religious hypocrisy and display (ll. 10–22,

82–7, 100–26, 181–98); he opposes the force of sexual and social instinct to the shams of pulpit rhetoric and 'polemical divinity'; and he builds these oppositions up out of the sustained irony of worship, drink, and fornication juxtaposed, which reaches its climax in ll. 235–43. (Kinsley, 1095)

*   *   *

Holy fairs were an integral part of eighteenth-century Scotland and Mauchline's holy fair conformed to a well-established pattern which, in practice, was chaotic. In 1785 Mauchline had around 400 communicant church members but for the annual communion service – the Sunday climax to days of celebration – more than thrice that number came to receive the sacrament, arriving from within and without the parish and refreshing themselves at Nanse Tinnock's tavern by the churchyard. Since the church could not accommodate such a press of people, a tent was set up on church grounds and rival preachers, representing Auld Licht and New Licht notions, addressed the crowd. For many of those present, the occasion was an entertainment with religious overtones. A document published in 1759, *A Letter from a Blacksmith to the Ministers and Elders of the Church of Scotland*, indicates the incongruity of the holy fair:

> In Scotland they run from kirk to kirk, and flock to see a Sacrament, and make the same use of it that the papists do of their pilgrimages and processions – that is, indulge themselves in drunkenness, folly, and idleness . . . . In this sacred assembly there is an odd mixture of religion, sleep, drinking, courtship, and a confusion of sexes, ages and characters . . . in a word, there is such an absurd mixture of the serious and comick, that were we convened for any other purpose than that of worshipping the God and Governor of Nature, the scene would exceed all power of farce. (cited by Snyder, 176)

Noting the details contained in the *Letter from a Blacksmith*, Snyder describes the document as the prose source of Burns's poem but Burns drew more from personal experience and observation than from the prose and poetry that undoubtedly influenced him. Gilbert Burns confirmed that 'The farcical scene . . . was often a favourite field of [Burns's] observations, and the most of the incidents he mentions had actually passed before his eyes' (cited by Kinsley, 1094).

For example, he surpassed the efforts of his acknowledged master

Fergusson. Burns borrowed the Christis Kirk stanza as used by Fergusson in 'Hallow-Fair' and 'Leith Races' – following a rhyme-scheme of *ababcdcde* with the short last line (the tag, or tail) always ending in 'day' – and the nature of Burns's debt to Fergusson is obvious from a comparison of the opening quatrains of 'Leith Races' and 'The Holy Fair'. First, Fergusson:

> In July month, ae bonny morn,
> Whan Nature's rokelay green
> Was spread o'er ilka rigg o' corn
> To charm our roving een . . .

Then Burns:

> Upon a summer Sunday morn,
> When Nature's face is fair,
> I walked forth to view the corn,
> And snuff the caller air.

In his poem Fergusson meets Mirth who becomes his companion (his 'mate') for a humorous day at Leith Races. Burns, aiming for ecclesiastical satire rather than urban amusement, meets not one but 'Three hizzies': Fun (the equivalent of Fergusson's Mirth) who introduces him to Supersition and Hypocrisy, obligatory presences at Mauchline Holy Fair. Whereas Fergusson dwells on the particular in 'Hallow-Fair' and 'Leith Races', Burns aspires to the universal in 'The Holy Fair'.

It is a hallmark of Burns's poetic genius that he was able to comment on the human condition by sharply observing then satirically extending an actual parochial event. Not only is the poem rooted in the landscape of Mauchline, but local characters are involved in the action (though the ecclesiastical names were indicated by asterisks in the Kilmarnock Edition): 'Racer Jess' (Janet Gibson, the dimwitted daughter of Poosie Nansie); Rev Alexander Moodie (Auld Licht minister of Riccarton and one of the protagonists of 'The Twa Herds'); Rev George Smith (New Licht minister of Galston); Rev William Peebles (Auld Licht clerk of the Ayr Presbytery); Rev Alexander Miller (a man seeking the security of an Auld Licht parish); Rev John Russell (Auld Licht minister of the High Church in Kilmarnock and Moodie's antagonist in 'The Twa Herds').

Burns's vivid verbal portraits are damning. Rev Alexander Miller is presented as an intelligent man cynically using the Auld Licht credo to advance his career:

> Wee Miller niest, the guard relieves,
>   An Orthodoxy raibles,
> Tho in his heart he weel believes,
>   An thinks it auld wives' fables:
> But faith! the birkie wants a manse,
>   So, cannilie he hums them;
> Altho his carnal wit and sense
>   Like hafflins-wise o'ercomes him
>   At times that day.

Miller was duly ordained minister of Kilmaurs parish church in 1788, but maintained that Burns's remarks had harmed his career.

'The Holy Fair' suggests that Calvinism, with its vision of a cruelly selective God who sends preordained sinners to 'A vast, unbottom'd boundless pit,/Fill'd fou o lowin brunstane', brings no comfort to the common people who turn instead to the consolations of drink and the saving grace of sex. Although he ridicules the tavern gossips as 'yill-caup commentators' he celebrates the liberating power of alcohol:

> Leeze me on drink! it gies us mair
>   Than either school or college;
> It kindles wit, it waukens lear,
>   It pangs us fou o knowledge:
> Be't whisky-gill or penny wheep,
>   Or onie stronger potion,
> It never fails, on drinkin deep,
>   To kittle up our notion
>   By night or day.

Similarly, although he is distracted by the sight of 'twa-three whores' and 'tittlin jads,/Wi heavin breasts an bare neck' at a supposedly sacred event, he ends his poem by absolving sins in the pleasures of the flesh:

> How monie hearts this day converts
>   O sinners and o lasses!
> Their hearts o stane, gin night, are gane
>   As saft as onie flesh is:
> There's some are fou o love divine;
>   There's some are fou o brandy;
> An monie jobs that day begin,

May end in houghmagandie
Some ither day.

That final stanza is a synthesis of what has gone before in a poem that depends on counterpoint.

Throughout the poem Burns contrasts religious ceremony with social celebration, Calvinist condemnation with the natural vitality of the common people, dogma with drink, the concept of sin with the actuality of intercourse ('houghmagandie'). 'The Holy Fair' satirises the self-appointed moral guardians of parochial life by separating the preachers from those they preach at. As the Auld Licht strives to shine, 'Common-sense has taen the road' (Common Sense is a personification of the poet's friend Dr John Mackenzie, but obviously much more than that). Burns sees Calvinism as essentially antisocial and offers the alternative of booze and bed.

In doing so he touches inventively on various traditions. The catalogue of preachers, ultimately deriving from a medieval tradition that was imaginatively renewed in Dunbar's 'Lament for the Makars' (accessible to Burns in Allan Ramsay's anthology *Ever Green*, 1724) allows the poet to advance through an accumulation of human evidence of intolerance. The traditional brawl has become an arid theological contest. The stanzaic pattern has acquired increased satirical tension. Above all, Burns's use of counterpoint is inspired: while the Auld Licht preachers send souls to 'Hell, whare devils dwell', Burns's sensual sympathies are with 'The lads an lasses, blythely bent/To mind baith saul an body'. Burns is no passive observer, but a poet intent on stamping his personality on the scene he evokes.

THE VISION

Text   62/CW, 114–21.

Composition   Kinsley dates the poem, on the evidence of the Stair Manuscript (sent to Mrs Stewart of Stair in September 1786), to 'after August 1785' (Kinsley, 1072).

Publication   First published in abbreviated form in the Kilmarnock Edition (31 July 1786) then, with restorations from the manuscript, and additional stanzas, in the First Edinburgh Edition (17 April 1787). 'Burns's rejection of many of these stanzas in 1786–7 is probably due, more than anything else, to his concern with the balance of the poem' (Kinsley, 1071).

Reception   James Currie, in *The Works of Robert Burns* (1800), thought the second Duan of 'The Vision' represented 'an elevated and solemn strain of poetry, ranking in all respects, excepting the harmony of numbers, with the higher productions of the English muse' (CH, 141). Francis Jeffrey, writing in the *Edinburgh Review* of January 1809, felt 'If Burns had never written any thing else, the power of description, and the vigour of the whole composition, would have entitled him to the remembrance of posterity' (CH, 190–1). George Gleig, *A Critique on the Poems of Robert Burns* (1812), found the poem flawed because the poet 'describes [Coila's] dress and apperance with great propriety; but he seems to have viewed herself and her actions, to use the words of Dryden, "through the spectacles of books"' (CH, 253). Allan Cunningham, *The Works of Robert Burns* (1834), wrote '"The Vision" reveals the Poet's plan of Providence, proves the worth of eloquence, bravery, honesty and beauty, and that even the rustic bard himself is an useful and ornamental link in the great chain of being' (CH, 413). Tom Crawford suggests:

> It is the very summit of Burns's work as a national poet – symbolised, not only by Coila, but by 'the Genius of this Land' . . . 'The Vision' displays an emotional and intellectual awareness of historical processes that can be paralleled among his contemporaries only in the work of William Blake. I should say that Blake is the greater poet [but in] this one magnificent but little-read poem, Burns attains something of Blake's visionary insight, though by very different means. (Crawford, 192)

*   *   *

'The Vision', as printed in the Kilmarnock Edition, comprises thirty-eight Standard Habbie stanzas divided into two Duans (a term Burns derived from James 'Ossian' Macpherson's 'Cath-loda'): fifteen stanzas in 'Duan First', twenty-three in 'Duan Second'. In the First Edinburgh Edition the poem comprises forty-six stanzas, twenty-two in 'Duan First'. Amusingly, the Kilmarnock text, published when Burns was estranged from Jean Armour, compares Coila's shapely leg to that of Elizabeth Paton: 'And such a *leg*! my BESS, I ween,/Could only peer it'; in the First Edinburgh

Edition this has become: 'And such a leg! my bonie Jean/Could only peer it'.

A prose account of the poetic impulse behind 'The Vision' is given in an entry, for August 1785, in the first Common Place Book where Burns deplores the literary neglect of his native Ayrshire:

> I am pleased with the works of our Scotch Poets, particularly the excellent Ramsay, and the still more excellent Ferguson, yet I am hurt to see other places of Scotland, their towns, rivers, woods, haughs, &c., immortalized in such celebrated performances, whilst . . . we have never had one Scotch Poet of any eminence, to make the fertile banks of Irvine, the romantic woodlands and sequestered scenes on Aire, and the heathy mountainous source, and winding sweep of Doon, emulate Tay, Forth, Ettrick Tweed, &c., this is a complaint I would gladly remedy but Alas! I am far unequal to the task both in native genius and education. (CB, 46–7)

Pursuing his determination to be just such a 'Scotch Poet', Burns names his muse Coila after Kyle, his own district of Ayrshire. In a letter of 7 March 1788 to Mrs Dunlop (CL, 141), Burns explained that he derived the notion of Coila from Dr James Beattie's use of the muse Scota in his vernacular poem 'To Mr Alexander Ross at Lochlee'.

Burns draws on the tradition of the muse-inspired poet, an idiom he had certainly encountered in Beattie's poem, possibly in Cowley's 'The Complaint' (he owned a copy of Cowley's works though when he acquired it is not known), obliquely in Pope's mock-epic *The Rape of the Lock*. Imaginatively renewing this tradition, Burns offers a series of contrasts. The first, and most compelling, is the contrast between the physical exhaustion of Burns the man and the visionary ecstasy of Burns the poet. Weary after a long day's work, Burns sits musing – the homely use of the habit of musing sets up the appearance of the poetic muse – on the ways he has wasted his time since he was a boy. As he looks into the fire in Mossgiel he sees smoke filling 'The auld, clay biggin'. As the flames of a fire frequently prompt the perceptive spectator to rearrange them in familiar forms, this reference to the 'auld, clay biggin' can be read as a flashback to the cottage built by his father at Alloway. Kinsley worries over the precise 'auld clay biggin' mentioned by

Burns, saying 'Burns's setting is more like the house at Lochlie, where he lived until 1784, than Mossgiel' (Kinsley, 1075). However, as Burns is giving a visionary, not documentary, account of his past it is appropriate that he should recall his father's house where he was born and where the muse claimed him (so 'The Vision' declares) at his 'natal hour'. Burns had moved into Mossgiel in March 1784, the month after his father's death; and Lochlea, the farm that ruined his father, would have distressing connotations at the time he composed 'The Vision'. It is safe to say that, staking his claim as a poet, Burns retreated to fondly-remembered territory, the'auld clay biggin' at Alloway.

By choosing the life of the rhymer he has denied himself a decent life and a rewarding career as, for example, a bank clerk. Though there is irony in the option of security through banking, the longing for financial stability is genuine enough and often mentioned in the poetry and prose of Burns. His melancholy mood, expressed in a catalogue of self-reproaches, is transformed by the appearance of Coila. The first stanza devoted to her is lively with internal rhymes (click/snick; tight/sight), much swifter than the preceeding stanzas:

> All in this mottie, misty clime,
> I backward mus'd on wasted time:
> How I had spent my youthfu prime,
>   An done naething,
> But stringing blethers up in rhyme,
>   For fools to sing.
>
> Had I to guid advice but harkit,
> I might, by this, hae led a market,
> Or strutted in a bank and clarkit
>   My cash-account:
> While here, half-mad, half-fed, half-sarkit,
>   Is a' th'amount.
>
> I started, mutt'ring 'Blockhead! coof!'
> An heav'd on high my waukit loof,
> To swear by a' yon starry roof,
>   Or some rash aith,
> That I henceforth would be rhyme-proof
>   Till my last breath –

When click! the string the snick did draw;
And jee! the door gaed to the wa;
And by my ingle-lowe I saw,
    Now bleezin bright,
A tight, outlandish hizzie, braw,
    Come full in sight.

Speechless by the sight, Burns recognises the apparition as indigenous, as 'some Scottish Muse' crowned with a wreath of holly and dressed in a large green gown and tartan robe. (Tartan had been proscribed after the defeat of the clans at Culloden, 1746, and permitted in 1782, so the outfit has a symbolic charge.)

In the muse's mantle Burns sees the becoming contours of Ayrshire rippling with the rivers Doon, Irvine, Ayr 'And many a lesser torrent'. He sees the 'ancient borough' of Ayr and reflects on the heroic figures associated with the place: Sir William Wallace, 'His Country's Saviour'; Adam Wallace of Riccarton, cousin of Sir William Wallace; Sir John Wallace, who 'glorious fell' at the Scottish victory over the English at Sark in 1448; Sir William Wallace Dunlop, forced to sell his Craigie estate in 1783, 'he whom ruthless fates expel/His native land'; the Montgomeries of Coilsfield, 'a martial race'; Alexander Boswell of Auchinleck, 'An aged Judge . . . Dispensing good'; Matthew Stewart and Dugald Stewart, 'learned Sir and Son', both Professors at Edinburgh University; Colonel William Fullarton, 'brave ward' of Patrick Brydone. With this catalogue of local heroes (the use of the catalogue being crucial to Burns's insistent approach) the first Duan ends.

Apart from its first and final stanzas, the second Duan reports the speech of the 'native Muse' who calls Burns to the exalted company of great Scots. She praises a soldier, Colonel William Fullarton (see 'The Burns Circle'); a patriotic orator, George Dempster, MP for Forfar Burghs from 1761–90; and Dr James Beattie, both as poet and philosophical opponent of 'The sceptic' David Hume. Compared to these public figures the poet takes his place with the common people:

'To lower orders are assign'd
The humbler ranks of human-kind,
The rustic bard, the laboring hind,
    The artisan;

> All chuse, as various they're inclin'd,
>   The various man.'

The work such folk do is crucial to the cultural development of
Scotland, which needs farmers and shepherds as well as its poets.
And its poets need 'A guide and guard'. That said, the Muse names
herself:

> 'Of these am I – Coila my name:
> And this district as mine I claim,
> Where once the Campbells, chiefs of fame,
>   Held ruling pow'r:
> I mark'd thy embryo-tuneful flame,
>   Thy natal hour.

(The reference to the Campbells refers to the fact that the poet's
farm, Mossgiel, was part of the Loudon estate, long associated with
the Campbell Earls of Loudon.)

Burns, then, according to Coila, was born a poet (the 'natal
hour' goes back to 'The auld, clay biggin'), singled out to sing
the praises of his own area. As such he cannot compete with
James Thomson's delineation of the landscape, or with William
Shenstone's 'bosom-melting' sentimental verse; or with Thomas
Gray's emotional power. However, he can perform wonders as 'A
rustic bard'. Coila's last words of advice dissolve into a departure
after which Burns will presumably wake from his dream and
practise his rustic art:

> 'To give my counsels all in one,
> Thy tuneful flame still careful fan;
> Preserve the dignity of Man,
>   With soul erect:
> And trust the Universal Plan
>   Will all protect.

> 'And wear thou *this*' – She solemn said,
> And bound the holly round my head:
> The polish'd leaves and berries red
>   Did rustling play;

And, like a passing thought, she fled
In light away.

'The Vision', with its hero-worship of the landed gentry of Ayrshire
and its humility before the supposedly superior poetic gifts of such
as Shenstone, is too diffident in outlook to be truly visionary. The
humble tone does not do justice to the poet's talent and he only
asserted himself adequately when he aspired to a larger, more
universal, ideal than that represented by Coila, a local muse. 'The
Vision' is one of Burns's most parochial poems, nostalgic rather than
prophetic, a fireside doze rather than an illuminating dream, and it
goes back to 'The auld, clay biggin' of his birth rather than forward
to the grandeur of being a national poet.

HALLOWEEN

Text   73/CW, 151–7.

Composition   Written at Mossgiel in 1785, probably late autumn.

Publication   First published in the Kilmarnock Edition (31 July
1786).

Reception   James Anderson (reviewing the Kilmarnock Edition in
the *Monthly Review*, December 1786) found the poem of considerable documentary interest: 'It is a valuable relic, which . . . will
preserve the memory of these simple incantations long after they
would otherwise have been lost' (CH, 73). Citing the stanza beginning 'Whyles owre a linn the burnie plays', James Currie (*The
Works of Robert Burns*, 1800) thought the passage 'to be one of the
finest instances of description, which the records of poetry affords'
(CH, 139).

Hazlitt (*Lectures on the English Poets*, 1818) admired the poem
for its 'striking and picturesque description of local customs and
scenery' (CH, 302). Carlyle, reviewing Lockhart's *Life of Burns* (in
the *Edinburgh Review*, December 1828), wrote: 'Our *Halloween* had
passed and repassed, in rude awe and laughter, since the era of the
Druids; but no Theocritus, till Burns, discerned in it the materials of
a Scottish Idyll' (CH, 360). Allan Cunningham (*The Works of Robert
Burns with his Life*, 1834) approved of the 'happy mixture of the
dramatic and the descriptive' and the way in which the poem
'hovers between the serious and the ludicrous' (CH, 404–5).

Snyder thought the poem 'a relatively unsuccessful attempt to record in verse popular customs which Burns considered little more than children's games' (Snyder, 461–2). Crawford considers that in 'Halloween' Burns is unable to raise the parochial material to a higher artistic level:

Here, for once [in connecting local and national themes], he fails: and he fails because, for all its movement and activity, the poem does not *develop*. It revolves upon a single spot; and, furthermore, it seems to narrow in smaller and smaller gyrations. (Crawford, 123)

Kinsley says:

The antiquarian bias of 'Halloween' is obvious, both in the head-note and in Burns's foot-notes . . . and this bias, which may partly account for the unusually heavy mixture of dialect, holds Burns a little too far out from the action and sentiment of 'Halloween'. (Kinsley, 1118)

Burns clearly projected 'Halloween' as a set piece he was proud of, since the Kilmarnock Edition introduces the poem with a paragraph ending:

The passion of prying into Futurity makes a striking part of the history of Human-nature, in its rude state, in all ages and nations; and it may be some entertainment to a philosophical mind, if any such should honour the Author with a perusal, to see the remains of it, among the more unenlightened in our own.

A footnote (the first of many) explains the title of the poem:

It is thought to be a night when Witches, Devils, and other mischief-making beings, are all abroad on their baneful, midnight errands; particularly, those aerial people, the Fairies, are said, on that night, to hold a grand Anniversary.

*   *   *

Halloween, marking the beginning of the winter half of the year, is the eve of All Hallows (All Saints), 31 October. A Christian festival deriving from the winter festival of the pagan Celts, it was celebrated in Scotland as the night on which humans were able to discover, through rituals, what the future held for them especially in terms of marriage. The festival was still celebrated in Burns's time though his own experience was influenced by the stories told him by his mother, by Betty Davidson and by his cousin Jenny Broun who is mentioned as 'Wee Jenny' in the thirteenth stanza. Composed in the Christis Kirk stanza, 'Halloween' contains more old Scots words than any other Burns poem, another indication of its linguistic roots in the memories of an older generation.

In the first stanza Burns locates the poem 'On Cassilis Downans' – that is the hillocks of Cassillis, six miles south of Ayr – where the fairies dance. The second stanza mentions Robert the Bruce, thus adding Scottish national history to fairy folklore. Burns is portraying a magical world that is part of the rural and historical reality of Scotland. It is in this context that the common 'country-folks' are seen to hold their Halloween, their robust physicality reinforcing the sense of reality:

> The lasses feat an cleanly neat,
>   Mair braw than when they're fine;
> Their faces blythe fu sweetly kythe,
>   Hearts leal, an warm, an kin:
> The lads sae trig, wi wooer-babs
>   Weel-knotted on their garten;
> Some unco blate, and some wi gabs
>   Gar lasses' hearts gang startin
>   Whyles fast at night.

Immediately the lads and lasses begin the ceremonies of Halloween, first pulling cabbage plants. When the girls come to pull cornstalks, sexual desire asserts itself. Burns explains, in a footnote, that if the third stalk lacks the top-pickle (the grain at the end of the stalk) the girl will lose her maidenhead, but clearly this occurs anyway regardless of the ritual.

> The lasses staw frae 'mang them a',
>   To pou their stalks o corn;
> But Rab slips out, an jinks about,

> Behint the muckle thorn:
> He grippet Nelly hard an fast;
> Loud skirl'd a' the lasses;
> But her tap-pickle maist was lost,
> Whan kiutlin in the fause-house
> Wi him that night.

Rab clearly does not stand on ceremony.

There follows the ritual of burning nuts which, according to whether they flame together or suddenly separate, determine the course of a courtship. Jean and Jock watch their nuts separate, as do Willie and Mallie. Nelly, however, her mind on erotic adventures in the fause-house, watches her nut flaming with Rab's:

> Nell's heart was dancin at the view;
> She whisper'd Rob to leuk for't:
> Rob, stownlins, prie'd her bonie mou,
> Fu cozie in the neuk for't,
> Unseen that night.

Burns's humour has a serious point in showing the atrophy of ancient rituals for while the lads and lasses decide their own destinies, the old wives, like Jenny Broun's granny, take the rituals seriously. She recalls a Halloween harvest before 'the Sherra-moor' (the battle of Sheriffmuir in 1715) when the chief harvester went insane by mocking the ceremony of sowing a handful of hemp-seed to bind a relationship. Dismissing this story as 'nonsense', Jamie Fleck goes out to sow hemp-seed but he eventually takes fright, so fearful of the power of the custom that a pig's grunt alarms him.

Anecdotes proliferate, with Meg searching for the Devil in the barn, Will mistaking an old moss-oak for his intended, the wanton widow Leezie plunging into a pool while looking for a lover. As all this goes on while Rab is caressing Nelly in the fause-house, the scenario is shared by the shrewd lads and lassies; and the daft older folk. 'Halloween' shows a communal way of life in transition, superstition losing its grip on a new generation. Burns himself, who was sceptical of supersition while enthusiastic about its artistic power, ends the poem by showing the social strength of the Halloween ceremony in bringing the community together, if only for this night.

> Wi merry sangs, an friendly cracks,

I wat they did na weary;
And unco tales, an funnie jokes –
Their sports were cheap an cheery:
Till butter'd sow'ns, wi fragrant lunt,
Set a' their gabs a-steerin;
Syne, wi a social glass o strunt,
They parted aff careerin
Fu blythe that night.

Burns's attitude is ambivalent. The headnote and footnotes are directed towards readers of 'a philosophic mind' who need information about 'the more unenlightened': by implication a writer capable of providing such information is himself of 'a philosophic mind'. Moreover Burns was writing about a subject already explored in John Mayne's 'Halloween', printed, in November 1780, in Walter Ruddiman's *Weekly Magazine* (in which many of Fergusson's poems were first published). Still, the poem has an emotional as well as an antiquarian and literary interest: the erotic encounter of Rab and Nelly is a poetic piece of wishful thinking reaching back to Burns's infatuation with Nelly Kilpatrick during a Mount Oliphant harvest of 1774, the event that prompted his first song.

THE TWA DOGS

Text   71/CW, 140–6.

Composition   Listed as complete in Burns's letter of 17 February 1786 to John Richmond: 'I have likewise compleated my Poem on the dogs, but have not shown it to the world' (CL, 76). This remark leads Kinsley to argue that the poem was 'begun earlier than the other poems [in his list] and that it was planned, and probably in part written, before Richmond left Ayrshire in November 1785' (Kinsley, 1105).

Publication   First published in the Kilmarnock Edition (31 July 1786).

Reception   James Currie, *The Works of Robert Burns* (1800), enthused over Burns's combination of realism and ridicule:

The dogs of Burns, excepting in their talent for moralizing, are downright dogs; and not the Horses of Swift, or the *Hind and*

Panther of Dryden, men in the shapes of brutes. It is this circumstance that heightens the humour of the dialogue. The 'twa dogs' are constantly kept before our eyes, and the contrast beween their form and character as dogs, and the sagacity of their conversation, heightens the humour, and deepens the impression of the poet's satire. Though in this poem the chief excellence may be considered as humour, yet great talents are displayed in its composition; the happiest powers of description, and the deepest insight into the human heart. (CH, 135)

Josiah Walker, *Account of the Life and Character of Robert Burns* (1811), was similarly impressed:

Whether [Burns] addresses, or supplies language to inanimate and irrational objects, it is so suitable and unforced, and appears so gravely in earnest, as to render the fable more delusive, and the personifications more credible, than is commonly the case in similar attempts. His 'Twa Dogs' exercise their reason with the most sober propriety. (CH, 230)

Lecturing 'On Burns, and the Old English Ballads', at the Surrey Institution in 1817, William Hazitt declared: 'His "Twa Dogs" is a very spirited piece of description, both as it respects the animal and human creation, and conveys a very vivid idea of the manners both of high and low life' (CH, 302). Allan Cunningham, *The Works of Robert Burns* (1834), stressed the moral point of the poem: 'His "Twa Dogs" prove that happiness is not unequally diffused"' (CH, 413).

Modern critics have been less impressed by the poem: Snyder makes no judgement of it, Hecht mentions it in passing, Crawford compares it to Cervantes's *Colloquy of the Dogs* (Crawford, 169-74).

*　　　　　*　　　　　*

Gilbert Burns said that 'The Twa Dogs' was written after the poet had decided to publish a volume of verse:

Robert had had a dog, which he called Luath, that was a great favourite. The dog had been killed [on 12 February 1784] by the wanton cruelty of some person the night before my father's death. Robert said to me, that he should like to confer such immortality as he could bestow upon his old friend Luath, and that he had a great mind to introduce something into the book under the title of 'Stanzas to the Memory of a quadruped Friend'; but this plan was given up for the 'Tale' as it now stands. Caesar was merely the creature of the poet's imagination. (cited by Kinsley, 1104)

Burns modelled the poem structurally on Fergusson's 'Mutual Complaint of Plainstanes and Causey, in their Mother-Tongue', a Scots dialogue in octosyllabic couplets between Edinburgh street and pavement. The poem, however, is inventive rather than derivative; Fergusson's dialogue (between inanimate objects, not animals) is fanciful whereas Burns's is deeply felt, and no previous Scots-speaking poetic animals (in Henryson's *Moral Fables* or Hamilton of Gilbertfield's 'Bonnie Heck' for example) have the authority of Caesar. Burns was obviously proud of the poem: he placed 'The Twa Dogs, A Tale' first in the Kilmarnock Edition, a book he arranged with care.

The poem opens with a passage placing the time in summer ('a bonie day in June') and setting the scene in the Ayrshire district of Kyle, 'that place o Scotland's Isle,/That bears the name of auld King Coil'; King Coil was an imaginary figure who Burns relates to the nursery-rhyme hero, thus preparing the reader for an imaginative encounter between two dogs who meet (again the nursery-rhyme reference) 'ance upon a time'. The first dog is a Newfoundland, 'whalpit some place far abroad,/Whare sailors gang to fish for cod'. Caesar, the Newfoundland, is a the pride and joy of his wealthy master and himself a 'gentleman and scholar' though free from stand-offish snobbery: 'nae pride had he;/But wad hae spent an hour caressin,/Ev'n wi a tinkler-gipsy's messan'.

Luath, the other dog, is the 'friend and comrade' of a ploughman-poet who has named the collie 'After some dog in Highland sang,/Was made lang syne – Lord knows how lang': James 'Ossian' Macpherson had given Fingal a dog named Luath but though Burns (like most of his contemporaries) enjoyed *Fingal* (1762) his joke about its antiquity suggests he was sceptical of Macpherson's claim to have translated, rather than fabricated, the Ossianic original. Luath is the animal equivalent of the poor-but-honest man Burns admired:

> He was a gash an faithfu tyke,
> As ever lap a sheugh or dyke.

> His honest, sonsie, baws'nt face
> Ay gat him friends in ilka place.

After nosing around the ground, the two dogs 'set them down upon their arse' and begin 'a lang digression/About the "lords of the creation"'.

Caeser speaks first, and immediately criticises the privileged life of the laird, defining him as a man whose comforts are achieved by exploitation:

> Our laird gets in his racked rents,
> His coals, his kain, an a' his stents:
> He rises when he likes himself;
> His flunkies answer at the bell;
> He ca's his coach; he ca's his horse;
> He draws a bonie silken purse,
> As lang's my tail, whare, thro the steeks,
> The yellow letter'd Geordie keeks.

Luath replies that the poor cotter, though living under the constant threat of 'cauld and hunger', still manages to keep his family 'wonderfu contented' (as, of course, he does through religious and domestic ritual in 'A Cotter's Saturday Night').

Caesar does not accept Luath's sentimental idyll and speaks forcefully in a passage that has a bitter biographical dimension. When William Burnes's landlord, Provost William Fergusson, died on 7 November 1769, the poet's father was answerable to the factor who handled the affairs of Mount Oliphant farm. Burns told Dr John Moore how Mount Oliphant 'proved a ruinous bargain; and, to clench the curse, we fell into the hands of a Factor who sat for the picture I have drawn of one in my Tale of two dogs' (AL). Burns's anger is obvious through Caesar's observation:

> I've notic'd, on our laird's court-day,
> (An monie a time my heart's been wae),
> Poor tenant bodies, scant o cash,
> How they maun thole a factor's snash:
> He'll stamp an threaten, curse an swear
> He'll apprehend them, poind their gear;
> While they maun stan, wi aspect humble,

> An hear it a', an fear an tremble!
> I see how folk live that hae riches;
> But surely poor-folk maun be wretches!

(The last couplet quoted uses a pararhyme as ingenious as any in Wilfred Owen.)

Luath argues that the poor are so accustomed to misery that it loses its terror. Conditioned from birth to expect the worst they make the best of the little they have, deriving comfort from the company of 'Their grushie weans an faithfu wives'; from drink and discussion of politics, 'patronage an priests'; from seasonal celebrations. Still, Luath concedes

> There's monie a creditable stock
> O decent, honest, fawsont folk,
> Are riven out baith root an branch,
> Some rascal's pridefu greed to quench,
> Wha thinks to knit himsel the faster
> In favor wi some gentle master,
> Wha, aiblins thrang a parliamentin,
> For Britain's guid his saul indentin –

Caesar denies that good comes into it, listing the time-wasting, money-draining, soul-destroying ways of the far-from-gentle masters: 'For Britain's guid! for her destruction!/Wi dissipation, feud an faction.' That argumenative exchange clarifies the characters of the two dogs and shows the potential playwright in Burns.

Bowing to Caesar's superior knowledge, Luath asks his friend to assess the human condition of 'great folk'. Sarcastically, Caesar obliges with an image of death by decadence, showing the gentry boring themselves to death by avoiding useful work:

> But gentlemen, an ladies warst,
> Wi ev'n down want o wark are curst.
> They loiter, lounging, lank an lazy;
> Tho deil-haet ails them, yet uneasy:
> Their days insipid, dull an tasteless;
> Their nights unquiet, lang an restless.

By the end of Caesar's speech 'the sun was out o sight' and the two friends get up: 'When up they gat an shook their lugs/Rejoic'd they were na *men* but *dogs*'. The reminder still comes as a surprise, as the reader inevitably suspends disbelief during the lively debate.

The poem has psychological subtlety for Burns reverses expectations by putting the case for the poor in the mouth of the rich character, thus reinforcing the impression the poor dog gives of being conditioned into submission by the poverty the rich dog condemns. Stylistically the poem shows a skill with the octosyllabic couplet that will become mastery in 'Tam o Shanter'. Politically, the poem has maturity in expanding a personal experience (of the Factor) into an objective critique of inequality. As for the dogs, they function on two levels: as fabulous creatures they have the charm of their kind; as human-substitutes they have a commendable kindness. Luath's humility looks back to older animal fables, Caesar's political bite looks forward to Orwell and *Animal Farm*.

THE JOLLY BEGGARS

Text   84/CW, 182–91.

Composition   Burns probably composed the sequence in Autumn 1785, before November when John Richmond left Ayrshire for Edinburgh. According to Richmond it was prompted by a visit the poet made to Poosie Nansie's tavern in Mauchline (possibly in September or October 1785) where he was greatly amused by 'much jollity amongst a company who by day appeared abroad as miserable beggars' (cited by Snyder, 163). After a few days Burns recited part of the poem to Richmond who said the work, at that time, included songs by a sweep and a sailor.

Publication   Published, by Thomas Stewart, as *The Jolly Beggars: or Tatterdemallions. A Cantata* (1799) and included in Stewart's edition of *Poems ascribed to Robert Burns, the Ayrshire Bard* (1801). It is titled 'Love and Liberty' in Burns's fair copy in Edinburgh University Library.

Reception   Sir Walter Scott, in the first issue of the *Quarterly Review* (February 1809), confessed himself at a loss as to why Currie had omitted the poem from his edition of Burns. For Scott, 'The Jolly Beggars' was 'inferior to no poem of the same length in the whole range of English poetry' (CH, 197). Scott's son-in-law Lockhart, in *Peter's Letters to His Kinsfolk* (1819), took a similar view:

> By the way, this inimitable Cantata is not to be found in Currie's edition, and I suspect you are a stranger even to its name; and

yet, had Burns left nothing more than this behind him, I think he would still have left enough to justify all the honour in which his genius is held. There does not exist, in any one piece throughout the whole range of English poetry, such a collection of true, fresh, and characteristic lyrics. (CH, 307)

Reviewing Lockhart's *Life of Burns*, in the *Edinburgh Review* (December 1828), Thomas Carlyle acclaimed the work:

The subject truly is among the lowest in Nature; but it only the more shews our Poet's gift in raising it into the domain of Art. To our minds, this piece seems thoroughly compacted; melted together, refined; and poured forth in one flood of true *liquid* harmony. It is light, airy, soft of movement; yet sharp and precise in its details; every face is a portrait; that *raucle carlin*, that *wee Apollo*, that *Son of Mars*, are Scottish, yet ideal; the scene is at once a dream, and the very Ragcastle of 'Poosie-Nansie'. Farther, it seems in a considerable degree complete, a real self-supporting Whole, which is the highest merit in a poem. (CH, 368)

Matthew Arnold ('The Study of Poetry', in *Essays in Criticism*, Second Series, 1888) preferred the cantata to 'Tam o Shanter':

In the world of 'The Jolly Beggars', there is more than hideousness and squalor, there is bestiality; yet the piece is a superb poetic success. It has a breadth, truth, and power which makes the famous scene in Auerbach's cellar, of Goethe's *Faust*, seem artificial and tame beside it, and which are only matched by Shakespeare and Aristophanes. (ed. P. J. Keating, *Matthew Arnold: Selected Prose*, Harmondsworth, 1970, p. 364)

Modern critics have been equally enthusiastic. Referring to Matthew Arnold's description of the cantata as a 'puissant and splendid production', Snyder exclaimed: 'Never again was he to give such sure indication of his genius as in this "puissant production", which he wrote and suppressed!' (Snyder, 165). Crawford calls it 'a great lyrical dramatic poem' (Crawford, 132). Fitzhugh is equally ecstatic, asking 'Where at all . . . is there anything to approach *Love and Liberty*?' (Fitzhugh, 293). Kinsley writes:

Burns's setting and characters, and even more the attitudes they express, make an anti-pastoral – or a 'true' pastoral – of 'Love and Liberty' [also known as 'The Jolly Beggars']. The cantata celebrates an old myth: the belief in the content and 'truest happiness' of vagabond life which underlies the tradition of beggar-songs, and which Burns expressed more than once ['Epistle to Davie, a Brother Poet', ll. 29–70; 'Extempore Epistle to Mr McAdam of Craigengillan', ll. 17–20). But for all that, and despite the reflection of current revolutionary ideas in the songs, there is nothing mythical or idealized about Burns's beggars. (Kinsley, 1150)

*   *   *

Burns planned to publish 'The Jolly Beggars' in the First Edinburgh Edition of 1787 but was persuaded against its inclusion by Hugh Blair who commented:

> The Whole of What is called the Cantata, the Songs of the Beggars and their Doxies, with the Grace at the end of them, are altogether unfit in my opinion for publication. They are by much too licentious; and fall below the dignity which Mr Burns possesses in the rest of his poems & would rather degrade them. (CH, 82)

By September 1793, writing to George Thomson, Burns professed himself ignorant of the work:

> I have forgot the Cantata you allude to, as I kept no copy, & indeed did not know that it was in existence; however, I remember that none of the songs pleased myself, except the last – something about,
>
>   'Courts for cowards were erected,
>   Churches built to please the priest' (CL, 644)

By then, of course, he was an exciseman whose political opinions had caused offence in Dumfries and he may well have preferred, in the circumstances, to put such a subversive sequence as 'The Jolly Beggars' behind him for obvious reasons.

There are various precedents for Burns's presentation of beggars: the sixteenth-century vernacular songs 'The Gaberlunzie Man' and 'The Jolly Beggar'; seventeenth-century ballads; eighteenth-century burlesque cantatas; the choric song 'The Happy Beggars' and the cantata 'Merry Beggars' in Allan Ramsay's *The Tea-Table Miscellany* (1724–37); and John Gay's *The Beggar's Opera* (which Burns mentions in his letters). Like Brecht in the twentieth century, with his *Threepenny Opera*, Burns (with his frequently expressed resentment of the rich and sympathy with the poor) saw a revolutionary point in the condition of poverty and made it forcefully by shaping his cantata towards a political end. The chorus, by his own admission the most memorable section of the sequence, offers Liberty as a feast to the hungry and condemns the privileged as the enemy of the people.

Structurally, the cantata consists of eight arias linked by eight recitativos. The songs are (with the exception of the fiddler's song and the tinker's song) largely composed in a Scots-accented English. The recitativos are in broad Scots and show Burns as a master of various metrical forms: the first recitativo ('When lyart leaves bestrow the yird') adapts the Cherrie and the Slae stanza, the fifth recitativo ('A pigmy scraper on a fiddle') uses the Standard Habbie stanza, the seventh recitativo ('The caird prevail'd: th'unblushing fair') adapts the Christis Kirk stanza. Surprisingly, the stanzaic variety brings unity to the sequence, sharply individualising each speaker and indicating the swift shifts of mood typical of a motley gathering in a Scottish tavern.

The energy of the occasion is simulated in Burns's first recitato which uses alliteration to convey the cold outside the tavern, and internal rhyme to suggest the warmth inside:

> When lyart leaves bestrow the yird,
> Or, wavering like the bauckie-bird,
>   Bedim cauld Boreas' blast;
> When hailstanes drive wi bitter skyte,
> And infant frosts begin to bite,,
>   In hoary cranreuch drest;
> Ae night at e'en a merry core
> O randie, gangrel bodies,
> In Poosie-Nansie's held the splore,
> To drink their orra duddies:
>   Wi quaffing and laughing;
>   They ranted as they sang,
>   Wi jumping and thumping,
>   The vera girdle rang.

Having set the scene, Burns focuses on the first two singers, a soldier and his doxy. Each detail is significant, for example the soldier wears not just any old rags, but 'auld red rags', the tatters of the uniform he wore 'when I us'd in scarlet to follow a drum'. As he does throughout the sequence, Burns not only indicates the appearance and character of the singers, but involves them in action: the soldier hugs and kisses his doxy, she encourages his kisses with 'her greedy gab'.

That scenario is repeated with the third singer, the professional fool who 'Sat guzzling wi a tinkler-hussy'. These couples heighten the isolation of the fourth singer, the weeping widow whose appearance excites the interest of the fifth and sixth singers, the fiddler ('The wee Apollo') and the tinker ('a sturdy caird'), so much so that a brawl erupts in the pivotal sixth recitativo:

> Her charms had struck a sturdy caird,
>   As well as poor gut-scraper;
> He taks the fiddler by the beard,
>   An' draws a roosty rapier;
> He swoor by a' was swearing worth,
>   To speet him like a pliver,
> Unless he would from that time forth
>   Relinquish her for ever.

Typically, the drunken beggars fight among themselves but the squabbling ceases at the entrance of the bard who unites the beggars, first in applause, then in singing the revolutionary chorus that ends the cantata.

The songs themselves have the character of dramatic monologues, each revealing something about the singer. The soldier's song ('I am a son of Mars, who have been in many wars') uses a quatrain rich in internal rhymes to present a character who is unconsciously absurd in his unthinking willingness to sacrifice life and limb for any cause his country (or region of North Britain) imposes on him (Admiral Sir Roger Curtis's destruction of the French floating batteries in 1782, General George Elliot's defence of Gibraltar in 1783):

> I lastly was with Curtis among the floating batt'ries,
>   And there I left for witness an arm and a limb;
> Yet let my country need me, with Elliot to head me,
>   I'd clatter on my stumps at the sound of the drum.

Such bravado was not original for in the ballad 'Chevy Chase' (widely available in broadsides during the eighteenth century) one quatrain explains:

> For Witherington needs must I wayle
> As one in dolefull dumpes,
> For when his leggs were smitten of,
> He fought upon his stumpes.

Seeing the dark comedy in that convention, Burns allows his soldier of misfortune to make a bizarre example of himself by his boasts.

Repeating the phrase 'at the sound of the drum' in each quatrain, Burns simulates the regular march of the soldier preparing for battle. With his active service a thing of the past this particular soldier is only a casualty of war. He has learned nothing positive from his experiences – except the use of drink to dull what senses he retains. Though he is reduced to to the ranks of the beggar, and handicapped with his 'wooden arm and leg' (the spoils of war), this old soldier persuades himself that he is forever marching on, 'happy with my wallet, my bottle and my callet'. The irony is at its most intense in the last line of the soldier's song as the man boasts 'I could meet a troop of Hell, at the sound of a drum'. He has already been through hell without ever emerging from it.

Sung by the soldier's doxy, the second song ('I once was a maid, tho I cannot tell when') is poignant and ironical whereas the effect of the soldier's song is pitiful and ironical. Like her old soldier ('my old boy') the doxy ('the martial chuck') sings in a Scots-accented English rather than broad Scots, using the Scots 'sodger' (soldier) in the phrase that ends each quatrain. Two lines – one from the first stanza, the other from the fourth – best sum up the doxy's life: 'Some one of a troop of dragoons was my daddie'; 'The regiment at large for a husband I got'. Fathered by some soldier or other, she has followed her mother's example and received all comers until, worn out, she has been impoverished by the peace that makes paupers out of fighting men:

> But the Peace it reduc'd me to beg in despair,
> Till I met my old boy in a Cunningham Fair:
> His rags regimental they flutter'd so gaudy,
> My heart it rejoic'd at a sodger laddie.

A camp whore has become a beggar on the tramp, having nothing but holding on shakily to the comfort of drink: the spectacle of advanced alcoholism is vividly present in the line 'But whilst with

both hands I can hold the glass steady'. As sorry a spectacle as
her soldier, the doxy is projected by Burns as a victim of social
circumstances.

The fool's song ('Sir Wisdom's a fool when he's fou') plays games
with the notion of folly. Andrew, 'a fool by profession', is well
placed to observe the idiocy of those who take themselves seriously
so he mocks the Prime Minister ('A tumbler called the Premier') and
the local minister ('yon reverend lad') as his rivals in confusing 'the
mob' with absurd antics. Like Shakespeare's fools, Andrew is not so
'daft' as he seems for he has read books and been to school. Like
Burns himself he is fond of a drink ('For drink I would venture
my neck') and has been 'abus'd i' the kirk/For towsing a lass i'
my daffin'. If the irony here is self-conscious, the conclusion is still
effective:

> And now my conclusion I'll tell,
> For faith! I'm confoundedly dry:
> The chiel that's a fool for himself,
> Guid Lord! he's far dafter than I.

Andrew is well differentiated from the soldier and his doxy.
Whereas they are human ruins, he is his own construction, wise
about his own folly ('wise enough to play the fool', like the clown
in *Twelfth Night*).

Fourth in the sequence of songs is 'A highland lad my love
was born', sung by a sturdy old woman, 'a raucle carlin'. Taking
the date of the composition of 'The Jolly Beggars' as the date of
its action, then an old woman who mourns her widowhood in
1785 would have been young forty years before at the time of
the Jacobite rebellion. After the catastrophic defeat of the clans at
Culloden, the Hanoverian government, supported by the Scottish
Lowland establishment, prohibited clansmen from carrying arms
or wearing the tartan. The old woman's John Highlandman seems
more a symbol of political rebellion than a particular individual.
Despite the persecution of the clans, John Highlandman 'still was
faithfu to his clan'; despite the ban on Highland dress, he wore 'his
philibeg an tartan plaid'; despite the Disarming Act he had his 'guid
claymore down by his side'. He cared nothing for the 'lalland laws',
and 'For a lalland face he feared none'.

Encouraging this reading of John Highlandman as a symbol, the
old woman's song specifies two apparently contradictory penalties
inflicted on her hero: 'They banished him beyond the sea'; 'They've

hang'd my braw John Highlandman'. Exile and execution were two ways of dealing with recalcitrant clansmen and John Highlandman is thus portrayed as a tragic representative of his race. By this reckoning, the old woman is symbolic of a broken-hearted Scotland. Her tears are 'pearls', linking with a vanished way of life ('We ranged a' from Tweed to Spey,/An liv'd like lords and ladies gay'). The weeping widow's eyes are unfocused, her curse is directed against all the enemies of Scotland (English government and Lowland establishment):

> My curse upon them every one –
> They've hang'd my braw John Highlandman!

Far from bringing the sequence to a 'purely personal level' (Crawford, 137) the old woman's song speaks of the passion of a persecuted people.

The fifth song begins with the fiddler's response to the weeping widow:

> Let me ryke up to dight that tear,
> An go wi me an be my dear;
> An then your every care an fear
> May whistle owre the lave o't.

In the fiddler's song individual opportunism is offered as an alternative to tragic mourning. Like the birds of prey, in the ballad 'The Twa Corbies', gloating over the feast that lies behind a dyke, the fiddler and his companion will pick the bones of life clean:

> Sae merrily the banes we'll pyke,
> An sun oursels about the dyke;
> An at our leisure, when ye like,
> We'll – whistle owre the lave o't.

Confronted by cold, hunger and illness, the fiddler eagerly grabs whatever creature comforts come his way.

Jealous of the fiddler's overtures to the widow, a tinker ('a sturdy caird') asserts himself by threatening the fiddler, embracing the widow and singing the sixth song ('My bonie lass, I work in brass') to her. He advises her to reject the fiddler ('that shrimp, that wither'd imp') and, being in no position to offer financial security, promises sexual satisfaction:

> An by that stowp! my faith an houpe!

> And by that dear Kilbaigie!
> If e'er ye want, or meet wi scant,
>   May I ne'er weet my craigie.

The widow duly succumbs to the tinker but spares time for the fiddler who takes her behind the hen-coop.

The last two songs are sung by a bard, a travelling ballad-singer, 'a care-defying blade' as fond of the bottle as he is of his ballads. The bard's first song ('I am a Bard of no regard') establishes him as a poet of the common people, a poet sustained by alcoholic drink rather than the Castalian stream sacred to Apollo and the Muses:

> I never drank the Muses' stank,
>   Castalia's burn, an a' that;
> But there it streams, and richly reams –
>   My Helicon I ca' that.

The song ('See the smoking bowl before us') with which he concludes the whole cantata is, appropriately enough, a tribute to the sexual warmth and human worth of the common people, the rhetorical questions and the chorus condemning the established social structure as a strategy for suppressing such folk:

> With the ready trick and fable,
>   Round we wander all the day;
> And at night, in barn or stable,
>   Hug our doxies on the hay.
>
> Does the train-attended carriage,
>   Thro the country lighter rove?
> Does the sober bed of marriage
>   Witness brighter scenes of love?
>
> Life is all a variorum,
>   We regard not how it goes;
> Let them prate about decorum,
>   Who have character to lose.
>
> Here's to budgets, bags and wallets!
> Here's to all the wandering train!
> Here's our ragged brats and callets!
>   One and all, cry out, Amen!
>
> *A fig for those by law protected!*

> *Liberty's a glorious feast!*
> *Courts for cowards were erected,*
> *Churches built to please the priest!*

Thus the cantata ends with the spectacle of the assembled company on their feet with the bard – He 'rising, rejoicing', they 'Impatient for the chorus' – to join in a song whose revolutionary implications offer an alternative to the drunken condition and limited consciousness of the beggars.

Four years before the French Revolution, then, Burns is singing a song of Liberty celebrating the fraternity of the poor, and asserting the equality of humankind. His revolutionary song is inspired not only by the American example but by a direct contact with the vulnerable victims of an institutionalised inequality. It must have occured to Burns that he, given a less enlightened father, might have become a beggar, jolly or otherwise, and his instincts told him that such characters were not born as contemptibly inferior beings but bred to be exploited by a viciously divided society.

THE COTTER'S SATURDAY NIGHT

Text   72/CW, 147–51.

Composition   Composed during the winter of 1785–6 (the second stanza begins by invoking 'November chill') the poem was listed as complete in Burns's letter of 17 February 1786 to John Richmond (CL, 76).

Publication   First published in the Kilmarnock Edition (31 July 1786).

Reception   John Logan, Scottish minister and writer, singled the poem out for special praise in the *English Review* (February 1787): '"The Cotter's (Cottager's) Saturday Night" is, without exception, the best poem in the collection. It is written in the stanza of Spenser, which, probably our bard acquired from Thomson's "Castle of Indolence" and Beattie's "Minstrel"' (CH, 77). David Irving, *The Lives of the Scottish Poets* (1804), considered the poem 'The most exquisite of his serious poems . . . . The incidents are well selected, the characters skilfully distinguished, and the whole composition is remarkable for the propriety and sensibility which it displays' (CH, 164–5).

Writing in the *Edinburgh Review* (January, 1809) Francis Jeffrey invoked the poem to illustrate Burns's use of pathos: 'The exquisite description of "the Cotter's Saturday Night" affords, perhaps, the finest example of this sort of pathetic. Its whole beauty cannot, indeeed, be discerned but by those whom experience has enabled to judge of the admirable fidelity and completeness of the picture' (CH, 187). George Gleig assured readers of his *A Critique on the Poems of Robert Burns* (1812) that 'The "Saturday Night" is indeed universally felt as the most interesting of all the author's poems' (CH, 253). William Hazlitt, lecturing 'On Burns and the Old English Ballads' in 1818, responded to the moral tone of the poem: '"The Cotter's Saturday Night" is a noble and pathetic picture of human manners, mingled with a fine religious awe. It comes over the mind like a slow and solemn strain of music' (CH, 303). John Wilson, comparing the work of Burns and James Hogg in *Blackwood's Magazine* (February 1819), declared: 'there is in that immortal poem a depth of domestic joy – an intensity of the feeling of home – a presiding spirit of love – and a lofty enthusiasm of religion, which are all peculiarly Scottish, and beyond the pitch of mind of any other people' (CH, 310).

Modern critics have been less responsive to the poem. Snyder judged it a distressingly uneven work:

> The best of Burns and virtually the worst of Burns lie side by side in unseemly incongruity . . . . The Burns who wrote 'Anticipation forward points the view' was in bondage to a literary tradition utterly foreign to Scottish vernacular poetry as well as to his own genius . . . . In short, 'The Cotter's Saturday Night' lacks the unity and simplicity which Burns instinctively imparted to his best productions. (Snyder, 171–3)

Edwin Muir (*Scott and Scotland*, 1936; rept. Edinburgh, 1982, p. 10) felt that Burns's poetic use of Scots was inferior to Fergusson's: '"The Farmer's Ingle" is, in any case, a far better poem than "The Cotter's Saturday Night", which is roughly upon the same theme. The two poems, indeed, furnish excellent examples of the genuine and the false use of language.' Others, such as David Daiches and Maurice Lindsay, have followed Muir's example and found Fergusson's 'Farmer's Ingle' a finer work than the Burns poem it prompted (BE, 130).

Kinsley defends the poem, pointing out that its modern critics are out of sympathy with Augustan ideas of poetic imitation and with the sentimental mode of the eighteenth century:

> Here is the sober, virtuous aspect of Scottish rural life, described with the observation and understanding of a writer to whom the scene was home, in a linguistic convention established and accepted as proper to the theme. Fergusson provided a model for the *description* of country life in Scots; precedents for poetical *comment* on rural manners were English. . . . The poem is a bold linguistic experiment within an accepted mode; Burns's movement from Scots to English and back, between stanzas and sometimes subtly within them, has a 'propriety' of its own. (Kinsley, 1112)

*   *   *

The nine-line Spenserian stanza (eight pentameters plus one hexameter, rhyming *ababbcbcc*), devised by Spenser for *The Faerie Queene* (1589, 1596), was largely ignored in the seventeenth century but restored to poetic fashion in the eighteenth with Prior's 'Ode on the Glorious Success of Her Majesty's Arms' (1706), Shenstone's descriptive 'The Schoolmistress' (1742), Thomson's *Castle of Indolence* (1748) and James Beattie's *The Minstrel* (1771, 1774), a sentimental poem greatly admired by Burns. Burns certainly knew his Beattie, and his use of a formal English to stress a simple stoicism owes much to Beattie's example, as witness the third stanza of the first book of *The Minstrel*:

> The rolls of fame I will not now explore;
> Nor need I here describe in learned lay,
> How forth *the minstrel* fared in days of yore,
> Right glad of heart, though homely in array;
> His waving locks and beard all hoary grey:
> While from his bending shoulder, decent hung
> His harp, the sole companion of his way,
> Which to the whistling wind responsive rung:
> And ever as he went some merry lay he sung.

In a Preface to the poem, Beattie commended the 'difficult' Spenserian stanza because 'It admits both simplicity and magnificence of sound and of language, beyond any other stanza that

I am acquainted with.' Burns, less concerned with euphonic 'magnificence' than Beattie, saw in Robert Fergusson's 'The Farmer's Ingle' (1773) a way of combining Beattie's sentimental 'simplicity' with the vigour of the Scots vernacular. Fergusson's hero comes home in the second stanza of 'The Farmer's Ingle':

> Frae the big stack, weel winnow't on the hill,
> Wi' divets theekit frae the weet and drift,
> Sods, peats, and heath'ry trufs the chimley fill,
> And gar their thick'ning smeek salute the lift;
> The gudeman, new come hame, is blyth to find,
> Whan he out o'er the halland flings his een,
> That ilka turn is handled to his mind,
> That a' his housie looks sae cosh and clean;
> For cleanly house looes he, tho' e'er sae mean.

Burns's poem, which follows both the 'artificial note' of Beattie and the 'hamely strain' of Fergusson, reads as an uneasy union of the thematic pathos of *The Minstrel* and the verbal panache of 'The Farmer's Ingle'.

Comprising twenty-one Spenserian stanzas, 'The Cotter's Saturday Night' alternates between Scots and English, whereas Burns's 'The Farmer's Ingle' is written throughout in Lowland Scots. Noting the impact of the adoption of an English Bible by the Scottish Reformers in 1560, David Murison (*The Guid Scots Tongue*, Edinburgh, 1977, p. 5) drew attention to 'the split mind' Scots have applied to their native language since that time:

> A classic example [of the split mind] is Burns's 'The Cotter's Saturday Night', where the domestic scene is described in Scots, but as soon as the big ha' Bible is brought out the poem glides into English by the association of the Bible with the English language, which had gained spiritual prestige through the Reformation.

Recalling the composition of the poem, Gilbert Burns stressed its biblical and patriarchal connotations:

> Robert had frequently remarked to me that he thought there as something peculiarly venerable in the phrase, 'Let us worship God!' used by a decent, sober head of a family, introducing family worship. To this sentiment of the author, the world is indebted for 'The Cotter's Saturday Night' . . . .The cotter in the 'Saturday Night' is an exact copy of my father in his manners,

his family devotion, and exhortations; yet the other parts of the description do not apply to our family. (BE, 82)

From its inception, then, the poem was characterised by contradictions: Burns's wish to employ the dignified measure of the Spenserian stanza after the fashion of Beattie; his usual desire to emulate Fergusson's Scots poems; and his need to expand on an English injunction of his father's. The result is a work flawed by linguistic and psychological inconsistency.

Dedicated to Robert Aitken (see his entry in 'The Burns Circle') and prefaced with a quotation from Gray's *Elegy Written in a Country Churchyard*, the poem opens in English with a promise to 'sing, in simple Scottish lays' and show 'What Aiken in a cottage would have been' – presumably a man like the cotter in the poem, poor but contented with his honest poverty. The second stanza is in Scots, giving a vivid verbal picture of a Scottish winter as the grim natural environment of 'The toil-worn Cotter'. It is the third stanza that shows Burns falling to the sentimental occasion, stressing the small scale of the humble surroundings with his homely epithets ('wee' appears twice in three lines) and domestic diminutives ('his thrifty wifie'). Surrounded by his infants and his wife, the cotter is able to 'forget his labor and his toil' and, thus placed, he is joined in the fourth stanza by 'the elder bairns' and Jenny, 'woman grown,/In youthfu bloom, love sparkling in her e'e'. Like their father, the children (the 'elder bairns' working as farm labourers, Jenny in service) arrive home to escape from their everyday pressures. In assembling the family Burns has turned from the descriptive realism of Fergusson to the narrative sentimentality of the novelists (such as Henry Mackenzie) he most admired ('My favourite authors are of the sentimental kind' [CL, 55] he told John Murdoch in 1783.)

The humble household described by Burns is a small part of a rural idyll (the facts of a life of farm labour are ignored in this poem). Brothers and sisters come together in a common concern for the family welfare; the mother mends old clothes and makes them as good as new; the father gently asserts his authority which, since he is the Godlike head of the house, amounts to a warning 'to fear the Lord alway'. Suddenly the idyll is interrupted:

> But hark! a rap comes gently to the door;
>   Jenny, wha kens the meaning o the same,
> Tells how a neebor lad came o'er the moor,
>   To do some errands and convoy her hame.

222   *A Burns Companion*

Seeing Jenny blush, the mother asks the name of the visitor and is
pleased to hear he is 'nae wild, worthless rake'. This section of the
poem is a scene worthy of a place in a rural fiction.

Having assessed the credentials of this 'strappin youth', the father
and mother make him at home in their humble abode. Burns, however, stands back from the narrative to deliver a sermon in English:

> Is there, in human form, that bears a heart,
>   A wretch! a villain! lost to love and truth!
> That can, with studied, sly, ensnaring art,
>   Betray sweet Jenny's unsuspecting youth?
>   Curse on his perjur'd arts! dissembling, smooth!
> Are honor, virtue, conscience, all exil'd?
>   Is there no pity, no relenting ruth,
> Points to the parents fondling o'er their child?
> Then paints the ruin'd maid, and their distraction wild?

Kinsley's observation that this is an 'eighteenth-century set piece'
(Kinsley, 1115) – with precedents in Johnson's 'The Vanity of Human
Wishes', Goldsmith's *The Citizen of the World* and 'The Deserted Village', Sterne's *A Sentimental Journey* – does not affect the inadvertent
irony of the passage. At the time he wrote 'The Cotter's Saturday
Night' Burns was the father of an illegitimate daughter (by Elizabeth
Paton) and had certainly slept with Jean Armour (who was pregnant
by March 1786). Read in a biographical context, the description of
the wretch with 'studied, sly, ensnaring art' becomes a subconscious
self-portrait, Burns indulging in what Freud called 'projection' (the
attribution to others of faults one recognises in oneself).

After the moralistic aside, which is more of an intrusion into the
narrative than a comment on the 'strapping youth', the poem returns
to its idyllic manner. The family sit at the table to enjoy porridge
('chief o Scotia's food'), milk from their only cow, and cheese. Burns
then gives pride of place in the happy household to the cotter (who
bears some resemblance to Beattie's minstrel, see above):

> The chearfu supper done, wi serious face,
>   They, round the ingle, form a circle wide;
> The sire turns o'er, wi patriarchal grace,
>   The big ha'-Bible, ance his father's pride.
> His bonnet rev'rently is laid aside,
>   His lyart haffets wearing thin and bare;
> Those strains that once did sweet in Zion glide,

>He wales a portion with judicious care;
>'And Let us worship God!' he says with solemn air.

That stanza is the centrepiece of the poem, linking the cotter to his earthly father and his heavenly father. He is a God in his own house with his own good book.

The family sing psalms from the Scottish psalters before the 'priest-like father' reads from the Bible and, in the process of praying, becomes 'The saint, the father, and the husband'. Burns declares that the simple heart-felt faith of the cotter is more worthy than the pompous ritual of religion as observed in the kirk. The cotter speaks 'the language of the soul', 'The cottage leaves the palace far behind'. In his penultimate stanza (in English, like all those following the appearance of the 'big ha'-Bible) Burns makes an appeal to Scotia, the spirit of Scotland addressed as a deity in the final stanza:

>O Thou! who pour'd the patriotic tide,
>   That stream'd thro Wallace's undaunted heart,
>Who dar'd to, nobly, stem tyrannic pride,
>   Or nobly die, the second glorious part:
>(The patriot's God, peculiarly Thou art,
>His friend, inspirer, guardian, and reward!)
>   O never, never Scotia's realm desert;
>But still the patriot, and the patriot-bard
>In bright succession raise, her ornament and guard!

It is the duty of the patriot-bard to praise the finest qualities of Scotland, and these Burns finds embodied in the cotter and his family, folk who value companionship more than commerce. The rousing last stanza is an appropriately sermonising conclusion to a moralistic poem. Apart from his passages of Fergussonian description, Burns sounds more like a preacher than a poet, albeit a preacher familiar with the sentimental fiction of the time.

TO A MOUSE

Text   69/CW, 131–2.

Composition   Burns dates the poem in his full title, 'To A Mouse, *On turning her up in her Nest, with the Plough, November, 1785.*' Gilbert Burns recalled that his brother wrote it 'while holding the plough' at Mossgiel farm; John Blane, once a farm servant at Mossgiel, claimed to have chased after the mouse to kill it, before being admonished by Burns who then became 'thoughtful and abstracted' (cited in Donald A. Low's edition of *Robert Burns: The Kilmarnock Poems*, London, 1985, p. 153).

Publication   First published in the Kilmarnock Edition (31 July 1786).

Reception   James Currie (*The Works of Robert Burns*, 1800) considered the poem a combination of comic and serious effects, and judged it 'one of the happiest, and most finished of his productions' (CH, 140); Allan Cunningham (*The Works of Robert Burns*, 1834) took it entirely seriously, since it 'preaches to us the instability of happiness on earth' (CH, 413). Acclaiming it as the most outstanding achievement of the Kilmarnock Edition, Snyder pronounced it 'in its way . . . as superbly inimitable as *Hamlet* or "The Rime of the Ancient Mariner". Like them, it bears the marks of stark genius . . . . There is nothing else in the Kilmarnock volume quite so notable as "To a Mouse"' (Snyder, 179). Crawford praises the emotional authenticity of the poem and feels it can only be fully understood in the context of the Scottish Agrarian Revolution. Quoting the lines 'Till crash! the cruel coulter past/Out thro thy cell', Crawford comments: 'The coulter is in reality Burns's equivalent of [Blake's dark Satanic] mills – part of the metaphorical plough of social change that breaks down the houses of both Lowland and Highland cotters' (Crawford, 167).

*   *   *

Behind what still reads, thanks to its brilliance, as an unusually inspired occasional poem is a philosophical position. For informing the address is Burns's Deistic belief in a natural religion, a notion reinforced by his reading of favourite poets such as Thomson and Pope. Thomson, in 'Winter' (1726), from *The Seasons*, links Nature with 'th' eternal Scheme,/That dark perplexity, that mystic maze'. In the first of his *Moral Essays* (1731), Pope asserts that 'God and Nature only are the same'; and, in the first epistle of *An Essay on Man* (1733), Pope contemplates the 'Vast Chain of Being! which from God began', and warns 'From Nature's chain whatever link you strike,/Tenth or ten thousandth, breaks the chain alike'. Pope's 'Nature's chain' becomes Burns's 'Nature's social union'.

'To A Mouse' is composed in eight Standard Habbie stanzas.

The opening line of the poem is pictorially precise in its evocation of the 'Wee sleekit, cow'rin, tim'rous beastie': the three epithets describing the mouse are followed by two that divide the vulnerable creature from its tormentor, for it flees with 'bickering brattle' while he is associated with 'murdering pattle'. It is Burns's triumph to overcome this division between beast and man.

In the first two lines of the second stanza he moves from epithet to abstraction and in doing so shifts from broad Scots to Augustan English as he makes his apology: 'I'm truly sorry man's dominion/Has broken Nature's social union'. These lines have been criticised because they 'fail to ring true [and] smell of the lamp' (Snyder, 179) but the poet's tonal modulation is entirely appropriate. Burns's concept of Nature is obviously organic since the mouse has been disturbed by a mechanical, not a natural, intrusion and the abstractions are justifiably unnatural in their artificiality. Man's dominion is not only generally destructive but self-destructive, hence the poet linking himself to the mouse as 'thy poor, earth-born companion,/An fellow mortal'.

Burns has, then, a zoomorphic view of himself and an anthropomorphic view of the mouse. The fourth stanza, ostensibly addressed to the mouse, is a passionate lament for homelessness everywhere:

> Thy wee-bit housie, too, in ruin!
> Its silly wa's the win's are strewin!
> An naething, now, to big a new ane,
> O foggage green!
> An bleak December's win's ensuin,
> Baith snell an keen!

The mouse, indeed, has been ejected ('turn'd out') from its home, a fate that might well have befallen the poet's father towards the end of his life and might, in the future, befall Burns himself. As a vulnerable victim of 'man's dominion' the mouse is made in the social image of poor men in general, and one poor man – namely Burns – in particular.

> But Mousie, thou art no thy lane,
> In proving foresight may be vain:
> The best-laid schemes o' mice an men
> Gang aft agley,
> An lea'e us nought but grief an pain
> For promis'd joy!

> Still thou art blest, compar'd wi me!
> The present only toucheth thee;
> But och! I backward cast my e'e,
> On prospects drear!
> An forward, tho I canna see,
> I guess an fear!

These last two stanzas gain poignancy from the uncertainty of Burns's own position in November 1785: the previous year his father had died, worn out by hard work and the psychological strain of tenant-farming; and in October 1785 his youngest brother, John, had died at the age of fourteen. Burns's own future was far from certain.

In composing these two stanzas, Burns drew on two sources (see Crawford, 167n). The aphorism about the best-laid schemes derives from lines ('The best-concerted schemes men lay for fame/Die fast away') from Robert Blair's long poem *The Grave* (1743), a work often quoted by Burns in his letters. The final stanza probably owes something to Dr Johnson's *Rasselas* (the Prince tells the animals, 'Ye are happy and need not envy me . . . I sometimes shrink at evils recollected, and sometimes start at evils anticipated').

All the sources (Thomson, Pope, Blair, Johnson), however, have been transformed by Burns in a short and startlingly imaginative poem that sums up his sympathetic view of his fellow creatures. It eschews spurious sentimentality by drawing on the actual experience ('fields laid bare and waste,/An weary winter comin fast') of working on the land. 'Nature's social union' was something Burns encountered every working day of his life as a farmer.

TO A LOUSE

Text   83/CW, 181–2.

Composition   Written at the end of 1785, a year in which the name of Lunardi was celebrated in Scotland (see below).

Publication   First published in the Kilmarnock Edition (31 July 1786).

Reception   Dorothy Wordsworth, in a letter of December 1787 to Jane Pollard, mentions her delight on reading Burns's poems in the Kilmarnock Edition her brother showed her: 'I was very

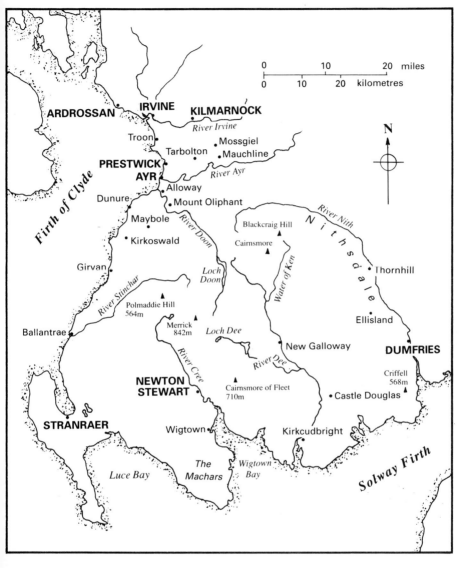

PLACES ASSOCIATED WITH ROBERT BURNS

BURNS MUSEUM
Alloway, Ayrshire

BURNS COTTAGE
Alloway, Ayrshire

BURNS MONUMENT
Alloway, Ayrshire

BRIG O DOON
Alloway, Ayrshire

ALLOWAY KIRK
Alloway, Ayrshire

BACHELORS' CLUB
Tarbolton, Ayrshire

TAM O SHANTER INN
Kirkoswald, Ayrshire

SOUTER JOHNIE'S HOUSE
Kirkoswald, Ayrshire

ELLISLAND FARM
Dumfriesshire

BURNS HOUSE
Burns Street, Dumfries

BURNS MAUSOLEUM
St. Michael's Churchyard, Dumfries

ROBERT BURNS CENTRE
Mill Road, Dumfries

2. (*left*) Agnes Broun, the poet's mother, married William Burnes in 1757 and went to live with him in the 'auld clay biggin'. Though she had little interest in books, she sang old Scottish songs to her children.

3. (*below*) The Alloway cottage where Burns was born on 25 January 1759, and where he spent the first seven years of his life, was built by the poet's father, William Burnes. It was acquired in 1881 by the Alloway Burns Monument Trustees and restored.

4. Mount Oliphant farm, on the Ayrshire estate of Doonholm, was occupied by William Burnes and his family from 1766 until 1777, eleven years during which Burns endured, as his brother Gilbert said, 'hard labour and sorrow' as 'principal labourer on the farm'.

5. Lochlea farm, Tarbolton, Ayrshire, was rented by William Burnes from 1777 until his death in 1784. It was here that Burns first asserted his independence, seeking the society of women and annoying his father by attending a country dancing class in Tarbolton.

6. While their father encountered legal problems at Lochlea, Robert and Gilbert Burns secretly arranged to lease Mossgiel farm, moving into it in March 1784. Here Burns wrote some of his finest poems before transferring his share of the farm to Gilbert in July 1786.

7. (*left*) Robert Fergusson (1750–74, portrait attributed to Alexander Runciman). Burns bought the Second Edition of Fergusson's *Poems* (1782) and wrote (letter of 2 August 1787 to John Moore) 'meeting with Fergusson's Scotch Poems, I strung anew my wildly-sounding, rustic lyre with emulating vigour'.

Curse on ungrateful man, that can be pleas'd,
And yet can starve the author of the pleasure!

Mr ROBERT FERGUSSON
Ætat. XXIV.

O thou, my elder brother in Misfortune,
By far my elder Brother in the muse,
With tears I pity thy unhappy fate!
Why is the Bard unfitted for the world,
Yet has so keen a relish of its Pleasures!

8. Fergusson's *Poems*. Burns sent his own copy of Fergusson's *Poems* (1782) to Rebekah
Carmichael on 19 March 1787, writing, under the engraving of Fergusson, 'O thou, my
elder brother in Misfortune,/By far my elder Brother in the muse.' (Book owned by
Rt. Hon the Earl of Rosebery.)

9. As illustrated by David Allan (1744–1796), the Scottish genre-painter, 'The Cotter's Saturday Night' becomes a domestic sermon. Allan incorporated the poet's features in the face of the eldest son who sits next to his father.

10. As this etching by W. B. Scott indicates, the Burns cult has long demanded images of the poet's amorous adventures. On the second Sunday of May 1786, Burns and 'Highland Mary' Campbell made a matrimonial gesture by clasping hands and exchanging Bibles over the Fail water.

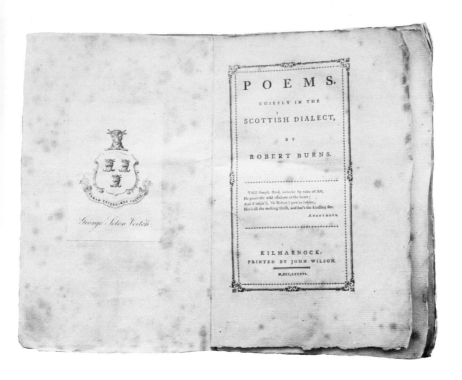

11. The Kilmarnock Edition of *Poems, Chiefly in the Scottish Dialect* was printed and issued by John Wilson on 31 July 1786 in an edition of 600 selling at three shillings per copy. Burns made around £50 from the book.

12. (*left*) Gilbert Burns took
    Mossgiel farm in July 17..
    He was able to run it u..
    1798 and look after Bur..
    illegitimate daughter E..
    beth thanks to a loan..
    around £200 from ..
    brother.

13. (*right*) Burns was, by his own
    admission, on the point of
    emigrating to Jamaica when
    a letter, of September 1786
    from Dr Thomas Blacklock
    in praise of the Kilmarnock
    Edition, persuaded him to
    seek literary fame and for-
    tune in Edinburgh.

14. Peter Taylor's portrait of Burns, in Edinburgh in 1786, is the earliest painting of the poet. When the portrait was issued as an engraving in 1829, Mrs McLehose, and Sir Walter Scott pronounced it an excellent likeness.

15. (*left*) Henry Mackenzie's essay in the *Lounger* (9 December 1786) celebrated Burns as 'this Heaven-taught ploughman'. For Burns, Mackenzie's *The Man of Feeling* (1771) was 'a book I prize next to the Bible' (letter of 15 January 1783 to Murdoch).

16. (*right*) Mrs Frances Dunlop was recently widowed when, finding solace in 'The Cotter's Saturday Night', she wrote to Burns who replied on 15 November 1786. He wrote more letters to her than to any other correspondent, eventually offending her with his revolutionary politics.

(*right*) Burns saw Margaret Chalmers at the Edinburgh home of Dr Blackclock for whom she sang and played the piano. In January 1787 he wrote to tell her 'your Piano and you together have play'd the deuce somehow, about my heart'.

18. (*left*) Commissioned by William Creech to be engraved for the First Edinburgh Edition, Alexander Nasmyth's bust-portrait of Burns was finished by February 1787 and is an authentic likeness of the poet at the age of twenty-eight.

19. (*above*) Based on Nasmyth's bust-portrait of Burns, John Beugo's engraving of February 1787 for the first Edinburgh Edition (17 April 1787) was checked against the living original who was delighted by it.

20. (*above right*) John Miers's silhouette of 1787 was first published in Allan Cunningham's 1834 edition of Burns. In a letter of 23 June 1788, Burns told Bob Ainslie 'when I sat to Mr Miers, I am sure he did not exceed two minutes'.

21. (*right*) Neil Gow (1727–1807), here portrayed by Sir Henry Raeburn, was a celebrated fiddler and composer whose tunes Burns used in his songwriting. Burns met Gow on 31 August 1787 at Dunkeld and found him 'a short, stout-built, honest highland figure'. Gow's son Nathaniel, also a fiddler, met Burns in Dumfries in 1794.

2. (*right*) William Smellie, printer of the First Edinburgh Edition, in whose office, in Anchor Close off the High Street, Burns corrected his proofs: 'Yet, tho his caustic wit was biting rude,/His heart was warm, benevolent, and good' ('William Smellie—A Sketch').

3. (*below right*) William Creech, publisher of the First and Second Edinburgh Editions, and a notoriously mean man as Burns found out to his cost: 'O, Willie was a witty wight,/And had o things an unco sleight!' ('Lament for the Absence of William Creech').

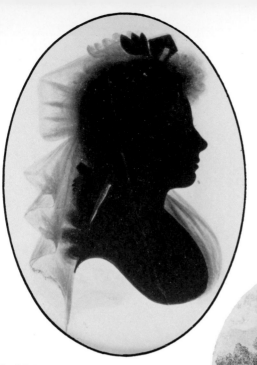

24. (*left*) Mrs Agnes McLehose, Clarinda to Burns's Sylvander, met the poet in Edinburgh on 4 December 1787. On 6 December 1791 the two met in Edinburgh for the last time and, on 27 December, Burns sent 'Ae Fond Kiss', the finest of the ten songs he wrote for her.

25. (*right*) Burns signed the lease for Ellisland farm, on the banks of the River Nith, Dumfriesshire, on 18 March 1788 and renounced the lease on 10 September 1791. As the soil was exhausted it was a bad bargain, but here Burns wrote 'Tam o Shanter' as well as some fine songs.

26. (*left*) Sir Thomas Lawrence's portrait of Maria Riddell shows the beauty that captivated Burns when he met her at Friars' Carse in 1791. Her 'Memoir Concerning Burns' (August 1796) declared that 'fascinating conversation', not poetry, was his *forte*.

(*right*) After composing 'Tam o Shanter', in late autumn 1790, Burns made several copies for friends. This holograph is from the Afton Manuscript (now in the Burns Cottage Museum), presented by the poet to 'Mrs General Stewart of Afton' in 1791. The poem was first published in the *Edinburgh Herald* of 18 March 1791.

(*below*) Kirk Alloway, the setting of 'Tam o Shanter', as illustrated in the second volume of Francis Grose's *The Antiquities of Scotland* (1791). Grose agreed to include a picture of the kirk in his book on condition that Burns supply a witch-story to accompany it.

Tam o' Shanter. - A Tale. -

Alloway-kirk, the scene of the following Poem, is an old Ruin in Ayr-shire, hard by the great road from Ayr to Maybole, on the banks of the river Doon, & near the old bridge of that name. - A Drawing of this Ruin will make its appearance in Grose's antiquities of Scotland. -

When chapmen billies leave the street,
And drouthy neebors neebors meet,
As market-days are wearing late,
And folk begin to tak the gate;
While we sit bousing at the nappy,
And getting fou, & unco happy,
We think na on the lang Scots miles,
The mosses, waters, slaps & styles,
That lie between us & our hame,
Where sits our sulky, sullen dame,
Gathering

29. (*above*) The Theatre Royal in Shakespeare Street, Dumfries, was officially opened on Saturday, 29 September 1792. Burns, thanks to his friend Robert Riddell, was on the free list of patrons and was fascinated by the notion of a national drama (see 'Burns and the Theatre').

30. (*below*) On 19 May 1793 Burns moved into a red sandstone house in Millbrae Vennell (now Burns Street), Dumfries, and died there on 21 July 1796. Busy with Excise work and his song lyrics, Burns still found time for social pleasures. The house is now a museum.

31. This scale model – in the Robert Burns Centre, Dumfries – shows Dumfries in 1794, the year Burns was promoted to Acting Supervisor of Excise.

32. (*right*) Dr William Maxwell, who had applied his revolutionary principles in France, settled in Dumfries in 1794 and became friendly with Burns whom he treated during his final illness, prescribing sea-bathing at Brow on the Solway coast.

33. (*left*) Jessy Lewars an 18-year-old neigh▌ brought in to nurse the d poet and help the preg▌ Jean with the house▌ in the summer of 179▌ was hearing Jessy sing inspired Burns to write penultimate song, 'O, ▌ Thou in the Cauld Blast'.

34. (*left*) Alexander Reid's miniature was painted in Dumfries the year before the poet died. Writing to George Thomson, in May 1795, Burns described it as 'the most remarkable likeness of what I am at this moment, that I think ever was taken of any body'.

35. (*right*) Alexander Skirving's red-chalk portrait of Burns, based on Nasmyth's bust-portrait, was executed around 1797, after the poet's death. Nevertheless, Sir Walter Scott thought it 'the only good portrait of Burns'.

36. (*left*) Jean Armour: this portrait shows the poet's widow in 1821, by which time 'my bonie Jean' ('The Vision') was a 54-year-old grandmother. As a young woman she inspired fourteen songs by Burns.

37. Originally buried in an ordinary grave in St Michael's Churchyard, Dumfries, Burns's body was disinterred in 1815 and moved to a vault in the Mausoleum erected to his memory. The sculptured group, by Turnerelli, depicts the Muse of Poetry finding Burns at the plough.

much pleased with them indeed, the one which you mentioned to me is I think very comical, I mean the address to a Louse' (CH, 92). Josiah Walker (*Account of the Life and Character of Robert Burns*, 1811) admired Burns's ability to humanise supposedly insignificant creatures: 'His *Louse* is a well-scolded intruder.' (CH, 230)

Hecht found it a 'somewhat jarring poem' (Hecht, 82), Crawford calls it 'a delightful little satiric gem' (Crawford, 155). Considering Burns's addresses to a louse, mouse and mountain daisy, Fitzhugh writes '"To a Louse" is artistically by far the best, and by far the least popular' (Fitzhugh, 114).

*   *   *

'To a Louse', comprising eight Standard Habbie stanzas like its companion 'To a Mouse', is an extraordinary poetic act of empathy. Though the poem is gloriously funny it is never merely whimsical, deriving its strength from serious circumstances. At the end of 1785, Burns must have felt something like the louse, 'Detested, shunn'd, by saunt an' sinner'. On 22 May, Elizabeth Paton had given birth to the poet's first illegitimate child (Bess) and (according to 'The Fornicator') he had done public penance in Mauchline Kirk, the setting for 'To a Louse'.

The full title of the poem, in the Kilmarnock Edition, is 'To A Louse, On Seeing one on a Lady's Bonnet at Church'. This bonnet is crucial to the poem: it is a Lunardi, so-called in honour of Vincenzo Lunardi, the Italian aeronaut who, in 1785, made balloon ascents from sites in Edinburgh and Glasgow. Appropriately, the Lunardi bonnet was balloon-shaped. Burns's contemporary readers would have been well aware that a Lunardi was an extremely fashionable piece of headwear, a possession to be worn with pride. It is this pride that is punctured by the louse the poet observes crawling on the Lunardi, the crowning glory of Jenny's Sunday best:

> Ha! whare ye gaun, ye crowlin ferlie?
> Your impudence protects you sairly;
> I canna say but ye strunt rarely
>   Owre gauze and lace,
> Tho faith! I fear ye dine but sparely
>   On sic a place.

Burns's tone is that of amused tolerance. Sitting in a Scottish kirk, as a pompous preacher performs for self-satisfied parishioners like

Jenny, the louse is entitled to its 'impudence' since the minister sets an impudent tone in 'sic a place'. The second stanza is intended ironically, mocking the indignant tone of self-righteous moralists:

> Ye ugly, creepin, blastit wonner,
> Detested, shunn'd by saunt an sinner,
> How daur ye set your fit upon her –
>   Sae fine a lady!
> Gae somewhere else and seek your dinner
>   On some poor body.

There is, so Burns suggests, an incongruity in the spectacle of a louse setting foot on a lady when the poor are readily available as a source of food. Avoiding overburdening the poem with social comment, Burns nevertheless indicates the squalid poverty that exists, alongside affluence, in a self-styled Christian society. He advises the louse to move from the lady in the church to 'some beggar's hauffet' (beggar's temple, note the oxymoron).

This louse, however, has the presumption to come to the kirk and there climb to whatever heights it can, in a grotesquely humorous travesty of the worshipper who wishes to come closer to God. It ascends to 'The vera tapmost, tow'rin height/O Miss's bonnet'. Many of Burns's poems tack a conclusion onto a humorous series of observations. Like 'To a Mouse', 'To a Louse' allows the conclusion to evolve from a succession of highly prejudiced, and mischievous, observations. The final three stanzas are among the finest Burns ever produced and the conclusion that emerges is no platitude but a profoundly enduring reflection of human behaviour.

> I wad na been surpris'd to spy
> You on an auld wife's flainen toy;
> Or aiblins some bit duddie boy,
>   On's wyliecoat;
> But Miss's fine Lunardi! fye!
>   How daur ye do't?
>
> O Jenny, dinna toss your head,
> An set your beautie's a' abread!
> Ye little ken what cursed speed
>   The blastie's makin!
> Thae winks an finger-ends, I dread,
>   Are notice takin!

> O wad some Power the giftie gie us
> To see oursels as ithers see us!
> It wad frae monie a blunder free us,
>   An foolish notion:
> What airs in dress an gait wad lea'e us,
>   An ev'n devotion!

Part of the power of these lines comes from the conversational sound of a man speaking commonsense: 'O Jenny, dinna toss your head' is a warning full of folk wisdom. It is significant, too, that in a Scottish kirk Burns appeals not to the kirk-given God but to 'some Power', a notion natural to his Deism.

THE AULD FARMER'S NEW-YEAR MORNING SALUTATION TO HIS AULD MARE, MAGGIE

Text   75/CW, 158–61.

Composition   Early January 1786 at Mossgiel: the title specifies New Year's morning; the manuscript in the Kilmarnock Monument Museum places it alongside a group of poems listed as complete in a letter of 17 February 1786 to John Richmond (CL, 76).

Publication   First published in the Kilmarnock Edition (31 July 1786).

Reception   James Currie (*The Works of Robert Burns*, 1800) found, in the poem, a 'union of tenderness and humour' (CH, 135). Thomas Carlyle, reviewing Lockhart's *Life of Burns* in the *Edinburgh Review* (December 1828), wrote: 'In respect of mere clearness and minute fidelity, the *Farmer's* commendation of his *Auld Mare*, in plough or in cart, may vie with Homer's Smithy of the Cyclops, or yoking of Priam's Chariot' (CH, 362).

Snyder described the poem as 'a perfect piece of *genre* painting' and noted:

> Nor indeed is it without a universal audience; for despite the definitely Scottish flavour imparted by the broad and consistently maintained dialect, its fundamental theme is the sympathy that exists the world over between man and the beasts that labour for him. (Snyder, 174)

Christina Keith (*The Russet Coat*, London, 1956, p. 54) declared the poem shared, with 'Halloween', 'the honour of having the finest Lallans Burns ever wrote'. Crawford, unlike Snyder, finds the poem limited in its appeal:

> [It] is photography, not painting; it is documentary, not art of the most highly creative or imaginative kind . . . . it does not rise above the local and the particular as the greatest of Burns's works certainly do. (Crawford, 117)

*   *   *

The full title of the poem, as given in the Kilmarnock Edition, is 'The Auld Farmer's New-Year-Morning Salutation to his Auld Mare, Maggie, on Giving her the Accustomed Ripp of Corn to Hansel in the New Year'. Conveying the conversational intimacy of Burns's verse epistles, the poem is a dramatic monologue spoken by an old farmer (Burns was a young farmer approaching his twenty-seventh birthday when the poem was written) who inevitably empathises with his old horse: the description of the horse as 'howe-backit' (hollow-backed) in the first stanza could apply to the speaker as well as the subject. Both of them have seen better days.

Maggie, of course, is female and Burns dwells on the attractions she once possessed, stressing her former shapliness by anthropomorphising – or, rather, gynandromorphising – the mare.

> Thou ance was i' the foremost rank,
> A filly buirdly, steeve an swank:
> An set weel down a shapely shank,
>   As e'er tread yird;
> An could hae flown out-owre a stank,
>   Like onie bird.

This says as much about the mentality of the man as the appearance of the mare and demonstrates Burns's dramatic gift of inhabiting a character. The old farmer perceives the world as it 'ance was'; the past means more to him than the present which amounts only to marking time with memories.

Having seen the mare as a woman, the old farmer goes further by specifically associating the animal with his wife Jenny. Maggie the mare was a gift, twenty-nine years before, from his father-in-law and the farmer recalls wife and mare as a pair:

> That day, ye pranc'd wi muckle pride,
> When ye bure hame my bonie bride:
> An sweet an gracefu, she did ride,
>> Wi maiden air!
> Kyle-Stewart I could bragged wide,
>> For sic a pair.

So the poem develops stanza by stanza as a meditation on the atrophy of ageing and its impact on man and woman as well as beast. The first line of the eighth stanza addresses the mare by recalling the time 'When thou an I were young and skeigh'. By sharing the experience of time passing, man and beast are (in the man's imagination) bound by a sentimental union.

Like most of the old men Burns would have encountered, the farmer romanticises the golden days of his youth and, in doing so, his tenderness for the mare becomes increasingly reverential: 'Thou was', 'thee and I'. In those distant days, so the farmer supposes, he and Maggie were heroic in their labours, swift and sturdy while working incessantly without complaint:

> In cart or car thou never reestit;
> The steyest brae thou wad hae fac't it:
> Thou never lap, an sten't, an breastit,
>> Then stood to blaw;
> But just thy step a wee thing hastit,
>> Thou snoov't awa.

> My pleugh is now thy bairntime a',
> Four gallant brutes as e'er did draw;
> Forbye sax mae I've sell't awa,
>> That thou hast nurst:
> They drew me thretten pund an twa,
>> The vera warst.

> Monie a sair darg we twa hae wrought,
> An wi the weary warl' fought!

> An monie an anxious day, I thought
>   We wad be beat!
> Yet here to crazy age we're brought,
>   Wi something yet.

Burns has succeeded brilliantly (note the metaphorical density of 'My pleugh is now thy bairntime a'') in realising the psychology of the speaker, allowing him to move from sentimental valuation of Maggie to a shrewd assessment of the profit he has made from the mare's offspring. The coupling imagery (mare and cart, horse and plough, mare and sire) leads to a connexion between man and beast, united now by 'crazy age' ('crazy years' in the final stanza).

In the two concluding stanzas the old farmer, projecting onto the mare his own dread that his days 'may end in starvin', promises to look after her by providing food and comfort ('tentie care'). Both stoic and sentimental by nature, the old farmer's promise reveals his fear that he will succumb to an unproductive old age without the sustenance he offers Maggie. Ostensibly an address to an animal, the poem is actually a poignant reflection on the vulnerability that comes with old age. Burns had seen his own father worn out by toil and knew that many tenant-farmers faced starvation and poverty when unable to do the physical work on the farm. A whole social psychology lies behind the poem which uses the Standard Habbie stanza to suggest pathos rather than pawky humour.

ADDRESS TO THE DEIL

Text   76/CW, 161–4.

Composition   Written at Mossgiel in the winter of 1785–6; writing to John Richmond on 17 February 1786 Burns refers to the poem as complete (CL, 76).

Publication   First published in the Kilmarnock Edition (31 July 1786).

Reception   Reviewing the Kilmarnock Edition in the *English Review* (February 1787) John Logan praised the timeless humour of the poem (CH, 77), an opinion endorsed by other critics. David Irving (*The Lives of the Scottish Poets*, 1804) admired its 'original vein of satirical humour' (CH, 167) and Allan Cunningham (*The Works of*

Robert Burns with his Life, 1834) said the poem 'indulges in religious
humanities, in which sympathy overcomes fear' (CH, 413).

Snyder thought it 'one of Burns's half dozen masterpieces'
(Snyder, 169), Hecht said that Burns 'lets a gentle ray of hope
of redemption fall upon the Prince of Hell himself, thus echoing,
unconsciously perhaps, ideas already expressed by Origenes'
(Hecht, 58). Crawford writes: 'If there is some reason for supposing
that Burns identified himself imaginatively with Satan . . . then a
peculiar interest attaches to the much-quoted final stanza of the
address' (Crawford, 218).

*   *   *

Burns's irreverent address to the devil plays verbal games with the
moral conventions of his time. According to the preachers, God
was ubiquitous; according to the evidence available in Ayrshire,
however, it was Satan who was omnipresent, 'ranging like a roaring
lion' through the landscape; rattling at church doors; and lurking,
unseen but palpably there, 'in the human bosom'. Burns sees the
devil as a tiresome practical joker who has been at his tricks since
he tormented Job ('the man of Uzz').

The manuscripts of the poem (in the Irvine Burns Museum and
the Kilmarnock Monument Museum) show that Burns tinkered with
the text before publication. Originally, the eleventh stanza offered
an explicitly sexual joke about a bridegroom's erect penis (warklum
is Scots for tool) being softened by evil spells:

> Thence, knots are coosten, spells contriv'd,
> An' the brisk bridegroom, newly wived
> Just at the kittle point arriv'd,
> Fond, keen, an' croose,
> Is by some spitefu' jad depriv'd
> O's warklum's use.

As printed in the Kilmarnock Edition the stanza reads:

> Thence, mystic knots mak great abuse
> On young guidmen, fond, keen an croose;
> When the best wark-lume i' the house,
> By cantraip wit,
> Is instant made no worth a louse,
> Just at the bit.

This was still too bawdy for Hugh Blair who urged Burns to omit the stanza 'as indecent' (CH, 81), advice Burns ignored when including the poem in the First Edinburgh Edition.

At the period the Kilmarnock Edition was being prepared for the printer, Burns had been repudiated by James Armour and had broken with Jean, a 'shocking affair' (AL) that led to changes in the poem. Originally the fifteenth stanza referred to Jean:

> Langsyne, in Eden's happy scene,
> When strappin Edie's days were green,
> An' Eve was like my bonie Jean,
>> My dearest part,
> A dancin, sweet, young, handsome quean
>> Wi' guileless heart.

In the Kilmarnock Edition the stanza became impersonal:

> Lang syne in Eden's bonie yard,
> When youthfu lovers first were pair'd,
> An all the soul of love they shar'd
>> The raptur'd hour,
> Sweet on the fragrant flow'ry swaird,
>> In shady bow'r.

The loss of Jean in the poem simply postpones the subjective point Burns wishes to drive home as he works towards his conclusion.

Burns prefaces the poem with a quotation from Milton's *Paradise Lost*, one of his favourite works. He not only liked to have his pocket Milton about his person, but he was an admirer of Milton's Satan, enthusing over 'my favourite hero, Milton's Satan' (CL, 118) and 'the intrepid, unyielding independance [of Milton's] great Personage, Satan' (CL, 344). Whereas Milton's Satan, however, has the stature of a tragic hero, Burns's has the presence of a familiar friend which is why the poet addresses him on intimate terms throughout – as 'Auld Hornie, Satan, Nick, or Clootie', Auld Hangie, 'auld, snick-drawing dog', Auld Cloots, Auld Nickie-ben. The devil, in Burns's poem, is reduced to an imp of hell. Burns's tone is mock-heroic.

It is the contrast between the devil's reputation and his Ayrshire activities that grants the poem its comic dimensions. Burns gives the devil his due of fame but places him parochially 'In lanely glens', 'yont the dyke', 'Ayont the lough'. If hell is wherever the devil haunts then these corners of the countryside are indeed damned, but Burns does not force this notion of an infernal Ayrshire. Instead he lists the little crimes of a devil who ruins the butter in the churn, interrupts the bridegroom at his lovemaking, expends his diabolic powers on drunks:

> And aft your moss-traversing spunkies
> Decoy the wight that late an drunk is:
> The bleezin, curst, mischievous monkies
>   Delude his eyes,
> Till in some miry slough he sunk is,
>   Ne'er mair to rise.

This thought disturbs the often-inebriated poet who tells the devil that he will outsmart him by constantly being wary of his omnipresence and by self-consciously putting Satan behind him in the last two stanzas:

> An now, Auld Cloots, I ken ye're thinkin,
> A certain Bardie's rantin, drinkin,
> Some luckless hour will send him linkin
>   To your black Pit;
> But, faith! he'll turn a corner jinkin,
>   An cheat you yet.

> But fare-you-weel, Auld Nickie-ben!
> O, wad ye tak a thought an men'!
> Ye aiblins might – I dinna ken –
>   Still hae a stake:
> I'm wae to think upo' yon den,
>   Ev'n for your sake!

If, as the Ayrshire evidence indicates, the devil exists – and Burns's parenthetical 'I dinna ken' leave this issue unsettled – then he presents only a limited challenge to the individual. The lightness of touch Burns displays towards his subject should be considered in the context of the Auld Licht vision of hell. An earlier poem, 'The Holy Fair', had depicted the Calvinist hell as 'A vast, unbottom'd, boundless pit,/Filled fou o lowin brunstane'. At the beginning of 'Address to the Deil', the devil is seen playfully splashing about in 'the brunstane cootie' and by the end of the poem hell is a domestic 'den'. Burns's mock-heroic poem not only mocks the Calvinist notion of an awesome and terrifying devil but, by implication, ridicules the credulity of those who take such a figure seriously and presumably deserve the hell they hold in their minds.

THE AUTHOR'S EARNEST CRY AND PRAYER

Text   81/CW, 174–9.

Composition   Written during the winter of 1785–6; a note by Burns in the First Edinburgh Edition explains that the poem 'was wrote before the Act anent the Scotch Distillieries, of Session 1786'.

Publication   First published in the Kilmarnock Edition (31 July 1786).

Reception   James Currie's *The Works of Robert Burns* (1800) says that 'chusing to exalt whisky above wine [Burns] sinks into humour, and concludes the poem with [a] most laughable, but most irreverent apostrophe . . . . . *"Freedom* and *whisky* gang thegither,/Tak aff your dram!"'' (CH, 136) Quoting the penultimate stanza of the Postscript (the lines beginning 'Sages their solemn een may steek') Josiah Walker, in *Account of the Life and Character of Burns* (1811), suggests that the 'bad effect of this stanza is heightened by its position between a passage of exalted pathos, and one of exquisite humour' (CH, 235). Allan Cunningham, in *The Works of Robert Burns* (1834), notes 'The patriotic feelings of the Bard were touched [in this poem which] shows the keen eye which humble people cast on their rulers' (CH, 406, 413). Crawford praises the ingenious irony of the poem and, quoting the last two lines ('Freedom and whisky gang thegither/Tak aff your dram!'), writes:

> The reader inevitably asks – what kind of Freedom? Freedom from 'royal George', or from the 'unco guid'? National freedom, or freedom for the individual to do as he likes? The probability is that Burns means not one but all of these things, and that the ambivalence of the ending is an intentional part of the poem's comic effect. (Crawford, 153–4)

*   *   *

The Wash Act of 1784 (Burns calls it 'that curst restriction/On acqua-vitae' in his third stanza), which formally divided Scotland into Lowlands and Highlands, restricted the size of Highland stills and deprived distillers of privileges under the excise laws; the Scotch Distillery Act of 1786, which applied to all Scotland, imposed more taxes on the whisky trade and regulated whisky sales between Scotland and England. Burns deplored the first Act and dreaded the

second (which paradoxically, in practice, encouraged Scottish distillers to increase their rate of production). Burns begins his protest
(written throughout in the Standard Habbie stanza) by addressing the Irish lords (who had Scottish seats in Parliament while
the eldest sons of Scottish peers were ineligible) and the Scottish
'knights an squires': 'To you a simple Bardie's prayers/Are humbly
sent.' This simulation of simplicity and affectation of humility are
meant ironically for Burns had no reverence for the men who sat
in the English parliament. In this mood he urges the Irish lords
and Scottish knights to make an appeal to the Prime Minister,
William Pitt:

> Stand forth, an tell yon Premier youth
> The honest, open, naked truth:
> Till him o mine and Scotland's drouth,
>   His servants humble:
> The muckle deevil blaw you south,
>   If ye dissemble!

What Pitt is to be told is the story of the sorry state of contemporary
Scotland, deprived of sufficient drink because 'damn'd excisemen'
(in enthusiastically applying the Wash Act) are forever seizing
stills.

   This most eloquent of poets projects himself as an inarticulate out-
sider who needs his superiors to speak for him, an irony underlined
by the catalogue of orators that Burns produces: James Boswell, then
active in Ayrshire politics; George Dempster, Whig MP for the Forfar
Burghs; Sir Adam Ferguson of Kilkerran, Whig MP for Ayrshire;
James Graham, one of Pitt's ministers in 1783; Henry Dundas, MP
for Midlothian and Pitt's Treasurer of the Navy; Thomas Erskine,
MP for Portsmouth; Lord Frederick Campbell, MP for Argyll; Sir
Ilay Campbell, MP for the Glasgow burghs and Lord Advocate; Sir
William Cunninghame of Livingston, MP for Linlithgow; 'sodger
Hugh' Montgomerie of Coilsfield, MP for Ayrshire. Burns's words
to these self-important worthies comes with a warning:

> Arouse, my boys! exert your mettle,
> To get auld Scotland back her kettle;
> Or faith! I'll wad my new pleugh-pettle,
>   Ye'll see't or lang,
> She'll teach you, wi a reekin whittle,
>   Anither sang.

This other song is a song of Scottish independence, a strident theme swelled by the resentment over English interference in Scottish domestic affairs. Personifying Scotland as a 'poor auld mither' capable of rising to the national occasion Burns writes ominously:

> An Lord! if ance they pit her till't,
> Her tartan petticoat she'll kilt,
> An durk an pistol at her belt,
>   She'll tak the streets,
> An rin her whittle to the hilt,
>   I' the first she meets!

In other words, if Scotland does not get satisfaction from her parliamentary representatives she will opt for the revolutionary alternative.

Burns advises the parliamentarians to ignore the taunts of Pitt's rival Charles James Fox (out of office at this time, passing his time in gambling and womanising) and to put the Scottish case to Pitt, humorously referred to not by his own name but by the Cornish estate of his grandfather, Robert Pitt of Boconnoc:

> Tell yon guid bluid of auld Boconnock's,
> I'll be his debt twa mashlum bonnocks,
> An drink his health in auld Nanse Tinnock's
>   Nine times a-week,
> If he some scheme, like tea an winnocks,
>   Wad kindly seek.

(Nanse Tinnock, the Mauchline tavern-hostess, told that Burns proposed to toast the Scottish members nine times a week in her tavern, said 'Him drink in my house! I hardly ken the colour o' his coin' [CH, 406]; the reference to tea and windows alludes to Pitt's Commutation of Act of 1784 which reduced the import duty on tea and imposed a tax on windows.) This plea comes with a promise of support from Scotland which Burns compares to a woman with 'a raucle tongue' capable of loyalty if treated decently. Burns ends this part of the poem with a mock-tribute to the forty-five Scottish MPs, hoping they will always have 'sowps o kail and brats o claes', food and dress usually associated with the common people.

The Postscript to the poem contrasts the whisky-drinking Scots with 'half-starved slaves in warmer skies'. Wine-drinkers are, according to Burns, passive individuals unsuited to war. Scots, however, are easily led into war under the influence of Scotch courage. Burns explores the implications of this in a stanza charged with ambiguity:

> But bring a Scotsman frae his hill,
> Clap in his cheek a Highland gill,
> Say, such is royal George's will,
>   An there's the foe!
> He has nae thought but how to kill
>   Twa at a blow.

This can be taken as meaning that an inebriated Scotsman is so stupefied he will fight for any cause, right or wrong, when it is sanctioned by the king; or that he can be galvinised into combat by the thought of the Hanoverian king, so that 'royal George' (a kinsman of Butcher Cumberland who persecuted the Scottish clans at, and after, Culloden) is himself 'the foe'; or that drink simply reduces him to a homicidal wretch with 'nae thought but how to kill'. Most of Burns's readers no doubt understood the stanza to be a loyal tribute to 'royal George' but the subversive sub-text is inescapably there.

The last stanza of the poem returns to the personification of Scotland as the 'poor auld mither' of the ninth stanza.

> Scotland, my auld, respected mither!
> Tho whiles ye moistify your leather,
> Till whare ye sit on craps o heather,
>   Ye tine your dam;
> Freedom and whisky gang thegither
>   Tak aff your dram!

That is a more humane image than the image of the Scotsman coming down from his hill with murder on his mind. Burns's sympathies give the feminine spirit of Scotland, not the masculine mentality of the soldier, the last word which is a cup of kindness in honour of the quality that unites freedom and whisky. It is interesting to note that Burns changed the ending in a holograph in his copy of the Second Edinburgh Edition (now in the Henry E. Huntington Library, San Marino, California):

> Till when ye speak, ye aiblins blether;
>   Yet deil-mak-matter!

Freedom and whisky gang thegither,
Tak aff your whitter.

Still, the message is the same. Fergusson (in 'Auld Reekie')
facetiously linked 'drink and sense'; Burns, associating a love of
drink with an historic thirst for independence, gives a symbolic
charge to the spirit of Scotland.

THE ORDINATION

Text   85/CW, 192–4.

Composition   Composed probably early February 1786; in a letter
of 17 February 1786 to John Richmond, Burns says 'I have been
very busy with the muses since I saw you, and have composed,
among several others, The Ordination, a poem of Mr Mckinlay's
being called to Kilmarnock' (CL, 76).

Publication   Omitted from the Kilmarnock Edition as Burns did
not wish 'to compromise his friends, and needlessly to exasperate
his – and their – enemies' (Snyder, 160). Included in the First
Edinburgh Edition (17 April 1787).

Reception   A rhymed attack 'On the Ayr-shire Ploughman Poet,
or Poetaster, R. B.', in James Maxwell's *Animadversions on Some Poets
and Poetasters of the Present Century* (1788), cited 'The Ordination' as
an example of Burns's irreligious attitude: 'This infidel mocks at the
Psalmist so sly,/Like fiddles and baby-clouts hung up to dry' (CH,
94). David Irving, in *The Lives of the Scottish Poets* (1804), called the
poem an 'ecclesiastical satire, remarkable for its wit and humour'
(CH, 166). Crawford praises it as 'one of the finest and freshest
things Burns ever did' (Crawford, 63).

*   *   *

After the death of the Rev John Mutrie in June 1785, the Earl of
Glencairn presented the Rev James Mackinlay (1756–1841) – an
Auld Licht conservative – to the second charge at Kilmarnock,
that of the Laigh Kirk (Low Church). A moderate, Glencairn made
the appointment on the assumption that the parishioners wanted
an Auld Licht minister; however, Mackinlay's presentation to the
charge, in August 1785, was bitterly opposed by the moderates

and the ordination did not take place until 6 April 1786. Burns, who later described Mackinlay as one of the 'ill-digested lumps of Chaos . . . strongly tinged with bituminous particles, and sulphureous effluvia' (CL, 270), wrote his poem in anticipation of the ordination. It is a sustained prolepsis.

Like 'The Holy Fair', 'The Ordination' has a purely parochial dimension in its parade of the names of local characters: Maggie Lauder, wife of Rev William Lindsay, a former Auld Licht minister of the Laigh Kirk; Rev James Oliphant, Auld Licht minister of Kilmarnock High Church from 1764–73; Rev John Russell, Auld Licht minister of Kilmarnock High Church after Oliphant; Rev William Boyd, New Licht minister at the parish Church of Fenwick; Rev John Robertson, New Licht minister of the first charge at Kilmarnock; and, of course, Mutrie and Mackinlay.

Burns brings these particular individuals into a general attack on the viciously vindictive attitude of the Auld Licht creed. It was, in Burns's view, a punitive rather than a positive creed and he portrays the Auld Licht luminaries as self-righteous floggers of the people: Mackinlay 'taks the flail', fornicators are to receive 'sufficient threshin', Patronage has a 'rod o airn', Orthodoxy is 'swingein thro the city' with a 'nine-tailed cat'. Remaking Kilmarnock in the image of a cow, Burns ironically promises the town a generous feeding of theological fare:

> Now auld Kilmarnock, cock thy tail,
>   An toss thy horns fu canty;
> Nae mair thou'lt rowte out-owre the dale,
>   Because thy pasture's scanty:
> For lapfu's large o gospel kail
>   Shall fill thy crib in plenty,
> An runts o grace the pick an wale,
>   No gi'en by way o dainty,
>   But ilka day.

The animal image is effective, suggesting that a docile town willing to endure such a minister as Mackinlay deserves its avoidable destiny. Burns also uses the fame of Kilmarnock as a carpet-making town, advising the moderate minister Robertson to renounce his religious calling, since there is no place for the New Licht in Mackinlay's Kilmarnock, and instead 'to the Netherton repair,/And turn a carpet weaver'. (Netherton was the carpet-making district of Kilmarnock.)

The coming of Mackinlay, the poet is certain, means the defeat of Common-sense who, personified as a woman, leaves Kilmarnock to seek the company of James Beattie, the prominent Common Sense philosopher and poet admired by Burns. After an ironical celebration of the 'torture' about to be inflicted by the Auld Lichts, Burns ends the poem by increasing the irony in a toast to the prospect of the moderates being burned in the flame of the Auld Licht and boiled 'Like oil':

> Come, bring the tither mutchkin in,
>   And here's – for a conclusion –
> To ev'ry New-Light mother's son,
>   From this time forth, confusion!
> If mair they deave us wi their din
>   Or patronage intrusion,
> We'll light a spunk, and ev'ry skin,
>   We'll rin them aff in fusion,
>   Like oil some day.

Burns's use of irony reinforces his ingenuity in persuasively integrating personifications (Heresy, Patronage, Orthodoxy, Learning, Common-sense, Morality) into the poem as individuals, not disembodied abstractions. Learning, for example, is seen as an irascible pedagogue unable to relate to reality: 'Learning, with his Greekish face,/Grunts out some Latin ditty'.

In 'The Ordination' Burns uses the descriptive Christis Kirk stanza for a didactic purpose that emerges through irony. A local squabble becomes a moral issue going much further than 'auld Kilmarnock' and its 'gospel kail'. The heavy alliteration, on the 'k' consonant, follows logically from the opening word 'Kilmarnock', quickly followed by 'creeshie', 'Kirk', 'tak', 'Curst Common-sense', 'king', 'clangor', 'kicks'. The effect of this is a clicking noise suggestive of head-shaking disgust, appropriate to the sarcastic intention of the poem.

ADDRESS OF BEELZEBUB

Text   108/CW, 225–6.

Composition   Dated 'HELL, June 1st, Anno Mundi 5790' by Burns: that is the 'year of the world' 1786.

Publication   Posthumously published in February 1818 (Crawford, 160n); 'to publish the poem [in his lifetime] would have been
to challenge powers with which Burns dared not risk a conflict'
(Snyder, 159).

Reception   Snyder, discussing Burns's diplomatic suppression of
an outspoken poem, wrote admiringly of the Address: 'There was
a sting, a lash, in the couplets which Pope or Juvenal might have
admired; Burns rarely wrote more feelingly or more eloquently'
(Snyder, 158). Crawford calls it 'the most savage of all Burns's
satires' (Crawford, 162).

                    *   *   *

Burns explains the topical significance of the poem in a scathing
introductory note addressed to John Campbell, fourth Earl of
Breadalbane, one of the sixteen representative Scottish peers and
President of the Highland Society which, on 23 May 1786, met in
London

> to concert ways and means to frustrate the designs of five hun-
> dred Highlanders who, as the Society were informed by Mr
> M'Kenzie of Applecross, were so audacious as to attempt an
> escape from their lawful lords and masters whose property they
> are, by emigrating from the lands of Mr Macdonald of Glengary
> to the wilds of Canada, in search of that fantastic thing – LIBER-
> TY.

Unable to support themselves on an overcrowded and agriculturally
impoverished land, the Highlanders (so the *Edinburgh Advertiser* for
30 May 1786 explained) had raised money and purchased ships to
take them to Canada. Concerned at the imminent loss of so many
tenants, the Scottish lairds and landowners wished to persuade the
government to prevent this plan by improving fishing, agriculture
and industry in the Highlands and so persuading the Highlanders
to remain as crofters under the control of 'their lawful lords and
masters'. Some commentators have found it ironic that Burns, the
self-proclaimed poet of the common people, should have savaged
the Scottish aristocracy for attempting to prevent emigration when
later writers condemned the lairds and landowners for forcing the
Highlanders to emigrate during the Highland Clearances. However,
both injustices are the result of the same proprietorial mentality

which Burns alludes to in his note, referring to the Highlanders as
'property'.

The poem derives its irony from its form as a dramatic monologue
delivered by the devil (Beelzebub) who is firmly and enthusiastically on the side of Breadalbane. Addressing Breadalbane, the devil
supports his strategy to keep the wretched Highlanders servile on
the land, rather than allowing them to breathe the exhilarating air of
revolution overseas after the manner of John Hancock (supposedly
the first to sign the American Declaration of Independence), Benja-
min Franklin (who helped draft the Declaration), George Washington (commander of the American forces) and Major-General Richard
Montgomery (an Irishman who served in the British Army then
joined the American side in the War of Independence):

> Long life, my lord, and health be yours,
> Unskaith'd by hunger'd Highland boors!
> Lord grant nae duddie, desperate beggar,
> Wi dirk, claymore, or rusty trigger,
> May twin auld Scotland o a life
> She likes – as lambkins like a knife!
>
> Faith! you and Applecross were right
> To keep the Highland hounds in sight!
> I doubt na! they wad bid nae better
> Than let them ance out owre the water!
> Then up amang thae lakes and seas,
> They'll mak what rules and laws they please:
> Some daring Hancock, or a Franklin,
> May set their Highland bluid a-ranklin;
> Some Washington again may head them,
> Or some Montgomery, fearless, lead them;
> Till (God knows what may be effected)
> Poor dunghill sons of dirt and mire
> May to Patrician rights aspire!

Inexorably, the couplets accumulate expressions of contempt for
the Highlanders and the enjambement after 'life', in the fifth line,
breaks the confines of the couplet on the most crucial word in
the passage. It is the gift of life itself that must be stolen from
the 'hunger'd Highland boors'; specifically a life that lets them
'mak what rules and laws they please', a revolutionary concept
threatening the authority of autocrats like Breadalbane – and the

devil. Indeed the devil regrets the paucity of reactionary warriors 'To cowe the rebel generation,/An save the honor o the nation'.

It is the devil's contention that Glengarry's economic measures are too mild to subjegate the Highlanders. Inhabiting the character of a vindictive devil with a skill that makes the reader regret Burns's reluctance to develop his histrionic gifts, the poet articulates the essence of oppression. The devil advises Glengarry to break the spirit of the Highlanders:

> But smash them! crush them a' to spails,
> An rot the dyvors i' the jails!
> The young dogs swinge them to the labour:
> Let wark an hunger mak them sober!
> The hizzies, if they're aughtlins fawsont,
> Let them in Drury-lane be lesson'd!
> An if the wives an dirty brats
> Come thiggin at your doors an yetts,
> Flaffin wi duds, and grey wi beas',
> Frightin awa your ducks an geese;
> Get out a horsewhip or a jowler,
> The langest thong, the fiercest growler,
> An gar the tatter'd gypsies pack
> Wi a' their bastards on their back!

The spectacle of young men treated as slaves and young women trained as prostitutes (Drury-lane was then a notoriously depraved district of London) powerfully makes the point that landowners like Glengarry are well placed, socially and politically, to do the devil's work. Burns's savage couplets still have the power to arouse indignation since his description of women and children being driven away by horsewhips and bulldogs has a contemporary relevance as well as a historical pathos.

After the angry intensity of that passage the poem ends with slyly subversive humour as the devil invites Glengarry to sup with him at home, thus taking his rightful place in hell. Burns, at the time he wrote 'Address of Beelzebub', had no personal contact with the aristocracy but was politically conscious of their mercenary motives. He was, however, painfully familiar with the concept of an interfering devil. In making a Scots-speaking devil (whose conspiratorial tone has much in common with that of Holy Willie addressing his God) declare his political affiliations with an opportunistic aristocrat Burns makes an imaginative leap from the limitations of his parish to produce a brilliant satire on cynicism and, obliquely, a celebration of the American revolution. Even in 1786, three years before the French followed the American example, Burns was worldly enough to conceal his revolutionary political faith from the public he aimed to please in the Kilmarnock Edition.

A DREAM

Text   113/CW, 233–6.

Composition   Written in June 1786 in response to Thomas Warton's 'Ode XVII for His Majesty's Birthday, June 4th, 1786'.

Publication   Published in the Kilmarnock Edition (31 July 1786).
Reception   David Irving (*The Lives of the Scottish Poets*, 1804) classed the poem 'among [Burns's] happier efforts' (CH, 166). Linking it with 'The Author's Earnest Cry and Prayer', Snyder found both poems 'timely, and in places at least, brilliant, examples of that rare sort of political satire which remains readable after the conditions which occasioned it have ceased to exist' (Snyder, 166). Crawford commented:

'A Dream' has often been considered a Jacobite effusion, but its mood seems to be that of a romantic Jacobite nationalism in the process of turning into something politically radical and uncompromising – the sort of attitude which, seven years after the Kilmarnock Edition, would be termed Jacobinical. It is closer to 'Courts for cowards were erected' [from 'The Jolly Beggars'] than to the sentimental worship of Bonnie Prince Charlie. (Crawford, 159–60)

*   *   *

Though he 'set little by kings' (CL, 136) Burns had a sentimental attachment to the Royal House of Stewart and believed his father's family had suffered because of its Jacobite sympathies. The Hanoverian kings he regarded as usurpers though George I, who became king of Great Britain in 1714, was a great grandson of James VI and I. Burns was, like many Scots, stirred by the story of 'Bonnie Prince Charlie' – Charles Edward Stuart, James II's grandson – who came to Scotland in 1745 and, with the support of the Scottish clans, proclaimed his father (James Francis Edward Stuart, the Old Pretender) king and himself regent on 19 August. By 4 December, Bonnie Prince Charlie had reached Derby and George II was ready to return to Hanover. However, at this point the Jacobites retreated and their hopes were destroyed, along with the Scottish clans, on the battlefield of Culloden on 16 April 1746. George III, who succeeded his grandfather George II in 1760, was (to Burns and others) a Hanoverian autocrat who oppressed America and opposed parliamentary reform.

For the forty-eighth birthday of George III – marked by national parades of loyalty – the Poet Laureate, Thomas Warton, produced a Pindaric ode. Burns's headnote in the Kilmarnock Edition explains how his own poem was written:

On Reading, in the Public Papers, the Laureate's Ode with the other Parade of June 4th, 1786, the Author was no sooner dropt asleep, than he imagined himself transported to the Birthday Levee; and, in his dreaming Fancy, made the following address.

The note itself mocks Warton's Ode, so soporific in celebrating 'the Monarch's natal morn' that it sent Burns into a deep sleep. It is ostensibly as a mere dreamer, 'A humble poet', that he converses with the king though the poem undermines this conceit with irony and the currency of malicious gossip.

Using the Christis Kirk stanza, Burns bids 'Guid-mornin to your Majesty' and (second and third stanzas) brings the gift of sardonic verse to the birthday party. He warns the king to beware of easy flattery then informs him that he sits on a throne that would be better occupied by one 'better/Than you', that is Bonnie Prince Charlie who had been regarded by Jacobites as Charles III since 1766, when the Old Pretender died (the Young Pretender died in Rome on 31 January 1788, not so long after the publication of Burns's poem).

> I see ye're complimented thrang,
>   By monie a lord an lady;
> 'God save the King' 's a cuckoo sang
>   That's unco easy said ay:
> The poets, too, a venal gang,
>   Wi rhymes weel-turn'd an ready,
> Wad gar you trow ye ne'er do wrang,

> But ay unerring steady,
>   On sic a day.
>
> For me! before a Monarch's face,
>   Ev'n there I winna flatter;
> For neither pension, post, nor place,
>   Am I your humble debtor:
> So, nae reflection on your Grace,
>   Your Kingship to bespatter;
> There's monie waur been o the race,
>   And aiblins ane been better
>   Than you this day.

This is courageously said, though Burns attempts to defuse a potentially explosive attack by claiming dream-status for his poem and prefacing it with an apologetic couplet: 'Thoughts, words and deeds, the Statue blames with reason;/But surely Dreams were ne'er indicted Treason.'

Reminding George III that 'facts are chiels that winna ding,/And downa be disputed', Burns describes the sorry spectacle displayed by the 'royal nest': the American colonies have gone; The Tory 'ministration' (of Pitt) is run by men more suited to cleaning out a cowshed; 'sair taxation' fleeces the nation; Pitt is 'a true guid fallow's get' about to cut back spending on the Navy (the king's 'bonie barges'). Burns hopes, ironically considering the evidence, that the king will allow Freedom to toss her head and will destroy Corruption. Turning to other members of the royal family, the poet presents his compliments to the Queen and predicts that George, Prince of Wales (later George IV), 'young Potentate o Wales' will regret his affairs (he seduced Mme Hardenberg in 1781 and secretly married Mrs Fitzherbert in 1785) and the time he has wasted throwing 'dice wi Charlie' (Charles James Fox, leader of the Whig opposition to Pitt). Ironically, Burns suggests that the Prince might surprise his critics, the way Prince Hal did on becoming Henry V, 'him at Agincourt wha shone'.

Frederick Augustus, Duke of York and Bishop of Osnaburg, is advised to 'get a wife to hug' lest he 'stain the mitre'. As for Prince William (later Duke of Clarence and William IV) – in the Navy since 1779 and rumoured to be having an affair with Sarah Martin, daughter of the Commissioner of Porstmouth dockyard – he is advised to go ahead with the sexual voyage Burns evokes with nautical metaphors.

> Young, royal Tarry-breeks, I learn,
> Ye've lately come athwart her –
> A glorious galley, stem an stern,
> Well rigg'd for Venus' barter;
> But first hang out that she'll discern
> Your hymeneal charter;
> Then heave aboard your grapple-airn,
> An, large upon her quarter,
> Come full that day.

The penultimate stanza urges George III's daughters (Charlotte, Augusta, Elizabeth, Mary, Sophia, Amelia) to favour 'British boys' over 'German gentles'. Burns then closes the poem on a note of caution, recalling that a full feast of flattery can become as empty as a dish scraped clean.

The poem offended two of Burns's friends. Advising the poet on the contents of the First Edinburgh Edition, Hugh Blair suggested deleting the stanza beginning 'Young, royal Tarry-breeks, I learn' as it was 'coarse' (CH, 81). Mrs Dunlop, writing to Burns on 26 February 1787, observed: 'numbers at London are learning Scots to read your book, but they don't like your Address to the King, and say it will hurt the sale of the rest' (cited by Kinsley, 1191). Burns, however, retained the poem in the First Edinburgh Edition.

'A Dream' is a poetic gesture that makes two main points, one personal, the other political. First, its irreverent attitude to the reigning monarch conveys the independence Burns valued as an essential part of his character (compare his boast 'I was bred to the Plough, and am independent' in the Dedication to the First Edinburgh Edition). Secondly, Burns implies that no Hanoverian king can assume he is irreplaceable. On the first point, Burns had to compromise in his subsequent career; on the second, he had to make do with wishful thinking (and his thoughts included republican action as well as the claim of Bonnie Prince Charlie, 'Charles III', to the throne). Technically, the poem is mistitled for Burns addresses a (geographically and psychologically) distant king without any dream-like delusions.

ADDRESS TO THE UNCO GUID

Text 39/CW, 74–6.

Composition   Composed in the late summer of 1786, according to
Snyder's conjecture that 'it was not written till after his experience
in doing penance for the Armour affair' (Snyder, 160): Burns's last
penitential appearance before the Mauchline congregation was on 6
August 1786.

Publication   Included in the First Edinburgh Edition (17 April
1787).

Reception   Quoting the last twelve lines of the poem Wordsworth
(*A Letter to a Friend of Robert Burns*, 1816) suggested that Burns's
biographer Currie should have considered them before producing
'a revolting account of a man of exquisite genius . . . sunk into the
lowest depths of vice and misery' (CH, 281). Quoting lines 49–60
of the poem, thus focusing on the same sentiments as Wordsworth,
Thomas Campbell (*Specimens of the British Poets*, 1819) wrote: 'Nor
should his maxims, which inculcate charity and candour in judging
of human frailties, be interpreted as a serious defence of them'
(CH, 324).

  Snyder thought it 'a plea, as eloquent as can well be conceived, for
"Poor Frailty"' (Snyder, 160). Similarly, Crawford sees it as a highly
personal poem which 'reiterates the timeless plea of a young and
passionate man to his intolerant elders' (Crawford, 65).

*   *   *

Burns's full title, 'Address to the Unco Guid or the Rigidly Righteous', is self-explanatory and comes complete with a quotation from
Solomon translated into Scots and versified in the eight-line stanza
(*ababcdcd*) of the poem. If the poem was prompted by his penitential appearances before the Mauchline congregation in July–August
1786 it explored a theme he had considered for some time. Snyder
finds a 'prose first draft' (Snyder, 87) for the poem in an entry for
March 1784 in the first Common Place Book:

> Let any of the strictest character for regularity of conduct among
> us, examine impartially how many of his virtues are owing to
> constitution and education; how many vices he has never been
> guilty of, not from any care or vigilance, but from want of
> opportunity, or some accidental circumstance intervening; how
> many of the weaknesses of mankind he has escaped because he
> was out of the line of such temptation; and what often, if not

always, weighs more than all the rest; how much he is indebted to the world's good, because the world does not know all; I say, any man who can thus think, will scan the failings, nay the faults and crimes of mankind around him, with a brother's eye. (CB, 9)

Though the words 'temptation', 'scan' and 'faults' appear in both the prose passage and the poem, the entry in the first Common Place Book is not so much a prose draft of a specific poem as a summary of Burns's general ideas on tolerance and fraternity.

Through his friendship with lawyers such as Bob Ainslie and Gavin Hamilton, Burns developed an interest in forensic techniques and put his knowledge to poetic use in the Address. From the first phrase, 'O ye wha are sae guid yoursel', the poem is confrontational, constructed as a spirited speech for the defence of common humanity before prejudiced judges representing the rigidly righteous. In the second stanza Burns declares himself 'counsel for poor mortals' who would 'here propone defences' and he then urges the unco guid to consider his argument. 'Think', he cautions them at the beginning of the fourth stanza: think how you behaved when you were young enough to feel the blood coursing through your veins, then try to empathise with the youth whose 'veins convulse' with the pressure of passion. The following stanza suggests that what the unco guid see as 'Debauchery and Drinking' is only their prejudiced perception of harmless 'Social Life and Glee'. With age, Burns implies, comes an atrophy of tolerance.

The sixth stanza, the most forceful in the poem, exchanges forensic argument for pointed sarcasm. Temptation, Burns scornfully insists, can only be understood by those it touches:

> Ye high, exalted, virtuous dames,
>   Tied up in godly laces,
> Before ye gie poor Frailty names,
>   Suppose a change o cases:
> A dear-lov'd lad, convenience snug,
>   A treach'rous inclination –
> But, let me whisper i your lug,
>   Ye're aiblins nae temptation.

These lines are brilliantly charged with poetic meaning by Burns. The women are prisoners of their fancy clothes, helplessly 'Tied up' in them, an image that makes them victims of their own self-denying morality. Cunningly, Burns presents the lusty lad but leaves his sentence hanging in the air as he comically parodies the Bible. In Genesis the serpent 'more subtil than any beast of the field' (Genesis 3:1) whispers words of temptation into the ear of Eve. Burns, whom the unco guid would consider a sinner on the side of the serpent, whispers a very different message into the ear of the self-righteous women.

In the last two stanzas of the poem, Burns gives his peroration, moving from Scots to Augustan English and appealing, finally, to a higher judge than the self-appointed judges comprising the unco guid.

> Then gently scan your brother man,
> Still gentler sister woman;
> Tho they may gang a kennin wrang,
> To step aside is human:
> One point must still be greatly dark,
> The moving *Why* they do it;
> And just as lamely can ye mark,
> How far perhaps they rue it.
>
> Who made the heart, 'tis He alone
> Decidedly can try us;
> He knows each chord, its various tone,
> Each spring, its various bias:
> Then at the balance let's be mute,
> We never can adjust it;
> What's done we partly may compute,
> But know not what's resisted.

The linguistic balance is well judged by Burns here and the use of English is appropriate to the legalistic tone of the poem. Only one line in the penultimate stanza is in Scots – 'Tho they may gang a kennin wrang' – and its homely accent stresses the human appeal of the aphorism that follows it. By the end of the poem the reader is persuaded that Burns has made his case and that any decently human verdict on him and his kind must absolve them of guilt.

Structurally, the poem is solid, moving persuasively from table-turning accusation ('O ye wha are sae guid yoursel'), through anec-dotal illustration ('A dear-lov'd lad, convenience snug') to pero-ration ('Then at the balance let's be mute'). With the rhetorical

cunning of an accomplished lawyer Burns makes the case for view-
ing youthful passion with mature compassion; and, in doing so,
enlarges his poetic repertoire.

THE CALF

Text   125/CW, 252.

Composition   Written on Sunday, 3 September 1786. Burns sent
'The Calf' to Robert Muir on 8 September 1786, noting 'This Poem
was nearly an extemporaneous production, on a wager with Mr
[Gavin] Hamilton that I would not produce a poem on the subject
in a given time' (CL, 87).

Publication   First published the First Edinburgh Edition (17 April
1787); reprinted in a chapbook of 1787 with a note saying the
Glasgow Advertiser had rejected it, as being too personal, 'some time
ago' (Kinsley, 1211).

Reception   The indifference of early critics to this poem has been
emulated in modern books about Burns. Snyder makes no value
judgement of it, noting only that 'the first and third of [it] had
certainly been written before the Kilmarnock volume appeared,
but had been excluded from it' (Snyder, 229). Crawford calls it 'a
spirited piece of essentially verbal tomfoolery . . . important mainly
as proving that Burns had by the end of 1786 lost interest in the
[anti-Calvinist satirical] *genre*' (Crawford, 75–6).

*   *   *

On Sunday, 3 September 1786, the Rev James Steven (1761–1824)
– assistant to the Rev Robert Dow of Ardrossan – preached at
Mauchline (probably on exchange with Rev Auld) on the text 'and
ye shall go forth, and grow up as calves of the stall' (Malachi 4:2).
Gavin Hamilton wagered that Burns could not produce a poem on
the same text in a given time. Burns won the wager, sending a copy
of the poem to Dr John Mackenzie on the day of Steven's sermon:
'The fourth, and the last Stanzas are added since I saw you today'
(CL, 113).

The poet's hostility to the Auld Licht preacher is articulated in a
series of animal metaphors identifying Steven as the embodiment

of his own sermon: the preacher's name was a gift to Burns since 'steven', in Scots, means an uproar. Each quatrain, apart from the fourth, ends with Steven as an animal: 'an unco *calf*', 'a *stirk*', 'a *stot*', 'among the *nowte*', 'a famous *bullock*'. The fourth quatrain is the most malicious of all, suggesting, through the commonplace connotation of horns, that Steven is destined to be a cuckold rather than a bull:

> Tho, when some kind connubial dear
>   Your but-an-ben adorns,
> The like has been that you may wear
>   A noble head of *horns*.

In other ecclesiastical satires ('Holy Willie's Prayer', for example) Burns implies that the Auld Lichts are sly. In 'The Calf' he is content to condemn their representative as stupid, thus so far below contempt as to be harmless. Hence the concluding stanza which has the concise quality of Burns's mischievous epitaphs:

> And when ye're number'd wi' the dead,
>   Below a grassy hillock,
> Wi' justice they may mark your head –
>   'Here lies a famous *bullock*!'

'The Calf', despite Snyder's assertion that two-thirds of it predated the Kilmarnock Edition, has the confidence that comes with being a published poet. Burns is no longer anguished by the antics of the Auld Lichts; he is serenely above them, at least in his art. Over his life he did not exert so much control. In the evening of the Sunday of the sermon he had satirised, Burns was at Mossgiel when he was visited by a brother of Jean Armour who told him she had just given birth to twins.

As for the Rev Steven, the cuckold-cum-bullock of the poem, he moved to London in 1787 and became a founder of the London Missionary Society. The poet's brother William heard the Rev Steven preach in London in March 1790 and noted that he had 'grown very fat and . . . as boisterous as ever' (BE, 342). In 1803 Rev Steven returned to Ayrshire as minister of Kilwinning.

THE BRIGS OF AYR

Text   120/CW, 244–9.

Composition   Written in the autumn of 1786 when the construction of the new bridge of Ayr was underway. It was sent to the dedicatee, John Ballantine, on 27 September 1786 (CL, 97).

Publication   First published in the First Edinburgh Edition (17 April 1787).

Reception   James Currie (*The Works of Robert Burns*, 1800) noted it was suggested by Fergusson's 'Mutual Complaint of Plainstanes and Causey' and commented:

> This poem, irregular and imperfect as it is, displays various and powerful talents, and may serve to illustrate the genius of Burns. In particular it affords a striking instance of his being carried beyond his original purpose by the powers of imagination . . . . Incongrous as the different parts of the poem are, it is not an incongruity that displeases, and we have only to regret that the poet did not bestow a little pains in making the figures more correct, and in smoothing the versification. (CH, 138)

Josiah Walker (*Account of the Life and Character of Robert Burns*, 1811) also found the poem flawed:

> A desire to pay compliments to his friends made him sometimes choose improper and unexpected places for them, without considering how far he would be accompanied by the feelings of his reader. In this manner he disturbs the process of imagination, in the 'Brigs of Ayr', to praise a favourite fiddler; and he injures the unity of that poem, as well as of his 'Vision', by mixing real with fancied persons. The effect is nearly the same, as if a painter of some historical event should injudiciously compose his group of portraits of his friends, whether their phisiognomy might suit the characters or not. (CH, 234–5)

Snyder judged it 'the most pretentious of the poems written too late for the Kilmarnock volume . . . a less readable example of the old *débat* than "The Twa Dogs' (Snyder, 230). Crawford admired sections of the poem but found it, as a whole, 'lacking in design and general proportion' (Crawford, 198). Kinsley described it simply as 'a late, provincial variant of the ancients-and-moderns debate' (Kinsley, 1200).

*   *   *

'The Brigs of Ayr' is dedicated to John Ballantine who, as Dean of Guild in Ayr, was prominent in promoting the building of a new bridge over the Ayr in 1786 as the old bridge, dating from the fifteenth century, was regarded as unsafe. A design for the new bridge by Robert Adam was paid for but, according to local tradition, the mason Alexander Steven, who built the bridge, worked from his own plans. Interestingly, the prophecy of the old bridge in Burns's poem – 'I'll be a brig when ye're a shapeless cairn!' – was fulfilled in 1877 when the New Brig collapsed after flood-damage to the arch at the south end. It was replaced by the present bridge in 1881–2 and, in 1910, the Auld Brig was restored.

Writing to Robert Aiken, in October 1786, Burns regretted that John Wilson, the printer of the Kilmarnock Edition, was not prepared to publish a second edition without a financial guarantee. Thinking of how Ballantine had encouraged him, Burns added:

> There is scarcely any thing hurts me so much in being disappointed of my second edition, as not having it in my power to shew my gratitude to Mr Ballantine, by publishing my poem of *The Brigs of Ayr*. I would detest myself as a wretch, if I thought I were capable, in a very long life, of forgetting the honest, warm and tender delicacy with which he enters into my interests. (CL, 92)

The poem, then, was regarded as the artistic payment of a debt to a patron, a theme articulated in the dedicatory first verse-paragraph where Burns projects himself as 'The simple Bard, rough at the rustic plough' and humbly salutes his benefactor:

> Still, if some patron's gen'rous care he trace,
> Skill'd in the secret to bestow with grace;
> When Ballantine befriends his humble name,
> And hands the rustic stranger up to fame,
> With heartfelt throes his grateful bosom swells:
> The godlike bliss, to give, alone excels.

Here the heroic couplets plod along dutifully but elsewhere Burns shortens and lengthens the iambic pentameter in the interests of an irregularity appropriate to a 'simple Bard, rough at the rustic plough'. What critics like Currie (see above) took for carelessness is a deliberate attempt to go against the grain of the heroic couplet.

After the Augustan English of the opening verse-paragraph, the poem switches to an English enriched with Scots words. Burns dwells on the savagery of human nature as 'Man, that tyrant o'er the weak' (a notion explored in the poetry of Pope and Thomson) prepares for winter by dispensing death:

> The thundering guns are heard on ev'ry side,
> The wounded coveys, reeling, scatter wide;
> The feathered field-mates, bound by Nature's tie,
> Sires, mothers, children, in one carnage lie

The sentiment is strong in eighteenth-century verse: Pope, in *Windsor Forest* (1713) refers to 'slaught'ring Guns' as does Burns in his song 'Now Westlin winds', written in celebration of an affair of 1775. As in 'To a Mouse', Burns sees a natural order disturbed by the activities of man.

It is late autumn, then, 'that season, when a simple Bard,/Unknown and poor . . . left his bed and took his wayward route'. Having evoked autumn atmospherically (in lines influenced by Thomson's description of autumn in *The Seasons*: compare Burns's 'The hoary morns precede the sunny days' with Thomson's 'The western sun withdraws the shortened day'), Burns gives his meditation a precise time and place. (The Dungeon-Clock was on the Tolbooth steeple which was demolished in 1826; the Wallace Tower, which contained a clock, stood at the corner of High Street and Mill Vennel until 1834 when it was replaced.)

> The drowsy Dungeon-Clock had number'd two,
> And Wallace Tower had sworn the fact was true;
> The tide-swoln Firth, with sullen-sounding roar,
> Through the still night dash'd hoarse along the shore;
> All else was hush'd as Nature's closed e'e;
> The silent moon shone high o'er tower and tree;
> The chilly frost, beneath the silver beam,
> Crept, gently-crusting, o'er the glittering stream.

Suddenly the 'list'ning Bard' hears the swish of wings and sees 'Two dusky forms dart thro the midnight air'. These are 'The Sprites that owre the Brigs of Ayr preside': the spirit of the Auld Brig, 'of ancient Pictish race', has wrinkled Gothic features; the spirit of the New Brig, dressed in a fine new coat, has elaborately decorative features. Thus introduced as architectural opposites, the two bridges embark on a dialogue of the old versus the new.

The Auld Brig begins the conversation, which develops as a mild form of the 'flyting' (fulminating) exchanges so popular with such great Scots makars as Dunbar (see his 'The Flyting of Dunbar and Kennedie' in Kinsley's edition of *The Poems of William Dunbar*, Oxford, 1979). To the Auld Brig's accusation of frivolity, the New Brig replies with an insult to its opponent's 'ugly, Gothic hulk'. The Auld Brig then prophesies (accurately, see above) that the New Brig will fall to floods and the New Brig produces a powerful critique of Gothic architecture:

> 'Gaunt, ghastly, ghaist-alluring edifices,
> Hanging with threat'ning jut like precipices;
> O'er-arching, mouldy, gloom-inspiring coves,
> Supporting roofs fantastic – stony groves;
> Windows and doors in nameless sculptures drest,
> With order, symmetry, or taste unblest;
> Forms like some bedlam statuary's dream,
> The craz'd creations of misguided whim . . . '

Linguistically, the New Brig uses a less dense Scots than the Auld Brig and is more erudite. Burns, a poet who renewed rather than renounced tradition, does not allow the New Brig to win the argument for novelty without a struggle.

Speaking on behalf of a positive tradition, the Auld Brig condemns the superficiality of the gentry in whose frivolous image the New Brig is apparently made:

> 'Nae langer thrifty citizens, an douce,
> Meet owre a pint, or in the council-house;
> But staumrel, corky-headed, graceless gentry,
> The herryment and ruin of the country;
> Men three-parts made by tailors and by barbers,
> Wha waste your weel-hain'd gear on damn'd New Brigs and
>   harbours!'

This is well said and Burns, always able to inhabit a character even if unsympathetic, clearly endorses this criticism. Yet if the Auld Brig has some valid observations, it is too tied to an oppressive past to be accepted uncritically. So Burns gives the last word to the New Brig who advocates the liberal cause of 'Common-sense', sick of the 'Plain, dull stupidity' of the past.

At this point the dispute – described by the poet as nonsensical 'clish-ma-claver' – ends and Burns rounds off his poem with a parade of personifications led by the Genius of the Stream, a catalogue introducing the allegorical figures of Female Beauty,

Spring, Rural Joy, Summer, Plenty, Autumn, Winter, Hospitality, Courage, Benevolence, Learning, Worth:

> Last, white-rob'd Peace, crowned with a hazel wreath,
> To rustic Agriculture did bequeath,
> The broken, iron instruments of death:
> At sight of whom our Sprites forgat their kindling wrath.

The gift of the iron instruments of death is ambiguous, depriving war of its weapons but emphasising the bitter battles of the impoverished tenant-farmer.

Linguistically, the poem shows Burns using, with considerable success, the various verbal options open to him. There are echoes of Pope and there is the Scots precedent of Fergusson's 'Mutual Complaint of Plainstanes and Causey, in their Mother Tongue' (a dialogue between Edinburgh street and pavement). Whereas the combination of English and Scots is awkward in 'The Cotter's Saturday Night' here it is allows appropriate shifts in tone so the poet (who uses Augustan English and descriptive Scots) is distanced from the conversation between the combative Auld Brig and the more reasonable New Brig. The formal English frame (provided by the dedicatory lines of the opening and the catalogue of personifications at the close) emphasises the exuberance of the Scots used in the dialogue.

A WINTER NIGHT

Text   130/CW, 258–60.

Composition   Completed by 20 November 1786 when it was sent, with a letter, to John Ballantine (CL, 98).

Publication   First published in the First Edinburgh Edition (17 April 1787).

Reception   Writing to Burns on 23 May 1787, Dr John Moore described the poem as 'very beautiful' (Snyder, 217). Josiah Walker (*Account of the Life and Character of Robert Burns*, 1811) wrote:

> In his 'Winter Night' he contrives, by a masterly description of its severity, to lead us gradually on from the sufferings of the innocent songsters, to commiserate those even of the kite and the carrion crow, and to acknowledge that their voracious

cruelty has been more than expatiated by the merciless lash of the elements . . . . The 'Winter Night', like the 'Brigs [of Ayr]', sets out with description very powerfully executed, and in language decidedly Scotch, but it passes abruptly to English, and, in my apprehension, to a tone more nearly within the compass of an ordinary poet. (CH, 224, 242)

Thomas Carlyle (reviewing Lockhart's *Life of Burns* in the *Edinburgh Review*, December 1828) praised the poem's emotional power:

How touching it is, for instance, that, admidst the gloom of personal misery, brooding over the wintry desolation without him and within him, he thinks of the 'outrie cattle' and 'silly sheep', and their sufferings in the pitiless storm! . . . The tenant of the mean hut, with its 'ragged roof and chinky wall', has a heart to pity even these! This is worth several homilies on Mercy: for it is the voice of Mercy herself. Burns, indeed, lives in sympathy; his soul rushes forth into all realms of being; nothing that has existence can be indifferent to him. (CH, 365)

Hecht saw the poem as 'an impressive variation on the theme of man's inhumanity to man' (Hecht, 121), Crawford thought 'the separation between the first and second half is so absolute that one feels they almost belong to two entirely different poems – a Scottish descriptive lyric, and a neo-classic ode' (Crawford, 215). In Kinsley's opinion 'Burns's strophes have rhythmical strength [but] his images are too predictable, his diction too conventional' (Kinsley, 1216).

*   *   *

Burns described 'A Winter Night' as 'my first attempt in that irregular kind of measure in which many of our finest Odes are wrote' (CL, 98) and this poem alone makes nonsense of Burns's projection of himself (in the preface to the Kilmarnock Edition and elsewhere) as a poetic primitive. It is prefaced with a quotation from *King Lear*, alludes ('Blow, blow, ye winds') to a song from *As You Like It* ('Blow, blow, thou winter wind') and has echoes of Cowper, Goldsmith, Thomson, Young and Blair. Compare, for example, Burns's 'Luxury . . . With all the servile wretches in the rear,/Looks o'er proud Property, extended wide' with Goldsmith's 'The man of wealth and pride,/Takes up a space that many poor supplied;/Space for his lake, his park's extended bounds' (*The Deserted Village*).

Structurally 'A Winter Night' presents an English Pindaric ode framed by Scots verse with a concluding quatrain in English. The first part of the poem comprises six Standard Habbie stanzas in Scots, beginning with an evocation of a snowstorm, chillingly conveyed in such images as the sun 'Dim-dark'ning thro the flaky show'r,/Or whirling drift'. Burns does not, in this section, dwell on his own discomfort but thinks of the farm animals and the birds wasted by winter:

> Ilk happing bird, wee, helpless thing! –
> That in the merry months o spring,
> Delighted me to hear thee sing,
>   What comes o thee?
> Whare wilt thou cow'r thy chittering wing,
>   An close thy e'e?

The use of Scots is highly charged, 'chittering' (for instance) meaning both shivering from cold and trembling from fear. Burns, however, turns from Scots as the moon dimly hangs over the winter landscape. His thoughts turn inward from 'the dreary plain' and he hears a 'plaintive strain' – the Pindaric ode that is the centre-piece – and set-piece – of the work.

Burns's ode begins by adapting the song 'Blow, blow, thou winter wind' from *As You Like It*:

> Blow, blow, ye winds, with heavier gust!
> And freeze, thou bitter-biting frost!
> Descend, ye chilly, smothering snows!
> Not all your rage, as now united, shows
>   More hard unkindness, unrelenting,
>   Vengeful malice, unrepenting
> Than heaven-illumin'd Man on brother Man bestows!

Shakespeare thought the winter wind kind in comparison to 'man's ingratitude'. Burns goes further in attributing to 'heaven- illumin'd man' a relentless and deliberate cruelty to his brother man.

There is, in this switch from Scots to English, a loss of atmospheric intensity. In place of the bleak winter scene with shivering animals, Burns offers a series of abstractions, focusing on personifications like Oppression, Ambition, 'Woe, Want, and Murder', Truth, Luxury, Flattery, Property, Honour, Love, 'Maiden-Innocence', Pity, Misery, Guilt, Misfortune and Affliction. Moving from poignantly descriptive Scots verse to indignantly didactic English verse Burns becomes more formal and less persuasive. The points Burns makes – about the vicious nature of man and the immorality of 'pamper'd Luxury' – were made before by Shakespeare and Goldsmith ('Thus fares the land, by luxury betrayed', *The Deserted Village*) and have become commonplace. This is not to question the sincerity of Burns's attack on injustice, but to put it into the context of his period.

Even though Burns attempts a verbal portrait of wretchedness, the image is blurred by the surrounding abstractions so that what is meant to be the clinching couplet becomes a weak excuse for an argument: 'Affliction's sons are brothers in distress;/A brother to relieve, how exquisite the bliss!' The Pindaric ode reads, then, as an exercise, not an imaginative achievement; Burns ('not up to this kind of poetry', Kinsley, 1216) does not successfully realise his ambition of competing, in English, with the English poets he admired. It is with a sense of relief that the reader returns to the Scots of the penultimate stanza as sunlight breaks through the 'pouthery shaw'. Finally, Burns reverts to English to deliver the platitudinous conclusion to the poem:

> But deep this truth impress'd my mind:
> Thro all His works abroad,
> The heart benevolent and kind
> The most resembles God.

The style, as well as the sentiment, proceeds from a sense of duty that informs all the English lines of the poem. It is difficult to resist the conclusion that, had Burns not encountered the Scots muse of Fergusson in 1782, he would have been content to turn out pale imitations of the Augustans.

THE KIRK'S ALARM

Text   264/CW, 359–61.

Composition   Written in July 1789 at Ellisland; on 17 July, Burns sent 'the first rough-draught' (CL, 176) to Mrs Dunlop; on 7 August, enclosing a fair copy of the finished product to John Logan, he wrote 'I have, as you will shortly see, finished, "The KIRK'S ALARM"' (CL, 124).

Publication   First published in Dumfries, in abbreviated form and with the title 'The Ayrshire Garland, an Excellent New Song: tune, "The Vicar and Moses"', as an anonymous broadside of 1789; two further stanzas given in *Poems and Songs by Alexander Tait* (1790). A broadside-based text was given in Thomas Stewart's edition of *Poems ascribed to Robert Burns, the Ayrshire Bard* (1801) and an authoritative text was published in Allan Cunningham's *The Works of Robert Burns* (1834).

Reception   Snyder thought the first two stanzas 'in Burns's best satiric vein: brilliant in execution, both personal and general in application, and so phrased as to place before the reader at a glance the fundamental issue around which the controversy was raging' (Snyder, 338). Hecht notes 'with what gusto Burns attacks the old hated enemy' (Hecht, 138). For Crawford, the poem 'is mainly of local and historical interest, and is essentially an example of rather crude "flyting" or name-calling, which suggests that by 1789 Burns's heart was no longer in ecclesiastical satire' (Crawford, 75).

*   *   *

Two years after Burns was born, Rev William McGill (1732–1807) was ordained to the second ministry of Ayr, as the colleague of Rev William Dalrymple (see his entry in 'The Burns Circle') who had baptised the poet: like Dalrymple, McGill was listed on the side of the New Licht liberals in 'The Twa Herds' (1785). In 1786, McGill published *A Practical Essay on the Death of Jesus Christ* (1786) which was found, by Auld Lichts, to contain dangerous traces of Socinianism by emphasising Christ's teaching rather than his divinity:

> To suffer many indignities in the world, and to die on the cross, were not the chief and ultimate ends of our Saviour's mission [but rather] to confirm his doctrine by proper evidences; to set an example of what he taught; [and to] promote the salvation of sinners. (cited by Kinsley, 1306–7)

Disgruntled by the groundswell of orthodox opinion against his 'learned and truly worthy friend' McGill, Burns wrote to Mrs Dunlop, on 24 November 1787, that if the hostility continued 'I shall keep no measure with the savages, but fly at them with the faulcons of Ridicule, or run them down with the bloodhounds of Satire' (CL, 138). Mrs Dunlop counselled caution.

In November 1788 Rev William Peebles – clerk of the Ayr Presbytery, a man dismissed as superficial in 'The Twa Herds' and ridiculed, on 'the holy rostrum', in 'The Holy Fair' – denounced McGill and his *Practical Essay* as heretical. McGill defended himself in *The Benefits of the Revolution* (1789) but he was charged with heresy before the synod of Glasgow and Ayr. That May, the General Assembly of the Church of Scotland 'quashed the synod's order to the presbytery of Ayr to investigate the charge, but instructed the presbytery to maintain purity of doctrine' (Kinsley, 1307) and a committee of the presbytery was set up to examine McGill's teaching. The poet had his opportunity to unleash 'the bloodhounds of Satire', though not openly since 'Burns was eagerly awaiting orders that would put him on active duty in the Excise; a public challenge to the establishment . . . would have been inopportune' (Snyder, 338).

Burns's comments to his correspondents show clearly his predicament at being both a poet and a family man anxious to embark on an official career. To Mrs Dunlop, on 17 July, he said 'I am thinking to throw off two or three dozen copies [of 'The Kirk's Alarm'] at a Press in Dumfries, & send them as from Edinburgh to some Ayr-shire folks on both sides of the question' (CL, 176). To John Logan, on 7 August, he said:

> I am determined not to let it get into the Publick; so [request] that you will only read it to a few of us, and do not on any account, give, or permit to be taken, any copy of the Ballad . . . . I have enemies enow, God knows, tho' I do not wantonly add to the number. (CL, 124)

To Robert Aiken, in August, Burns claimed that McGill's foes were shielded by 'Ignorance, supersition, bigotry, stupidity, malevolence, self-conceit, envy' and that 'to such a shield, humour is the peck of a sparrow, and satire the pop-gun of a school-boy' (CL, 95). On 1 September Burns began work as an Excise officer and to Robert Graham of Fintry, on 9 December, he said:

> I think you must have heard of Dr Mcgill, one of the clergymen of Ayr, and his heretical book [*A Practical Essay on the Death of*

Jesus Christ]. – God help him, poor man! though he is one of the worthiest as well as one of the ablest, in the whole priesthood of the Kirk of Scotland, in every sense of that ambiguous term, yet, for the blasphemous heresies of squaring Religion by the rules of Common Sense, and attempting to give a decent character to Almighty God and a rational account of his proceedings with the Sons of Men, the poor Doctor and his numerous family are in imminent danger of being thrown out to the mercy of the winter winds. – The inclosed Ballad ['The Kirk's Alarm'] on that business is I confess too local, but I laughed at some conceits in it myself, though I am convinced in my conscience that there are several heavy stanzas in it too. (CL, 431)

Finally, to Lady Elizabeth Cunningham, on 23 December, he said (enclosing a copy of the poem) 'Dr Mcgill . . . is my particular friend, & my Ballad on his persecution has virulence enough if it has not wit' (CL, 499). From these remarks it is clear that Burns was not responsible for the anonymous broadside publication of the poem (or part of it) that year; and that his boast, to Mrs Dunlop, about taking a public stand on the issue, had to be abandoned for the selfish cause of careerism. Perhaps, for all the kind words he heaped on McGill, Burns anticipated that the minister would ultimately capitulate – again for the sake of careerism and domestic security, since Burns refers to McGill's large family. In April 1790, less than a year after the composition of Burns's poem, a diffident McGill – described by Mrs Dunlop as 'a poor little white rabbit' (Kinsley, 1308) – apologised to the church and the case against him was dropped.

Burns's poem (or song, for he matched it to various tunes including 'The hounds are out' and 'Push about the brisk bowl') rattles along on internal rhymes as it expresses mock-horror at the verbal assault on the kirk by 'Doctor Mac' (McGill). The first two stanzas explain the supposedly alarming situation, as Burns, laying on the irony, articulates the orthodox position:

> Orthodox! orthodox! what believe in John Knox –
>   Let me sound an alarm to your conscience:
> A heretic blast has been blown i' the Wast,
>   That what is not sense must be nonsense –
> Orthodox! That what is not sense must be nonsense.

> Doctor Mac! Doctor Mac, you should stretch on a rack,
> 　To strike wicked Writers wi terror;
> 　To join Faith and Sense, upon onie pretence,
> 　　Was heretic, damnable error –
> Doctor Mac! 'Twas heretic, damnable error.

As in his earlier ecclesiastical satires, Burns proceeds by listing a catalogue of names. The first four names are those of men he admired: Doctor Mac; Provost John Ballantine of Ayr; 'Orator Bob' Aiken; Rev William Dalrymple. They are on the side of Common Sense which leads Burns to the other faction, the Auld Lichts:

> Calvin's sons! Calvin's sons! seize your sp'ritual guns,
> 　Ammunition you never can need;
> Your hearts are the stuff will be powther enough,
> 　And your skulls are storehouses o lead
> Calvin's sons! Your skulls are storehouses o lead.

Each succeeding stanza is devoted to one of Calvin's sons: Rev John Rusell, (here 'Rumble John', previously 'wordy Russell' of 'The Twa Herds' and 'Black Russell' of 'The Holy Fair'), Auld Licht minister of the High Kirk, Kilmarnock; Rev James Mackinlay (of 'The Ordination'), Auld Licht minister of the Laigh Kirk, Kilmarnock; Rev Alexander ('Sawnie') Moodie (of 'The Twa Herds'), Auld Licht minister of Riccarton; Rev William Auld, Auld Licht minister of Mauchline and Burns's old adversary; Rev James Young ('Jamie Goose'), Auld Licht minister of New Cumnock; Rev David Grant ('Davie Rant'), Auld Licht minister of Ettrick; Rev William Peebles, whose line 'And bound in *Liberty's* endearing chain', in a poem on the Centenary of the Glorious Revolution, Burns alludes to; Rev Andrew Mitchell ('Andrew Gowk'), Auld Licht minister of Monkton; Rev Stephen Young ('Barr Steenie'), Auld Licht minister of Barr; Rev George Smith, 'Cessnock-side' (described as a turn-coat in 'The Twa Herds', damned with faint praise in 'The Holy Fair'), Auld Licht minister of Galston; Rev John ('Muirland Jock') Shepherd,, Auld Licht minister of Muirkirk; 'Holy Will' Fisher (of 'Holy Willie's Prayer'). Finally – in a framing stanza that connects with the listing of McGill, Ballantine, Aiken and Dalrymple at the beginning of the poem – comes the poet himself.

> Poet Burns! Poet Burns, wi your priest-skelpin turns,

Why desert ye your auld native shire?
Your Muse is a gipsy, yet were she e'en tipsy,
She could ca' us nae waur than we are –
Poet Burns! ye could ca' us nae waur than we are.

As the catalogue in the poem (and the above paragraph) demonstrates Burns assumed a working knowledge of ecclesiastical
politics and, with the passing of time, many of the references have
lost their point. The names on Burns's theological hate-list would
have been forgotten long since had he not preserved them in his
satirical poems. 'The Kirk's Alarm' is not the best of Burns: the
pun of 'Davie Rant', for Davie Grant, is childish and the accusation that Holy Willie Fisher 'pilfer'd the alms of the poor' simply
repeats the malicious gossip that the man had stolen money from
the Mauchline Kirk poor-box. The most effective insults are those
with scatological or sexual connotations. Thus the poetic pretensions of the Rev William Peebles (the villain of the piece) are
dismissed: 'O'er Pegasus' side ye ne'er laid a stride,/Ye but smelt,
man, the place where he shit'. Thus the phallic pride of Rev George
Smith is deflated: 'Cessnock-side! Cessnock-side, wi your turkey-
cock pride/Of manhood but sma' is your share'.

In clarifying Burns's hatred of Calvinistic orthodoxy, the poem
adds nothing to the earlier ecclesiastical satires, though it matches
the intolerance of the enemy with its own combative intolerance of
the Auld Lichts. In returning to the catalogue-technique of those
satires, it suggests that Burns never lost his conviction that the
most appalling aspect of the Auld Lichts was their collective conspiratorial existence so that to name them is enough to damn them.
In showing that Burns never lost his fascination with his 'auld native
shire' it is psychologically revealing for, even at Ellisland, the poet
could not forget the 'bark' of Daddie Auld or the hypocrisy of
Holy Willie. The strident stanzaic form ('common in squibs and
drinking-songs', Kinsley, 1308) is handled adroitly: stylistically, if
not intellectually, the poem is impressive, showing an abundance
of energy and an ingenuity with internal rhyme.

ELEGY ON CAPTAIN MATTHEW HENDERSON

Text 239/CW, 337–40.

Composition   Completed on 23 July 1790, as Burns explained in a letter to Robert Cleghorn (CL, 275) sending him a fair copy of the poem.

Publication   Published in the *Edinburgh Magazine*, August 1790; revised for the Second Edinburgh Edition (18 February 1793).

Reception   In a letter of 10 October 1796 to his kinsman James Currie (then planning his edition of Burns) Thomas Duncan, a tutor in a Liverpool family, wrote:

> [Burns] does not *always* suit the measure of his verses to the subject on which they treat. The elegy on Capt. M. H. for instance, is composed in a metre which custom has appropriated to humour & which is therefore perfectly incongruous with the gravity of the language. Its effect was, to me, extremely unpleasant. (CH, 114)

Allan Cunningham, *The Works of Robert Burns* (1834), took a more positive view of the poem:

> Others of his poems have a still grander reach . . . the divine 'Elegy on Mathew Henderson' unites human nature in a bond of sympathy with the stars of the sky, the fowls of the air, the beasts of the field, the flowery vale, and the lonely mountain'. (CH, 413)

Hecht called the poem 'a deeply felt elegy' (Hecht, 113) and Crawford thought it 'worthy of being considered as one of the greatest elegies to have been produced in the British Isles' (Crawford, 212). Comparing the elegy to Allan Ramsay's 'Elegy on Lucky Wood' and Fergusson's 'Elegy, on the Death of Scots Music', Kinsley writes:

> Burns's invocation to Nature is much more sustained, and well ordered; moving from natural features to flowers, animals and birds, the four seasons and finally the planets through whose 'orbs' Henderson has 'taen his flight'. (Kinsley, 1287)

*   *   *

The subject of the elegy, Matthew Henderson (1737–88) was the son of David Henderson of Tannoch, Ayrshire, and Tannochside,

Lanarkshire. He inherited both properties but had to sell them to pay for his convivial pleasures and by the time Burns met him in Edinburgh 1787, when he became a neighbour of Henderson's in St James's Square, the Captain (who had been a lieutenant in the Earl of Home's regiment and a civil servant) was subsisting on a pension. Henderson was buried in Greyfriars churchyard on 27 November 1788.

Sending a fair copy of the poem to Robert Cleghorn on 23 July 1790 from Ellisland, Burns explained:

> You knew Matthew Henderson. At the time of his death I com-posed an elegiac Stanza or two, as he was a man I much regarded; but something came in my way so that the design of an Elegy to his memory gave up. – Meeting with a fragment the other day among some old waste papers, I tried to finish the Piece, & have this moment put the last hand to it. (CL, 275)

Sending another copy to Dugald Stewart, from Ellisland on 30 July 1790, Burns paid further respects to his late friend:

> I dare say if you have not met with Captain Matthew Henderson about Edinburgh, you must have heard of him. – He was an intimate acquaintance of mine, & of all Mankind I ever knew, he was one of the first, for a nice sense of honour, a generous contempt of the adventitious distinctions of Men, and sterling tho' sometimes outré Wit. – The inclosed Elegy has pleased me beyond any of my late poetic efforts. – Perhaps 'tis 'the memory of joys that are past', and a friend who is no more, that biasses my criticism. – It is likewise, ever since I read your, Aiken on the poetical use of Natural history [in John Aikin's *Essays on Song-Writing*, 1772], a favorite study of mine, the characters of the Vegetable & the manners of the Animal kingdoms. (CL, 449)

In the copy he sent Mrs Dunlop, Henderson is described as 'a much-valued acquaintance' (CL, 190), in the copy he sent Dr John Moore, Henderson is 'a Man I loved much' (CL, 261) and the copy sent to Graham of Fintry (from the Globe Inn, 4 September 1790) came with a touching tribute:

> Poor Matthew! – I can forgive Poverty for hiding Virtue and Piety. – They are not only plants that flourish best in the shade,

but they also produce their sacred fruits more especially for another world. – But when the haggard Beldam throws her invidious veil over Wit, Spirit, &c. but I trust another world will cast light on the subject. (CL, 434)

All this confirms what the elegy indicates, that the loss of Henderson was profoundly distressing to Burns.

Composed, like Fergusson's 'Elegy, on the Death of Scots Music' (which influenced it) in the Standard Habbie stanza, Burns's poem is a sustained application of the pathetic fallacy (to borrow Ruskin's phrase of 1856) after the manner of Milton's 'Lycidas' ('And Daffadillies fill their cups with tears,/To strew the Laureat Herse where Lycid lies'). Burns begins what develops into a catalogue with an image from Dunbar's great catalogue-poem 'Lament for the Makars' (which he knew from Allan Ramsay's anthology *Ever Green*, 1724). Dunbar described Death as 'That strang unmercifull tyrand', Burns begins his 'Elegy on Captain Matthew Henderson, A Gentleman who held the Patent for his Honours immediately from Almighty God' (to give the full title) with a similarly grim acknowledgement of Death:

> O Death! thou tyrant fell and bloody!
> The meikle devil wi' a woodie
> Haurl thee hame to his black smiddie,
>   O'er hurcheon hides,
> And like stock-fish come o'er his studdie
>   Wi thy auld sides!

The second stanza announces the departure of Henderson from a natural order that will mourn him:

> He's gane, he's gane! he's frae us torn,
> The ae best fellow e'er was born!
> Thee, Matthew, Nature's sel' shall mourn,
>   By wood and wild,
> Where, haply, Pity strays forlorn,
>   Frae man exil'd.

What Burns (in 'To a Mouse') described as 'Nature's social union' has been disturbed by the death of a dear friend. In memory of the man, Burns arranges 'Nature's sturdiest bairns' as a chorus of lamentation.

Conducting this chorus, Burns points to the hills, the cliffs, the groves, the brooks and commands mournful song from the creatures that haunt these places. Inevitably he concentrates on birdsong, the music of the 'wee songsters o the wood', curlews and patridges and other birds:

> Mourn, sooty coots, and speckled teals;
> Ye fisher herons, watching eels;
> Ye duck and drake, wi airy wheels
>   Circling the lake;
> Ye bitterns, till the quagmire reels,
>   Rair for his sake!

> Mourn, clam'ring craiks, at close o day,
> 'Mang fields o flow'ring clover gay!
> And when you wing your annual way
>   Frae our cauld shore,
> Tell thae far warlds wha lies in clay,
>   Wham we deplore.

> Ye houlets, frae your ivy bower
> In some auld tree, or eldritch tower,
> What time the moon, wi silent glowr
>   Sets up her horn,
> Wail thro the dreary midnight hour,
>   Till waukrife morn!

The first stanza quoted has been described as 'one of the most verbally melodious stanzas in British – perhaps in any – literature' (Crawford, 213) and it alludes to Thomson's 'Spring' (where the poet pictures 'The bittern . . . with bill engulfed/To shake the sounding marsh'). The second is heavily textured with alliteration ('clam'ring', 'craiks', 'clover', 'cauld', 'clay'). The third, with its unearthly ('eldritch') atmosphere, its supernatural scenario (the tree, the haunted tower, the moon) has the ring of the ballads. Burns is juxtaposing literary and oral traditions, and informing his poem with direct observation. The touches of realism – or naturalism – save the poem from becoming an empty elegiac exercise.

In the eleventh stanza there is a falling off in quality as Burns looks at nature not as a poetic farmer but as a man made in the image of Harley, the lachrymose hero of Henry Mackenzie's *The Man of Feeling* (1771); Harley sees the world through a 'moistened eye', Burns despairs that 'frae my een the drapping rains/Maun ever flow'. This hyperbolic image determines the rest of the elegy

as the seasons are asked to weep for Henderson, an abstract concept
weak in comparison to the catalogue of the sadly singing birds. The
third last stanza of the elegy proper, however, introduces an impressive philosophical note, sending Henderson not to some theological
heaven but into a universal infinity:

> Mourn him, thou Sun, great source of light!
> Mourn, Empress of the silent night!
> And you, ye twinkling starnies bright,
> My Matthew mourn!
> For through your orbs he's ta'en his flight,
> Ne'er to return.

The elegy ends by comparing the ostentatious state funerals of the
'Great', with the humble passing of the 'man of worth', the honest
man who lies beneath the 'honest turf'.

This contrast between the posthumous pomp of the rich and the
humble graves of the poor is, of course, influenced by Gray's *Elegy
Written in a Country Churchyard*. Following Gray's example, Burns
attaches an epitaph to his elegy, an epitaph rhythmically compelling
on account of the clever variations in the refrain that defines the dead
man: 'For Matthew was a great man . . . . For Matthew was a poor
man . . . . For Matthew was a brave man . . . . For Mathew was a
bright man . . . . For Matthew was a kind man . . . . For Matthew
was a true man . . . . For Matthew was a queer man . . . . For
Matthew was a rare man.' Thus finally, the catalogue becomes an
incantation for a character who displayed the qualities Burns most
admired. Writing the poem he clearly identified with his friend.
Despite occasional lapses into literary pastiche, the elegy (with its
effective epitaph) is one of Burns's most memorable meditations on
death, a presence seen as the antithesis of the natural vitality of a
particular man and the artistic vitality of a singular poet.

TAM o SHANTER

Text   321/CW, 410–15.

Composition   Burns wrote this poem in late autumn, 1790, having
met Francis Grose in the summer and promised him a witch tale
to accompany a drawing of Kirk Alloway in the second volume of
his *The Antiquities of Scotland*. In June 1790 Burns sent Grose three

prose witch stories; in November he sent Mrs Dunlop an incomplete copy of 'Tam o Shanter'; on 1 December 1790 he sent Grose 'Tam o Shanter' which he described as 'one of the Aloway-kirk Stories, done in Scots verse' (CL, 559). According to Lockhart's *Life of Burns* (1828) 'Tam o Shanter' was composed in a single session at Ellisland:

> The poem was the work of one day, and Mrs Burns well remembers the circumstances. He spent most of the day on his favourite walk by the river . . . Her attention was presently attracted by the strange and wild gesticulations of the bard, who, now at some distance, was *agonized* with an ungovernable access of joy. He was reciting very loud, and with the tears rolling down his cheeks, those animated verses which he had just conceived. (cited by Snyder, 327)

Snyder dismisses this story as dubious and notes that the poet told Mrs Dunlop the poem had 'a finishing polish that I despair of ever excelling' (CL, 194). The two statements are not, however, mutually exclusive.

Publication   First published in the *Edinburgh Herald* on 18 March 1791 then as a footnote (pp. 199–201) to the account of Kirk Alloway in the second volume of Francis Grose's *The Antiquities of Scotland* (April 1791). It was included by Burns in the Second Edinburgh Edition (16 February 1793).

Reception   Burns named the poem as his 'own favourite' (CL, 578) of his own works and said 'I look on "Tam o Shanter" to be my standard performance in the Poetical line' (CL, 194). This assessment has been endorsed by generations of critics beginning with A. F. Tytler who wrote to Burns, on 12 March 1791, 'when you describe the infernal orgies of the witches' sabbath and the hellish scenery in which they are exhibited, you display a power of imagination that Shakespeare himself could not have exceeded' (CH, 95). Sir Walter Scott (in the first issue of the *Quarterly Review*, February 1809) also compared the Burns of 'Tam o Shanter' with Shakespeare: 'No poet, with the exception of Shakespeare, ever possessed the power of exciting the most varied and discordant emotions with such rapid transitions' (CH, 207).

For James Montgomery (*Eclectic Review*, May 1809) 'Tam o Shanter' was 'that miracle of the muse of Burns' (CH, 213); for Byron (letter of 7 February 1821) the poem was Burns's 'opus magnum' (CH, 326). Carlyle, however, was critical of the poem (when reviewing Lockhart's *Life of Burns* in the *Edinburgh Review*, December 1828):

> It is not so much a poem, as a piece of sparkling rhetoric; the heart and body of the story lies hard and dead. He has not gone back, much less carried us back, into that dark, earnest, wondering age, when the tradition was believed, and when it took its rise; he does not attempt, by any new-modelling of his supernatural ware, to strike anew that deep mysterious chord of human nature, which once responded to such things, and which lives in us too, and will forever live, though silent now, or vibrating with far other notes, and to far different issues . . . . The piece does not properly cohere: the strange chasm which yawns in our incredulous imagination between the Ayr public-house and the gate of Tophet, is nowhere bridged over, nay the idea of such a bridge is laughed at; and thus the Tragedy of the adventure becomes a mere drunken phantasmagoria, or many-coloured spectrum painted on ale-vapours, and the Farce alone has any reality. We do not say that Burns should have made much more of this tradition; we rather think that, for strictly poetical purposes, not much *was* to be made of it. (CH, 367–8)

Modern critics, however, have been united in their applause. This single sustained narrative by Burns has been described as 'swift, brilliant, dramatic [in moving] from an entirely human and plausible introduction to an absolutely unbelievable and supernatural conclusion' (Snyder, 471). It has been acclaimed as 'worthy to stand beside the best tales in the history of the world' (Hecht, 176). It has been acclaimed as 'a work of genius' on account of 'its synthesis of rapid motion, high energy, pure comedy, imaginative fantasy, and a sense of the stubborn realities of everyday life that never departs altogether from the poem' (Crawford, 221). Kinsley stresses the stylistic and textural complexity of the poem:

> In feeling, [the narrator] moves from objective moral comment to enthusiastic engagement and back; in style, between the naturalistic and the mock-heroic; and in diction, between a brisk, concrete vernacular and artificial 'Augustan' English. (Kinsley, 1353)

*   *   *

On 6 September 1789, Burns told Mrs Dunlop how much he wanted 'to write an epic poem of my own composition' (CL, 178). He never achieved that ambition but he did write a masterly mock-epic in 'Tam o Shanter'. On one level, the poem is a comical odyssey (Burns had read Pope's translations of Homer) following the homewards journey of a farmer to Kirkoswald, Carrick, Ayrshire from the county town of Ayr. (Kinsley, 1357, has reconstructed Tam's ride: he left Ayr by the Foul Vennel, rode south over the Burrowfield to Slaphouse Burn and then into the barony of Alloway, passing the 'meikle stane' and keeping the Cambusdoon cairn on his right until he reached the wooded bank of the Doon and St Mungo's Well before coming to the kirk and passing it on the south side; from the south-west he went forward to see the Devil in the east of the ruined kirk and, when chased by the witches held to his road over the Doon by the Auld Brig and south-west on the long ride to Kirkoswald.)

Burns's letter of June 1790 to Grose gives three witch stories, the second of which begins by stressing the geographical nature of the odyssey:

> On a market day in the town of Ayr, a farmer from Carrick, and consequently whose way lay by the very gate of Aloway kirk-yard, in order to cross the river Doon at the old bridge, which is about two or three hundred yards further on than the said gate, had been detained by his business, 'till by the time he reached Aloway, it was the wizard hour, between night and morning. (CL, 558)

This parenthetical English prose is transmuted into this poetic passage, complete with vivid characterisation and atmosphere and replacing business with pleasure, from 'Tam o Shanter':

> But to our tale: – Ae market-night,
> Tam had got planted unco right,
> Fast by an ingle, bleezing finely,
> Wi reaming swats, that drank divinely;
> And at his elbow, Souter Johnie,
> His ancient, trusty, drouthy cronie:
> Tam lo'ed him like a very brither;
> They had been fou for weeks thegither.

It is evident from this that Burns has found the octosyllabic couplet the perfect form for a narrative that moves easily and swiftly from the natural to the supernatural, from the earthly to the other-worldly, thus giving Tam's odyssey a timeless dimension.

In the first stanza (or verse-paragraph) of the tale Burns introduces a crucial character who will remain 'off-stage' during the poem: the 'sulky, sullen dame,/Gathering her brows like gathering storm,/Nursing her wrath to keep it warm'. Odysseus has to win home to Penelope and Tam, even in his cups, knows he has to win home to Kate. Tam himself appears in the second stanza and is awarded the poet's favourite epithet: he is 'honest Tam o Shanter' and (prior to his eventful ride to Kirkoswald) he is passing his time enjoyably in Ayr, which Burns praises, for its honesty, in a parenthesis: '(Auld Ayr, whom ne'er a town surpasses,/For honest men and bonie lasses.)'

Burns had produced the poems in the Kilmarnock Edition without ever straying from his native Ayrshire. Significantly, his most mature masterpiece (technically and thematically, as well as chronologically), though written in Dumfriesshire, goes back to Ayrshire and the scenes he knew as a child when he lived in the cottage near Kirk Alloway and listened to the tales, told by Betty Davidson, of 'devils, ghosts, fairies, brownies, witches, warlocks' (AL). That oral tradition of supernatural belief is infinitely more pertinent to the poem than the notion that Burns modelled Tam on Douglas Graham, Souter Johnie on John Davidson, Kate on Graham's wife Helen McTaggart (see entries in 'The Burns Circle') and the witch Nannie on Katie Steven of Laighpark, Kirkoswald (see Kinsley, 1363).

But to our tale. Tam, the hero of a mock-epic, is identified as an epic drinker, never sober on a market-day in Ayr. Boozing with Souter Johnie, he finds that pressures and problems dissolve into drink:

> The Souter tauld his queerest stories;
> The landlord's laugh was ready chorus:
> The storm without might rair and rustle,
> Tam did na mind the storm a whistle.

The scenario, with drinkers protecting themselves from the external cold by warming themselves internally by imbibing before a fire, is familiar from Burns (see the opening of 'The Jolly Beggars') and, indeed, from the Scots tradition. The sixth stanza of 'The Testament of Cresseid', by Robert Henryson (*c*.1420–*c*.1490), begins:

> I mend the fyre and beikit me about,
> Than tuik ane drink my spreitis to comfort,
> And armit me weill fra the cauld thairout.

Burns makes no mention of Henryson in his letters but certainly knew poets of that period: 'Tam o Shanter' is prefaced by a quotation ('Of Brownyis and of Bogillis full is this Buke') from Henryson's near-contemporary Gavin Douglas (*c*.1474–1522) and Burns knew early and Middle Scots poetry from Allan Ramsay's anthology *Ever Green* (1724).

After his splendid Scots couplets celebrating the companionship and comfort of drink, Burns switches to Augustan English:

> But pleasures are like poppies spread:
> You seize the flow'r, its bloom is shed;
> Or like the snow falls in the river,
> A moment white – then melts for ever;
> Or like the borealis race,
> That flit ere you can point their place;
> Or like the rainbow's lovely form
> Evanishing amid the storm.

These four similes, on the ephemeral nature of pleasure, interrupt the narrative flow in order to distance the reader from the story which Burns seems to want to be read objectively rather than empathically. They led Edwin Muir, an Orkney poet who wrote most effectively in English, to the curious conclusion that the intellectual content of the English passage could not have been expressed in Scots 'which was to [Burns] a language for sentiment but not for thought' (Edwin Muir, *Scott and Scotland*, 1936; rept. Edinburgh, 1982, p. 13). A survey of the opening stanzas of the poem will show that Burns had no trouble in expressing equally portentous ideas in Scots. Consider:

> While we sit bousing at the nappy,
> An getting fou and unco happy,
> We think na on the lang Scots miles,
> The mosses, waters, slaps, and styles,
> That lie between us an our hame . . .

Or these lines in the stanza that immediately precedes the English passage, showing a personified Care crazed by drink then a couplet combining a simile and a metaphor about the intensity of sensual enjoyment:

> Care, mad to see a man sae happy,

> E'en drown'd himself amang the nappy.
> As bees flee hame wi lades of treasure,
> The minutes wing'd their way wi pleasure.

Burns did not show the divided self of the Scot in turning briefly to English: indeed Muir's argument could be reversed and the passive platitudinous English passage advanced as a deliberate contrast to the dynamic Scots of the main narrative. Certainly, Burns abandons the English abruptly to set his hero in motion:

> Nae man can tether time or tide,
> The hour approaches Tam maun ride:
> That hour o night's black arch the key-stane,
> That dreary hour Tam mounts his beast in:
> And sic a night he taks the road in,
> As ne'er poor sinner was abroad in.

The repetition of 'hour', in three successive lines, cleverly pressurises Tam by bringing him back to the 'real' world he abandoned in his cups.

Tam, however, may have won free from the company of Souter Johnie but he is still under the influence of alcohol, a narrative fact Burns supplies in order to emphasise the ambiguity of Tam's infernal vision which may be an alcoholic hallucination or may be a supernatural experience. Burns makes it clear that the boozy Tam is superstitious and that, therefore, his perception of the world is prejudiced by ghostly preconceptions as well as distorted by drink: as he rides towards Kirk Alloway he sings an old Scots song to comfort himself while he looks around 'Lest bogles catch him unawares'. As he rides, 'on his grey mare Meg', he is aware of the nightmarish associations of the area (where drunken Charlie broke his neck, where hunters found a murdered child, where Mungo's mother hanged herself) but is himself possessed by a spirit, namely the Scotch courage induced by alcohol:

> Inspiring bold John Barleycorn,
> What dangers thou canst make us scorn!
> Wi tippeny, we fear nae evil;
> Wi usquabae, we'll face the Devil!
> The swats sae ream'd in Tammie's noddle,

Fair play, he car'd na deils a boddle.

His horse, though, has more sense than him and 'right sair aston-ished' is reluctantly urged forward to Kirk Alloway, lit up and looking like nothing on earth.

Burns's description of the diabolic dance in Kirk Alloway is one of his finest achievements. By identifying the devil – 'Auld Nick, in shape o beast' – as a shaggy dog ('touzie tyke') playing the part of a frenzied Scottish piper, it satirises the wild Scottish folk-musical tradition. By locating the diabolic dance in a Scottish kirk (even if 'Witches frequently meet in or round a church', Kinsley, 1358) it rebukes religious complacency. By putting horrific objects (a murderer's bones, two unchristen'd babies, a thief cut from the rope) on a 'haly table' it ridicules the worship of religious relics. By making an intoxicated Scot the witness to all this it questions the reliability of the Scottish gossip. What Tam sees is not necessarily true; but Tam's perception of what he sees is relevant as well as the substance of a riotously funny tale. Burns is using folk material with considerable intellectual sophistication, allowing the story to involve the reader on several levels.

Having earlier distanced the reader with his English similes, Burns now distances the reader again by drawing back from the narrative and addressing his hero as he watches the 'Warlocks and witches in a dance', especially the witches:

> Now Tam, O Tam! had thae been queans,
> A' plump and strapping in their teens!
> Their sarks, instead o creeshie flannen,
> Been snaw-white seventeen hunder linen! –
> Thir breeks o mine, my only pair,
> That ance were plush, o guid blue hair,
> I wad hae gien them off my hurdies,
> For ae blink o the bonie burdies!

In admonishing Tam, Burns introduces himself as the creator of the poem, an ironical aside since the events are apparently beyond his control. Burns disdains the witches as old hags, but acknowledges that the intoxicated Tam spots one beauty among the hideous bunch, for 'There was ae winsome wench and wawlie'. Having introduced the witch Nannie in her short shift (a seductive contrast to Tam's sullen wife) Burns again pulls back to let the narrative run along on its own irrational logic:

> But here my Muse her wing maun cour,
> Sic flights are far beyond her power:
> To sing how Nannie lap and flang
> (A souple jade she was and strang),
> And how Tam stood like ane bewitch'd,
> And thought his very een enrich'd;
> Even Satan glowr'd, and fidg'd fu fain,
> And hotch'd and blew wi might and main:
> Till first ae caper, syne anither,
> Tam tint his reason a' thegither,
> And roars out, 'Weel done, Cutty-sark!'
> And in an instant all was dark:
> And scarcely had he Maggie rallied,
> When out the hellish legion sallied.

Earlier in the poem Burns had used the image of bees ('As bees flee hame wi lades o treasure') to convey the pleasures of drink; now he recalls that image in a series of similes that are as telling as the previous English similes Muir admired:

> As bees bizz out wi angry fyke,
> When plundering herds assail their byke;
> As open pussie's mortal foes,
> When, pop! she starts before their nose;
> As eager runs the market-crowd,
> When 'Catch the thief!' resounds aloud:
> So Maggie runs, the witches follow,
> Wi monie an eldritch skriech and hollow.

That said, Burns issues a warning to Tam – 'Ah, Tam! Ah, Tam! thou'll get thy fairin!/In hell they'll roast thee like a herrin!' – before escorting him over the bridge to his wife Kate, a final journey made possible by the old supersitition that a witch cannot cross a running stream. Nevertheless, the young witch Nannie, 'far before the rest', grabs hold of the horse's 'ain grey tail' and pulls it off, leaving 'poor Maggie scarce a stump'. That detail about the horse allows Burns to move, through a pun on tail/tale, to his mock-moralistic ending about the dangers of drink and sex:

> Now, wha this tale o truth shall read,
> Ilk man, and mother's son, take heed:

> Whene'er to drink you are inclin'd,
> Or cutty sarks in in your mind,
> Think! ye may buy the joys o'er dear:
> Remember Tam o Shanter's mare.

The humour of this derives from a knowing manipulation of folk sources and popular superstitions. Burns is evidently, considering what has gone before, being ironical.

The poem shows Burns's mastery of the Scots language for the poem is unusually rich in Scots words; and it demonstrates his technical skill as never before (or after). It puts new life into old expressions (Tam is supernaturally 'bewitch'd' when watching Nannie in her cutty sark), uses puns (tail/tale), introduces distancing asides that put the folk content in a sceptical context, offers moralistic statements ironically. Clearly, Burns was in complete command of his medium and that medium was Scots verse informed by a rare intelligence and remarkable sense of humour.

It is not necessary to identify one consistent narrative voice in the poem, as its ambiguity conveys both Tam's inebriation and Burns's creative energy (able to see several possibilities simultaneously). Burns knew the poem was unlike anything else he had done for his 'own favourite poem [was] an essay in a walk of the muses entirely new to him' (CL, 578). It was not the supernatural treatment that was 'entirely new' (think of 'Death and Doctor Hornbook'), nor was it use of irony (think of 'Holy Willie's Prayer'), nor was it the combination of Augustan English and earthy Scots (think of 'The Brigs of Ayr'). What was new was the aesthetic imposition of a multifaceted imagination and folk sophisticated intellect on material, a brilliant literary restructuring of an anecdotal adventure along Homeric, or mock-epic, lines (thus linking across the centuries with Joyce's Ulysses and MacDiarmid's A Drunk Man Looks at the Thistle which follows Burns in tracing the unsteady journey of a drunken Scot to the arms of a nagging wife). Burns hoped he might 'persevere in this species of poetic composition' (CL, 578) but never again found such a suitable subject as Tam o Shanter and his astonishing homecoming.

THE TREE OF LIBERTY

Text   625/CW, 478–80.

Composition   Probably written in 1793; the reference to the execution of Louis XVI places it after 21 January 1793.

Publication   First published in Robert Chambers's edition of *The Life and Works of Robert Burns* (Edinburgh, 1838, p. 86).

Reception   Accepting his manuscript source as reliable, Chambers judged 'The Tree of Liberty' to be

> One piece which was probably written or at least freely touched up by Burns and which, but for the ultra-Jacobinal fashion in which it introduces the name of the unfortunate Louis XVI, might have been read by the poet's contemporaries without any pain, as expressing only the feelings of a man who was too sanguine about the success of the popular cause in France. (*The Life and Works of Robert Burns*, ed. Robert Chambers and revd. William Wallace, Edinburgh, 1896, vol. 4, p. 133)

Auguste Angellier, in his 1893 study of Burns, thought it 'a genuine revolutionary song [in a] tone composed of a mixture of dynamic vulgarity, heroic defiance, and cynical mockery' (cited by Crawford, 250). In their edition of *The Poetry of Robert Burns* (Edinburgh and London, 1896–7, vol. 4., p. 107) W. E. Henley and T. F. Henderson say 'we may charitably conclude that Burns neither made the trash nor copied it'. Crawford suggests 'If this work . . . is ever definitely proved to be by Burns, it will have to be recognised as the most extreme development of his political thought and emotions that we possess' (Crawford, 246). Kinsley's opinion is inconclusive:

> Some lines in the poem – notably ll. 1–8 – have a Burnsian quality, and there are some correspondences with his acknowledged work; but I do not share Angellier's enthusiasm over the style. Such a device as the allegorical tree of liberty was unlikely to raise Burns to his highest powers, but the manner here is less firmly and finally expressive and less richly vernacular than that of Burns when he is fully engaged. In my view the question of authorship remains open. (Kinsley, 1528)

            *   *   *

Writers with revolutionary sympathies have no doubts that 'The Tree of Liberty' is the work of Burns. Hugh MacDiarmid (*Burns Today and Tomorrow*, Edinburgh, 1959, p. 107) enthused:

The most important event in [Burns's] life-time was undoubtedly the great French Revolution of 1789. Its effect was comparable to that of the Russian Revolution in 1917 [and] it inspired that important poem ['The Tree of Liberty'].

Similarly, in their study of *The Scottish Insurrection of 1820* (London, 1970, p. 55) P. Berresford Ellis and Seumas Mac a' Ghobhainn write:

The sympathy Scotland felt towards the [French] revolution was . . . reflected in the poetry of the day, particularly in the work of the nationalist poet Burns [whose] 'The Tree of Liberty' and 'A man's a man for a' that' are . . . famous in this context.

It is evident to such writers that the revolutionary sympathies of the work are consistent with what is known of Burns's political views on the French Revolution. Nevertheless, the evidence of Burns's authorship is internal.

'The Tree of Liberty' was communicated to Chambers by 'the mysterious Mr Duncan of Mosesfield' (Crawford, 246) and there is no extant manuscript. Consequently, many editors and commentators have avoided the poem: Snyder makes no mention of it and Kinsley, while printing it in his section of 'Undated Poems and *Dubia*' considers it of uncertain attribution. Crawford, however, argues that it is probably by Burns since the political sentiments are his and it exhibits (in the last couplet of the eighth stanza: 'That sic a tree can not be found,/'Twixt London and the Tweed, man') 'a devastating subtlety which, as much as anything else in the poem, tells in favour of Burns's authorship' (Crawford, 249).

Crawford concedes that the author of 'The Tree of Liberty' apparently uses 'England' as a synonym for Britain and grants that this does not accord with Burns's usage; however, he suggests that some textual corruption may have taken place during the transcription of James Duncan of Mosesfield or, more persuasively, that 'England' was deliberately used in order to point a contrast with Scotland. Crawford also points out that the poem has a documentary dimension since Trees of Liberty were erected in Scottish towns during the height of the Reform agitation. In November 1792 (the month, incidentally, that the French Convention offered assistance to all peoples wishing to overthrow their government) Trees of Liberty – decorated with garlands of flowers, emblems of freedom and various inscriptions – were set up by radicals in Perth and Dundee. Several events of 1793 affected Burns profoundly: on 21 January

Louis XV1 was executed, on 1 February France declared war on Britain; on 16 October Marie Antoinette was executed. Burns's opinion of the executions is well-known from his remark about the deserved fate of 'a perjured Blockhead & an unprincipled Prostitute' (CL, 214). As he had been in trouble, in December 1792, because of his allegedly unpatriotic opinions he had decided to keep his views to himself: 'I have set, henceforth, a seal on my lips, as to these unlucky politics' (cited by Kinsley, 1381). If he wrote 'The Tree of Liberty' in 1793 then he would not have wished to circulate it in Scotland and Crawford considers that that the poem may have been written 'for dispatch to one of Burns's correspondents in England' (Crawford, 249).

The poem begins with a celebration of the fall of the Bastille on 14 July 1789. The Tree of Liberty has taken the place of the Paris prison:

> It stands where ance the Bastile stood,
>   A prison built by kings, man,
> When Superstition's hellish brood,
>   Kept France in leading strings, man.

The tree bears fruit that 'raises man aboon the brute' and offers the peasant a chance to rise above 'a lord' – a statement that, in associating 'a lord' with 'the brute', shows a poetic skill characteristic of Burns and consistent with his oft-expressed indignation about the arrogant ignorance of the gentry (compare the association of 'a lord' with 'a coof' in 'A Man's a Man for a' that'). The line 'It raises man aboon the brute' echoes a phrase in the *Manual of Religious Belief* composed by the poet's father, William Burnes, who warned that sin reduced man to 'a level with the brute beasts' (cited by Kinsley, 1013–4).

Also characteristic of Burns is the use of personification, as in the tribute to the work of 'Fair Virtue' who has watered the tree and watched its branches spreading wide. In condemning the 'vicious folks' who oppose the work of Virtue, the poem cites Louis XVI who attempted to cut down the tree when it was still small and fragile. The poem declares, triumphantly, 'For this the watchman cracked his crown,/Cut aff his head and a', man.' As stated above, Burns considered Louis XVI 'a perjured Blockhead'.

The poem reflects on the battles of revolutionary France then condemns the absence of liberty in reactionary England where no Tree of Liberty can be found. Without this tree, the poem laments, life is dire and desperate with poor people working in the service of their self-styled superiors. In expressing this the poem defines the kind of life led by such men as Burns's father:

> We labour soon, we labour late,
>   To feed the titled knave, man;
> And a' the comfort we're to get
>   Is that ayont the grave, man.

The penultimate stanza calls for an international brotherhood of man and the last four lines plead for a coming of liberty to England (the first of the four lines quoted uses the same internal rhyme as 'Then let us pray that come it may' from 'A Man's a Man for a' that'):

> Syne let us pray, auld England may
>   Sure plant this far-famed tree, man;
> And blythe we'll sing, and hail the day
>   That gave us liberty, man.

'The Tree of Liberty' is not, as Henley and Henderson contend, 'trash'. It strongly sustains the theme of international revolution, it uses the 'Gilliecrankie' measure competently, it contains a typically Burnsian contrast between the poor, but honest, peasant and the rich, but perfidious, lord. As Crawford says, to exclude the poem from the Burns canon is to attribute its qualities 'to some talented literary criminal of the early nineteenth century, or to some anonymous democrat of the seventeen-nineties who wrote nothing else of value which has been preserved' (Crawford, 251). Without the authority of an authentic manuscript, final judgement must be suspended but there are compelling thematic and stylistic reasons for considering 'The Tree of Liberty' to be by Burns.

Verse Epistles

During the time of Dunbar (c.1460–c.1520) Scottish poets indulged in furious 'flyting' sessions, exchanging abusive and vituperative poems (the best known being the four-part 'The Flyting of Dunbar and Kennedy'). By the eighteenth century, the flyting tradition had given way to a milder tradition of verse epistles, generally full of personal praise and occasional in manner. Both Ramsay and Fergusson wrote verse epistles that began and ended in salutation and offered comments on particular subjects or occasions. The 'Familiar Epistles between Lieut. Hamilton and Allan Ramsay' are cast in the Standard Habbie stanza and expand on enthusiastic openings (like Ramsay's):

> Sonse fa' me, witty, Wanton Willy,
> Gin blyth I was na as a filly;
> Not a fou pint, nor short-hought gilly,
>   Or wine that's better,
> Could please sae meikle, my dear Billy,
>   As thy kind letter.

Burns basically followed Ramsay's example in heartily (or ironically) hailing a friend, then offering him pungent asides that actually comprise the substance of the poem, then looking foward to further physical or epistolary contact. As Burns did not, initially at least, know skilful poets, his verse epistles were often prompted by prose or unprompted. Occasionally (as with the epistles to the Guidwife of Wauchope House, Dr Blacklock and Thomas Walker) Burns did respond to poems.

Burns included seven verse epistles in the Kilmarnock Edition (Snyder counts nine verse epistles by including 'A Dedication to Gavin Hamilton' and 'Address to the Deil' in their number, but the first is a 'complimentary effusion' and the second an address to an idea rather than an individual) and shows a mastery of the idiom, combining a conversational – even conspiratorial – tone with a meditative mood. The early epistles proclaim his poetic faith in nature, assert his nationalism, demonstrate his hostility to the Calvinist excesses of the kirk and – in the case of the 'Epistle to a Young Friend' – show a capacity for cunning.

Later epistles, written after the publication of the Kilmarnock Edition, range from the obsequious ('Epistle to Robert Graham, Esq., of Fintry'), through the irreverent ('Reply to a Trimming Epistle) and the expedient ('Epistle to Dr Blacklock'), to the admirable ('Epistle to Colonel de Peyster'). What follows is a chronological consideration of the most interesting epistles.

EPISTLE TO JOHN RANKINE

Included in the Kilmarnock Edition, Burns's earliest verse epistle (47/CW, 82–4) also appeared in subsequent editions despite the advice of Hugh Blair who urged the poet to drop it from the First Edinburgh Edition on the grounds of indecency:

> The Description of shooting the hen is understood, I find, to convey an indecent meaning: tho' in reading the poem, I confess, I took it literally, and the indecency did not strike me. But if the Author meant to allude to an affair with a Woman, as is supposed, the whole Poem ought undoubtedly be left out of the new edition. (CH, 81)

Blair was right about 'an affair with a Woman'. Burns wrote the poem, at the end of 1784, during the pregnancy of Elizabeth Paton, serving-girl to William Burnes at Lochlea, who bore him a daughter (the 'bonie, sweet, wee dochter' of 'A Poet's Welcome to his Love-begotten Daughter') on 22 May 1785.

'Epistle to John Rankine' was addressed to the tenant-farmer of Adamhill, near Tarbolton. Rankine (who died in 1810) got to know the poet well during his Lochlea period and teased Burns with gossip about Elizabeth Paton's pregnancy. Burns's response was to send his amusing allegorical epistle on the subject, a poem that describes Rankine (in the second line) as 'The wale o cocks for fun and drinkin' and spends the first six stanzas mischievously establishing Rankine's credentials as a 'wicked sinner' and 'unregenerate heathen', the enemy of the kirk and 'The lads in black'. The perfect man, in fact, to whom to confess a sexual adventure.

The seventh stanza introduces the allegory that offended Blair:

> 'Twas ae night lately, in my fun,
> I gaed a rovin wi the gun,
> An brought a paitrick to the grun' –
> A bonie hen;
> And, as the twilight was begun,
> Thought nane wad ken.

Obviously enough (at least with the hindsight denied Blair) the gun stands for the penis, the partridge for the shapely girl he brought to the ground. Burns sustains the allegory by telling how the bird was hardly hurt and how he stroked it 'for sport'. Alas for his sporting instinct, somebody told 'the Poacher-Court' (that is, the Kirk Session) of his action and he was made to pay for it.

Rising sexually to his theme, Burns declares that he will take revenge on the moralistic men of the parish by regarding all the women as fair game for his gun:

> But, by my gun, o guns the wale,
> An by my pouther and my hail,
> An by my hen, an by her tail,
> I vow and swear!
> The game shall pay, owre moor an dale,
> For this, niest year!

After all, he pleads in his own defence, the bird he brought to the ground received attention rather than injury: 'neither broken wing nor limb,/But twa-three chaps about the wame'. The epistle establishes Burns as a sexual adventurer at odds with parochial conventions of behaviour. Snyder thought it outstanding: 'Burns rarely wrote with more *verve* than when composing the thirteen stanzas of this clever but blackguardly epistle. Never again was he so successful in this vein' (Snyder, 118).

EPISTLES TO DAVIE

Dated January – that is January 1785 – by Burns in the Kilmarnock

Edition, 'Epistle to Davie, a Brother Poet' (51/CW, 86–9) was drafted the previous summer according to a letter of 2 April 1789 from Gilbert Burns to Currie:

> Among the earliest of his poems was the *Epistle to Davie* . . . . It was, I think, in summer, 1784, when in the interval of hardest labour, he and I were working in the garden (kail-yard), that he repeated to me the principal part of this epistle. I believe the first idea of Robert's becoming an author was started on this occasion. (cited by Snyder, 100–1)

Burns cast the poem in the complicated fourteen-line Cherrie and the Slae stanza, having read Alexander Montgomerie's poem 'The Cherrie and the Slae' in Allan Ramsay's anthology *The Ever Green* (1724).

The Davie, to whom two epistles were addressed, was David Sillar (1760–1830), a fiddler who also wrote poems. Sillar was born on his father's farm at Spittleside, Tarbolton (near Lochlea), and taught for a time in the parish school; when the permanent appointment went to John Wilson (Burns's Dr Hornbook) Sillar set up his own school. In 1781 he became a member of Tarbolton Bachelors' Club, which Burns had helped to found, and became friendly with the poet.

On the failure of his school, Sillar moved in 1783 to Irvine where he set up as a grocer. Burns's reference, in the epistle, to 'your Meg' refers to Margaret Orr, a nursemaid Sillar planned to marry (eventually she broke the engagement and Sillar married another). Burns used Sillar's original tune, 'A Rosebud', for his lyric 'A Rosebud by My Early Walk' in the second volume of the *Scots Musical Museum* (1788). Like John Lapraik, to whom Burns addressed three epistles, Sillar attempted to emulate Burns by having a volume of his verse, *Poems* (1789), brought out by John Wilson, printer of the Kilmarnock Edition. Shortly after the publication of his poems, Sillar became bankrupt but inherited a small fortune on the death of his uncle. He served for some years on Irvine Town Council and, in 1827, helped found the Irvine Burns Club.

Burns uses the Cherrie and the Slae stanza with splendid atmospheric effect in beginning the poem (just as he does, with the same stanzaic form in the opening of 'The Jolly Beggars'). The winds blow from the north, 'frae aff Ben-Lomond'; the doors are

sealed 'wi drivin snaw'; the frost drifts 'Ben to the chimla lug'.
Burns, sitting by the fire and passing his time in rhyming, resents
the comforts of the rich and condemns 'their cursed pride', a theme
clarified in the second stanza which contrasts the human decency of
the poor with the inhumanity of the rich.

Having stated his theme, Burns develops it in the following five
stanzas by suggesting that poor people are in touch with nature in
a way impossible for the rich, and thus have access to a wealth that
is evident in the landscape and the creatures that inhabit it. Burns
insists that such treasures are stored in the heart and are therefore
more valuable than profits stored in banks.

> It's no in titles, nor in rank:
> It's no in wealth like Lon'on Bank,
>   To purchase peace and rest,
> It's no in makin muckle, mair;
> It's no in books, it's no in lear,
>   To make us truly blest:
> If happiness hae not her seat
>   An centre in the breast,
> We may be wise, or rich, or great,
>   But never can be blest!
>   Nae treasures nor pleasures
>   Could make us happy lang;
>   The heart ay's the part ay
>   That makes us right or wrang.

The relentlessly moralistic praise of the poor is relieved in the eighth
stanza where Burns moves from the general to the particular and
cites as priceless joys the company of such women as 'your Meg
[and] my darling Jean', that is Margaret Orr and Jean Armour. As
the final three stanzas (the first two of them in English) elaborate
Burns's love for Jean, whom he did not meet until April 1785,
it looks as if the last four stanzas were tacked onto a poem he
otherwise considered complete by January 1785. Probably Burns
first composed the poem as a meditation on poverty, subsequently
decided to address it to David Sillar, then rounded it off with a
routine tribute to Jean. It is certainly uneven in tone and falls off
in intensity when it reaches the eighth stanza.

A 'Second Epistle to Davie' (101/CW, 213–4), written prior to the publication of the Kilmarnock Edition but omitted from that volume, uses the Standard Habbie stanza. Burns, sometimes dazed with love and sometimes dazed with drink, cites poetry as his greatest pleasure:

> Leeze me on rhyme! it's ay a treasure,
> My chief, amaist my only pleasure;
> At hame, a-field, at wark or leisure,
>   The Muse, poor hizzie!
> Tho rough an raploch be her measure,
>   She's seldom lazy.

Accordingly he advises David Sillar to follow his example and 'Haud to the Muse' as the one constant in his life.

EPISTLES TO J. LAPRAIK

Burns wrote three epistles, in the Standard Habbie measure, to John Lapraik (1727–1807), a farmer and (to Burns) 'an old Scotch bard'. Ruined by the failure of the Ayr Bank in 1783, Lapraik was forced to sell his farm at Dalfram, Muirkirk (nine miles from Mauchline), and was briefly imprisoned for debt in 1785, passing his time in prison by writing poems. In 1788 he brought out his *Poems on Several Occasions* with John Wilson, printer of the Kilmarnock Edition. After leasing a farm at Muirkirk he became innkeeper and postmaster at Muirsmill. The first 'Epistle to J. Lapraik, An Old Scotch Bard' (57/CW, 101–4) is dated 1 April 1785 in the first Common Place Book and was included in the Kilmarnock Edition. It begins by describing how nature inspires Burns's Muse then states the reason for the poet writing to a stranger, 'an unknown frien''. At 'a rockin' – that is, a musical evening – Burns has heard a love song that seems to him worthy of Pope, Steele or Beattie. He recalls how excited he became on hearing that the song (Lapraik's 'When I upon thy Bosom Lean', later published in *Poems on Several Occasions* and included, as improved by Burns, in the *Scots Musical Museum*) is by 'an odd kind chiel/About Muirkirk'. Recognising a man after his own heart – a spontaneous poet of the people – Burns invokes his own Muse.

Describing his approach to poetry, Burns produces a personal credo and does so with a brilliance that demonstrates the quality, as well as the courage, of his convictions.

I am nae poet, in a sense;
But just a rhymer like by chance,
An hae to learning nae pretence;
        Yet, what the matter?
Whene'er my Muse does on me glance,
        I jingle at her.

Your critic-folk may cock their nose,
And say, 'How can you e'er propose,
You wha ken hardly verse frae prose,
        To mak a sang?'
But, by your leaves, my learned foes,
        Ye're maybe wrang.

What's a' your jargon o your schools,
Your Latin names for horns an stools?
If honest Nature made you fools,
        What sairs your grammars?
Ye'd better taen up spades and shools,
        Or knappin-hammers.

A set o dull, conceited hashes
Confuse their brains in college-classes,
They gang in stirks, and come out asses,
        Plain truth to speak;
And syne they think to climb Parnassus
        By dint o Greek!

Gie me ae spark o Nature's fire,
That's a' the learning I desire;
Then, tho I drudge thro dub an mire
        At pleugh or cart,
My Muse, tho hamely in attire,
        May touch the heart.

That magnificently assertive passage puts in a creative context the diffident apology for ignorance of Latin and Greek in the Preface to the Kilmarnock Edition. Here Burns declares that a passionate response to nature has more poetic relevance than a classical education. He confidently places his own gifts above learning acquired by rote in universities where students (the animal imagery is telling) are transformed from bullocks to asses.

After linking Lapraik with his own favourite Scots poets, Allan Ramsay and Robert Fergusson, Burns extends the hand of friendship. Since he has listed his poetic virtues, he cites his principal human failing, his love of 'the lasses'. Having established himself as an amorous poet he invites Lapraik to meet him, at Mauchline Race or Mauchline Fair, for an exchange of 'rhymin-ware'.

Lapraik replied to this epistle with a letter which his son delivered to Burns as he was sowing in a field at Mossgiel. On 21 April 1785 Burns wrote his 'Second Epistle to J. Lapraik' (58/CW, 104–7), also included in the Kilmarnock Edition. Since he has already projected himself as the inspired poet of nature in the first epistle, Burns now turns to the conditions he has to endure as part of the poverty into which he was born. The reality of the nature the farmer has to cope with is a grimmer affair than the nature celebrated by the poet:

> Forjesket sair, with weary legs,
> Rattlin the corn out-owre the rigs,
> Or dealing thro amang the naigs
> Their ten-hours bite;
> My awkward Muse sair pleads and begs,
> I would na write.

As indicated in the first epistle, he jingles at his Muse who, worn out with poetic work, assumes the form of an exhausted servant-girl: 'The tapetless, ramfeezl'd hizzie,/She's saft at best an something lazy'. Burns, however, presses the Muse into his service.

As well as invoking the Muse as a servant-girl, Burns sees Fortune as 'but a bitch' and himself as a man surviving despite the aggravation of sexual problems and malicious gossip:

> Now comes the sax-and-twentieth simmer
> I've seen the bud upo' the timmer,
> Still persecuted by the limmer
> Frae year to year;
> But yet, despite the kittle kimmer,
> I, Rob, am here.

Burns contrasts his economically poor human condition with the unsightly commercial contortions of the rich. Nature, he is sure, favours the 'social, friendly, honest man' and places no value on wealth. Poor poets, like Burns and Lapraik, are transfigured while rich people are wretched:

> O mandate glorious and divine!
> The followers o the ragged Nine –
> Poor, thoughtless devils! – yet may shine
> In glorious light;
> While sordid sons o Mammon's line
> Are dark as night!

In a future incarnation, the rich will return as wolves, the poor as gentle souls united by friendship. If the poem ends optimistically with some wishful thinking, the thrust of Burns's argument is clearly that the angels are on the side of the poor souls who will inherit the earth they have cultivated.

The 'Third Epistle to J. Lapraik' (67/CW, 127–8), dated 13 September 1785 and first published in Cromek's *Reliques* (1808), concludes the epistolary trilogy by anticipating a boozy session between the two poets. The friendship offered in the first epistle and eulogised in the second, will lead to a shared celebration of the inspirational qualities of whisky. Burns ends by turning from dreams of the 'Muse-inspirin aqua- vitae' to the reality of his life on the farm:

> But stooks are cowpet wi the blast,
> And now the sinn keeks in the wast;
> Then I maun rin amang the rest,
> An quat my chanter;
> Sae I subscribe myself in haste,
> Yours, Rab the Ranter.

All three epistles are rich in Scots words thus defining, as well as discussing, the linguistic wealth that Burns treasures above all material possessions.

TO WILLIAM SIMSON, OCHILTREE

Dated May 1785 by Burns, in the Kilmarnock Edition, the epistle 'To William Simson, Ochiltree' (59/CW, 107–11) was written in response to a verse epistle from William Simson (1758–1815) in praise of Burns's ecclesiastical satire 'The Holy Tulzie'. Simpson, a farmer's son who had gone to Glasgow University with the intention of entering the ministry, became schoolmaster in his native Ochiltree in 1780. Eight years later he became schoolmaster in Cumnock, where he died.

Burns's epistle, in the Standard Habbie stanza, explores his own identity and ambitions as a Scottish poet. After thanking 'winsome Willie' for his flattering words, Burns modestly compares himself to Allan Ramsay, William Hamilton of Gilbertfield and Robert Fergusson then laments Fergusson in a bitter parenthesis:

> (O Fergusson! thy glorious parts
> Ill suited law's dry, musty arts!
> My curse upon your whunstane hearts,
>   Ye E'nbrugh gentry!
> The tythe o what ye waste at cartes
>   Wad stow'd his pantry!)

Thoughts of Ramsay and Fergusson immortalising the rivers Forth and Tay in verse encourages Burns to invoke his own Ayrshire Muse, Coila, and take up the challenge of doing the same for 'Irwin, Lugar, Ayr an Doon' (a view also expressed in the first Common Place Book and 'The Vision'). Though devoted to the beauty of his area, the Ayrshire bard will not, however, be of only limited local appeal. He will 'sing auld Coila's plains an fells' but also show the national significance of 'glorious Wallace'. So the poetic pantheon (Ramsay and Fergusson) has a political dimension of nationalism.

Above all, Burns continues, he will be the poet of Nature, finding in the natural harmony of the landscape a more appealing energy than the fiercely competitive clamour of the crowd:

> The warly race may drudge an drive,
> Hog-shouther, jundie, stretch, an strive,
> Let me fair Nature's face descrive,
>   And I, wi pleasure,
> Shall let the busy, grumbling hive
>   Bum owre their treasure.

With his ambitions articulated, Burns offers 'love fraternal' to his friend, William Simson.

A long Postscript to the epistle clarifies Burns's concept of a liberal theology, 'this New-Light'. He likens the 'Auld-Licht' theology to the antiquated and superstitious view of the moon as an object periodically replaced in the heaven. The New Lichts,

by comparison, understand that the moon changes as it turns in
the sky:

> Some herds, weel learn'd upo' the Beuk,
> Wad threap auld folk the thing misteuk;
> For 'twas the auld moon turn'd a neuk
>   An out o sight,
> An backlins-comin to the leuk,
>   She grew mair bright.

Burns makes fun of the squabbles between the two schools of
thought and concludes that 'a' this clatter/Is naething but a
"moonshine-matter"' of little interest to poets.

EPISTLE TO JOHN GOLDIE

Burns used the Standard Habbie to treat some grimly serious matters in a light-hearted manner as can be seen from the ecclesiastical
epistles to John Goldie and the Rev John McMath, both omitted
from the Kilmarnock Edition. In August 1785, he sent his 'Epistle
to John Goldie, in Kilmarnock' (63/CW, 121–2), in support of the
second edition of the Kilmarnock wine-merchant's *Essays on various
Important Subjects, Moral and Divine* (1779, second edition 1785).
Endorsing the liberal New Licht theology of this work, Burns
advises Goldie (1717–1809) to ignore the attacks on him and even
to increase the ferocity of his onslaught on the dogmatic divines,
seen as a pack of snarling dogs:

> E'en swinge the dogs, and thresh them sicker!
> The mair they squeel ay chap the thicker,
> An still 'mang hands a hearty bicker
>   O something stout!
> It gars an owthor's pulse beat quicker,
>   An helps his wit.

EPISTLE TO THE REV JOHN McMATH

The epistle 'To the Rev John McMath' (68/CW, 129–31), sent on 17
September 1785 with a copy of 'Holy Willie's Prayer', is a statement
of Burns's religious position and an affirmation of the honesty he

always opposed to hypocrisy. McMath (1755–1828) was a New Licht minister at Tarbolton Parish Kirk so the poet addresses him as an ecclesiastical ally. He admits it was foolish for him to risk the wrath of the Auld Licht luminaries by writing 'Holy Willie's Prayer' but indignantly expresses his anger at their vindicative antics and confusion of ritual with religion:

> But I gae mad at their grimaces,
> Their sighin, cantin, grace-proud faces,
> Their three-mile prayers, an hauf-mile graces,
>   Their raxin conscience,
> Whase greed, revenge, an pride disgraces
>   Waur nor their nonsense.

Burns's anger is expressed in the first line, but the third line is poised, showing him to be an unusually intelligent judge of the Auld Lichts.

Having produced such a balanced line, he has no need to invoke the satirical muse of Pope, though he does so, emphasising that he, unlike the arrogant preachers, is a modest man. If religion came down to a choice between the Auld Licht travesty and atheism, Burns would rather be 'An atheist clean' than conceal himself behind the Auld Licht creed. However, he believes in a humane religion as he demonstrates by personifying Religion as a divine virgin ('Maid divine') and offering his allegiance:

> Tho blotch't and foul wi monie a stain,
> An far unworthy of thy train,
> With trembling voice I tune my strain,
>   To join with those
> Who boldly dare thy cause maintain
>   In spite of foes:
>
> In spite o crowds, in spite o mobs,
> In spite o undermining jobs,
> In spite o dark banditti stabs
>   At worth an merit,
> By scoundrels, even wi holy robes,
>   But hellish spirit!

Burns achieves an appropriate intensity here by carrying over the catalogue of obstacles from one stanza to the other. Having addressed a personified Religion he addresses his friend in formal terms, thus linking him with the personification. McMath, as a member of 'A candid lib'ral band . . . Of public teachers', sits easily within the circle described by the affirmative spirit of religion: 'Sir, in that circle you are nam'd;/Sir, in that circle you are fam'd'.

TO J. SMITH

Written around March 1786 – it announces Burns's determination to publish his poems, 'To try my fate in guid, black prent' – the epistle 'To J. Smith' (79/CW, 169–73) is one of the poet's happiest productions and was duly included in the Kilmarnock Edition. James Smith (1765–c.1823), ten years old when his father was killed in an accident, was brought up in Mauchline by his strict stepfather. Rejecting his stepfather's notions of morality, Smith became – as did his friends Burns and John Richmond – a notoriously obstreperous character in Mauchline where, at the time of the epistle, he ran a linen draper's shop, almost opposite Nanse Tinnock's Inn. Smith was a member ('Procurator Fiscal' to Burns's 'Perpetual President' and Richmond's 'Clerk of the Court') of the Court of Equity, the secret bachelors' association that met in the Whitefoord Arms, Mauchline. Burns wrote several intimate letters to Smith about his affair with, and marriage to, Jean Armour. Like Richmond, Smith left Mauchline under censure of the Kirk Session. After living at Linlithgow he emigrated to Jamaica and died there.

Burns addresses Smith irreverently as 'the slee'st, pawkie thief,/ That e'er attempted stealth or rief' and counts the cost of his friendship with a fellow reprobate. That said, he also considers himself blessed with the company of such eccentrics, and twice-blessed with the glorious gift of poetry. Whereas in the epistles to Davie Sillar and John Lapraik, Burns rails bitterly against the rich, here he optimistically proclaims the human quality of his poverty:

> The star that rules my luckless lot,
> Has fated me the russet coat,
> And damn'd my fortune to the groat;
> But, in requit,
> Has blest me with a random-shot
> O countra wit.

He is prepared for a hostile critical reception to the publication of his poems, resigned to being an unknown bard singing 'My rustic sang', since he is capable of relishing the life he leads:

> This life, sae far's I understand,
> Is a' enchanted fairy-land,
> Where Pleasure is the magic-wand,
> That, wielded right,
> Makes hours like minutes, hand in hand,
> Dance by fu light.

Pleasure, for Burns, is to be found in 'vacant, careless roamin'', in 'cheerfu tankards foamin'', in 'dear, deluding Woman,/The joy of joys'.

Some stanzas (cast mainly in English) reflect, with rather feeble personifications (Young Fancy, Caution, Fortune, Keen Hope), on the inevitable decline into old age but Burns overcomes such thoughts by declaring himself the enemy of those who become old and inactive before their time:

> O ye douce folk that live by rule,
> Grave, tideless-blooded, calm an cool,
> Compar'd wi you – O fool! fool! fool!
> How much unlike!
> Your hearts are just a standing pool,
> Your lives, a dyke!

The poet, made vital through his verse, prefers to be one of 'The hairum-scairum, ram-stam boys,/The rattling squad' and enjoy life with friends such as the ram-stam boy to whom the epistle is addressed. Though the gravely reflective parts of the poem amount to unnecessary padding, the strongly colloquial Scots stanzas impressively convey Burns's affirmative human presence. 'Where,' asked Josiah Walker in his *Account of the Life and Character of Robert Burns* (1811), 'can we find a more exhilarting enumeration of the enjoyments of youth, contrasted with their successive extinction as age advances, than in "the Epistle to J. S[mith]"?' (CH, 223).

TO GAVIN HAMILTON, ESQ., MAUCHLINE

Written in three Cherry and the Slae stanzas, the epistle 'To Gavin

Hamilton, Esq., Mauchline, Recommending a Boy' (102/CW, 215–6) is dated 3 May 1786. A light-hearted character reference for 'yon lad . . . 'Bout which ye spak the tither day', the poem warns Hamilton (see 'The Burns Circle') that another potential employer has his eye on the boy: 'Master Tootie,/*Alias* Laird M'Gaun' (an unscrupulous cattle-dealer in Mauchline). Burns suggests sarcastically that the boy will be best placed with Hamilton, a far from flawless model for the young and a man who had been criticised by the kirk in 1784 for failing to attend church regularly, hence Burns's little jest:

> Altho I say't, he's gleg enough,
> An 'bout a house that's rude an rough,
> The boy might learn to swear;
> But then wi *you* he'll be sae taught,
> An get sic fair example straught,
> I hae na onie fear.
> Ye'll catechise him, every quirk,
> An shore him weel wi 'Hell';
> An gar him follow to the kirk –
> Ay, when ye gang yoursel!
> If ye, then, maun be then
> Frae hame this comin Friday,
> Then please, Sir, to lea'e, Sir,
> The orders wi your lady.

Burns ends by telling Hamilton he has discussed the deal in 'Paisley John's that night at e'en' (Paisley John was John Dow, landlord of the Whitefoord Arms). Like 'A Dedication to Gavin Hamilton' in the Kilmarnock Edition, the epistle is an expression of Burns's intimate friendship with Hamilton but was too inconsequential to be included in the Kilmarnock or Edinburgh editions.

EPISTLE TO JAMES TENNANT OF GLENCONNER

According to Kinsley this epistle was completed before 15 May 1786 as Burns, addressing a man who had recently married (Margaret Colville in 1785), 'writes almost certainly in anticipation of their first child's birth (15 May 1786)' (Kinsley, 1172). Omitted from the Kilmarnock Edition, the 'Epistle to James Tennant of Glenconner' (90/CW, 200–2) comprises a series of octosyllabic couplets addressed to the eldest son of John Tennant of Glenconner, the farmer who advised Burns to take Ellisland. James Tennant (1755–1835), known as 'The miller' because he had Ochiltree Mill, was once described by a neighbour as 'a dungeon of wit' (BE, 354).

Parts of the poem are taken up with greetings to mutual friends and Tennant's relatives but there is an amusing aside on Common Sense philosophy. Sending Tennant books by Adam Smith and Thomas Reid, Burns elaborates:

> Smith, wi his sympathetic feeling,
> An Reid, to common sense appealing.
> Philosophers have fought and wrangled,
> An meikle Greek and Latin mangled,
> Till, wi their logic-jargon tir'd
> As in the depth of science mir'd,
> To common sense they now appeal –
> What wives and wabsters see and feel!

With good humour, Burns requests the rapid return of his philosophical books as he is currently 'Perusing Bunyan, Brown an Boston' and in danger of grunting 'a real gospel groan': John Brown's *The Self-Interpreting Bible* and Thomas Boston's *The Four-fold State of Man* were treatises on divinity, Burns elsewhere condemning Boston's book as 'stupid' (CL, 260) and 'trash' (CL, 318).

The poem ends weakly with moralistic advice to 'cousin Kate, an sister Janet' to value their virginity ('To grant a heart is fairly civil,/But to grant a maidenhead's the devil') and the hope that Tennant will enjoy laughter, drink 'And ay eneugh o needfu clink'.

EPISTLE TO A YOUNG FRIEND

Dated May 1786 by Burns in the Kilmarnock Edition – and, more precisely, 15 May 1786 in the manuscript in the Kilmarnock Monument Museum – the 'Epistle to a Young Friend' (105/CW, 221–3), was addressed to Andrew Hunter Aiken, the eldest son of Ayr lawyer Robert Aiken (to whom 'The Cotter's Saturday Night' is dedicated). In later years Andrew became a merchant in Liverpool and British Consul in Riga, where he died in 1831.

Comprising eleven eight-line stanzas, rhyming *ababcdcd* and using 'abundant feminine rhyme' (Kinsley, 1180), the epistle shows Burns striking a moralistic pose, unconvincing in the context of the Kilmarnock Edition where elsewhere he projects himself as one of 'The hairum-scairum, ram-stam boys,/The rattling squad' ('Epistle to J. Smith'). Dispensing advice gratuitously to his 'youthfu friend', Burns issues a warning about the weakness of the human race and stresses the integrity of being true to oneself. Characteristically, he associates honesty with poverty ('A man may hae an honest heart,/Tho poortith hourly stare him') and, hypocritically, he condemns 'illicit' love (at the time the poem was composed Jean Armour was pregnant by Burns who was currently involved with Mary Campbell).

After saying his platitudinous piece on the subject of love, Burns turns to the topic of thrift, suggesting that the honourable accumulation of wealth is justified 'for the glorious privilege/Of being independent'. He urges respect for God, if not for canting preachers, and suggests 'An atheist-laugh's a poor exchange/For Deity offended'. The final stanza sums up all the arguments Burns has advanced in his poetic sermon:

> Adieu, dear, amiable youth!
>   Your heart can ne'er be wanting!
> May prudence, fortitude, and truth,
>   Erect your brow undaunting!
> In ploughman phrase, 'God send you speed',
>   Still daily to grow wiser;
> And may ye better reck the rede,
>   Than ever did th' adviser!

Only the humour of the last two lines saves the poem from total banality. Written after Burns had (3 April 1786) sent Proposals for the Kilmarnock Edition to the printer, 'Epistle to a Young Friend' was evidently composed to please the sort of reader who might be offended by the rakish Burns of other epistles.

REPLY TO A TRIMMING EPISTLE

Thomas Walker (who died around 1812) was a tailor who lived at Pool, near Ochiltree. Knowing that his schoolmaster friend William Simson (see section on 'To William Simson, Ochiltree' above) had exchanged verse epistles with Burns, Walker sent a twenty-six stanza poem which Burns ignored. After the appearance of the

Kilmarnock Edition, Walker (encouraged and advised by Simson) tried again, sending an epistle (119A) which referred to the poet's plan to emigrate, condemned his sexual indiscretions, and predicted that he would 'gang to hell'. This time Burns reacted and his 'Reply to a Trimming Epistle received from a Tailor' (119B/CW, 242–4) – collected in Thomas Stewart's *Poems ascribed to Robert Burns, the Ayrshire Bard* (1801) – was probably composed in the early autumn of 1786.

Burns's first stanza fairly seethes with indignation, protesting against the unprovoked assault as more irksome than his recent stint before Rev William Auld and the Mauchline congregation (his last penitential appearance was on 6 August 1786):

> What ails ye now, ye lousie bitch
> To thresh my back at sic a pitch?
> Losh, man, hae mercy wi your natch!
>   Your bodkin's bauld:
> I didna suffer half sae much
>   Frae Daddie Auld.

That sounds a flyting note more combative than other verse epistles. However, Burns does not attempt the character assassination of Walker, merely dismissing him as typical of his trade: 'ye prick-the-louse,/An jag-the-flae'. Leaving Walker to his sexually suggestive work of pricking and jagging, Burns turns to a survey of his own supposed sins.

Recalling that sexually active men like 'King David o poetic brief' have been subsequently celebrated, Burns feels he himself is a sinner who might some day 'sit amang the saunts'. Indeed, he cannot take his own sins seriously. He recalls how he answered the call of the Kirk Session and agreed to stand three times before the Mauchline congregation as a condemned fornicator. Burns then reports an imaginary conversation between himself and Daddie Auld. When the 'fornicator-loun' jokingly says that only gelding could eliminate his sexual appetite, the minister takes the suggestion seriously:

> 'Geld you!' (quo he) 'an what for no?
> If that your right hand, leg, or toe
> Should ever prove your sp'ritual foe,
>   You should remember
> To cut if aff – an what for no
>   Your dearest member!'

The insane logic of the fanatical fundamentalist is superbly conveyed by the rhetorically appropriate identical rhyme ('an what for no'). It is characteristic of Burns's ability to convey a character that the most effective stanza in the poem is attributed to Daddie Auld.

Predictably, Burns finds castration too drastic a solution and offers an alternative:

> 'Or, gin ye like to end the bother,
>   To please us a' – I'e just ae ither:
> When next wi yon lass I forgather,
>   Whate'er betide it,
> I'll frankly gie her 't a' thegither,
>   An let her guide it.'

This has the same irrational logic as the minister's cure-by-castration and Burns leaves the matter there, having taken intolerance to its own absurd conclusion.

EPISTLE TO CAPTAIN WILLIAM LOGAN

Written, like the 'Reply to a Trimming Epistle', after the publication of the Kilmarnock Edition, 'Epistle to Captain William Logan' (129/CW, 256–8), is dated Mossgiel, 30 October 1786. William Logan (who died in 1819) was, at that time, a lieutenant (Kinsley, 1214, points out that 'Captain' is a courtesy title used by Burns in recognition of Logan's status as an officer), a raconteur and a fiddler who lived at the house of Park, Ayr, with his mother Lucky and his unmarried sister Susan to whom Burns sent the poem 'Again the silent wheels of time' with a New Year's gift of Beattie's *Poems* in 1787. The epistle (entitled 'Epistle to Major Logan', a rank relating to Logan's service in the West Lowland Fencibles from 1794–9) was printed in Allan Cunningham's *The Works of Robert Burns* (1834)

As is his epistolary custom, Burns greets his friend with appropriate epithets: 'Haill, thairm-inspirin, rattlin Willie!' Just as Burns has his poetry to sustain him through 'this vile warl', Willie Logan has his fiddle, a conceit that allows Burns to introduce musical imagery and restate his familiar theme of the triumph of honest poverty over grim money-grubbing:

> A' blessings on the cheery gang

Wha dearly like a jig or sang,
An never think o right an wrang
But square an rule,
But as the clegs o feeling stang,
Are wise or fool.

My hand-wal'd curse keep hard in chase
The harpy, hoodock, purse-proud race,
Wha count on poortith as disgrace!
Their tuneless hearts,
May fireside discords jar a bass
To a' their parts!

The poor, as usual, are part of a natural harmony; the rich have 'tuneless hearts'. Having made this oft-repeated point Burns ends the epistle with a celebration of friendship and a promise to come to Park to see 'sentimental sister Susie,/An' honest Lucky' as well as Willie Logan.

TO THE GUIDWIFE OF WAUCHOPE HOUSE

Written in March 1787 and cast, like 'Epistle to Davie', in the Cherrie and the Slae stanza, 'To the Guidwife of Wauchope House' (147B/CW, 271–2), is addressed to Elizabeth Scott (1729–89), *née* Rutherford. The wife of Walter Scott of Wauchope House (near Jedburgh, Roxburghshire), and a cousin of poet Alison Cockburn, Mrs Scott had read the Kilmarnock Edition and, in February 1787, sent Burns a flattering verse epistle (147A) beginning 'My canty, witty, rhyming ploughman' and offering to send him 'a marled plaid'. Burns responded with his epistle 'To the Guidwife of Wauchope House' and visited Wauchope House, on 10 May 1787, during his Border tour.

This epistle combines an artistic statement with important autobiographical details. Burns recalls his youthful days of farm labour, then abruptly declares his lifelong ambition to be the national poet of Scotland:

E'en then, a wish (I mind its pow'r),
A wish that to my latest hour
Shall strongly heave my breast,

That I for poor auld Scotland's sake
Some usefu plan or book could make,
    Or sing a sang at least.
The rough burr-thistle spreading wide
    Amang the bearded bear,
I turn'd the weeder-clips aside,
    An spar'd the symbol dear.
    No nation, no station,
        My envy e'er could raise;
    A Scot still, but blot still,
        I knew nae higher praise.

Without naming her, he credits Nelly Kilpatrick with provoking him into poetry. Described as 'a young girl' (CB, 4) in the first Common Place Book and as 'a bewitching creature' (AL) in the Autobiographical Letter, Nelly is here 'the sonsie quean/That lighted up my jingle'. The memory of Nelly prompts Burns into a romantic meditation on Woman, 'The saul o life, the heav'n below'. The final stanza accepts the offer of the marled plaid.

EPISTLE TO HUGH PARKER

On 11 June 1788 Burns moved to his recently-leased farm of Ellisland but, as no farmhouse was ready for himself and Jean, went to live alone (until December when Jean joined him) in a hut near the tower of Isle (a mile down river from his farm), moving into the Ellisland farmhouse after April the following year. Burns described his temporary accomodation in a letter of 16 September 1788 to Peggy Chalmers: 'this hovel that I shelter in while occasionally here, is pervious to every blast that blows, and every shower that falls; and I am only preserved from being chilled to death, by being suffocated with smoke' (CL, 238).

'Epistle to Hugh Parker' (222/CW, 322–3), written in June 1788 (before 24 June since Burns promises a meeting in Tarbolton on that date), describes the situation in a series of octosyllabic couplets to a Kilmarnock banker friend:

Here, ambush'd by the chimla reek,
Hid in an atmosphere of reek,
I hear a wheel thrum i' the neuk,
I hear it – for in vain I leuk:

The red peat gleams, a fiery kernel
Enhusked by a fog infernal.
Here, for my wonted rhyming raptures,
I sit and count my sins by chapters;
For life and spunk like ither Christians,
I'm dwindled down to mere existence:
Wi nae converse but Gallowa' bodies,
Wi nae kend face but Jenny Geddes.

Jenny Geddes was the horse Burns named after the woman who –
on 23 August 1637 in St Giles Cathedral, Edinburgh – threw a stool
at the Bishop of Edinburgh while, on the instructions of Charles I, he
tried to impose The Book of Common Prayer on the Scottish Church.
The poem, saved from self-pity by Burns's sense of humour, ends
with the usual flourish of friendship.

EPISTLE TO ROBERT GRAHAM, ESQ., OF FINTRY

On 10 September 1788 (the poem is dated two days earlier), Burns
sent a letter, enclosing his 'Epistle to Robert Graham, Esq., of
Fintry' (230/CW, 330–3), to Graham (see his entry in 'The Burns
Circle'), the Excise Commissioner he had met, at Athole House,
on 1 September 1787. The letter explains, after a recital of Burns's
financial difficulties:

> I live here, in the very centre of a country Excise Divison . . . and
> as the [present Officer, Leonard Smith], owing to some legacies,
> is quite opulent, a removal could do him no manner of injury:
> and on a month's warning, to give me a little time to look again
> over my Instructions, I would not be afraid to enter on business.
> (CL, 426)

Burns had already (7 January 1788) asked Graham to use his
influence to secure him an Excise post, so the letter and verse
epistle amounted to an appeal to a patron already well disposed
to him.

Written in couplets of iambic pentameter, the epistle to Graham
has the stylistic rigidity of Burns's conventional Augustan English
poems and an unpleasantly fawning manner. Invoking Nature as
the creator of 'her last, best work, the human mind' Burns moves, by
way of platitudinous personifications ('plodding Industry', 'sober

Worth') to a projection of the poet as 'A mortal quite unfit for Fortune's strife'. What the poet needs, above all, is a patron of the quality of 'bounteous Graham': 'I know my need, I know thy giving hand,/I tax thy friendship at thy kind command.'

Burns's epistle is, then, a metrical version of a begging letter. He claims to be more independent than most poets but closes by implying that his artistic development is dependent on Graham's assistance:

> I trust, meantime, my boon is in thy gift:
> That, plac'd by thee upon the wish'd-for height,
> With man and nature fairer in her sight,
> My Muse may imp her wing for some sublimer flight.

It is obvious why Burns had to write such inferior occasional verse. It is less obvious why he thought so highly of the epistle that he showed a draft of it to Mrs Dunlop and sent copies of it to various correspondents including the highly intelligent Dugald Stewart. Perhaps Burns thought the predicament described in the epistle would alert others to his problems.

EPISTLE TO DR BLACKLOCK

Sent from Ellisland on 21 October 1789, the 'Epistle to Dr Blacklock' (273B/CW, 370–2) was a response to a verse epistle in English (273A) from Thomas Blacklock, dated Edinburgh, 24 August 1789. Blacklock (1721–91) – see his entry in 'The Burns Circle' – was the man whose letter, of 4 September 1786 in praise of the Kilmarnock Edition, persuaded Burns to abandon plans to emigrate to Jamaica and, instead, seek literary fame (if not fortune) in Edinburgh. Burns begins with the usual salutation, then expresses his annoyance that Robert Heron (see 'The Burns Circle') failed to deliver a letter he had promised the poet he would take to Blacklock ('He tauld myself by word o mouth,/He'd tak my letter'). After all Burns has significant news for Blacklock since he has 'turn'd a gauger', becoming an exciseman on 1 September 1789.

Burns dismisses as spurious any suggestion that he has prostituted his gifts by selling his intelligence for 'fifty pounds a year' to the Excise, a point he repeated in a letter of 23 December 1789 to Lady Elizabeth Cunningham: 'People may talk as they please of the ignominy of the Excise, but what will support my family and keep me independant of the world is to me a very important matter' (CL, 498). To Blacklock, Burns declares that 'strang necessity supreme is/'Mang sons o men'. Domestic duty, he claims, must take priority over poetic ambition for the man born into poverty even though the human cost of this is depressingly high:

> I hae a wife and twa wee laddies;
> They maun hae brose and brats o duddies:
> Ye ken yourself my heart right proud is –
> I need na vaunt –
> But I'll sned besoms, thraw saugh woodies,
> Before they want.
>
> Lord help me thro this warld o care!
> I'm weary-sick o't late and air!
> Not but I hae a richer share
> Than monie ithers;
> But why should ae man better fare,
> And a' men brithers.

The disgust (emphasised by the coupling 'weary-sick') at his dilemma is utterly convincing and an appropriate prelude to his assertion of human equality. Less convincing is his appeal to a personified Resolve ('Thou stalk o carl-hemp in man') and his deification of domesticity:

> To make a happy fireside clime
> To weans and wife,
> That's the true pathos and sublime
> Of human life.

That sentimentality has encouraged the worst excesses of Burns's imitators; the kindest thing that can be said about it is that, occuring in the context of a poem about 'strang necessity', it is capable of an ironical interpretation.

TO ALEXANDER FINDLATER

Alexander Findlater (1754–1839) – born, the son of an excise officer, in Burntisland, Fife – was Excise Supervisor at Dumfries from 1787–97. In February 1790, Burns sent Findlater a gift of eggs with a covering letter:

Mrs B[urns], like a true good wife, looking on my taste as a
Standard, & knowing that she cannot give me any thing – *eatable*
– more agreeable than a new-laid egg, she begs your acceptance
of a few. – They are all of them *Couch*; not thirty hours out.
(CL, 540)

It is possible that the epistle 'To Alexander Findlater' (281/CW,
378–9) was sent from Ellisland at the same time. Comprising five
Standard Habbie stanzas, the epistle indicates a relaxed relationship
between the poet and his official superior. After offering Lucky's
new-laid eggs in the first stanza, Burns humorously puts himself
in the place of the cock, stressing the sexual connotations of
the image:

> Had Fate that curst me in her ledger,
> A Poet poor, and poorer Gager,
> Created me that feather'd Sodger,
>   A generous Cock,
> How I wad craw and strut and roger
>   My kecklin Flock!

The obvious implication – that the cock has a better time of it than
a poor poetry-writing exciseman – is stressed in the penultimate
stanza:

> Nae cursed Clerical Excise
> On honest Nature's laws and ties;
> Free as the vernal breeze that flies
>   At early day,
> We'd tasted Nature's richest joys,
>   But stint or stay.

However, Burns decides, the subject is too provocative to pursue
('Our wisest way 's to say but little') and closes the poem as 'Your
Friend and Servant – Robt. Burns'.

    Though Burns is treating lightly the suggestion that a poet-cock
comparison is fraught with danger, there is a serious point he might
well have pursued had he had more creative time at his disposal.
His domestic life was far from blissful and he may have felt
emasculated in his capacity as an exciseman obliged to play the part
of an irreproachably respectable citizen. Findlater was occasionally
critical of Burns's excise work though he defended the poet when
his political opinions were the subject of an official enquiry.

EPISTLE TO COLONEL DE PEYSTER

Burns's last verse epistle, the 'Epistle to Colonel de Peyster' (517/CW, 564–5), was written towards the end of his life, in response to a letter of January 1796 from Colonel Arent Schuyler de Peyster enquiring after the poet's health. De Peyster (1736–1822) was born in New York of French Protestant descent and served in the British Army from 1755 to 1794 when he retired to Mavis Grove, on the Nith, three miles from Dumfries. He became Major Commandant of the Dumfries Volunteers which Burns helped found in 1795 and led the Volunteers at the poet's funeral. In 1813 de Peyster published a volume of his own verse, *Miscellanies by an Officer*.

Whereas early epistles begin by addressing the correspondent irreverently, the epistle to de Peyster opens with a respectful nod to 'My honor'd Colonel'. Burns, surrounded 'by bolus pill/And potion glasses', reflects on the vagaries of fate and how he has been unfairly treated by Dame Life. His melancholy is lifted, however, by an impressive image of life being determined by diabolic temptations as Man, the fly, wanders in the web woven by the poet's old adversary, the devil:

> Ah Nick! Ah Nick! it is na fair,
> First showing us the tempting ware,
> Bright wines and bonie lasses rare,
>   To put us daft;
> Syne weave, unseen, thy spider snare
>   O Hell's damn'd waft!

> Poor Man, the flie, aft bizzes by,
> And aft as chance he comes thee nigh,
> Thy auld damn'd elbow yeuks wi' joy
>   And hellish pleasure;
> Already in thy fancy's eye
>   Thy sicker treasure!

> Soon, heels o'er gowdie, in he gangs,
> And, like a sheep-head on a tangs,
> Thy girning laugh enjoys his pangs
>   And murdering wrestle,
> As, dangling in the wind, he hangs
>   A gibbet's tassle.

The imagery has a pictorial quality that indicates the imaginative power Burns possessed, even when agonised by illness in his last months.

The Songs

The bulk of Burns's songs were contributed to two rival publications. *The Scots Musical Museum*, edited by the Edinburgh engraver James Johnson, and published in six volumes (Edinburgh 1787, 1788, 1790, 1792, 1796, 1803) contains some 200 songs and fragments written, revised or communicated by Burns. *A Select Collection of Original Scottish Airs for the Voice*, edited by Edinburgh clerk George Thomson and published in eight parts (Edinburgh 1793, 1798, 1799, ?1799, 1802, 1803, 1805, 1818) contains more than 70 songs by Burns; after Burns's death 'Thomson meddled and muddled, impudently and sometimes disastrously, with the manuscripts Burns had left in his hands' (Kinsley, 991).

Kinsley's three-volume and one-volume editions of Burns (see 'Select Bibliography') give the tunes the songs match. An ambitious attempt to record all 323 songs associated with Burns is in progress as *The Songs of Robert Burns*, researched by Serge Hovey (1920–89) and sung by Jean Redpath, and available on long-playing records and cassettes from Philo/Rounder Records, Cambridge, Massachusetts; and Greentrax Records, Edinburgh. Another project, *Burns Songs from The Scots Musical Museum*, sung by Jean Redpath with notes on the songs by Donald A. Low, is available (cassettes and booklets) from Scottish Records, Brig o Turk, Perthshire; as is *Songs of Robert Burns* sung by William McCue.

Burns's own notes on Scottish songs can be consulted. The poet wrote to Johnson in 1792:

In the mean time, at your leisure, give a copy of the Museum to my worthy friend Mr Peter Hill, Bookseller, to bind for me interleaved with blank leaves, exactly as he did the laird of Glenriddell's, that I may insert every anecdote I can learn, together with my own criticisms and remarks on the songs. A copy of this kind I shall leave with you, the Editor, to publish at some after period, by way of making the Museum a book famous to the end of time, and you renowned for ever. (CL, 297)

In an interleaved copy of the first four volumes of the *Scots Musical Museum* Burns wrote his explanatory notes on Scottish song for Robert Riddell, 'the laird of Glenriddell' of the letter to Johnson. As transcribed as 'Strictures on Scottish Songs and Ballads' in R. H. Cromek's *Reliques of Robert Burns* (1808) the notes were queried in James C. Dick's *Notes on Scottish Song by Robert Burns* (1908) which suggested that Cromek had forged some of them. However, Davidson Cook ('Annotations of Scottish Songs by Burns', *Burns Chronicle*, 1922) and J. DeLancey Ferguson ('In Defense of R. H. Cromek', *Philological Quarterly*, July, 1930) showed the supposedly spurious notes were indeed by Burns though derived from other sources than the interleaved *Museum*. Burns's notes on Scottish song can, then, be read by consulting both Cromek and Dick.

*   *   *

As a child Burns heard the songs and ballads of Scotland sung by his mother who, the poet's sister affirmed, 'possessed a fine musical ear, and sang well' (BE, 36); and by Betty Davidson, his mother's friend, whose folk repertoire comprised 'tales and songs' (AL). Dugald Stewart noted that Burns's 'memory was uncommonly retentive [for] ballads, and other pieces in our Scottish dialect [which] he had learned in his childhood, from his mother' (cited by Kinsley, 1535).

From an early age Burns was an avid reader of songbooks including Allan Ramsay's *The Tea-Table Miscellany* (1724–37), James Oswald's *The Caledonian Pocket Companion* (9 vols, 1743–59) and Robert Bremner's collections of Scots songs (several of Bremner's volumes were published in Edinburgh in the 1750s). Of *The Lark: being a Select Collection of the most celebrated and newest songs, Scots and English* (published in Edinburgh, 1765) Burns wrote:

The Collection of Songs was my vade mecum. – I pored over them, driving my cart or walking to labor, song by song, verse by verse; carefully noting the true tender or sublime from affectation and fustian. – I am convinced I owe much to this for my critic-craft such as it is. (AL)

By his adolescence, then, he was familiar with traditional songs and printed songbooks. Later he took an informed interest in the technique of songwriting, describing John Aikin, author of *Essays on Song-Writing* (1772), as 'A great critic' (CL, 669) in a letter of 1795 to George Thomson.

The Kilmarnock Edition contains only a sprinkling of songs, including the admirable 'Now Westlin Winds' and the splendid 'The Rigs o Barley' (see below), but the volume was specifically entitled *Poems, Chiefly in the Scottish Dialect* which explains the omissions. In the last nine years of his life Burns's creative energies were almost entirely devoted to songwriting: beginning in 1787 he wrote for Johnson's *Scots Musical Museum*; and, beginning in 1792, he wrote for George Thomson's *Select Scottish Airs*. To this prolific output can be added other songs and ballads (including political ballads) Burns wrote throughout his life. Indeed his first lyric, 'Handsome Nell' (see below), written at the age of fifteen, was composed to fit a tune sung by Nelly Kilpatrick: 'Among her other love-inspiring qualifications, she sung sweetly; and 'twas her favorite reel to which I attempted giving an embodied vehicle in rhyme' (AL). In his first Common Place Book, discussing the genesis of the lyric, Burns noted that 'Rhyme and Song were, in a manner, the spontaneous language of my heart' (CB, 3).

Comprising discursive prose punctuated by song and verse, the first Common Place Book also expatiates thoughtfully on the subject of Scottish song in the entry for September 1785:

> There is a certain irregularity in the Old Scotch Songs, a redundancy of syllables with respect to that exactness of accent and measure that the English Poetry requires, but which glides in, most melodiously with the respective tunes to which they are set . . . . There is a degree of wild irregularity in many of the compositions and fragments which are daily sung to them by my compeers, the common people – a certain happy arrangement of Old Scotch syllables, and yet, very frequently, nothing, not even *like* rhyme, or sameless of jingle at the ends of the lines. This has made me some times imagine that perhaps, it might be possible for a Scotch Poet, with a nice, judicious ear, to set compositions to many of our most favorite airs, particularly that class of them mentioned above, independent of rhyme altogether. (CB, 49)

Later that month Burns attempted, in fitting words to the tune 'Galla Water', to imitate the irregularity he so admired. His 'Montgomerie's Peggy' runs:

> Altho my bed were in yon muir,
>   Amang the heather, in my plaidie,
> Yet happy, happy, I would be,
>   Had I my dear Montgomerie's Peggy.
>
> When o'er the hill beat surly storms,
>   And winter nights were dark and rainy,
> I'd seek some dell, and in my arms
>   I'd shelter dear Montgomerie's Peggy.
>
> Were I a Baron proud and high,
>   And horse and servants waiting ready,
> Then a' 'twad gie o joy to me
>   The sharin 't with Montgomerie's Peggy.
>   (22/CW, 60)

While his verbal virtuosity is not in doubt, it is not known for sure how much Burns knew about musical technique though one tradition supposes that, sometime before 1781, he attempted to learn the violin (Snyder, 90). If this tradition is true, he probably made little advance beyond the rudimentary stage for, when working on a collection of Highland airs for Johnson, he says 'I have had an able Fiddler two days already on it' (CL, 294) which suggests he was not himself an able fiddler. Although John Murdoch insisted that 'Robert's ear, in particular, was remarkably dull, and his voice untunable' (cited by Snyder, 43) he did demonstrate an understanding of musical notation, as when he alerted Johnson to alterations in an Argyllshire air:

> The alterations are: in the fourth bar of the first and third strains, which are to be the tune, instead of the crotchet C, and the quavers G and E, at the beginning of the bar make an entire minim in E, I mean E, the lowest line. (cited by Fitzhugh, 312)

This contradicts Burns's statement, to Thomson, that 'my pretensions to musical taste, are merely a few of Nature's instincts, untaught & untutored by Art' (CL, 638). He was not a musical illiterate.

Burns's most celebrated statement on his songwriting is contained in a letter of September 1793 to Thomson:

> Untill I am compleat master of a tune, in my own singing, (such as it is) I never can compose for it. – My way is: I consider the poetic Sentiment, correspondent to my idea of the musical expression;

then chuse my theme, begin one Stanza; when that is composed, which is generally the most difficult part of the business, I walk out, sit down now & then, look out for objects in Nature around me that are in unison or harmony with the cogitations of my fancy & workings of my bosom; humming every now & then the air with the verses I have framed: when I feel my Muse beginning to jade, I retire to the solitary fireside of my study, & there commit my effusions to paper; swinging, at intervals, on the hind-legs of my elbow-chair, by way of calling forth my own critical strictures, as my pen goes on. (CL, 643)

The reference to a natural harmony is particularly relevant to Burns's songs. Nature is the beautiful backdrop to the tormented emotions of human beings, as in 'The Winter it is Past' (published as the last song in the second volume of *Scottish Musical Museum* and matched to a hauntingly beautiful tune Burns found in *The Caledonian Pocket Companion* of 1759):

> The winter it is past, and the summer's come at last,
>   And the small birds sing on ev'ry tree;
> The hearts of these are glad, but mine is very sad,
>   For my lover has parted from me.
>
>   (218/CW, 321)

Occasionally, Burns felt it necessary to defend his musical taste, as he did in a letter of September 1794 to Thomson:

> I am sensible that my taste in Music must be inelegant & vulgar, because people of undisputed & cultivated taste can find no merit in many of my favorite tunes. – Still, because I am cheaply pleased, is that any reason why I should deny myself that pleasure? (CL, 656)

The rhetorical question answers itself just as surely as Burns's songs speak volumes for his genius as a songwriter. The following comments concentrate on the poetic nature of some of the songs and the arrangement is chronological so far as a chronology can be established.

HANDSOME NELL

Composed in the autumn of 1774, when Burns was fifteen and

fancied himself in love with Nelly Kilpatrick, his partner in the Mount Oliphant harvest, 'Handsome Nell' (1/CW, 43) is mainly interesting as an apprentice work which promises better things to come. Like Burns's greatest songs, it is a lyric to a pre-existing tune ('I am a man unmarried') and it deals with the notion of love. The first quatrain, with its jaunty opening, repeatedly refers to love:

> O once I lov'd a bonie lass,
>   Ay, and I love her still!
> And whilst that virtue warms my breast,
>   I'll love my handsome Nell.

The weak word there is 'virtue' ('passion' would have been stronger) and it determines the theme of the song which falls off into affectation as Burns claims the chief attraction of Nell is moral rather than physical. Nell is no more beautiful than other girls 'But for a modest gracefu mien/The like I never saw'. Burns, the apprentice poet, is now at the mercy of his theme: what matters about Nell is that 'Her reputation is complete', that her 'innocence and modesty' are enchanting. Burns had yet to learn how to transcend sentimental conventions and assert his passions. Significantly, the Scots swagger of the first two lines is rapidly replaced by a polite, lightly Scotticised English, leading to the declaration, in the seventh and final stanza, 'For absolutely in my breast/She reigns without controul'.

Transcribing the song in his first Common Place Book, Burns subjected it to criticism. He acknowledged the flaws in the final stanza, but declared 'I never recollect it, but my heart melts, and my blood sallies at the remembrance' (CB, 6).

NOW WESTLIN WINDS

Written in August 1775 to the tune 'Port Gordon', 'Now Westlin Winds' (2/CW, 44) celebrates Peggy Thomson (see her entry in 'The Burns Circle') who, when Burns was studying at Hugh Rodger's school in Kirkoswald, distracted the sixteen-year-old scholar from his studies and caused him sleepless nights (see AL). Unlike 'Handsome Nell', 'Now Westlin Winds' was included in the Kilmarnock Edition as Burns clearly appreciated its technical and thematic superiority to the earlier song. Not only does it use internal rhyme intelligently but it begins with an image of slaughter that allows the poet to counter with an affirmation of human tenderness.

> Now westlin winds, and slaught'ring guns
> Bring Autumn's pleasant weather;
> And the moorcock springs, on whirring wings,
> Amang the blooming heather:
> Now waving grain, wide o'er the plain,
> Delights the weary Farmer;
> And the moon shines bright, when I rove at night,
> To muse upon my Charmer.

That first stanza is packed with telling detail: the gentry with their 'slaught'ring guns' (Pope has 'slaught'ring guns' in his *Windsor Forest*) are contrasted with 'the weary Farmer' who delights in the sight of 'waving grain'; the rural bustle of the day is contrasted with the solitude of night when the sleepless poet muses on his sweetheart. That ability to set various figures in the landscape indicates a poetic maturity surprising in a sixteen-year-old.

In the second stanza (which Burns slightly revised by replacing 'The Patridge loves' with the Scots 'The Paitrick lo'es' for the appearance of the song in the *Scots Musical Museum*, 1792) the poet associates birds (partridge, plover, woodcock, heron, wood-pigeon, thrush, linnet) with the landscape they love, a lyrical flight threatened by the 'slaught'ring guns' of the first line. Burns returns to this threat in the third stanza, indignantly referring to 'The Sportsman's joy, the murd'ring cry,/The flutt'ring, gory pinion!' It is a detail that greatly distinguishes the song, showing Burns to be no mere lovesick poet of convention.

The last two stanzas turn away from the slaughter of nature and present human passion in a way that accords with 'the charms of Nature'. This placing of human beings in a natural union leads Burns to end the poem with thoughts of the union between himself and his sweetheart. Structurally and thematically, 'Now Westlin Winds' is an impressive performance for a teenage poet, one of Burns's best songs in English since he pressurises the language with his outrage at 'Tyrannic man's dominion' over nature.

THE LASS OF CESSNOCK BANKS

First published in R. H. Cromek's *Reliques of Robert Burns* (1808). 'The Lass of Cessnock Banks' (matched to the tune 'The Butcher Boy') was probably written in 1781 in honour of Alison Begbie (see

'The Burns Circle') who was a servant in a household on the banks of the Cessnock near Lochlea. The song (11/CW, 51–2), built around the refrain 'An she has twa sparkling, rogueish een', begins with a conventional catalogue of the Lass's charms: 'sweeter than the morning dawn . . . stately like yon youthful ash . . . spotless like the flow'ring thorn'.

In the ninth stanza (as edited by William Scott Douglas, *The Works of Robert Burns*, 1877–9, substituting 'bosom' for 'teeth') Burns declares a sexual, as well as a poetic, interest in the Lass:

> Her bosom's like the nightly snow,
>   When pale the morning rises keen,
> While hid the murm'ring streamlets flow –
>   An she has twa sparkling, rogueish een.

After this compliment, very much a piece of the period, Burns continues:

> Her lips are like yon cherries ripe,
>   That sunny walls from Boreas screen;
> They tempt the taste and charm the sight –
>   An she has twa sparkling, rogeuish een.

Clearly, the Lass embodies what is best in nature, even surpassing nature since, in addition to the shapely physical charms evoked through similes, she has 'rogueish' eyes that mesmerise the poet with their vitality.

The effect of the catalogue of similes and the insistent refrain is to present the Lass as not only a paragon of nature but a desirable woman. Yet Burns ends the song (as he ended his first song, 'Handsome Nell') by praising the mind above the body of the sweetheart:

> But it's not her hair, her form, her face,
>   Tho matching Beauty's fabled Queen:
> 'Tis the mind that shines in ev'ry grace –
>   An chiefly in her rogeuish een.

The conclusion owes more to convention than to conviction.

MARY MORISON

Sending 'Mary Morison' (30/CW, 69) to Thomson, on 20 March 1793, Burns described the song as 'one of my juvenile works', adding 'I do not think it very remarkable, either for its merits, or demerits' (CL, 623). However, Hugh MacDiarmid (*Burns Today and Tomorrow*, Edinburgh, 1959, p. 33) acclaimed 'the supreme power of Burns's finest line – *Ye arena Mary Morison*'; and Crawford called it 'the finest of his early songs' (Crawford, 9). Kinsley dates the poem to around 1784 though in that year the poet was twenty-five and far from 'juvenile'.

At that time, too, the Mary Morison traditionally identified as the heroine of Burns's song was thirteen and thus an unlikely candidate for the poet's passion (even less likely if the song was written earlier than 1784). This Mary Morison (1771–91), who died of consumption and is buried in Mauchline churchyard, was the daughter of Adjutant John Morison of the 104th Regiment.

A more plausible heroine is Alison Begbie (see 'The Burns Circle' and remarks above on 'The Lass of Cessnock Banks'), for it 'is possible that Burns's brief infatuation for Alison Begbie was . . . responsible for [the song]' (Crawford, 9). It was in 1781 that Burns made romantic overtures to Alison Begbie who then, he lamented, 'jilted me with peculiar circumstances of mortification' (AL). In 1781 Burns was twenty-two, not 'juvenile' psychologically though still learning the poetic trade he had started at the age of fifteen. As to why Burns should prefer the name Mary Morison to the name Alison Begbie in a song: the former is more mellifluous; it is also conveniently general for 'Morison is a not uncommon name, and many Morisons are Marys' (Kinsley, 1022). If written in 1781 (the year before he acquired the Second Edition of Fergusson's *Poems*) it shows Burns a period when he was exploring the dramatic potential of Scottish song.

The first stanza is an urgent declaration of love – indeed lust – for the woman he addresses.

> O Mary, at thy window be!
>   It is the wish'd, the trysted hour.
> Those smiles and glances let me see,
>   That makes the miser's treasure poor.
> How blythely wad I bide the stoure,
>   A weary slave frae sun to sun,
> Could I the rich reward secure –
>   The lovely Mary Morison.

The theme is one that animates the body of Burns's work: the poor man will endure his burden as 'A weary slave frae sun to sun' if he can escape from it through erotic excitement. Lacking material wealth, the poor seek the only treasure available to them, the 'rich reward' of sex.

Burns introduces a dramatic situation in the second stanza of the song. The previous night, as 'The dance gaed thro the lighted ha'', he looked at beautiful women but rejected them all since none was equal to his sweetheart: 'I sigh'd, and said amang them a'/–"Ye are na Mary Morison".' Finally, Burns makes an emotional appeal to Mary to give him the gift of sexual love, to offer him 'the rich reward':

> O, Mary, canst thou wreck his peace
> Wha for thy sake wad gladly die?
> Or canst thou break that heart of his
> Whause only faut is loving thee?
> If love for love thou wilt na gie,
> At least be pity to me shown:
> A thought ungentle canna be
> The thought o Mary Morison.

If Alison Begbie was the sweetheart in question, then her answer to the two questions in the first four lines was a rejection of Burns. Traditional in technique (the octosyllabic ballade-stanza was used in several poems in Allan Ramsay's anthology *Ever Green*, 1724) the song gives the conventional lovesick lament a powerful sexual thrust. It is possible that 'The Lass of Cessnock Banks' and 'Mary Morison' were written, respectively, before and after Alison Begbie jilted Burns.

THE RIGS o BARLEY

Composed around 1782, 'The Rigs o Barley' (8/CW, 49–50) was included in the Kilmarnock Edition. Burns cites the traditional tune 'Corn rigs are bonie' and knew the song 'My Patie is a Lover Gay', in Allan Ramsay's *The Gentle Shepherd*, ending 'Then I'll comply, and marry Pate,/And syne my Cockernonny,/He's free to touzel air or late,/Where Corn-riggs are bonny.' Writing to Thomson, on 7 April 1793, Burns declared this version 'far unworthy of Ramsay' (CL, 627), preferring his own 'Rigs o Barley'. The honour of being the Annie of Burns's song was claimed by Anne Rankine, youngest daughter of the man addressed in 'Epistle to John Rankine'. She married John Merry, an inkeeper in Cumnock where she died in 1843.

Burns shows his ability to put a memorable lyrical gloss on an erotic experience. The song begins expansively 'It was upon a Lammas night', as if a narrative adventure was about to unfold; the first stanza, however, ends intimately with Annie since 'Wi sma' persuasion she agreed/To see me thro the barley.' The detail about 'sma' persuasion' is psychologically revealing: Burns is describing a shared pleasure rather than a seduction. He is not, initially at any rate, indulging in sexual boastfulness, as he does in his blatantly bawdy poems; he is celebrating the tenderness of the experience.

One way Burns emphasises this tenderness is to show the erotic act as a regular part of the natural order. In the second stanza, nature is seen at her most serene – 'The sky was blue, the wind was still,/The moon was shining clearly' – which matches the mood of the couple (as it does not in those poems where Burns calls on nature as a witness to the internal insecurity of human nature). Here, nature seems at one with the passion of the couple: 'I kiss'd her owre and owre again,/Amang the rigs o barley.' The penultimate stanza introduces a sexually boastful note by predicting that Annie will recall 'the moon and stars so bright' and bless her 'happy night/Amang the rigs o barley'.

The last stanza is an uncomplicated statement of Burns's outlook, raising shared sexual ecstasy above other pleasures.

> I hae been blythe wi comrades dear;
> I hae been merry drinking;
> I hae been joyfu gath'rin gear;
> I hae been happy thinking:
> But a' the pleasures e'er I saw,
> Tho three times doubl'd fairly –
> That happy night was worth them a',
> Amang the rigs o barley.

Burns shows his great songwriting gift in making his heroine both an ideal and an individual figure.

GREEN GROW THE RASHES, O

Burns entered 'Green Grow the Rashes, O' (45/CW, 81) in his first Common Place Book, August 1784. Having divided young men into two classes, comprising the Grave and the Merry, he reflected 'I shall set down the following fragment which, as it is the genuine language of my heart, will enable any body to determine which of the classes I belong to' (CB, 21). The chorus derives from the ballad 'Cou thou me the rasyches grene', first listed in 1549; the air was first printed in Oswald's collection of 1740. Burns circulated a bawdy version of the song, see 'The Bawdy Burns'.

This song is a general reflection on the particular emotion expressed in 'The Rigs o Barley'. Sexual pleasure, Burns suggests, is a pursuit more worthy than the accumulation of wealth.

> But gie me a cannie hour at e'en,
> My arms about my dearie, O,
> An war'ly cares an war'ly men,
> May a' gae tapsalteerie, O!

Predictably, the last stanza (in the text from the First Edinburgh Edition) brings in nature as an ally of sensual pleasure. Whereas Pope, in *An Essay on Man*, asserted 'An honest man's the noblest work of God' (a statement that might have been Burns's motto and which he quoted in 'The Cotter's Saturday Night'), the song asserts a femininist alternative:

> Auld Nature swears, the lovely dears
> Her noblest work she classes, O:
> Her prentice han' she try'd on man,
> An then she made the lasses, O.

WHEN GUILFORD GOOD

Published in the First Edinburgh Edition under the title 'A Fragment', to the tune 'Gilliecrankie', the song 'When Guilford Good' (38/CW, 72–4) was written in 1784. Burns considered including it in the Kilmarnock Edition but was advised against it. Then, towards the end of 1786, he showed it to Glencairn:

> I showed [my] political ballad to my lord Glencairn, to have his opinion whether I should publish it; as I suspect my political tenets, such as they are, may be rather heretical in the opinion of some of my best Friends . . . . His Lordship seems to think the piece may appear in print. (CL, 224)

The song, which has been praised as 'daring' (Crawford, 147) and dismissed as 'merely a squib' (Kinsley, 1026), is Burns's scornful metrical history of Britain's misfortunes in the period stretching from the Boston Tea Party of 16 December 1773 to the Peace of Versailles, 3 September 1783, that officially ended the American War of Independence.

Guilford, named in the first line, is Lord North (son of the 1st Earl of Guilford), the Tory premier who, against his better judgement, pursued George III's provocative policy towards America. The opening stanza establishes the ironic tone since 'Guilford good', the pilot of state, loses his sense of direction when confronted with the Boston Tea Party ('Then up they gat the maskin-pat,/And in the sea did jaw, man'). There follows a tribute to Richard Montgomery, who died during the revolutionary assault on Quebec, and a parade of reactionary warriors: Governor Gage of Massachusetts; Sir William Howe, Gage's successor as Commander-in-chief; General John Burgoyne (who surrendered Saratoga in 1777); Brigadier Simon Fraser (killed during Burgoyne's campaign); General Charles Cornwallis (who surrendered Yorktown in 1781); General Sir Henry Clinton (who retreated on hearing of Cornwallis's surrender).

Having dealt with the military men, Burns turns to the political armchair warriors: John Montague, 4th Earl of Sandwich and North's First Lord of the Admiralty; North himself; Lord George Sackville, North's Secretary of State for the Colonies; Edmund Burke, forceful critic of North's American policy; Charles James Fox, leader of the opposition to North; Lord Rockingham, who succeeded North as premier in 1782 and died the same year; the Earl of Shelburne, appointed by George III as successor to Rockingham and defeated by the Fox–North coalition in 1783; William Pitt ('Chatham's boy'); Lord Grenville, Pitt's cousin and later his foreign minister; Henry Dundas, Shelburne's treasurer of the navy.

On 17 December 1783 (that is, shortly after the Peace of Versailles) Fox's India Bill was defeated in the Lords, the Fox–North coalition resigned and 'Willie' Pitt formed a ministry with himself, as Chancellor of the Exchequer, the sole member of the cabinet in the Commons. The ballad ends with an allusion to 'Willie' Pitt's successful election campaign of 1784:

> But, word an blow, North, Fox, and Co.
> Gowff'd Willie like a ba', man,

> Till Suthron raise, an coost their claise
> Behind him in a raw, man:
> An Caledon threw by the drone,
> An did her whittle draw, man;
> An swoor fu rude, thro dirt an bluid,
> To mak it guid in law, man.

As Burns sees it, the British generals are incompetent and the English politicians are absurd, playing politics as other men would play a game of golf. By using the catalogue format comically Burns disowns the military and disarms the armchair warriors. Devoid of lyricism, this ballad has more in common with Burns's Election Ballads than with his greatest songs.

MY HIGHLAND LASSIE, O

Unlike other songs he wrote about 'Highland Mary' Campbell (see her entry in 'The Burns Circle'), 'My Highland Lassie, O' (107/CW, 224) was probably written in the spring of 1786, while the subject of it was alive: 'Thou Lingering Star' (also known as 'To Mary in Heaven') was sent to Mrs Dunlop in November 1789; 'Will Ye Go to the Indies, My Mary' was sent to Thomson in October 1792; 'Highland Mary' was sent to Thomson in November 1792. Mary died in the late autumn of 1786, at the age of twenty-three. Written in lightly Scots-accented English quatrains (each comprising couplets the second of which rhymes throughout with the refrain 'Highland lassie, O'), 'My Highland Lassie, O' is not one of Burns's finest songs, indeed all the Highland Mary songs are intrinsically inferior to Burns's passionate Scots lyrics but remain popular with Mariolaters in love with the romantic legend of a tragic heroine.

Burns specifies that 'My Highland Lassie, O' was 'a composition of early life' (CL, 644) in a letter of September 1793 to Thomson. The interleaved *Scots Musical Museum* expands on the poem in a note (now accepted as genuine and identifying the unnamed heroine of the poem as Mary Campbell):

> This was a composition of mine in very early life, before I was known at all in the world. My Highland lassie was a warm-hearted, charming young creature as ever blessed a man with generous love. After a pretty long tract of the most ardent recip-rocal attachment, we met by appointment, on the second Sunday

of May [1786], in a sequestered spot by the Banks of Ayr, where we spent the day in taking farewell, before she should embark for the West-Highlands to arrange matters among her friends for our projected change of life. (cited by Kinsley, 1183)

Although this implies that Burns and Mary were to emigrate to Jamaica together (a suggestion strengthened on the evidence of the song 'Will Ye Go to the Indies, My Mary') the first song to Highland Mary (which matches the tune 'MacLauchlin's Scots-Measure') indicates that the poet anticipated leaving Scotland on his own:

> Altho thro foreign climes I range,
> I know her heart will never change;
> For her bosom burns with honour's glow,
> My faithful Highland lassie, O!

He could, after all, just as easily written 'we' instead of 'I' in that first line. However the succeeding stanza hopes that 'Indian wealth may lustre throw/Around my Highland lassie, O', which could mean either that she would join him or that he would return to Scotland a wealthy man.

Burns begins by raising his Highland lassie on a pedastal, above the level of 'gentle dames'. He then regrets that he is not a man of property able to show the world his love for his sweetheart, which brings him to his predicament:

> But fickle Fortune frowns on me,
> And I maun cross the raging sea;
> But while my crimson currents flow,
> I'll love my Highland lassie, O!

The poet explains that he is linked to his Highland lassie 'By secret troth' and he ends by bidding farewell to her Highlands and his Lowlands:

> Farewell the glen sae bushy, O!
> Farewell the plain sae rashy, O!
> To other lands I now must go,
> To sing my Highland lassie, O!

Fortunately, Burns found other subjects more poetically inspiring than Mary Campbell who seemed to provoke only insipid sentiments in him.

THE GLOOMY NIGHT IS GATH'RING FAST

'The gloomy night is gath'ring fast' (122/CW, 250–1), to the tune 'Roslin Castle', was a valedictory composition (of August 1786) as Burns explained in his letter of 2 August 1787 to Dr John Moore:

> I had taken the last farewel of my few friends, my chest was on the road to Greenock; I had composed my last song I should ever measure in Caledonia, 'The gloomy night is gathering fast', when a letter from Dr Blacklock to a friend of mine overthrew all my schemes by rousing my poetic ambition. (AL)

Burns was on the point, then, of emigrating to Jamaica when Dr Blacklock's letter of 4 September 1786, in praise of the poems in the Kilmarnock Edition, persuaded him to seek literary fame in Edinburgh.

Composed in octosyllabic couplets grouped in eight-line stanzas each ending on the phrase 'banks of Ayr', the song reveals Burns in one of his melancholy moods, sure that the wild and stormy weather perfectly matches his personal instability. As is customary in his English poems, he relies more on adjectival padding than on inspiration: 'gloomy night', 'wild inconstant blast', 'placid, azure sky', 'fatal, deadly shore'. The song is redeemed by the central image it sustains of water welling uncontrollably from a source. In the first stanza rain-clouds shift across the sky, in the second the waves swell with the storm, in the third there is a surge on the shore, in the fourth and final stanza the water Burns sees is in his own eyes (which are even more moist than those of Harley, the lachrymose hero of Henry Mackenzie's *The Man of Feeling*, one of his favourite novels):

> Farewell, old Coila's hills and dales,
> Her healthy moors and winding vales;
> The scenes where wretched Fancy roves,
> Pursuing past unhappy loves!
> Farewell my friends! farewell my foes!
> My peace with these, my love with those –
> The bursting tears my heart declare,
> Farewell, my bonie banks of Ayr!

RANTIN, ROVIN ROBIN

Burns wrote this lyric (140/CW, 267–8) in an entry for April 1787 in his second Common Place Book. It was matched to the tune of 'Dainty Davie' though Thomson subsequently quarrelled about the chorus which, Burns insisted, was to be sung to the low part of the tune. It is ostensibly a self-congratulatory song, composed when Burns – basking in the critical success of his poems – was in an autobiographical mood (the long Autobiographical Letter to Dr Moore was written in the same year as the song).

After the chorus rejoicing that Robin was a 'rantin, rovin' boy, the song establishes the region (Kyle) in which Burns was born then recalls the fact that, ten days after Burns's birth, a storm blew out the gable above the fireplace in the Alloway cottage. The blast of January wind is a gift to the bard, a breath of the spirit of Scotland. This notion is implied in the four last stanzas which are spoken by a local gossip – an old wife, the kind of woman central to the oral traditions of Scotland.

So the prophecies about Robin are prophecies emerging from the same source that sang the ballads of Scotland and told the tales of folklore. Giving the gossip a larger dimension than that of one neighbour strengthens the line 'He'll be a credit till us a'': that is, he will be a credit to the Scottish folk, not simply to one gossip next door.

Similarly, the last two stanzas link Burns not only to a few women but to the glory of womankind – 'our kin'', as the gossip calls her sex. The gossip's discussion of Robin's sexuality is both spellbinding ('But sure as three times three mak nine' sounds like a spell) and specific: for him the woman will keep their legs apart for penetration. Burns is thus seen as a force capable of revitalising Scotland:

> 'But sure as three times three mak nine,
> I see by ilka score and line,
> This chap will dearly like our kin',
>   So leeze me on thee, Robin!'

> 'Guid faith', quo she, 'I doubt you gar
> The bonie lassies lie aspar ;
> But twenty faults ye may hae waur –
>   So blessins on thee, Robin!'

What sounds like an innocent song has remarkable national connotations when considered in the context of the folk tradition, something Burns had absorbed from his ballad-singing mother and his mother's cousin Betty Davidson – an old gossip expert at retelling the folk tales of the country.

WHERE, BRAVING ANGRY WINTER'S STORMS

After becoming infatuated by Peggy Chalmers (see 'The Burns Circle') Burns sent her two songs on 6 November 1787: 'My Peggy's Face' and 'Where, braving angry winter's storms' (182/CW, 298) which Burns calls 'Where, braving all the winter's harms' in the letter though Kinsley accepts Johnson's text in the *Scots Musical Museum* (1788) as authoritative. 'Where, braving angry winter's storms', Burns explained, was 'already set – the tune is Neil Gow's lamentation for Abercairny' (CL, 232). Composed in quatrains it shows Burns resorting to the platitudinous routine he was prone to when writing in a sentimental English diction. All the epithets in the first two quatrains are commonplace: 'angry winter', 'lofty Ochils', 'wondering eyes', 'savage stream', 'lonely gem'. The last eight lines work up, feebly, to a personified 'tyrant Death' whose proximity is less alarming than the thought of losing Peggy.

MY PEGGY'S FACE

The other song sent to Peggy Chalmers on 6 November 1787, 'My Peggy's Face' (181/CW, 297–8), appeared in *Select Scottish Airs* (1801) to an unauthorised air, and in the *Scots Musical Museum* (1803) to one of two tunes proposed by the musician Stephen Clarke. It would have been published at the same time as 'Where, braving angry winter's storms' had not Peggy 'protested against publication' (Kinsley, 1250). Like its companion-song 'My Peggy's Face' is written in English and relies on commonplace descriptions, resulting in one of the most lifeless lines ever written by Burns: 'Her face so truly heavenly fair'. After noting that nature's charms are ephemeral he asserts that Peggy's are immortal and defines them in more empty epithets:

> The tender thrill, the pitying tear,
> The generous purpose, nobly dear,
> The gentle look that rage disarms –
> These are all immortal charms.

The two songs to Peggy have none of the power of the prose in the letter Burns sent her on 16 September 1788 (quoted in her entry in 'The Burns Circle').

OF A' THE AIRTS THE WIND CAN BLAW

In the interleaved copy of the *Scots Musical Museum*, Burns wrote of 'Of a' the airts the wind can blaw' (227/CW, 329): 'This air is by Marshall, the song I composed out of compliment to Mrs Burns. N.B. It was during the honeymoon' (cited by Kinsley, 1277, who traces the air back to 'Alace I lie my alon', the basis for William Marshall's tune). Burns married Jean Armour at the end of March 1788, which places the poem chronologically. What is astonishing is that Burns could have written such a superlative lovesong for a woman he described one month before the marriage as follows: 'I, this morning, as I came home, called for a certain woman. – I am disgusted with her; I cannot endure her! . . . I have done with her, and she with me' (CL, 399). The song is widely regarded as the 'best of all the songs inspired by Jean Armour' (Crawford, 273). Jean, in this song, is associated with nature in general and the landscape around Mauchline in particular:

> Of a' the airts the wind can blaw
>   I dearly like the west,
> For there the bonie lassie lives,
>   The lassie I lo'e best.
> There wild woods grow, and rivers row
>   And monie a hill between,
> But day and night my fancy's flight
>   Is ever wi my Jean.

The second stanza emphasises the natural appeal of Jean: 'I see her in the dewy flowers . . . I hear her in the tunefu birds'. After his epistolary affair with Mrs McLehose (to whom Burns wrote the letter of disgust quoted above) Burns seems to have valued Jean for her uncomplicated earthiness:

> There's not a bonie flower that springs
>   By fountain, shaw, or green,
> There's not a bonie bird that sings,
>   But minds me o my Jean.

AULD LANG SYNE

Writing to Mrs Dunlop (7 December 1788) Burns congratulated
her on her description of a meeting with an old schoolfriend and
added:

> Apropos, is not the Scots phrase, 'Auld lang syne', exceedingly
> expressive. – There is an old song & tune which has often thrilled
> thro' my soul. – You know I am an enthusiast in old Scots songs.
> – I shall give you the verses on the other sheet . . . Light be the
> turf on the breast of the heaven-inspired Poet who composed this
> glorious Fragment! There is more of the fire of native genius in
> it, than in half a dozen of modern English Bacchanalians. (CL,
> 161, 163)

'Auld Lang Syne' (240/CW, 341) was subsequently sent to Johnson
who (having already printed Allan Ramsay's lovesong 'Auld Lang
Syne' in 1787) delayed its publication in the *Scots Musical Museum*
until the fifth volume which appeared some months after Burns's
death. Johnson matched the words to an old air collected in
Playford's *Original Scotch Tunes* (1700).

In September 1793 Burns sent 'Auld Lang Syne' to Thomson,
explaining:

> The air is but mediocre; but the following song, the old Song of
> the olden times, & which has never been in print, nor even in
> manuscript, until I took it down from an old man's singing; is
> enough to recommend any air. (CL, 646)

Thomson published the words in *Select Scotish Airs* in 1799, and
matched them to the tune still sung all over the world in this
celebration of companionship.

Burns certainly knew previous versions of the old song: Allan
Ramsay's song beginning 'Should auld acquaintance be forgot,/Tho'
they return with scars'; and John Skinner's 'The Old Minister's
Song' beginning 'Should auld acquaintance be forgot,/Or friendship
e'er grow cauld'. His version, however, is infinitely superior to
these and the song must be regarded as largely, though not all,
his own work.

The chorus and the first quatrain, too familiar to reproduce,
celebrate dear departed days with 'a cup of kindness' and the
second quatrain specifies the cup of kindness as a 'pint-stowp'.

It is in the three final quatrains that Burns actually explores the experience of a long companionship.

> We twa hae run about the braes,
>   And pou'd the gowans fine,
> But we've wander'd monie a weary fit,
>   Sin auld lang syne.

> We twa hae paidl'd in the burn
>   From morning sun till dine,
> But seas between us braid hae roar'd
>   Sin auld lang syne.

> And there's a hand my trusty fiere,
>   And gie's a hand o thine,
> And we'll tak a right guid-willie-waught,
>   For auld lang syne.

The first of these quatrains evokes youth when a couple are capable of running in a human race that eventually overwhelms them with weariness. A different contrast is evoked by the imagery of water in the lines about paddling in the burn as a prelude to being separated by the seas. These two quatrains comprise a flashback to the speaker's own experience, a nostalgic aside to the central affirmation of friendship which is reasserted in the last four lines.

Coming after the flashback, the shared drink takes on a new dimension, the liquid linking with the burn and the seas that, respectively, unite and separate the couple. Thus the song operates on two levels, as a general celebration of friendship with present company and a tribute to the memory of missing companions.

THE SILVER TASSIE

Sending 'The Silver Tassie' (242/CW, 342) to Mrs Dunlop on 7 December 1788, Burns cited 'two old Stanzas which please me mightily' (CL, 163). After the song had appeared as an anonymous traditional song in the *Scots Musical Museum* Burns described it, in a letter of September 1793 to Thomson, as 'a song of mine, & I think not a bad one' (CL, 643. (The lyric was first written for the tune 'The Stolen Kiss'; Burns told Thomson it could be fitted to the tune of 'Wae's my Heart that we should sunder'; Thomson preferred a third tune 'The Old Highland Laddie'). Snyder thought the song 'unexcelled by anything [Burns] ever wrote for sheer virtuosity of technique' (Snyder, 350) and it was a favourite of Sean O'Casey who named his play *The Silver Tassie* (1929) after this 'riotous and romantic song' (O'Casey, *Autobiographies* 2, 1963; rept. London, 1980, p. 270).

Spoken as an instruction in an inn in Leith, the first four lines have a splendid swagger which is qualified by the following four explaining that the singer's departure involves some distance:

> Go fetch to me a pint o wine,
>   And fill it in a silver tassie;
> That I may drink, before I go,
>   A service to my bonie lassie:
> The boat rocks at the Pier o Leith,
>   Fu loud the wind blaws frae the Ferry,
> The ship rides by the Berwick-law,
>   And I maun leave my bony Mary.

The opening quatrain of the second stanza offers the reason for this departure which is a response to the 'shouts o war', a phrase repeated in the closing quatrain:

> It's no the roar o sea or shore,
>   Wad make me langer wish to tarry;
> Nor shouts o war that's heard afar –
>   It's leaving thee, my bony Mary!

So the swagger of the opening line has given way to the sadness of the final line, for battles 'deep and bloody' have a fatal finality. In the space of sixteen lines Burns seems to run through the emotional range of parting.

THE BANKS o DOON

Burns wrote three versions of this song. The first, 'Sweet Are The Banks' (CW, 613), is quoted in a letter of 11 March 1791 to Alexander Cunningham in which Burns explains:

> I have this evening sketched out a Song . . . My song is intended to sing to a Strathspey reel of which I am very fond, called in Cummin's Collection of Strathspeys, 'Ballendalloch's reel'; & in other Collections that I have met with, it is known by the name of, 'Camdelmore' . . . I shall give the song to Johnson for the fourth

vol. of his Publication of Scots Songs, which he has just now in hand. (CL, 461)

This first version, comprising six quatrains, begins with the familiar Burnsian theme of personal misery amidst natural beauty:

> Sweet are the banks – the banks o Doon,
>   The spreading flowers are fair,
> And everything is blythe and glad,
>   But I am fu o care.

The second version, 'Ye Flowery Banks' (328A/CW, 419), revises the first quatrain and begins:

> Ye flowery banks o bonie Doon,
>   How can ye blume sae fair?
> How can ye chant, ye little birds,
>   And I sae fu o care?
>
> Thou'll break my heart, thou bonie bird,
>   That sings upon the bough:
> Thou minds me o the happy days
>   When my fause Luve was true!

Burns has opted for an inquisitive opening, questioning the landscape he merely observed in the first version. The effect of this is to intensify the singer's sensation of being out of harmony with the natural order.

The final version, 'The Banks o Doon' (328B/CW, 419–20), comprises four quatrains, deleting the incrementally repetitive third and sixth quatrains of 'Sweet Are The Banks'. This third version, matched to the tune 'The Caledonian Hunt's Delight', begins:

> Ye banks and braes o bonie Doon,
>   How can ye bloom sae fresh and fair?
> How can ye chant, ye little birds,
>   And I sae weary fu o care!
>
> Thou'll break my heart, thou warbling bird,
>   That wantons thro the flowering thorn!
> Thou minds me o departed joys,
>   Departed never to return.

Adding extra syllables for the sake of the melody, Burns has changed 'That sings upon the bough' to 'That wantons thro the flowering thorn' just as the third quatrain of the final version changes 'To see the woodbine twine' to 'To see the rose and woodbine twine'. Structurally, the final version is more compact if, stylistically, more florid in opting for longer lines instead of incremental repetition. What began as a poignant ballad ends as a decorative lyric, demonstrating Burns's ability to adapt a traditional measure to his own mood.

AE FOND KISS

Learning that Mrs Agnes McLehose intended to join her now prosperous husband in Jamaica, Burns made his last visit to Edinburgh where, on 6 December 1791, Sylvander and Clarinda met for the last time. On his return to Dumfries, he composed 'Ae Fond Kiss' (337/CW, 434), the finest of his ten love songs to her. Burns sent the song to Mrs McLehose (known as Nancy to her friends) on 27 December 1791 as one of three 'Songs I have just been composing for the Collection of Songs' (CL, 409). 'Ae Fond Kiss' appeared in Johnson's *Scots Musical Museum* (1792), matched to the tune 'Rory Dall's port'.

Characteristically, Burns created his song by improving on a precedent, 'The Parting Kiss' by the English poet Robert Dodsley, included in *The Charmer; a Choice Collection of Songs, English and Scots* (1749). Dodsley's poem begins

> One kind kiss before we part,
> Drop a tear, and bid adieu:
> Tho' we sever, my fond heart,
> Till we meet, shall pant for you.

Burns's song begins

> Ae fond kiss, and then we sever!
> Ae farewell, and then forever!

The first stanza, while an advance on Dodsley, still displays the emotional affectations of Burns's source. Dodsley has 'that falling tear', Burns has 'heart-wrung tears'; Dodsley says 'ev'ry wish shall pant for you', Burns offers 'Warring sighs and groans'.

It is the second stanza that represents the passionate Burns, transcending the timid diction of Dodsley and making a personal statement of a love that could only lead to the despair of parting:

> I'll ne'er blame my partial fancy:
> Naething could resist my Nancy!
> But to see her was to love her,
> Love but her, and love for ever.
> Had we never lov'd sae kindly,
> Had we never lov'd sae blindly,
> Never met – or never parted –
> We had ne'er been broken hearted.

Burns uses language economically here, thus concentrating the emotion: the third line is entirely monosyllabic; the fifth and sixth lines are identical apart from the rhyming words; the repetition of 'never' (four times in the last four lines, five times if 'ne'er' is included) emphasises the unacceptable alternative to love.

The third and final stanza is a farewell, Burns being a past master of the valedictory mood. Here he returns to the affected English of the first stanza, introducing abstractions ('Peace, Enjoyment, Love and Pleasure') then ending by repeating the first four Dodsley-derived lines. It is the central stanza that distinguishes the song which is thus constructed like a triptych with a superb middle panel surrounded on each side by sections of lesser intensity.

THE DEIL'S AWA WI TH' EXCISEMAN

According to Lockhart's *Life of Burns* (1828) Burns composed 'The Deil's awa wi' th' Exciseman' (386/CW, 467–8) in February 1792 while taking part in the capture of the smuggling brig *Rosamond*, a tale dismissed as a 'picturesque legend . . . invented by the ingenious brain of a romantic biographer' (Snyder, 396) but substantially true (see 'Burns and Politics'). Burns quotes the song in a letter of 1792 to Creech (CL, 307) and mentions it in a letter of March 1792 to John Leven, a Dumfries grocer and Supervisor of Excise:

> Mr Mitchell [that is, John Mitchell, Collector of Excise in Dumfries] mentioned to you a ballad which I composed & sung at one of his Excise-court dinners . . . If you honor my ballad by making it one of your charming, bon vivant effusions, it will secure it undoubted celebrity. (CL, 614)

Matched to the tune 'The Hemp-dresser' in the *Scots Musical Museum* (1792), the song is one of abandon that acknowledges the popular dislike of the Exciseman by making him a natural – or supernatural – partner of the devil. When the devil dances off with the Exciseman, the women of the town cheer and wish the devil luck. In the second quatrain they give thanks to the 'meikle black deil' for giving them the opportunity to brew their drink in peace. The last quatrain (of three, plus chorus) salutes the diabolic dance as the most pleasing of all to the common people:

> There's threesome reels, there's foursome reels,
> There's hornpipes and strathspeys, man,
> But the best dance e'er cam to the Land
> Was *The Deil's awa wi th' Exciseman.*

By incorporating the title of the song in its last line, Burns makes the diabolic dance a circular one.

THE CHEVALIER'S LAMENT

The first eight lines of 'The Chevalier's Lament' (220/CW, 322) are an expression, in English, of Burns's frequently expressed feelings of despair in a beautiful natural environment:

> The small birds rejoice in the green leaves returning,
> The murmuring streamlet winds clear thro the vale,
> The primroses blow in the dews of the morning,
> And wild scatter'd cowslips bedeck the green dale.
> But what can give pleasure, or what can seem fair,
> When the lingering moments are numbered by Care?
> No birds sweetly singing, nor flowers gayly springing,
> Can sooth the sad bosom of joyless Despair.

A draft of this was sent to Robert Cleghorn on 31 March 1788 with an explanatory note:

> Yesterday, my dear Sir, as I was riding thro' a parcel of melancholy joyless muirs, between Galloway and Ayrshire; it being Sunday, I turned my thoughts to 'Psalms and hymns and spiritual Songs'; and your favourite air, Captain Okean, coming in my head, I tryed these words to it. (CL, 274)

Cleghorn approved of the stanza, as matched to the air 'Captain O'Kean', and suggested (27 April) it could be expanded as a Jacobite piece. 'Suppose,' said Cleghorn, 'it should be sung after the fatal field of Culloden by the unfortunate Charles.' (cited by Kinsley, 1273) Burns was not able to respond immediately to this advice but, some time after April 1793, completed the song along the lines proposed by Cleghorn.

After the defeat of the Scottish clans by 'Butcher' Cumberland's army at Culloden on 16 April 1746, Bonnie Prince Charlie (albeit reluctantly) fled the battlefield, shedding tears over the Highlanders he left to shed their blood and face a sustained period of quasi-genocidal oppression. In the song Burns puts into the mouth of the Young Pretender, there is a sentimental supposition that Bonnie Prince Charlie could live with the loss of a kingdom but not with the calamity that was visited on the men he called his 'faithful Highlanders':

> The deed that I dar'd, could it merit their malice,
>   A king and a father to place on his throne?
> His right are these hills, and his right are those valleys,
>   Where the wild beasts find shelter, tho I can find none!
> But 'tis not my suff'rings thus wretched, forlorn,
>   My brave, gallant friends, 'tis your ruin I mourn;
> Your faith proved so loyal in hot, bloody trial,
>   Alas, can I make it no sweeter return!

The reference to the lack of shelter shows that the song is supposedly sung during Bonnie Prince Charlie's five months of wandering as a fugitive through the Western Highlands and Islands with a price of £30,000 on his head, a period when the 'faithful Highlanders' protected him regardless of the danger to themselves. Burns is not alone in finding the Prince's predicament poignant, but more tolerant than some of his countrymen in crediting Charles with remorse over the ruin of the clans. It is, like 'The Bonnie Lass of Albanie', one of the songs that celebrates Burns's love-affair with the unfortunate House of Stuart.

SCOTS WHA HAE

On Sunday, 26 August 1787, during his Highland tour with William Nicol, Burns visited Bannockburn, the site of Robert the Bruce's great victory over Edward II on 24 June 1314. Burns was well aware of the historic significance of a battle in which a relatively small Scottish army (5,500 trained men plus 2,000 untrained volunteers) defeated a huge English army (20,000 men including heavy cavalry, archers and spear-wielding foot soldiers). In his journal of the tour, Burns referred to 'the field of Bannockburn – the hole where glorious Bruce set his standard' (cited by Snyder, 244).

Around 30 August 1793, Burns wrote to George Thomson:

> There is a tradition, which I have met with in many places of Scotland, that [the old air, 'Hey tuttie taitie'] was Robert Bruce's March at the battle of Bannock-burn. – This thought, in my yesternight's evening walk, warmed me to a pitch of enthusiasm on the theme of Liberty & Independance, which I threw into a kind of Scots Ode, fitted to the Air, that one might suppose to be the gallant ROYAL SCOT's address to his heroic followers on that eventful morning. (CL, 638)

Burns then set down the words of 'Robert Bruce's march to BANN-OCKBURN – To its ain tune' (CL, 638). The first two stanzas of 'Scots Wha Hae' (425/CW, 500), this 'most thrilling and defiant of all the battle-songs of the nation' (Snyder, 419), simulate a determined march by rhythm and rhyme (the first three lines rhyme with each other, the fourth line rhymes with the last line of all succeeding stanzas):

> Scots, wha hae wi Wallace bled,
> Scots, wham Bruce has aften led,
> Welcome to your gory bed
>   Or to victorie!
>
> Now's the day, and now's the hour:
> See the front o battle lour,
> See approach proud Edward's power –
>   Chains and slaverie!

In the next two stanzas of his monologue, Bruce dismisses the cowards of the company and defines his genuine followers as those who 'Freedom's sword will strongly draw'. So far, so faithful to the patriotic spirit Burns so admired in Bruce.

Before considering the final two stanzas, it is worth citing Burns's postscript to his letter to Thomson. He explains that he had shown the air to Pietro Urbani who had asked him for 'soft verses' for it, a request Burns rejected when inspired by 'that glorious struggle [at Bannockburn] for Freedom, associated with the glowing ideas of some other struggles of the same nature, *not quite so ancient*' (CL,

639). Audaciously, Burns had made Bruce sing a song of freedom that was still being fought for in contemporary Scotland.

On 1 February 1793, the French Republic had declared war on Britain and the government increased its attempts to suppress the Friends of the People, a radical movement largely organised by the young lawyer, Thomas Muir of Huntershill. Muir's trial was fixed for 30 August, the date assigned by DeLancey Fergusson to Burns's letter to Thomson (enclosing 'Scots Wha Hae'). In that context, Burns was putting into the song his own faith in a radical solution to Scotland's current situation:

> By Oppression's woes and pains,
> By your sons in servile chains,
> We will drain our dearest veins,
> But they shall be free!
>
> Lay the proud usurpers low!
> Tyrants fall in every foe!
> Liberty's in every blow! –
> Let us do, or die!

Had Burns openly declared his radical sympathies he might well have been treated like Muir, who was sentenced to fourteen years' transportation for seditiously inciting the Scottish people to rise up and oppose the government. Significantly, Burns agreed to the *Morning Chronicle* (8 May 1794) publishing the song but insisted 'let them insert it as a thing they have met with by accident, & unknown to me' (CL, 699).

By making Bruce the spokesman for liberty Burns was protecting himself but still providing Scotland with a theme with practical political variations. It has been so received since its appearance in *Select Scottish Airs* (1799) though Thomson preferred the tune 'Lewie Gordon' to Burns's choice of 'Hey tutti taitie'.

A RED RED ROSE

Burns sent this lyric (453/CW, 517) in a letter of November 1793 to Alexander Cunningham, along with a long explanation about his discussions on Scottish songs with Pietro Urbani (see his entry in 'The Burns Circle'):

> I [gave Urbani] a simple old Scots song which I had pickt up in this country, which he promised to set in a suitable manner. – I

would not even have given him this, had there been any of Mr Thomson's airs, *suitable to it*, unoccupied . . . . I would, to tell the fact, most gladly have seen it in our Friend's publication; but, though I am charmed with it, is is a kind of Song on which I know we would think very differently. – It is the only species of Song about which our ideas disagree. – What to me appears the simple & the wild, to him, & I suspect to you likewise, will be looked on as the ludicrous and the absurd.' (CL, 468–9)

The song was first published in Urbani's *Scots Songs* (1794) to an original tune. Later, the first three stanzas appeared in Johnson's *Scots Musical Museum* (1796) to the Neil Gow tune 'Major Graham'. It then appeared in Thomson's *Select Scottish Airs* (1797), altered to fit William Marshall's tune 'Wishaw's Favourite'. It gained immense popularity when matched to the air 'Low down in the Broom' in Robert Archibald Smith's *Scottish Minstrel* (1821).

When Urbani anthologised the song he added a note on its origin, explaining

> the words of the RED, RED ROSE were obligingly given to him by a celebrated Scots Poet, who was so struck with them when sung by a country girl that he wrote them down, and, not being pleased with the air, begged the Author to set them to Music in the style of a Scots Tune, which he has done accordingly. (BE, 367)

Commenting on Burns's ability to rework folk material in an astonishingly original manner, Snyder suggests:

> There is hardly an idea or an image in Burns's stanzas which was not suggested by one of the earlier songs. But the old songs were crudely expressed, childish, inept. Burns took a phrase here, an adjective there, an entire line somewhere else, rearranged the material thus selected in a new and harmonious pattern, and the result is one of the world's perfect lyrics. (Snyder, 470)

Crawford concurs with this view, describing the work as 'a lyric of genius, made out of the common inherited material of folk-song by an author whose name we happen to know' (Crawford, 281).

Kinsley, however, suspects that the song was collected, not composed by Burns:

> Editors have turned up chapbook models for every stanza, and almost every line, of this song; and have treated it as an exquisite

example of Burns's art in raising folksong to perfection . . . . We
may, however, be doing an injustice to oral tradition in regarding
['A Red Red Rose'] even as a reconstruction by Burns . . . . There
is nothing in the letter to Cunningham to suggest that Burns made
any changes in the song; he had not even adjusted it to fit an air,
for he left the setting to Urbani. His comment to Cunningham
indicates, more positively, that he left it alone . . . (Kinsley, 1455)

If Burns simply 'pickt up' the song, then he had access to a truly
gifted recreative singer, one who possessed 'a fluid entity soluble
in the mind, to be concretely realized at will in words and music'
(to quote a description of the ballad-singer Mrs Brown of Falkland
by Bertrand Bronson, *The Ballad as Song*, Berkeley, 1969, p. 7).

   If Burns reworked the song from other sources, he had rich
material to work on. Consider: 'O, she's like a new-strung instru-
ment/That's newly put in tune' ('The Wanton Wife of Castle Gate',
a broadside ballad in the Roxburghe Collection); 'Altho' I go ten
thousand miles/I'll come again to thee, dear Love . . . The Day shall
turn to Night, dear Love,/And the Rocks melt with the Sun,/Before
that I prove false to thee' (song in *The Hornfield Garland*); 'Fare you
well, my own true love,/And fare you well for a while,/And I will
be sure to return back again,/If I go ten thousand mile' ('The
True Lover's Farewell', chapbook song of 1792). The evidence is
inconclusive but the song has touches of genius usually associated
with Burns: the printed variants, and Burns's letter to Cunningham,
demonstrate that such a song was in oral circulation in 1793 but
Burns probably impoved it (and, for once, there is no need for ironic
quotation marks round 'improved' with reference to a tinkering
with a text derived from an oral source). At any rate, minus the
well-known music, the song speaks eloquently for itself in four
quatrains in the ballad measure:

        O, my luve is like a red, red rose,
           That's newly sprung in June.
        O, my luve is like the melodie,
           That's sweetly play'd in tune.

        As fair art thou, my bonie lass,
           So deep in luve am I,
        And I will luve thee still, my dear,
           Till a' the seas gang dry.

        Till a' the seas gang dry, my dear,

And the rocks melt wi' the sun!
And I will luve thee still, my dear,
While the sands o life shall run.

And fare thee weel, my only love!
And fare thee weel, a while!
And I will come again, my luve,
Tho it were ten thousand mile!

What sounds like a simple love song gains power from its apparently effortless synthesis of argument and anticipation. The first six lines, relying on statements that will countenance no contradiction, dissolve into a prediction of the longevity of this love. Remarkably, the imagery of the seas drying up and the rocks melting in the sun is a prophecy that has gained scientific authority since the song was written. Astronomers estimate that, some six billion years from now, the sun's core will have exhausted its hydrogen and begin to burn helium, converting it into carbon and oxygen. Simultaneously, the sun's atmosphere will expand to one hundred times its present size as the sun becomes a red giant. Life on earth will be obliterated by the swollen sun which will boil away the oceans and melt the continents. It is an astonishing love that measures its life against the ability of the earth to endure.

The final quatrain is equally intense though it looks back to an indigenous tradition rather than forward to the destiny of the planet. What is meant by the promise to 'come again' is a determination to defeat death by spiritual means. In the Scottish folk tradition, as witness ballads like 'Sweet William's Ghost' (included in Allan Ramsay's *Tea-Table Miscellany*, 1750), lovers return to their sweethearts after death, especially after dying at some distance from Scotland: Sweet William says his bones are buried 'Afar beyond the sea'. There is, then, the hint that the singer who compares his love to a red rose expects to die far from his native land. Wherever he dies, and however distant it is, he will 'come again'. Seldom has so much meaning been packed into a sixteen-line lyric.

AS I STOOD BY YON ROOFLESS TOWER

Burns's ability to remake bawdy songs in a poignant manner is impressively shown in 'As I stood by yon roofless tower' (555/CW, 570). In September 1794 Burns sent Thomson a transcription of

'Cumnock Psalms' which, he explained, was 'a droll Scots song, more famous for its humour than delicacy' (CL, 656). 'Cumnock Psalms' opens:

> As I looked o'er yon castle wa'
> I spied a grey goose & a gled;
> They had a fecht between them twa,
> And O, as their twa hurdies gade.

After describing the unlikely encounter the song ends:

> He placed his Jacob whare she did piss,
> And his ballocks whare the wind did blaw,
> And he grippet her fast by the gooset o' the arse
> And he gae her cunt the common law.
> (CL, 657)

Burns told Thomson he intended to fashion 'decenter verses' for Johnson's *Scots Musical Museum* and shaped his haunting song from the raw material of 'Cumnock Psalms'. Burns's song, to the tune of 'Cumnock Psalms', opens with an atmospheric quatrain and a chorus of lamentation:

> As I stood by yon roofless tower,
> Where the wa'flow'r scents the dewy air,
> Where the houlet mourns in her ivy bower,
> And tells the midnight moon her care:
> *A lassie all alone, was making her moan*
> *Lamenting our lads beyond the sea: –*
> *'In the bluidy wars they fa', and our honor's gane an a',*
> *And broken-hearted we maun die.'*

The 'roofless tower' – on the river Nith, at Maxwelltown, outside Dumfries – is Lincluden abbey, where Margaret, Robert III's daughter, is buried.

However, Burns's 'lassie' sings of commoners, not kings: 'our lads beyond the sea' which Crawford (who believes the song was originally intended as a prelude to 'Ode for General Washington's Birthday') takes as a reference to 'the early stages of the contemporary war with France' (Crawford, 244). It requires too much reading between the lines to make of this song a revolutionary offering to the cause of France; had Burns wished to make such a song the clues would have been more obvious. In this case, the chorus is a general lament for Scottish soldiers who had fought and died overseas for the English government since the parliamentary union of 1707 (in the Seven Years War and the American War of Independence as well as the war with revolutionary France). That is the point of 'our honor's gane an a'': Scotland has lost its honour with its independence.

The evocation of the landscape is both factual and fantastic as in the quatrain indicating some agitation in the natural order:

> The winds were laid, the air was still,
> The stars they shot along the sky,
> The tod was howling on the hill,
> And the distant-echoing glens reply.

This image of shooting stars may have been prompted by a passage in *A Midsummer Night's Dream* where (after alluding to Mary Queen of Scots as a mermaid, Elizabethan slang for a prostitute) Shakespeare notes 'the rude sea grew civil at her song,/And certain stars shot madly from their courses' (II.i.52–3, the 'certain stars' in this instance being the rebellious northern lords of 1569). Nature, in Burns's song, is disturbed: the noise accompanying the Northern Lights is 'eerie'.

Burns has set the scene for a supernatural apparition which comes in the fifth stanza, moonlit ('pale-faced Cynthia') and menacing:

> Now, looking over firth and fauld,
> Her horn the pale-faced Cynthia rear'd,
> When lo! in form of minstrel auld
> A stern and stalwart ghaist appear'd.

The Scottish minstrel, the ghost of a ballad-singer, tells 'a tale of woe' which remains mysterious in the final stanza:

> He sang wi joy his former day,
> He, weeping, wail'd his latter times:
> But what he said – it was nae play!
> I winna ventur't in my rhymes.

What is the song that Burns cannot specify? For Crawford the stanza denotes a diplomatic revolutionary silence by Burns, 'a peculiarly moving depiction of the feelings of a liberal during a period of political reaction' (Crawford, 243). Yet Burns has given a clue in the contrast between the joyful 'former day' and the miserable 'latter times': once Scotland was an independent country, now it is a province that provides soldiers for the English army. The chorus of Burns's modern ballad is the song the minstrel sings and it is the lament of a 'lassie' for the lost honour of Scotland.

IT WAS A' FOR OUR RIGHTFU KING

Composed for Johnson's *Scots Musical Museum* in 1794, to the tune of 'Mally Stuart' (and partly based on the chapbook ballad of that name), 'It was a' for our rightfu king' (589/CW, 594–5) is the most hauntingly beautiful of Burns's Jacobite songs. Sung by a cavalier exiled to Ireland for the Roman Catholic cause of James VII and II, it poignantly demonstrates a personal response to a political situation. The first stanza indicates the cavalier's assumption of the divine rightness of his cause, the second stresses the consequences of fighting for the divine right of his king: 'My Love and Native Land fareweel,/For I maun cross the main'.

The first two and the last two stanzas are in the first-person and these two pairs are interrupted by the third stanza which Burns casts in the third-person to evoke, through the image of turning, the finality of the cavalier's exile from his native land. Here is the last stanza of the chapbook version:

> The trooper turn'd himself about all on the Irish shore,
> He has given the bridle-reins a shake, saying
> > 'Adieu for ever more, My dear,
> > Adieu for ever more.'

And here is Burns's compellingly rhythmic reworking of these lines in his central stanza:

> He turn'd him right and round about,
> Upon the Irish shore,
> And gae his bridle-reins a shake,
> > With, Adieu for evermore, my dear,
> > And adieu for evermore.

As the cavalier could conceivably be reunited with a human love, Burns provides a context that implies the lost love is Scotland (a reading encouraged by the third line of the second stanza: 'My Love and Native Land fareweel'). Thus the cavalier's lament 'I hae parted frae my Love,/Never to meet again'. His love is the land he has been forced to leave. The last stanza turns to the defeated king as the embodiment of Scotland:

When day is gane, and night is come,
  And a' folk bound to sleep;
I think on him that's far awa,
  The lee-lang night and weep, my dear,
  The lee-lang night and weep.

The lyric is a patriotic lovesong, rather than a personal one.

A MAN'S A MAN FOR A' THAT

One of the most potent reasons for the enduring reputation of
Burns as a revolutionary writer is the song 'A Man's a Man for
a' That' (482/CW, 535–6) written the year before the poet's death.
It is the summation of Burns's belief in human equality, the most
strident assertion of his hatred of a rank-ridden society, the most
uninhibited expression of his belief in a future liberated by the
revolutionary cause of the common people. For much of his life
– as a poor farmer's son, as a patron-seeking poet, as a farmer, as
an exciseman – he had to make compromises, sometimes 'kissing
the arse of a peer' (as he accused his enemies of doing in his second
Election Ballad for Patrick Heron).

At the beginning of 1795 Burns was in a revolutionary mood,
as witness his letter of 12 January 1795 describing the execution
of Louis XVI and Marie Antoinette as 'the deserved fate of . . . a
perjured Blockhead & an unprincipled Prostitute' (CL, 214). Accused
of political disaffection in 1792 Burns had protected his position so
well that, in December 1794, he was promoted to Acting Supervisor
of Excise. However, the song shows he had not been tamed as an
artist. The first stanza, indeed, consists of a rhetorical question and
angry answers:

Is there for honest poverty
  That hings his head, an a' that?
The coward slave, we pass him by –
  We dare be poor for a' that!
For a' that, an a' that,
  Our toils obscure, an a' that,
The rank is but the guinea's stamp,
  The man's the gowd for a' that.

The rush of passion is so swift it ignores conventional syntax though the meaning is clearly that honest poverty should never be associated with the coward slave that hangs his head – little wonder that Burns referred (see below) to thought being 'inverted' in his song.

The second stanza begins brilliantly with a poignant verbal picture of the condition of the poor, with whom Burns identifies by using the first person plural: 'What though on hamely fare we dine,/Wear hoddin grey, an a' that?' Fine wine and expensive clothes are a 'tinsel show' fit for fools. Burns declares that, despite appearances, 'The honest man . . . Is king o' men'.

That said, Burns provides revolutionary laughter fit for a king of men. The song gains immense strength by moving from a general contempt for the aristocracy to a beautifully observed caricature of a lord:

> Ye see yon birkie ca'd 'a lord',
>   Wha struts, an stares, an a' that ?
> Tho hundreds worship at his word,
>   He's but a cuif for a' that.
> For a' that, an a' that,
>   His ribband, star, an a' that,
> The man o independent mind,
>   He looks an laughs at a' that.

The ridicule has a Mozartian sublimity – coincidentally, of course (brother-mason Mozart's *Marriage of Figaro*, which gloriously holds up the Count to similar ridicule, was produced in Vienna in 1786 though not known to Burns who may, however, have heard of the Beaumarchais play, of 1778, on which it is based). Those are feelings Burns often suppressed in order to advance his career and protect his family. He is no longer speaking as a cautious careerist. He is singing as a revolutionary poet of the common people, encouraging them to see lords as preposterous clowns.

In the penultimate stanza Burns not only elevates the honest man above the lord but urges him never to underestimate himself. Real rank resides in 'The pith o sense an pride o worth'. Finally, Burns produces a prophetic stanza about the revolution that is 'comin yet'. The 'let us pray' gives the final chorus a spiritual dimension, the vision of 'the world' gives a promise of a paradise on earth:

> Then let us pray that come it may

> (As come it will for a' that),
> That Sense and Worth o'er a' the earth,
> Shall bear the gree an a' that.
> For a' that, an a' that,
> It's comin yet for a' that,
> That man to man, the world o'er
> Shall brithers be for a' that.

Sending 'A Man's a Man for a' That' to George Thomson, in early January 1795, Burns cited the authority of John Aikin's *Essays on Song-Writing* (1772) in defining his song as a didactic offering:

> A great critic, Aikin on songs, says, that love & wine are the exclusive themes for song-writing. – The following is on neither subject, & consequently is no Song; but will be allowed, I think, to be two or three pretty good *prose* thoughts, inverted into rhyme. (CL, 669)

Critics have been keen to track down the sources of these prose thoughts. Richard Hindle Fowler's *Robert Burns* (1988) points out persuasively that the last two lines of the first stanza, 'The rank is but the guinea's stamp/The man's the gowd for a' that', is derived from an image in the Epistle Dedicatory to Locke's *Essay Concerning Human Understanding* (1690): 'truth, like gold . . . though it be not yet current by public stamp, yet it may, for all that, be as old as nature, and is certainly not the less genuine'. Burns, creatively alert when reading Locke, has made a compact metaphor from the philosopher's simile and made a ringing refrain from a commonplace expression ('for all that') used by Locke.

That the prose thoughts were also suggested by Tom Paine's *The Rights of Man* (1791) has been stressed by J. MacCunn (in *Ethics of Citizenship*, 1921) and by Crawford (see Appendix II, Crawford, 365). Some of Burns's phrases share sentiments with those of *The Rights of Man*. For example, Paine refers to a love of titles leading to talk about 'its fine *blue ribbon* like a girl', Burns mocks the lord with 'His ribband, star, an a' that'. Paine links character to rank, Burns says that sense and worth 'Are higher rank than a' that'. Paine longs for 'one great Republic', Burns predicts 'That man to man, the world o'er/Shall brithers be for a' that.' Crawford also points out that the emphasis on brotherhood has masonic, as well as revolutionary, connotations.

Even more striking than the echoes from *The Rights of Man* is an apparent reference to Paine's earlier work, *Common Sense*. Burns's insistence that 'The honest man . . . Is king of men' reads like an allusion to Paine's statement 'Of more worth is one honest man to society and in the sight of God, than all the crowned ruffians that ever lived.' (Thomas Paine, *Common Sense*, 1776; rept. Harmondsworth, 1976, p. 81) The spotting of these sources does nothing to detract from the inspiriting quality of the song. Burns has transcended his sources, mastered his material to produce a song that is both distinctive and genuinely popular.

O, WERT THOU IN THE CAULD BLAST

In the summer of 1796 Burns was emaciated through illness and seriously worried about the state of his finances. Nevertheless he had to give up his Excise work and, because Jean was pregnant again, an eighteen-year-old neighbour, Jessy Lewars, was brought in to nurse the poet and help with the housework. Jessy was the younger daughter of John Lewars, Supervisor of Excise at Dumfries; after his death in 1789 Jessy stayed in Mill Vennell, opposite the poet's home, in the house of her brother John Lewars, a fellow excise officer of Burns. Burns mentioned Jessy in his last letter to Johnson, on 1 June 1796, asking for a copy of the *Scots Musical Museum* for this 'young lady who sings well' (CL, 303).

It was hearing Jessy sing 'The Robin cam' to the Wren's nest' that inspired Burns to write 'O, Wert Thou in the Cauld Blast' (524/CW, 567), his penultimate song and certainly his last great work. As Snyder says, 'it was a product of the same formula that had occasioned the earliest of his boyish atempts, "Handsome Nell": a scrap of an old tune, and a pretty girl' (Snyder, 386). The likelihood that it was written within weeks of the poet's death gives the work added poignancy.

The first eight lines amount to a promise to shelter a loved one from cold and misfortune, the poet offering his plaid and his person as comfort. The repeated phrases – 'On yonder lea, on yonder lea', 'Around thee blaw, around thee blaw' – give the effect of haunting echoes in a bleak landscape populated only by the poet and the woman he is addressing.

In the second stanza Burns reverses the situation. Now it is the poet who needs comfort in this bleak landscape, this 'wildest waste'.

If life offered him nothing more than love, he declares, he would be a poor man blessed with romantic riches:

> Or were I in the wildest waste,
>   Sae black and bare, sae black and bare,
> The desert were a Paradise,
>   If thou wert there, if thou wert there.
> Or were I monarch o the globe,
>   Wi thee to reign, wi thee to reign,
> The brightest jewel in my crown
>   Wad be my queen, wad be my queen.

The use of Scots words in both stanzas ('cauld', 'blaw', 'bield', 'sae', 'wad') gives the lyric a conversational mood so that the song, for all its elegant balance, sounds like an intimate assurance from one man to one woman.

FAIREST MAID ON DEVON BANKS

This, the last song written by Burns, was sent to George Thomson from the Brow Well on 12 July 1796 – nine days before the poet's death in Dumfries. In his covering letter Burns asked Thomson for £5 in return for which he intended to 'furnish you with five pounds' worth of the neatest song genius you have seen' (CL, 679). Meanwhile, he enclosed 'Fairest Maid on Devon Banks' (525/CW, 568) , which he had written that morning, matching his words to the tune of 'Rothiemurche's Lament'. 'The measure is so difficult,' Burns observed apologetically, 'that it is impossible to infuse much genius into the lines' (CL, 680). Thomson included the song in *Select Scottish Airs* (1802) and noted 'These I presume are the last verses which came from the great Bard's pen, as he died very soon after' (CL, 680n).

The song harks back to a visit Burns made to the Falls of Devon with Charlotte Hamilton, Gavin Hamilton's half-sister, on 27 August 1787. Charlotte, the close friend of Peggy Chalmers, lived at Harvieston, Clackmannanshire, on an estate bordered by the river Devon. Burns's first song in celebration of Charlotte and the Devon, a rather feeble tribute called 'The Banks of Devon', appeared in the *Scots Musical Museum* in 1788. His second attempt was even feebler.

After a chorus asking the fairest maid on Devon banks to 'smile as thou wert wont to do' Burns produces two quatrains:

> Full well thou know'st I love thee dear –
> Couldst thou to malice lend an ear!
> O, did not Love exclaim: – 'Forbear
> Nor use a faithful lover so!'

> Then come, thou fairest of the fair,
> Those wonted smiles, O, let me share,
> And by thy beauteous self I swear
> No love but thine my heart shall know!

In his dying days, then, Burns was unable to call on the inspired Scots that had sustained him in his most creative works. Instead he wrote an affected English tribute to a woman-friend he knew briefly and whose company he recalled nostalgically. The song is almost entirely composed of clichés – 'Full well', 'lend an ear', 'a faithful lover', 'wonted smiles', 'beauteous self' – and is ploddingly pedestrian in rhythm if not rhyme (he shows some ingenuity in linking the two quatrains with the terminal rhyme). In the circumstances (the terror of dying a debtor on top of the stress of his illness) it is hardly surprising that Burns was unequal to the occasion. What is significant is that his last song confirms by its weakness what his great work demonstrates by its strength: that in a creative context the self-consciously poetic English that Burns borrowed from the likes of Shenstone was a foreign language.

Election Ballads

Burns's broad political principles, as expressed in his finest poems, are invariably on the side of the common people, the oppressed, the poor. He lifted a band of drunken vagabonds to a revolutionary level at the end of 'The Jolly Beggars' and in such songs as 'Scots Wha Hae' and 'A Man's a Man for a' That' he affirmed his belief in national independence and individual liberty. Parochial politics, however, imposed limitations on him as can be seen in the various election ballads he composed for specific occasions.

In September 1789 an election contest commenced for parliamentary representation of the Dumfriesshire Burghs (Dumfries, Lochmaben, Annan, Kirkcudbright, Sanquhar). The Tory candidate was Sir James Johnstone of Westerhall, who had held the seat since 1784; the Whig candidate was Captain Patrick Miller of Dalswinton, son of Burns's landlord. Though Burns was sympathetic to the Whigs, he considered Miller 'a youth by no means above mediocrity in his abilities [with] a huckster-lust for shillings, pence & farthings' (CL, 432). Moreover, Burns detested Miller's patron, William Douglas, 4th Duke of Queensberry, as he explained on 9 December 1789 when sending a copy of 'The Five Carlins' (269/CW, 364–6) to Robert Graham of Fintry:

> The Election-ballad ['The Five Carlins'] alludes, as you will see, to the present canvass in our string of Boroughs. – I do not believe there will be a harder run match in the whole General Election. – The Great Man here, like all Renegadoes, is a flaming Zealot . . . . I beg your pardon, Sir, if I differ from you in my idea of this Great Man; but were you to know his sins as well of Omission as Commission to this outraged Land, you would club your curse with the execrating voice of the Country. (CL, 431–2)

Burns was inclined to prefer a decent Tory to a doltish Whig supported by a man like Queensberry.

'The Five Carlins' is a clever ballad parody, but not particularly biting as political satire. The poet's five carlins are personifications of the Dumfries burghs: proud Maggie is Dumfries, tough Marjorie is Lochmaben, Blinkin Bess is Annan, Brandy Jean is Kirkcudbright, Black Joan is Sanquhar. Meeting to 'send a lad to London town' they consider the merits of the two candidates. As introduced by Burns, Sir James Johnstone is the more attractive candidate:

> The first ane was a belted Knight,
>   Bred of a Border band;
> And he wad gae to London Town,
>   Might nae man him withstand.
>
> And he wad do their errands weel,
>   And meikle he wad say;
> And ilka ane at London court
>   Wad bid to him guid-day.

His opponent, Miller, is 'a Soger youth' who, lacking eloquence, offers 'an honest heart' and loyalty to 'his friend', a reference Burns's friends would have applied to Queensberry (since the use of the singular is significant). The carlins squabble until 'Marjorie o the Lochs' declares 'I will send to London town/Wham I lo'e best at hame'. Burns leaves it to his reader to decide which man is meant by this.

'Election Ballad for Westerha'' (270/CW, 367), written in December 1789 during the Dumfriesshire election, is addressed to Sir James Johnstone but directed at the Duke of Queensberry who had, that year, been dismissed as George III's Lord of the Bedchamber when the king, regaining his sanity in February, heard he had supported the Prince of the Wales in the Regency crisis. Burns presents Queensberry as a treacherous turncoat:

> The Laddies by the banks o Nith
>   Wad trust his Grace wi a', Jamie;
> But he'll sair them, as he sair'd the King –
>   Turn tail and rin awa, Jamie.

In the elections for the parliament of 1790–6, held on 12 July 1790, the young and foolish Captain Miller was successful. Shortly afterwards, Burns wrote his 'Election Ballad at Close of the Contest for Representing the Dumfries Burghs' (318/CW, 402–6). Addressed

to Graham of Fintry, the ballad attacks Queensberry, placing him at
Drumlanrig Castle, his hereditary seat in Dumfriesshire:

> All hail, Drumlanrig's haughty Grace,
> Discarded remnant of a race
>   Once godlike – great in story!
> Thy fathers' virtues all contrasted,
> The very name of Douglas blasted,
>   Thine that inverted glory!
>
> Hate, envy, oft the Douglas bore;
> But thou has superadded more,
>   And sunk them in contempt!
> Follies and crimes have stain'd the name;
> But, Queensberry, thine the virgin claim,
>   From aught that's good exempt!

Burns damns 'each ardent Whig/Beneath Drumlanrig's banner'
(thus condemning political expediency rather than Whig principles),
regrets that 'Tory ranks are broken' and ends with a general appeal
to free Scotland from those who exploit it:

> Now, for my friends' and brethren's sakes,
> And for my dear-lov'd Land o Cakes,
>   I pray with holy fire: –
> Lord, send a rough-shod troop o Hell
> O'er a' wad Scotland buy or sell,
>   To grind them in the mire!

Towards the end of his life Burns wrote four Election Ballads on
behalf of his friend Patrick Heron (see his entry in 'The Burns
Circle') who was thrice elected to parliament (1795, 1796, 1802).
In February 1795 Heron stood as Whig candidate in the election
for the Stewartry of Kirkcudbright, contesting the Stewarty with
the Tory, Thomas Gordon of Balmaighie. In March 1795, the poet
sent broadsides of 'a couple of political ballads' to Heron, explaining
his feelings about Pitt's repressive Tory policies:

> To pillory on Parnassus the rank reprobation of character, the
> utter dereliction of all principle, in a profligate junto which has
> not only outraged virtue, but violated common decency; which,
> spurning even hypocrisy as paltry iniquity below their daring; –
> to unmask their flagitiousness to the broadest day – to deliver
> such over to their merited fate, is surely not merely innocent, but

laudable; is not only propriety, but virtue. – You have already, as your auxiliary, the sober detestation of mankind on the heads of your opponents; and I swear by the lyre of Thalia to muster on your side all the votaries of honest laughter, and fair, candid ridicule! (CL, 715)

'Ballad First' (491/CW, 543–4) is a variant on (at times almost a parody of) 'A Man's a Man for a' That' (written a few months earlier, at the beginning of 1795). Whereas Gordon of Balmaighie is dismissed as a fool funded by his rich uncle, Murray of Broughton ('A beardless boy comes o'er the hills/Wi's uncle's purse and a' that'), Heron is presented as an 'independent patriot', an 'honest man', an 'independent commoner'. Despite his background in banking and his marriage to Lady Elizabeth Cochrane, Heron is acclaimed as a man of the people:

> But why should we to Nobles jeuk,
> And it against the law, that,
> And even a Lord may be a gowk,
> Wi ribban, star, and a' that?
> For a' that, and a' that,
> Here's Heron yet for a that!
> A Lord may be a lousy loon,
> Wi ribban, star, and a' that.

'Ballad Second' (492/CW, 545–6) continues the verbal assault on the Tory enemy, ridiculing the likes of the Douglas brothers, Sir William and James who had the name of the town Carlinwark changed to Castle Douglas by royal warrant; and who were constantly courting the favours of John Stewart, 7th Earl of Galloway, a representative Scottish peer:

> An there'll be Douglasses doughty,
> New christening towns far and near:
> Abjuring their democrat doings
> An kissing the arse of a peer!

(The phrase about 'kissing the arse of a peer' is inadvertently ironical in view of Burns's frequent deference to titles in his attitude to the Earl of Glencairn, Glencairn's sister Lady Elizabeth Cunningham, and indeed the dreaded Queensberry to whom the poet sent a respectful letter on 24 September 1791).

'Ballad Third: John Bushby's Lamentation' (493/CW, 547–8) is a mock lament, in ballad measure, over the defeated Tory candidate, Thomas Gordon of Balmaghie, supposedly spoken by John Bushby, a Dumfries lawyer and sheriff-clerk who had been a partner in Heron's bank and manager of the Dumfries branch. Burns is said to have disliked Bushby (see comments on the epitaph on John Bushby in 'Epitaphs and Epigrams') hence his pitiful monologue:

> 'Twas in the Seventeen Hunder year
> O grace, and Ninety-Five,
> That year I was the wae'est man
> Of onie man alive.
>
> In March the three-an-twentieth morn,
> The sun raise clear an bright;
> But O, I was a waefu man,
> Ere to-fa' o the night!

In May–June 1796, after the dissolution of Parliament, Heron stood for re-election, against the Tory candidate Montgomery Stewart, a younger son of the 7th Earl of Galloway. By that time Burns was dying but he obliged with another ballad, 'Ballad Fourth: The Trogger' (494/CW, 549) in which he sarcastically compares Tory election promises to the trash sold by pedlars and ends by assuming the devil will become the Tories' best customer: 'Hornie's turnin chapman: he'll buy a' the pack'. Heron was re-elected but Burns did not live to enjoy that success.

In the opinion of Alexander Young of Harburn – a Tory Writer to the Signet who, in 1834, composed a memoir of Burns – Heron was

> not likely to be aided in the attainment of [his parliamentary] object by the libels and lampoons of Burns, on all those who did not support, or were opposed to, Mr Heron's political interests, with which Burns had no more to do than he had with the affairs of the man in the moon. (cited by Kinsley, 1474–5)

There is some accuracy in that observation for Burns's Election Ballads are not strictly relevant to the issues of the campaigns. In the first Heron Election Ballad, Burns is thinking along the lines of 'A Man's a Man for a' That' and attributing to Heron great qualities he never possessed. In the second Heron Election Ballad, he produces a parade of Tories ('An there'll be black-nebbit Johnie . . . And there'll be Wigton's new sheriff . . . And there'll be Douglasses doughty'), thus returning to the catalogue format of his early ecclesiastical satires. However, the political enemies never come off the page the way the Auld Lichts did. Burns shows himself a good hater in his Election Ballads but does not convey anything more positive. He was, these propagandist pieces suggest, too intense a man to play the political game at a local level.

Epitaphs and Epigrams

Burns included a selection of epitaphs and epigrams at the end of the Kilmarnock Edition, demonstrating his talent for adroit rhyming as well as his sense of humour. Often these poems consist of one or two quatrains. 'Epitaph on a Henpecked Country Squire' (96/CW, 209) and 'Epigram on Said Occasion' (97/CW, 209) were written about a couple Burns had observed around Mauchline: William Campbell (d.1786) who lived at Netherplace, a mansion near Mauchline; and his wife Lilias Neilson (d.1826), daughter of a Glasgow merchant. The epitaph comprises one quatrain:

> As father Adam first was fool'd,
>   A case that's still too common,
> Here lies a man a woman ruled,
>   The Devil ruled the woman.

The epigram consists of two quatrains:

> O Death, had'st thou but spar'd his life,
>   Whom we this day lament!
> We freely wad exchanged the wife,
>   And a' been weel content.
>
> Ev'n as he is, cauld in his graff,
>   The swap we yet will do't:
> Tak thou the carlin's carcase aff,
>   Thou'se get the saul o boot.

That technique of building up swiftly to a clinching last line remained Burns's characteristic approach to the genres. For example, the epitaph 'On Wee Johnie' (34/CW, 71) – probably about John Wilson, the original of Dr Hornbook – reserves its satirical point for the final line:

> Whoe'er thou art, O reader, know,

That Death has murder'd Johnie;
And here his *body* lies fu' low –
For *saul* he ne'er had ony.

The Kilmarnock Edition contains two serious epitaphs. One, 'For the Author's Father' (35/CW, 71) – subsequently engraved on the tombstone of William Burnes in Alloway churchyard – solemnly celebrates 'The tender father, and the gen'rous friend'. The other, 'A Bard's Epitaph' (104/CW, 220) – the poem with which the Kilmarnock Edition ended – is an autobiographical meditation on the poet's own human flaws: 'But thoughtless follies laid him low,/And stain'd his name!'

Not included in the Kilmarnock Edition – for the reason it would offend, indeed enrage, the subject – is the 'Epitaph on Holy Willie (54/CW, 95), written in 1785 as an appendage to 'Holy Willie's Prayer'. Though William Fisher outlived Burns (until 1809 when, at the age of seventy-two, he froze to death in a ditch) the poet lost no time in sending him to hell: 'His saul has ta'en . . . the left-hand road'. In 'Holy Willie's Prayer', this hypocritical character congratulates himself on being chosen, according to the Calvinist creed of predestination, for a place in heaven. Burns, in the epitaph. is equally certain that Holy Willie will be claimed by the devil, 'Your brunstane Devilship'. Even so, he warns the devil that his infernal reputation could be compromised by such company as Holy Willie:

But hear me, Sir, Deil as ye are,
Look something to your credit:
A cuif like him wad stain your name,
If it were kent ye did it!

Compared to the subliminal psychology of 'Holly Willie's Prayer', the epitaph is inconsequential, a spiteful comment on an absurd enemy.

Friends as well as enemies were treated to Burns's concise comments. The 'Epigram on Captain Francis Grose' (323/CW, 415) makes fun of the obesity of a man (see 'The Burns Circle') Burns elsewhere described as 'a fine, fat, fodgel wight' ('On the late Captain Grose's Perigrinations Thro Scotland'). Burns invokes his old familiar, the devil, to the bedside of his friend:

The Devil got notice that Grose was a-dying,
So whip! at the summons, old Satan came flying;

But when he approach'd where poor Francis lay moaning,
And saw each bed-post with its burthen a-groaning,
Astonish'd, confounded, cries Satan – 'By God,
I'll want him ere take such a damnable load!'

Grose was delighted by the epigram, written (ironically enough) the
year before the antiquary died, in May 1791, in Dublin.

At the end of 1793, Burns was involved in the Rape of the Sabine
Women incident at Friars' Carse which outraged Elizabeth Riddell
(see her entry in 'The Burns Circle'). Elizabeth's sister-in-law Maria
Riddell felt duty bound to break with Burns and, infuriated by what
he saw as an unnecessary injustice, the poet took his revenge in
verse in 1794. At the end of his 'Monody on a Lady Famed for her
Caprice' (443/CW, 511–12) Burns placed 'The Epitaph', summing
up the essentially superficial character of the lady:

Here lies, now a prey to insulting neglect,
    What once was a butterfly, gay in life's beam:
Want only of wisdom denied her respect,
    Want only of goodness denied her esteem.

Walter Riddell, Maria's husband, was in the West Indies when the
Sabine Rape incident occurred but, because he was a member of a
family that had suddenly cast Burns in the role of a sinner, he was
excoriated in 'Epitaph for Mr Walter Riddell' (452/CW, 516):

So vile was poor Wat, such a miscreant slave,
That the worms even damn'd him when laid in his grave.
'In his scull there is famine!' a starved reptile cries;
'And his heart it is poison!' another replies.

It is unlikely that Burns would have sent these epitaphs to the
Riddells, though he did show them to sympathetic friends.

Inevitably, politics as well as personalities informed Burns's
vicious metrical miniatures. In April 1795 Warren Hastings, the
British imperial administrator in India, was acquitted after having
been impeached (in 1788) for corruption and cruelty. Burns used
the occasion to vent his venom on Edmund Burke who attacked
Hastings and who had long irritated Burns by his denunciation
of the French Revolution. Burns's epigram 'On Mr Burke by an
opponent and a friend to Mr Hastings' (478/CW, 534) reads:

Oft I have wonder'd that on Irish ground
No poisonous Reptile ever has been found:

Revealed the secret stands of great Nature's work:
She preserved her poison to create a Burke!

The epigram was not published in Burns's lifetime, but was preserved in a transcript made by John Syme.

Many of the epigrams and epitaphs preserve Burns's favourite prejudices. The 'Epitaph on Mr Burton' (541/CW, 521) ridicules, by caricature, a member of the gentry:

Here, cursing swearing Burton lies,
    A buck, a beau, or *Dem my eyes!*
Who in his life did little good,
    And his last words were, *Dem my blood!*

The 'Epitaph Extempore, On a person nicknamed the Marquis' (543/CW, 531) makes a similar protest against the pretensions of a Dumfries innkeeper:

Here lies a mock Marquis whose titles were shamm'd,
If ever he rise, it will be to be damn'd.

With his faith in the honest man, Burns was sure that the pompous and the pretentious would never inherit the earth in life, death or any afterlife.

A late epitaph, 'On John Bushby, Esq., Tinwald Downs' (544/CW, 521) is arguably the outcome of personal indignation. Bushby (who died in 1802) was a Dumfries lawyer and sherrif-clerk who had been a partner in Douglas, Heron and Co. and manager of its Dumfries branch before the Ayr-based bank collapsed in 1773. According to a story recorded in Robert Chambers's *The Life and Works of Robert Burns* (1851–2) Burns was friendly with Bushby until the lawyer played a cruel joke on the poet, telling him that a hot pudding was ice-cold, causing Burns to be scalded. Burns then got his own back in the Election Ballad 'John Bushby's Lamentation' and in the two-line epitaph which reads:

Here lies John Bushby – honest man,
Cheat him, Devil – if you can!

According to the Young manuscript in Edinburgh University Library, Bushby was amused rather than outraged by the epitaph, perhaps because Young misread, or substituted, 'Catch' for 'Cheat' in the second line.

A late epigram, 'The Toadeater' (553/CW, 569) – a variant of which was published in Allan Cunningham's *The Works of Robert Burns* (1834) – was said to have been provoked by an encounter with a young man who had made some £10,000 in speculation and 'vaunted of keeping the highest company [though] he was of low extraction' (John Syme, cited by Kinsley, 1496). As the crab louse (*pediculus pubis*) is an insect which attaches itself to pubic hair, it is simple enough to supply the missing word in the transcription:

> No more of your titled acquaintances boast,
> Nor of the gay groups you have seen;
> A crab louse is but a crab louse at last,
> Tho' stack to the [cunt] of a Queen.

The sentiment is a familiar one in Burns and this bawdy expression of it would have delighted his convivial companions in Dumfries.

Throughout his life, then, Burns entertained and amused himself and his friends with short pertinent poems, the best of which show him as a sharply observant friend and shrewd enemy.

The Letters

Almost to the day he died, Burns was a prolific letter-writer, regarding the act of correspondence as both an art – the 'Belle Lettre pursuit' (CL, 608) – and an intimate means of communication. It all depended on the correspondent. He could write pointedly private letters to cronies like Bob Ainslie and John McMurdo, and he could write formal and highly finished letters to ladies like Mrs Dunlop. He wrote Mrs Dunlop on 2 October 1789 on the value he placed on their correspondence:

> I beg your pardon, dear Madam, for this coarse paper, but I have no other large enough for a letter to you. – I have often said and thought that I had not time to write the letters I wished, when in fact, it was only the procrastinating, enfeebling tyranny of Indolence: now that excuse is literally true . . . . Still, Madam, be not afraid, as you are pleased to express so much satisfication in my correspondence, that this additional [pressure of Excise work] will in the least detach my heart from that friendship with which you have honored me, or even abridge my letters; though it must at times prevent the regularity of my answers to yours. – I hold the epistles of a Friend to be the SACRAMENTS of Friendship. – To deface or destroy the shortest Billet of yours would shock my feelings as glaring Sacriledge. (CL, 179)

There is an assumption there that Mrs Dunlop is preserving his own letters and those to whom Burns wrote generally did just that. James A. Mackay's one-volume edition of *The Complete Letters of Robert Burns* contains some 700 letters and the letters themselves run to almost 700 closely-printed pages. They range from the trivial note – 'I cannot be with you at tea tonight' (CL, 128) to the carefully considered autobiographical essay (see the Autobiographical Letter in Appendix C).

Thematically, Burns's letters are by turns sycophantic and scornful, superficial and serious, affected and earnest. Again, it all depended on the correspondent. Mrs Dunlop, for example, would have been shocked by the notorious 'horse litter' letter to Bob Ainslie; and Ainslie might have been sickened at the spectacle of Burns 'kissing the arse of a peer' (to use a phrase from 'Ballad Second: The Election') as he did in some letters to lords. When the broad-minded Lord Byron read some of 'Burns's unpublished and never-to-be published Letters' he was astonished: 'They are full of oaths and obscene songs. What an antithetical mind! – tenderness, toughness – delicacy, coarseness – sentiment, sensuality – soaring and grovelling, dirt and deity – all mixed up in that one compound of inspired clay!' (CH, 257–8) It is an excellent summary of all the surviving letters of Burns.

Yes, Burns could grovel. When the 11th Earl of Buchan, David Erskine, patronisingly praised the 'little doric pieces of yours' (CL, 266) in the Kilmarnock Edition, Burns replied 'My Lord, the honor your Lordship has done me by your notice . . . I shall ever gratefully remember' (CL, 266). Sending a copy of 'The Whistle' to the 4th Duke of Queensberry, a man he detested (see 'Election Ballads'), Burns wrote:

> My Lord Duke, Will your grace pardon this approach in a poor Poet, who perhaps intrudes on your converse with Princes to present you ['The Whistle']. Whatever might be my opinion of the poem, I would not have dared to take the liberty of presenting it thus, but for your Grace's acquaintance with the dramatis personae of the piece . . . . my sole motive is to shew how sincerely I have the honor to be, My Lord Duke, Your Grace's most devoted humble servant Robt Burns. (CL, 589)

James Cunningham, 14th Earl of Glencairn, was addressed (genuinely enough) by Burns as 'my noble Patron, my generous Benefactor' (CL, 226) for services (of patronage) rendered; Glencairn's sister, Lady Elizabeth Cunningham, was told (mendaciously) 'When I am tempted to do any thing improper, I dare not because I look on myself as accountable to your Ladyship and Family' (CL, 498). Lords and ladies, of course, expected to be treated with reverence by poetic tenant-farmers and Burns's toadying letters were exercises in an established epistolary genre. Still, they are curiously at odds with the emotions expressed in, say, 'A Man's a Man for a' That'.

Yes, Burns could soar. His fan letter of 22 November 1792 to the actress Louisa Fontenelle, enclosing 'The Rights of Woman', has more than merely period charm:

> In such a bad world as ours, those who add to the scanty sum of our pleasures, are positively our Benefactors. – To you, Madam, on our humble Dumfries boards, I have been more indebted for entertainment, than ever I was in prouder Theatres. – Your charms as a woman would insure applause to the most indifferent Actress, & your theatrical talents would secure admiration to the plainest figure. (CL, 682)

The compliments may be calculated to please, but have genuine touches of sexual exhilaration. Louisa was nineteen when she received the fan letter. With older women, such as Mrs Dunlop (fifty-six when Burns started writing to her) the tone was less teasing, the intimacy partly established through French phrases, since Mrs Dunlop had once been mildly sympathetic to revolutionary ideals (though she changed her tune when her daughters married French royalists). A letter of 5 January 1793 breaks into French:

> Oui! telles choses se font! Je viens d'en faire une epreuve maudite. – (By the way, I don't know whether this is French; & much would it go against my soul, to mar any thing belonging to that gallant people: though my real sentiments of them shall be confined alone to my correspondence with you.) (CL, 204)

Another (the letter of 1 January 1795 that offended Mrs Dunlop by enthusing over the execution of Louis XVI and Marie Antoinette) confidentally noted 'Entre nous, you know my Politics' (CL, 214).

The polite, formal letters, with their liberal sprinkling of French phrases, must be close to the conversastional style Burns cultivated in genteel company. Dugald Stewart, a man Burns admired and a philosopher he respected, praised the 'purity' of his conversation:

> [Burns] avoided more successfully than most Scotchmen, the peculiarities of Scottish phraseology . . . . He certainly possessed a smattering of French; and, if he had an affectation in any thing, it was in introducing occasionally a word or phrase from that language. (cited by Kinsley, 1535)

It took Burns a great deal of study to achieve his conversational and epistolary skills.

One of the favourite books of Burns's boyhood was Arthur Masson's *A Collection of Prose and Verse, from the Best English Authors* which contained – in addition to selections from Shakespeare, Shenstone and others – some of Elizabeth Rowe's *Moral Letters*. Burns memorised whole stretches of the verse and 'used Mrs Rowe's letters as models for many of his own "literary" attemps in prose' (Snyder, 44). From an early age, then, he was aware of the stylistic manners of literary sophisticates. It was one of his dearest ambitions to master the art of letter-writing. We have it on the authority of his brother Gilbert that, sometime after Murdoch left Alloway in 1768, Burns obtained

> a small collection of letters by the most eminent writers, with a few sensible directions for attaining an easy epistolary style. This book was to Robert of the greatest consequence. It inspired him with a strong desire to excel in letter-writing, while it furnished him with models by some of the first writers in our language. (GN)

Burns himself, discussing his return to Mount Oliphant from Kirkoswald in 1775, says:

> I returned home very considerably improved [and] engaged several of my schoolfellows to keep up a literary correspondence with me. – This last helped me much on in composition. – I had met with a collection of letters by the Wits of Queen Ann's reign, and I pored over them most devoutly. – I kept copies of any of my own letters that pleased me, and a comparison between them and the composition of most of my correspondents flattered my vanity. – I carried this whim so far that though I had not three farthings worth of business in the world, yet every post brought me as many letters as if I had been a broad, plodding son of Day-book & Ledger. (AL)

Burns kept up his letter-writing passion for the rest of his life.

Even such a sympathetic Burns scholar as Synder has complained of the poet's susceptibility to 'the somewhat rigid "epistolary" style of the late eighteenth century' and 'the unpleasant formalism usually associated with that style' (Snyder, 85–6). Burns described his poems and songs as 'the spontaneous language of my heart' (CB, 3) but would have been hard pressed to much such a claim for the bulk of his letters, though there are remarkable exceptions. Occasionally the dreary ritual of his relationship with Jean Armour

disgusted him and resulted in genuine emotional outbursts. On 16
September 1788 he wrote to Peggy Chalmers, an intelligent woman
with whom he was infatuated and to whom he had proposed:

> When I think . . . I have met with you, and have lived more of a
> real life with you in eight days, than I can do with almost any body
> I meet with in eight years – when I think of the improbability of
> meeting you in this world again – I could sit down and cry like
> a child! (CL, 237)

As Burns was, by then, a married man – 'I married "my
Jean" . . . not in consequence of the attachment of romance perhaps'
(CL, 237) – there was no question of him using the letter to soften
the resistance of such a woman as Peggy Chalmers. Months earlier,
before his marriage was recognised by the Mauchline Kirk Session,
he had written to Agnes McLehose (23 February 1788) on the subject
of Jean:

> Now for a little news that will please you. – I, this morning as I
> came home, called for a certain woman. – I am disgusted with
> her; I cannot endure her! I, while my heart smote me for the
> prophanity, tried to compare her with my Clarinda: 'twas setting
> the expiring glimmer of a farthing taper beside the cloudless glory
> of the meridian sun. – Here was tasteless insipidity, vulgarity
> of soul, and mercenary fawning; there, polished good sense,
> heaven-born genius, and the most generous, the most delicate,
> the most tender Passion. – I have done with her, and she with
> me. (CL, 399)

That is more calcalated than the outburst to Peggy Chalmers, Burns
possibly keeping his options open so far as Clarinda was concerned.
His correspondence with Mrs McLehose shows that Burns could be
calculating, even cunning, if necessary.

When, on 28 December 1787, Burns agreed to Mrs McLehose's
suggestion that he and she should adopt the Arcadian names of
Sylvander and Clarinda, he plunged into an prose full of affectation
and abstraction:

> My great constituent elements are Pride and Passion: the first I
> have endeavoured to humanize into integrity and honour; the
> last makes me a Devotee to the warmest degree of enthusiasm,
> in Love, Religion, or Friendship; either of them or all together as
> I happen to be inspired. (CL, 374)

A subsequent letter to Clarinda declared 'a friendly correspondence goes for nothing, except one write their undisguised sentiments' (CL, 376) but Burns was soon deeply into his epistolary affectations:

> My definition of Worth is short: Truth and Humanity respecting our fellow-creatures; Reverence and Humility in the presence of that Being, my Creator and Preserver, and who, I have every reason to believe, will one day be my Judge. (CL, 376)

Burns was anxious to impress Mrs McLehose as a man of absolute integrity, perhaps hoping to seduce her mind as a prelude to a seduction of her body. When she tried to rebuke him for making advances, he replied (25 January 1788) with a simulation of wounded pride calculated to comfort Clardinda:

> O Love and Sensibility, ye have conspired against My Peace! I love to madness, and I feel to torture! Clarinda, how can I forgive myself that I ever have touched a single chord in your bosom with pain! would I do it willingly ? Would any consideration, any gratification, make me do so? O, did you love like me, you would not, you could not deny or put off a meeting with the Man who adores you; who would die a thousands deaths before he would injure you; and who must soon bid you a long farewell! (CL, 390)

At the end of that letter he mentions bringing his 'bosom friend, Mr Ainslie' (CL, 390) to see Mrs McLehose and a comparison of the letters to Clarinda with a letter to Ainslie is extremely revealing.

On 3 March 1788, the day that Jean Armour gave birth to twin girl (who both died before the month was out), the poet wrote his notorious 'horse litter' letter to Bob Ainslie. The letter indicates that Burns had sexual intercourse with Jean when she was far advanced in pregnancy and also, by the extraordinary power of its phallic imagery, shows Burns's combative approach to sex:

> Jean I found banished, like a martyr . . . I have taken her to my arms. I have given her a mahogany bed. I have given her a guinea, and I have fucked till she rejoiced with joy unspeakable and full of glory . . . . I took the opportunity of some dry horse litter, and gave her such a thundering scalade that electrified the very marrow of her bones. Oh, what a peacemaker is a guide weel-willy pintle! It is the mediator, the guarantee, the umpire, the bond of union, the solemn league and covenant, the

plenipotentiary, the Aaron's rod, the Jacob's staff, the prophet Elisha's pot of oil, the Ahasuerus' Sceptre, the sword of mercy, the philosopher's stone, the Horn of Plenty, and Tree of Life between Man and Woman. (CL, 331–2)

The difference between that letter and the letters to Clarinda is startling: writing to Mrs McLehose Burns was performing the role of a hypersensitive poet; writing to Bob Ainslie, Burns was being himself, or at least that part of himself that was a highly-sexed farmer with an astonishing fund of erotic images.

Of the more than 700 extant letters of Burns only one, written to William Nicol in 1787, is in Scots. It is a virtuoso performance though of a literary rather than a conversational nature. In describing two girls he met, Burns not only gives them the benefit of vivid description: his evocation of one girl is heavily alliterative ('baith braw and bonie') and a simile he uses for the other girl – 'as blythe's a lintwhite on a flowrie thorn' – is an iambic pentameter. Writing to Nicol, a schoolteacher of classics, an 'obstinate Son of Latin Prose' (CL, 361), Burns aimed to be ingenious, rather than ingenuous, in Scots prose:

> I met wi' twa dink quines in particular, ane o' them a sonsie, fine fodgel lass, baith braw and bonie; the tither was a clean-shankit, straught, tight, weel-far'd winch, as blythe's a lintwhite on a flowrie thorn, and as sweet and modest's a new blawn plumrose in a hazle shaw. (CL, 343)

What Burns might have achieved in Scots prose, as well as Scots verse, is one more tantalising question mark over his career.

Another friend of Burns, Robert Muir, was obviously a more sensitive soul than either Ainslie or Nicol and Burns addressed him accordingly. Writing to this Kilmarnock wine merchant from Mossgiel on 7 March 1788 – that is, shortly before Muir's death from consumption on 22 April – Burns hoped the Spring would 'renew your shattered frame' and launched into a discourse on death:

> You and I have often agreed that life is no great blessing on the whole [so] an honest man has nothing to fear [from death]. If we lie down in the grave, the whole man a piece of broke machinery, to moulder with the clods of the valley, – be it so; at least there is an end of pain, care, woes and wants: if that part of us called Mind, does survive the apparent destruction of the man – away with old-wife prejudices and tales! Every age and

every nation has had a different set of stories; and as the many are always weak, of consequence they have often, perhaps always been deceived: a man, conscious of having acted an honest part among his fellow creatures; even granting that he may have been the sport, at times, of passions and instincts; he goes to a great unknown Being who could have no other end in giving him existence but to make him happy; who gave him those passions and instincts, and well knows their force. (CL, 90)

After Muir's death, Burns referred to his friend (as well as his father and Mary Campbell) in a letter of 13 December 1789 to Mrs Dunlop:

If there is another life, it must be only for the just, the benevolent, the amiable & the humane; what a flattering idea, then, is a World to come! Would to God I as firmly believed in it as I ardently wish it! There I should meet an aged Parent, now at rest from the many buffetings of an evil world against which he so long & bravely struggled. There should I meet the friend, the disinterested friend of my early life; the man who rejoiced to see me, because he loved me & could serve me. – Muir, thy weaknesses were the aberrations of Human-nature, but thy heart glowed with every thing generous, manly & noble; and if ever emanation from the All-Good Being animated a human form, it was thine! – There should I, with speechless agony of rapture, again recognise my lost, my ever dear MARY, whose bosom was fraught with Truth, Honor, Constancy & LOVE. (CL, 181–2)

Both these letters show more literary polish than spontaneity.

Burns wrote drafts of some letters, and carefully polished his epistolary prose. Before he sent his Autobiographical Letter to Dr Moore, he showed the original copy to Mrs Dunlop who pronounced it finer than Richardson or Fielding, thus rightly reading it as a well-crafted literary work and not a carelessly confessional missive. He told Mrs Dunlop of his plan to make the Glenriddell Manuscript of his letters, using 'those which I first sketched in a rough draught, & afterwards wrote out fair' (CL, 209). There are twenty-seven Burns letters, including a copy of the Autobiographical Letter, in the Glenriddell Manuscript but Burns must have had drafts of many more than that number. He told Mrs Dunlop 'I wrote always to you, the rhapsody of the moment' (CL, 209) so had only one draft of a letter to her. That statement was, the epistolary evidence suggests (leaving aside the letter on the execution of Louis XVI and Marie Antoinette) another of his affectations.

The letters Burns wrote to Mrs Dunlop are among his best, but they often read as premeditated performances designed to impress. For example, writing from Ellisland 4 March 1789 after a visit to Edinburgh, Burns launched into a highly-wrought set-piece that would have been more at home in an essay than a personal letter:

> often as I have glided with humble stealth through the pomp of Princes' street, it has suggested itself to me as an improvement on the present Human figure, that a man in proportion to his own conceit of his consequence in the world, could have pushed out the longitude of his common size, as a snail pushes out his horns, or as we draw out a perspective. – This trifling alteration; not to mention the prodigious saving it would be in the tear & wear of the neck and limb sinews of many of his Majesty's liege subjects in the way of tossing the head and tiptoe strutting, would evidently turn out a vast advantage in enabling us at once to adjust the ceremonials in making a bow or making way to a Great Man, and that too, within a second of the precise spherical angle of reverence, or an inch of the particular point of respectful distance, which the important creature itself requires; as a measuring glance at its towering altitude would determine the affair like instinct. (CL, 168)

Like his letters to other correspondents he respected, the letters to Mrs Dunlop tend to be ostentatiously erudite, punctuated with French phrases and quotations from, for example, Shakespeare, Milton, Pope, Shenstone, Gray, Young, Goldsmith, Thomson.

Burns had the diplomatic gift of addressing his main correspondents as intimates, implying that each of them was in some way special to him. Sometimes this had catastrophic consequences: as noted above, he told Mrs Dunlop, apropos 'that gallant people', the French, that 'my real sentiments of them shall be confined alone to my correspondence with you' (CL, 204) then fell out of favour with her precisely because of his enthusiasm for revolutionary France, because he described the execution of the French king and queen as 'the deserved fate [of] a perjured Blockhead & an unprincipled Prostitute' (CL, 214). George Thomson – with whom he corresponded on the art and craft of songwriting – he rebuked for sending him 'a pecuniary parcel' (CL, 631) containing £5 in payment for twenty-five songs. Having self-righteously refused to accept further money from Thomson, Burns was doubly distressed, towards the end of his life, when he had to turn to Thomson for financial help: 'After all my boasted independance, curst necessity compels me to implore you for five pounds' (CL, 679).

Sometimes Burns's letters reveal a capacity for hypocrisy, which cannot entirely be excused by pointing to his vulnerable position in society. For example Burns despised William Douglas, the 4th Duke of Queensberry (1724–1810). Queensberry, who succeeded his cousin to the Dukedom in 1786, was the biggest landowner in Nithsdale and used his influence unscrupulously to advance the interest of parliamentary candidates sympathetic to his principles. In 1789 Pitt dismissed him as George III's Lord of the Bedchamber after the king heard of Queensberry's support for the Prince of Wales in the Regency crisis. Queensberry turned against the king and the Tories, supporting Captain Patrick Miller, son of Burns's landlord, as Whig candidate in the election of 1790 for the Dumfries Burghs. On 4 September 1789, during the campaign, Burns expressed his opinion of Queensberry in a letter to Robert Graham of Fintry:

> The Great Man here, like all Renegadoes, is a flaming Zealot. – Kick'd out before the astonished indignation of his deserted Master, and despised I suppose by the Party who took him in to be a mustering faggot at the mysterious orgies of their midnight iniquities, and a useful drudge in the dirty work of their County Elections, he would fain persuade this part of the world that he is turned Patriot; and, where he knows his men, has the impudence to aim away at the unmistrusting manner of a Man of Conscience and Principle . . . . I am too little a man to have any political attachments; I am deeply indebted to and have the warmest veneration for, Individuals of both Parties; but a man who has it in his power to be the Father of a Country, and who is only known to that Country by the mischiefs he does in it, is a character of which one cannot speak with patience. (CL, 432)

The humble description of himself as an unimportant individual is not convincing, but the splendid dressing down of Queensberry is obviously sincere. Burns also ridiculed the Duke in his Election Ballads and is credited with a comment in the *Star* of 22 February 1790, describing Queensberry as 'degraded' (BE, 107). Nevertheless, Burns (again, as noted above) sent Queensberry a copy of 'The Whistle' with a sycophantic covering letter. A note by Burns in the Glenriddell Manuscript explained that this letter was written after being introduced to the Duke: 'Though I am afraid his Grace's character as a Man of worth is very equivocal, yet he certainly is a Nobleman of the first taste, & a Gentleman of the first manners' (CL, 589). This is yet another example of Burns 'kissing the arse of a peer'.

Sometimes he kissed less exalted arses. Receiving from Mrs Dunlop extracts from letters Dr John Moore had sent her, expressing a high opinion of the Kilmarnock Edition, Burns hesitated about getting in touch with the author of travel-books and the novel *Zeluco* (1786). As he told Mrs Dunlop (15 January 1787), 'I wished to have written Dr Moore . . . yet I could not for my soul set about it. I know his fame and character, and I am one of the "sons of little men"' (CL, 132). Eventually, before the month was out, Burns wrote to Moore with due humility:

> For my part, my first Ambition was, and still my strongest wish is, to please my Compeers, the rustic Inmates of the Hamlet . . . Still I know very well, the novelty of my character has by far the great- est share in the learned and polite notice I have lately got; and in a language where Pope and Churchill have raised the laugh, and Shenstone and Gray drawn the tear, where Thomson and Beattie have painted the landskip, and Littleton and Collins described the heart: I am not vain enough to hope for distinguished Poetic fame. (CL, 246–7)

There Burns was inhibited by Moore's reputation as a writer. When, in July 1793, Burns sent 'There was a lass, and she was fair', to his crony John McMurdo (the man he entrusted with his manu- script collection of bawdy verse) he explained that Jean, McMurdo's daughter, was the subject of the song. That said, he assessed his own importance:

> Kings give Coronets; Alas, I can only bestow a Ballad. – Still, however I proudly claim one superiority even over Monarchs: My presents, so far as I am a Poet, are the presents of Genius; & as the gifts of R. BURNS, they are the gifts of respectful gratitude to the WORTHY. – I assure you, I am not a little flattered with the idea, when I anticipate children pointing out in future Publications the tribute of respect I have bestowed on their Mothers. (CL, 495)

It was not simply the passing of years that made Burns address McMurdo more assertively than he did Moore; it was the knowledge that, with McMurdo, he was communicating with an equal whereas he could not entirely escape the feeling (unavoidable in one brought up as a farmer's son in a society divided by class) that men like Moore were his social superiors.

With tradesman he was at his ease. When Burns first met him, Peter Hill (see his entry in 'The Burns Circle') was a clerk in Creech's bookshop (which had been Allan Ramsay's shop). Hill set up his own business and became Burns's bookseller. The correspondence with 'my dear Bibliopolus' (CL, 313) was untroubled and fascinating for its indication of the poet's literary preferences. On 18 July 1788 Burns wrote to Hill, from Mauchline:

> I want only, Books; the cheapest way, the best; so you may have to hunt for them in the evening Auctions. – I want Smollett's works, for the sake of his incomparable humour. – I have already Roderick Random & Humphry Clinker. – Peregrine Pickle, Lancelot Greaves & Ferdinand Count Fathom, I still want; but as I said, the veriest ordinary Copies will serve me. – I am nice only in the appearance of my Poets. – I forget the price of Cowper's Poems, but I believe I must have them. (CL, 310)

Another letter urgently requested 'a Shakespear [and] an English dictionary, Johnson's I suppose is best' (CL, 314).

In 1789 Burns and Captain Robert Riddell set up the Monkland Friendly Society, in Dunscore parish, Nithsdale, for the purpose of running a circulating library for members. Burns, as Riddell acknowledged, was the Society's 'treasurer, librarian, and censor' (cited by Snyder, 325). Inevitably, Burns turned to Hill to order books for this society, explaining on 2 April 1789:

> The Library scheme that I mentioned to you is already begun, under the direction of Captain Riddel, & ME! – There is another in emulation of it, going on at Closeburn, under the auspices of Mr Mentieth of Closeburn, which will be on a greater scale than ours; I have likewise secured it for you. – Captain R[iddell] gave his infant society a great many of his old books, else I had written to you on that subject, but one of these days I shall trouble you with a Commission for 'the Monkland friendly Society.' – A copy of the Spectator, Mirror & Lounger, [Henry Mackenzie's] Man of feeling, [Mackenzie's] Man of the world, Guthrie's Geographical grammar, with some religious pieces, will likely be our first order. (CL, 314)

On 2 March 1790, Burns sent an order from Ellisland:

At a late meeting of the Monkland friendly Society, it was resolved to augment their Library by the following books which you are to send us as soon as possible. – The Mirror – The Lounger – Man of feeling – Man of the world (these for my own sake I wish to have by the first Carrier) Knox's history of the Reformation – [Peter Rae's] history of the Rebellion 1715 – Any good history of the Rebellion 1745 – A display of the Secession Acts & Testimony by Mr [Adam] Gib – Hervey's Meditations – [William] Beveridge's thoughts – & another copy of [Rev Thomas] Watson's body of Divinity . . . . In addition to the books I commissioned in my last, I want very much – An Index to the Excise laws, or An Abridgement of all the Statutes now in force relative to the Excise, by Jellinger Symons I want three Copies of this book. – If this book is now to be had, cheap or dear, get it for me . . . . I want likewise for myself, as you can pick them up, second-handed or any way cheap copies of Otway's dramatic works, Ben Johnson's Ditto Dryden's Congreve's, Wycherly's, Vanburgh's, Cibber's, or any Dramatic works of the more Moderns, Mackline Garrick, Foote, Colman, or Sheridan's. – A good Copy too of Moliere in French I much want. – Any other good Dramatic Authors, in their native language I want them; I mean Comic Authors chiefly, tho' I should wish Racine, Corneille & Voltaire too. – I am in no hurry for all or any of these, but if you accidentally meet with them very cheap, get them for me. (CL, 316)

And, again on 17 January 1791:

You will be so good then as send by the first Dumfries Carrier, all, or as many as you have by you, of the following books. – The Adventurer – Joseph Andrews – Don Quixote – The Idler – Arabian nights entertainment – Dr [Richard] Price's dissertations on Providence, prayer, Death & Miracles – Roderick Random – & – the 5th Volume of the Observer – for these books take your fair price, as our Society are no judges of the matter, & will insist on having the following damned trash, which you must also send us, as cheap as possible – Scots Worthies – [Rev Thomas] Boston's 4 fold State – Marrow of Modern divinity – [Elisha] Cole on God's Sovereignty – Newton's letters – [Philip] Doddridge's thoughts – Gib's Act & Testimony – Confession of faith – & Captain Robert Boyle. – I forgot to mention among the valuable books, [Hugh] Blair's Sermons & the latest edition of Guthrie's Geographical grammer, which two books be sure to send us. (CL, 318)

Burns was always fascinated by theological works but was clearly
able to discriminate between 'trash' (like Boston's Calvinistic treatise
Human Nature in its Four-fold State, 1790) and 'valuable books'.

In the autumn of 1791, Burns wrote an account of the Monkland
Friendly Society in a letter to Sir John Sinclair, compiler of *The Statistical Account of Scotland* (29 vols, 1791–9). Riddell was disappointed
with the account of Dunscore prepared by the parish minister, so
asked Burns to supplement it with details of the Monkland Friendly
Society. Burns's letter, published as an appendix to the third volume
of the *Statistical Account*, gives his views on the power of books to
enlarge the imagination and ends with a poignant image of the
unlettered man, such as he might have been but for the educational
interests of his father:

> To store the minds of the lower classes with useful knowledge, is
> certainly of very great consequence, both to them as individuals,
> and to society at large. Giving them a turn for reading and
> reflection, is giving them a source of innocent and laudable
> amusement; and, besides, raises them to a more dignified degree
> in the scale of rationality . . . . Mr Riddell got a number of his
> own tenants, and farming neighbours, to form themselves into
> a society, for the purpose of having a library among themselves.
> They entered into a legal engagement, to abide by it for 3 years;
> with a saving clause or two, in cases of removal to a distance,
> or of death. Each member, at his entry, paid 5s; and at each
> of their meetings, which were held every fourth Saturday, 6d.
> more. With their entry money, and the credit which they took
> on the faith of their future funds, they laid in a tolerable stock
> of books at the commencement. What authors they were to pur-
> chase, was always to be decided by the majority . . . . At the
> breaking up of this little society, which was formed under Mr
> Riddell's patronage, what with benefactions of books from him,
> and what with their own purchases, they had collected together
> upwards of 150 volumes. It will easily be guessed, that a good
> deal of trash would be bought. Among the books, however, of
> this little library, were, Blair's Sermons, Robertson's History of
> Scotland, Hume's History of the Stewarts, the Spectator, Idler,
> Adventurer, Mirror, Lounger, Observer, Man of Feeling, Man of
> the World, [Charles Johnstone's] Chrysal, Don Quixotte, Joseph
> Andrews, &c. A peasant who can read, and enjoy such books, is
> certainly a much superior being to his neighbour, who, perhaps,

stalks beside his team, very little removed, except in shape, from the brutes he drives. (CL, 586–7)

Burns's love of lists, seen in his catalogue of books, shows up in many of his letters, including the Autobiographical Letter where, thinking of Betty Davidson, he claims she had

> the largest collection in the country of tales and songs concerning devils, ghosts, fairies, brownies, witches, warlocks, spunkies, kelpies, elf candles, dead-lights, wraiths, apparitions, cantraips, giants, inchanted towers, dragons and other trumpery. (AL)

The same love of lists is evident in his poems, witness the list of ministers in 'The Holy Fair', the list of Scottish worthies in 'The Vision' or the list of local figures in the second Election Ballad for Heron. This accumulation of facts by catalogue is a strong feature of the Scottish literary tradition, and can be readily observed in Dunbar's 'Lament for the Makars', which Burns knew from Allan Ramsay's anthology *Ever Green*.

Another tradition associated with Dunbar (witness 'The Flyting of Dunbar and Kennedie') is flyting, or literary scolding. A letter (probably composed in 1788) from Burns to William Cruickshank (at whose house in St James's Square, Edinburgh, Burns stayed in 1787) is a spirited exercise in the genre:

> Thou Eunuch of language – Thou Englishman who never was south of the Tweed – Thou servile echo of fashionable barbarisms – Thou Quack, vending the nostrums of Empirical elocution – Thou Marriage-maker between vowels and consonants on the Gretna-green of Caprice – Thou Cobbler, botching the flimsy socks of bombast Oratory – Thou Blacksmith, hammering the rivets of Absurdity – Thou Butcher, embruing thy hands in the bowels of Orthography . . . (CL, 726)

And so on, nothing personal being intended. Like so many letters, this shows just one epistolary trick from a wide and varied repertoire.

Burns could be the musical scholar in his letters to James Johnson and George Thomson (see 'The Songs'). He could play the romantic lover in Sylvander's letters to Clarinda. He could act to perfection the part of the humble bard in letters to the aristocracy. He could write fan letters to an actress, fawning letters to the gentry. He could write in Scots, as he did to Nicol; he could sustain erotic imagery, as he did to Bob Ainslie. He could be frank and friendly with Mauchline friends like Gavin Hamilton, he could be deliberate and distant with Edinburgh associates like William Creech. He could write short stories as he did when sending Captain Francis Grose prose preludes to 'Tam o Shanter' in a letter of June 1790:

> Upon a stormy night, amid whirling squalls of wind and bitter blasts of hail, in short, on such a night as the devil would chuse to take the air in, a farmer or farmer's servant was plodding and plashing homeward with his plough-irons on his shoulder, having been getting some repairs on them at a neighbouring smithy. (CL, 557)

He could, in fact, strike a variety of poses in his letters and his polished performances are as revealing as his impulsive productions.

The most disturbing letters are, predictably, those Burns wrote at the end of his life. From 3–17 July he was at Brow, a hamlet on the shores of the Solway Firth, seeking a cure for his ill-health in sea-bathing. At that time he was almost demented with worry about his financial position, certain that he would end up in jail because of money he owed for a Dumfries Volunteers uniform. On 12 July 1796, nine days before he died, he wrote two letters from Brow about his predicament. To George Thomson, he wrote:

> After all my boasted independance, curst necessity compels me to implore you for five pounds. – A cruel scoundrel of a Haberdasher to whom I owe an account, taking it into his head that I am dying, has commenced a process & will infallibly put me into jail. – Do, for God's sake, send me that sum, & that by return of post. – Forgive me this earnestness, but the horrors of a jail have made me half distracted. (CL, 679)

To his cousin James Burness, he wrote a variant of this urgent appeal:

> When you offered me money-assistance little did I think I should want it so soon. – A rascal of a Haberdasher to whom I owe a considerable bill taking it into his head that I am dying, has commenced a process against me & will infallibly put my emaciated body into jail.– Will you be so good as to accomodate me, & that by return of post, with ten pounds. – O, James! did you know the pride of my heart, you would feel doubly for me! Alas! I am not used to beg! The worst of it is, my health was coming about

finely; you know & my Physician assures me that melancholy & low spirits are half my disease, guess then my horrors since this buei ness began . . . . Forgive me for once more mentioning by return of Post. – Save me from the horrors of jail! (CL, 64)

Both men sent the money as requested but Thomson annotated the begging letter to himself: 'This idea is exaggerated – he could not have been in any such danger at Dumfries nor could he be in such necessity, to implore aid from *Edinr*' (CL, 680). Burns was such a consummate role-player that Thomson's cynical remark was understandable. However, whatever the reality of the situation Burns seems to have been genuinely convinced that he was indeed in danger and in this state of mind he not only said exactly what he meant but said it twice, to two correspondents. These letters of a dying man, distracted and desperate, serve as a reminder to what artistic effort Burns put into his letters when he was fully alive and in command of his literary faculties.

The Common Place Books

Burns compiled two Common Place Books: the first, begun in April 1783 when he was living at Lochlea, was abandoned in October 1785 when he was at Mossgiel; the second, begun in Edinburgh on 9 April 1787, and sometimes referred to as the Edinburgh Journal, was abandoned in 1790 when he was employed as an exciseman and weary of working Ellisland, 'this accursed farm' (CL, 358).

The manuscript of the first Common Place Book was purchased, in 1868, by John Adam, Town Chamberlain of Greenock, who (with editorial assistance from Colin Daniel Lamont) transcribed the text and had it privately printed in 1872 as *Robert Burns' Common Place Book*. The Adam edition was reprinted, with corrections and an introduction by Raymond Lamont Brown (Wakefield, 1969, references to this volume).

Snyder suggests that the first Common Place Book was written with an audience in mind: 'the introductory paragraph suggests that he expected the booklet to be read by other eyes than his own' (Snyder, 86). Maurice Lindsay, however, is certain that the first Common Place Book 'was clearly not intended for publication' (BE, 79). Burns himself prepared an abridged version of the work for the prose volume of the Glenriddell Manuscript and said, 'I had meant the book should have lain by me, in the fond hope, that some time or other, even after I was no more, my thoughts would fall into the hands of somebody capable of appreciating their value' (CB, ii). The work was conceived, or more accurately developed, as a literary performance rather than an intimate journal.

Completed before the publication of the Kilmarnock Edition, the first Common Place Book shows the extent of Burns's ambitions. He wanted, in August 1785, to be the bard of Ayrshire, the poet of 'my dear native country, the ancient Baileries of Carrick, Kyle, and Cunningham' (CB, 46), a notion more fully articulated in 'The Vision'. In September 1785, that is more than a year before he started sending songs to Johnson, he also saw great artistic merit in writing words for Scottish songs: 'it might be possible for a Scotch Poet, with a nice, judicious ear, to set compositions to many of our most favorite airs' (CB, 49).

The Burns of the first Common Place Book projects himself as a a simple soul 'bred at a plough-tail' (CB, 1), a man who 'never had the least thought of inclination of turning Poet till I got once heartily in Love, and then Rhyme and Song were, in a manner, the spontaneous language of my heart' (CB, 3). He criticises the inadequacies of his own poems including the first of them, 'Handsome Nell', which he finds full of flaws but significant because 'I composed it in a wild enthusiasm of passion' (CB, 6). Yet the passionate 'ploughman' (CB, 1) is not lacking in sophistication, as witness his references to Adam Smith's *The Theory of Moral Sentiments* (1759) and to 'Ossian, Shakespeare, Thomson, Shenstone, Sterne' (CB, 22).

Intellectually, the book shows Burns looking beyond the theological horizons of Ayrshire towards a higher Being recognisable from Locke's *Essay Concerning Human Understanding* (1690) which he had read at Lochlea and which had recognised 'some knowing intelligent Being in the World'. Affirming Deism instead of dogma, Burns declares that 'the grand aim of human life is to cultivate an intercourse with that Being to whom we owe life' (CB, 23). Thematically, Burns stresses his own depressive nature, portraying himself as a man often at the mercy of his emotions:

> There was a certain period of my life, that my spirit was broke by repeated losses and disasters, which threatened and indeed affected the utter ruin of my fortune. My body, too, was attacked by that most dreadful distemper, a hypochondria, or confirmed melancholy; in this wretched state, the recollection of which makes me yet shudder, I hung my harp on the willow trees, except in some lucid intervals . . . (CB, 10)

As he never had a 'fortune' utterly to ruin, the passage shows Burns under the influence of the sentimental stylists he admired; he was devoted, after all, to Henry Mackenzie's *The Man of Feeling* (1771) in which people die of broken hearts to the consternation of Harley, the lachrymose hero. Nevertheless, the 'confirmed melancholy' was genuine enough and, in the summer of 1784, serious enough to bring the poet close to a nervous breakdown.

As well as meditative prose, the first Common Place Book contains twenty-five poems and songs: 'Handsome Nell', 'Remorse', 'A Penitential Thought', 'A Prayer Under the Pressure of Violent Anguish', 'Winter, A Dirge', 'My father was a farmer', 'My Nanie, O', 'Epitaph on a Celebrated Ruling Elder' 'Epitaph on James Grieve' 'Epitaph on Wm. Muir', 'Epitaph on my Honoured Father', 'Green grow the rashes', 'A Prayer, in the Prospect of Death', 'Stanzas on the same occasion', 'Tibby I hae seen the day', 'My girl she's airy', 'John Barleycorn', 'The Death and Dying Words of Poor Mailie', 'Epistle to J. Lapraik', 'Second Epistle to J. Lapraik', 'Man Was Made to Mourn', 'When first I came to Stewart Kyle', 'Now westlin winds', 'Montgomerie's Peggy', 'O raging Fortune's withering blast'. When Burns abandoned the first Common Place Book, in October 1785, he was well into his *annus mirabilis* as a poet and henceforth worked towards the Kilmarnock Edition (which contained some of the poems from the first Common Place Book).

If the first Common Place Book was the work of an aspiring poet, the second Common Place Book was the work of a literary celebrity and was started in the month the First Edinburgh Edition appeared. This second Common Place Book (the manuscript of which is kept in the Alloway Burns Cottage Museum) was included in the second volume of William Wallace's *The Life and Works of Robert Burns* (4 vols, 1896); according to Snyder, Burns never wished it to be made public for it 'was not intended for publication [but] intended for his own eye alone' (Snyder, 200, 287). As defined by Burns the purpose of the second Common Place Book was personal:

> As I have seen a good deal of human life in Edin[burgh], a great many characters which are new to one bred up in the shades of life as I have been, I am determined to take down my remarks on the spot [and] sketch every character, that in any way strikes me, to the best of my observation . . . . My own private story likewise [and] Poems and fragments that must never see the light, shall be occasionally inserted. (cited by Kinsley, 1224)

The folio of 170 pages (some missing, others blank) contains various observations and twelve poems by Burns: 'Rantin, Rovin Robin', 'Verses in Friars' Carse Hermitage', 'Epistle to Robert Graham, Esq., Requesting a Favour', 'Versicles on Sign-Posts', 'Castle Gordon', 'The Bonnie Lass of Albanie', 'The small birds rejoice in the green leaves returning', 'Stanzas on Naething', 'Sonnet to Robert Graham, Esq., of Fintry', 'Will ye go to the Indies, my Mary', 'The Wounded Hare', 'Elegy on Captain Matthew Henderson'.

The observations, some of them possibly intended for subsequent polish and publication, show Burns striking poses as a prose stylist, experimenting with different idioms. For example, he sums up the philosopher Dugald Stewart in the manner of an elegant essayist of the Enlightenment:

> The most perfect character I ever saw is Mr Stuart. An exalted judge of the human heart, and of composition. One of the very first public speakers; and equally capable of generosity as humanity. His principal discriminating feature is; from a mixture of benevolence, strength of mind, and manly dignity, he not only at heart values, but in his deportment and address bears himself to all the Actors, high and low, in the drama of Life, simply as they merit in playing their parts. Wealth, honours, and all that is extraneous of the man, have no more influence with him than they will have at the Last Day. His wit, in the hour of social hilarity, proceeds almost to good-natured waggishness; and in telling a story he particularly excells. (cited by Snyder, 200)

This is Common Sense prose for a Common Sense philosopher.

Considering the character of his parsimonious publisher William Creech, however, Burns opts for a more subjective approach, the confidential style popular in the epistolary novel. Here is a passage from Richardson's *Pamela*, the first novel Burns read (according to his brother Gilbert):

> You must know, then, that Mrs Arthur is a comely person, inclinable to be fat; but very easy with it, and has pretty good features, though a little too masculine, in my opinion. She has the air of a person of birth, and seems by it to shew, that she expects to be treated as such; and has a freedom and presence of mind in all she *says* or *does*, that sets her above being in the least conscious of imperfection in either. (Samuel Richardson, *Pamela*, 1740; rept. Harmondsworth, 1980, p. 83)

And here is Burns on Creech:

> My worthy bookseller, Mr Creech, is a strange, multiform character. His ruling passions of the left hand are an extreme vanity and something of the more harmless modification of selfishness. The one, mixed as it often is with great goodness of heart, makes him rush into all public matters, and take every instance of unprotected merit by the hand, provided it is in his power to

hand it into public notice; the other quality makes him, amid all
the embarrassment in which his vanity entangles him, now and
then to cast half a squint at his own interest. His parts as a man,
his deportment as a gentleman, and his abilities as a scholar, are
above mediocrity. Of all the Edinburgh literati, he writes most
like a gentleman. He does not awe you with the profoundness of
the philosopher, or strike your eye with the soarings of genius; but
he pleases you with the handsome turn of his expression and the
polite ease of his paragraph. His social demeanour and powers,
particularly at his own table, are the most engaging I have ever
met with. (BE, 85)

Burns, it is safe to say from that, could have written an epistolary
novel under the influence of Richardson but the letters in such a
novel would have lacked the incisive quality of his most passion-
ately personal letters.

Whereas the personal letters of Burns discuss his private life in
often frenzied terms, the second Common Place Book reflects on
marriage in the manner of a contemporary novelist:

Wedlock, the circumstance that buckles me hardest to Care, if
Virtue and Religion were to be anything with me but mere names,
was what in a few seasons I must have resolved on; in the present
case it was unavoidably necessary. Humanity, Generosity, honest
vanity of character, Justice to my own happiness for after-life,
so far as it could depend, which it surely will a great deal, on
internal peace, all these joined their warmest suffrages, their most
powerful solicitations, with a rooted Attachment, to urge the step
I have taken. Nor have I any reason on her part to rue it. I can fancy
how, but have never seen *where*, I could have made it better. (cited
by Snyder, 287)

Beneath the polish of the prose, Burns is dimly seen as a martyr to
marriage. He is distant in a way he never is in his most revealing
letters, those that pulsate with the emotional energy that runs
through his poetic masterworks.

Burns intended to preserve unpublishable poems in the second
Common Place Book but nothing remains in the folio (from which
pp. 23–6 and pp. 41–8 are missing) that would have given sexual
offence (nothing along the lines of 'My girl she's airy' in the first
Common Place Book). One song included in the second Common
Place Book, however, deals with a politically sensitive matter. 'The

Bonie Lass of Albanie' gives Burns's opinion of the Hanoverians and was possibly prompted by the news of the death of Bonnie Prince Charlie on 31 January 1788.

In 1753, the Prince's mistress Clementina Walkinshaw bore him a daughter, Charlotte, who was retrospectively legitimized in 1784 and recognised as Duchess of Albany by the French parliament in 1787. As a sentimental Jacobite, Burns championed Charlotte, 'This lovely maid', as being the rightful heir to the throne of Albany (Scotland). In the following stanzas (the last three of six) Burns ridicules Prince George (later George IV) as 'witless' and denounces George I, the first Hanoverian king, as a 'false usurper':

> But there is a youth, a witless youth,
>   That fills the place where she should be;
> We'll send him o'er to his native shore,
> And bring our ain sweet Albanie!
>
> Alas the day, and woe the day!
>   A false usurper wan the gree,
> Who now commands the towers and lands,
>   The royal right of Albanie.
>
> We'll daily pray, we'll nightly pray,
>   On bended knees most fervently,
> The time may come, with pipe and drum
> We'll welcome hame fair Albanie.
>
> (188/CW, 303)

The time never came, as Charlotte died, at the age of thirty-three, in 1789. Burns never published 'The Bonie Lass of Albanie' in his lifetime, for the obvious reason that it was not politically safe to insult the family of the reigning monarch.

The two Common Place Books, one written before and the other after the Kilmarnock Edition, contain philosophical fragments, psychological sketches and a fair sprinkling of fine poems. They show Burns at the literary workbench, trying out ideas and idioms, mastering his trade, lifting craft to the level of a fine art.

Part V:
Select Bibliography

Select Bibliography

BIBLIOGRAPHIES

Egerer, Joel Warren, *A Bibliography of Robert Burns* (Edinburgh, 1964).

Gibson, James, *The Bibliography of Robert Burns* (Kilmarnock, 1881).

Mitchell Library, *Catalogue of the Robert Burns Collection in the Mitchell Library, Glasgow* (Glasgow, 1959).

REFERENCE BOOKS

Craigie, William A., *A Primer of Burns* (London, 1896).

Cuthbertson, John, *Complete Glossary to the Poetry and Prose of Robert Burns* (Paisley, 1886).

Lindsay, Maurice, *The Burns Encyclopedia* (1959; rev., London, 1980).

Reid, John Brown, *A Complete Word and Phrase Concordance to the Poems and Songs of Robert Burns* (Glasgow, 1889; rpt. New York, 1968).

Ross, John D., *Who's Who in Burns* (Stirling, 1927).

Wilson, Sir James, *The Dialect of Robert Burns* (London, 1923).

MANUSCRIPTS

Some Burns manuscripts remain in private collections (mainly in the USA). The following list indicates important and accessible holdings; for further details see Kinsley's *The Poems and Songs of Robert Burns* (vol. 3, pp. 964–9).

British Library, London: the Autobiographical Letter to Dr John Moore; the Egerton Manuscript of three letters and fourteen poems; the Hastie Manuscript of nearly 200 songs and fragments sent to James Johnson.

Burns Cottage Museum, Alloway ('the finest single collection [of poetical holographs] in the world', Kinsley, 965): the Afton Manuscript, a collection of thirteen poems (including 'Tam o Shanter') presented by Burns to Mrs Alexander Stewart of Afton in 1791; the Stair Manuscript, a collection of eight early songs and poems (including 'The Vision') presented by Burns to Mrs Alexander Stewart of Stair in autumn 1786; the letters to Robert Graham of Fintry; the second Common Place Book.

City Museum, Edinburgh: the letters to James Burness.

Edinburgh University Library, Edinburgh: the Don Manuscript (Laing MSS), a collection of early letters presented by Burns to Lady Henrietta Don in 1787.

Henry E. Huntington Library, San Marino, California: sixty poems, including seventeen epigrams sent to Creech.

Irvine Burns Club: part of the holograph printer's copy for the Kilmarnock Edition.

Kilmarnock Monument Museum: a notebook containing fifteen poems, also letters and holographs of seven poems; the collection was edited by David Sneddon as *Burns Holograph Manuscripts in the Kilmarnock Monument Museum* (1889).

National Library of Scotland, Edinburgh: the Glenriddell Manuscript, made by Burns for Captain Robert Riddell, and consisting of two calf-bound quarto volumes, the first (copied 1791) containing fifty-two poems including 'Holy Willie's Prayer' and 'Tam o Shanter'; the Watson Manuscript (formerly in the National Portrait Gallery); the collection of C. R. Cowie of Glasgow, including eleven poems and fragments in holograph.

Pierpont Morgan Library, New York ('the largest single collection of Burns's letters', Kinsley, 966): the Dalhousie Manuscript of fifty-six letters from Burns to George Thomson, containing 107 songs in holograph (eight of the songs not by Burns); the Lochryan Manuscript of forty-two letters to Mrs Dunlop, containing thirty-seven poems.

BURNS'S VERSE

Three editions of *Poems, Chiefly in the Scottish Dialect* appeared during the lifetime of Burns: the Kilmarnock Edition, published by subscription, printed and issued by John Wilson, Kilmarnock, on 31 July 1786; the First Edinburgh Edition, published by subscription by William Creech on 17 April 1787; the Second Edinburgh Edition, published in two volumes by William Creech on 16 February 1793. Uncollected and unpublished poems were posthumously released in various volumes, beginning with James Currie's *The Works of Robert Burns* (1800, see below).

The indispensable scholarly edition is James Kinsley's *The Poems and Songs of Robert Burns* (3 vols, Oxford, 1968), the last volume of which comprises a detailed textual commentary. Kinsley's text is based on Burns's holographs and transcripts revised in his hand and on reliable printed texts (including the Kilmarnock and Edinburgh Editions and early printings in newspapers, periodicals and tracts).

As the three-volume Kinsley edition is expensive, two easily available and inexpensive texts are referred to in the present book. James Kinsley's *Burns: Poems and Songs* (Oxford, 1969) is a one-volume edition set from corrected proofs of the same editor's definitive three-volume work of 1968. Where numbers (obviously not dates) are given in parentheses after poems, they refer to Kinsley's numbering of Burns's poems and songs from 1–632.

Another text, aimed at the enthusiast rather than the scholar, is the Official Bicentenary Edition of *The Complete Works of Robert Burns* (Ayr, 1986) edited and introduced by James A. Mackay. Commissioned by the Burns Federation as a standard single-volume edition of the poems, it commemorates the bicentenary of the Kilmarnock Edition of *Poems, Chiefly in the Scottish Dialect*. Mackay has, with a few reservations, adhered to the chronological sequence established by Kinsley. The abbreviation CW refers to Mackay's edition.

Quotations generally adopt Mackay's modern orthography with its minimum of apostrophes but rely on the authority of Kinsley's texts.

A fascimile of the Kilmarnock Edition (reproduced from the copy in Glasgow University Library) – plus pages from the First Edinburgh Edition – was published as *Robert Burns: Poems 1786 and 1787* (Menston, 1971).

Burns's songs were written for two collections. *The Scots Musical Museum*, edited by James Johnson, was published in six volumes (Edinburgh, 1787, 1788, 1790, 1792, 1796, 1803). It includes some 200 songs and fragments (and some airs) written, revised, or communicated by Burns. A two-volume reprint of the *Scots Musical Museum* (Hatboro, 1962) is available.

A Select Collection of Original Scottish Airs for the Voice, edited by George Thomson, was published in eight parts (Edinburgh, 1793, 1798, 1799, ?1799, 1802, 1803, 1805, 1818). It includes more than 70 songs by Burns; as only the first part of *Select Scottish Airs* appeared in Burns's lifetime, 'Thomson meddled and muddled, impudently and sometimes disastrously, with the manuscripts Burns had left in his hands' (Kinsley, 991).

BURNS'S PROSE

Burns was a prolific and eloquent correspondent whose letters were garbled and toned down by early editors. However, the epistolary canon has been defined by modern scholars. J. DeLancey Ferguson's *The Letters of Robert Burns* (2 vols, Oxford, 1931) transcribed the originals of some 540 letters. G. Ross Roy's monumental edition of *The Letters of Robert Burns* (2 vols, Oxford, 1985), re-collated every letter from original manuscripts or first printed sources and scrupulously reproduced what Burns wrote, complete with lapses of spelling and syntax. The text referred to in the present book is James A. Mackay's *The Complete Letters of Robert Burns* (Ayr, 1987) – a single-volume edition and companion to the same editor's *The Complete Works of Robert Burns* (see above). Acknowledging the authority of Roy's text, Mackay eschews the chronological arrangement by individual letters; instead, he arranges some 700 letters in clusters according to correspondent, all letters to the same recipient then following in date order. The abbreviation CL refers to Mackay's edition.

Burns kept a journal of the Border tour he made with Robert Ainslie, 5 May–1 June 1787, and this was edited, by J. DeLancey Fergusson, as *The Journal of the Border Tour* in ed. Robert T. Fitzhugh's *Robert Burns: His Associates and Contemporaries* (Chapel Hill, 1943).

Burns also kept a journal of the Highland tour he made with William Nicol, 25 August–16 September 1787. This was published in fascimile, edited by J. C. Ewing, as *Journal of a Tour in the Highlands* (London, 1927).

Two volumes edited by Raymond Lamont Brown are devoted to the poet's tours: *Robert Burns's Tour of the Borders 5 May–1 June 1787* (Ipswich, 1972); and *Robert Burns's Tour of the Highlands and Stirlingshire 1787* (Ipswich, 1973).

Burns wrote two Common Place Books, the first covering the

period April 1783–October 1785, the second (sometimes called the Edinburgh Journal) written between 1787 and 1790. The first Common Place Book ('Observations, Hints, Songs, Scraps of Poetry, etc., by Robt. Burness') was transcribed by John Adam (with editorial assistance from Colin Daniel Lamont), as *Robert Burns' Common Place Book* (privately printed in Edinburgh, 1872); and the Adam edition was reprinted (Wakefield, 1969) with an introduction by Raymond Lamont Brown. A reproduction of the text in fascsimile was edited by J. C. Ewing and D. Cook, as *Robert Burns's Common Place Book, 1783–85* (Glasgow, 1938). The Ewing–Cook edition was reprinted (London, 1965) with an introduction by David Daiches.

The second Commonplace Book was included in the second volume of William Wallace's *The Life and Works of Robert Burns* (4 vols, Edinburgh, 1896).

In an interleaved copy of the first four volumes of Johnson's *Scots Musical Museum* Burns wrote explanatory notes on Scottish song. The poet's friend Robert Riddell acquired this copy (sometime before autumn 1792) and Burns's notes were transcribed as 'Strictures on Scottish Songs and Ballads' in R.H. Cromek's *Reliques of Robert Burns* (London, 1808). James C. Dick's *Notes on Scottish Song by Robert Burns* (London, 1908) produced a new scholarly transcription of the explanatory notes, suggesting that Cromek had been guilty of forgery. However, Davidson Cook ('Annotations of Scottish Songs by Burns', *Burns Chronicle*, 1922) and J. DeLancey Ferguson ('In Defense of R. H. Cromek', *Philological Quarterly*, July, 1930) showed the supposedly spurious notes were indeed by Burns though derived from other sources than the interleaved *Museum*. Burns's notes on Scottish song can, then, be read by consulting both Cromek and Dick; Dick's *Notes on Scottish Song* was reissued (Hatboro, 1962) together with the same editor's *The Songs of Robert Burns* (London, 1908).

BIOGRAPHICAL STUDIES

Adams, James, *Burns's 'Chloris', a Reminiscence* (Glasgow, 1893). A romantic account of Burns and Jean Lorimer.

Angellier, Auguste, *Robert Burns. La Vie. Les Oeuvres* (2 vols, Paris, 1893). The second volume is a critical biography much admired for its scholarly approach.

Brown, Hilton, *There Was a Lad* (London, 1949). Useful chapter on

'The Riddell Quarrel'.

Carswell, Catherine, *The Life of Robert Burns* (London, 1930). A highly
readable account by a pugnacious Scottish critic and novelist, it
has been faulted as unscholarly.

Crichton-Browne, Sir James, *Burns from a New Point of View* (London,
1926). Contests the Heron–Currie view of the alcoholic decline
and death of Burns and claims the poet died of rheumatic fever
terminating as rheumatic endocarditis.

Cunningham, Allan, *The Works of Robert Burns, with his Life* (4 vols,
London, 1834). A vivid portrait of the poet by a writer whose
father was a neighbour of Burns at Ellisland.

Currie, James, *The Works of Robert Burns, with an Account of his Life*
(4 vols, Edinburgh, 1800). Still controversial for its portrayal
of Burns 'Perpetually stimulated by alcohol' (I, 214). 'Here,'
said Wordworth's of Currie's biography, 'is a revolting account
of a man of exquisite genius, and confessedly of many high
moral qualities, sunk into the lowest depths of vice and misery!'
(CH, 281)

Daiches, David, *Robert Burns and his World* (London, 1971). A pictorial biography.

Ferguson, J. DeLancey, *Pride and Passion: Robert Burns* (New York,
1939). Scholarly and sympathetic.

Fitzhugh, Robert T., *Robert Burns: The Man and the Poet* (New York,
1970). A fluent narrative enriched by constant quotation.

Fowler, Richard Hindle, *Robert Burns* (London, 1988). Rejects the
Crichton-Browne diagnosis of the death of Burns and suggests the
poet contracted brucellosis which was exacerbated by habitually
drinking excessive quantities of lead-adulterated wine.

Hecht, Hans, *Robert Burns: The Man and his Work* (German edition,
1919; translated by Jane Lymburn, 1936; rept. Ayr, 1971). An
Appendix reprints Robert Heron's *A Memoir of the Life of the late
Robert Burns*.

Heron, Robert, *A Memoir of the Life of the Late Robert Burns*
(Edinburgh, 1797). The first formal biography, first published
as 'Original Memoirs of the Late Robert Burns' (*Monthly Magazine
and British Register*, London, January–June, 1797). Based on gossip,
it depicts the poet as a genius gradually destroyed by drink.
Reprinted in Hecht (see above).

Lindsay, Maurice, *Robert Burns: the Man, his Work, the Legend* (1954;
rev. London, 1979).

Lockhart, John G., *Life of Robert Burns* (Edinburgh, 1828). Highly readable but dismissed by Snyder as unreliable: 'It is inexcusably inaccurate from beginning to end, at times demonstrably mendacious, and should never be trusted in any respect or detail' (Snyder, 488–9).

Snyder, Franklyn Bliss, *The Life of Robert Burns* (New York, 1932; rpt. Hamden, Conn., 1968). Fiercely scholarly and sceptical of anecdotal material, this indispensable biography takes 'verifiable fact' (vii) as its priority.

Thornton, Robert D., *James Currie the Entire Stranger and Robert Burns* (Edinburgh, 1963).

Thornton, Robert D., *William Maxwell to Robert Burns* (Edinburgh, 1979). A spirited defence of the doctor who attended the dying poet.

CRITICAL STUDIES: GENERAL

Crawford, Thomas, *Burns: A Study of the Poems and Songs* (Edinburgh, 1960; rpt. Edinburgh, 1978). An enthusiastic and informative discussion of Burns's major works.

Daiches, David, *Robert Burns* (London, 1950; rev. London, 1966). Combines biographical readings with critical insights.

[Gleig, George], *A Critique on the Poems of Robert Burns* (Edinburgh, 1812). The first book on Burns's poetry.

Jack, R. D. S. and Noble, Andrew (ed.), *The Art of Robert Burns* (London and Totowa, 1982). Essays by various writers on aspects of Burns.

Keith, Christina, *The Russet Coat* (London, 1956).

Low, Donald A. (ed.), *Robert Burns: The Critical Heritage* (London, 1974). An annotated anthology of critical responses to Burns.

MacDiarmid, Hugh, *Burns Today and Tomorrow* (Edinburgh, 1959). A polemical demolition of the Burns cult.

Stevenson, Robert Louis, *Familiar Studies of Men and Books* (London, 1882). Contains the essay 'Some Aspects of Robert Burns'.

CRITICAL STUDIES: PARTICULAR

Brown, Mary Ellen, *Burns and Tradition* (London, 1984).

Daiches, David, *God and the Poets* (Oxford, 1984). In his seventh chapter ('Calvinism and the Poetic Imagination') the author discusses the religious background of Burns and finds him 'more of a deist than a theist' (p. 144).

Ericson-Roos, Catarina, *The Songs of Robert Burns: A Study of the Unity of Poetry and Music* (Uppsala, 1977).

Jamieson, A. Burns, *Burns and Religion* (Cambridge, 1931). This pugnacious little book denies that Burns was a Deist and argues that 'His democratic creed is, of course, bound up with his religion and is in harmony with the views of Knox and the Convenanters' (p.114).

Low, Donald A. (ed.), *Robert Burns: The Kilmarnock Poems* (London, 1985). Introduces and annotates the Kilmarnock Edition.

McGuirk, Carol, *Robert Burns and the Sentimental Era* (Athens, Georgia, 1985).

TOPOGRAPHY

Bold, Alan, *Scotland: A Literary Guide* (London, 1989).

Boyle, Andrew, *Burns-Lore of Ayrshire* (Ayr, 1985)

Mackay, James A., *Burns-Lore of Dumfries and Galloway* (Ayr, 1988)

McVie, John, *The Burns Country* (Edinburgh, 1962).

McVie, John, *Robert Burns and Edinburgh* (Kilmarnock, 1969).

Strawhorn, John (ed.), *Ayrshire in the Time of Robert Burns* (Ayr, 1959).

RELATED STUDIES

Bold, Alan, *MacDiarmid: A Critical Biography* (1988; rev. London 1990). Comments on the connexions between Burns and Scotland's greatest modern poet.

Craig, David, *Scottish Literature and the Scottish People, 1680–1830* (London, 1961). A thoughtful application of Marxist theory to Scottish culture.

Crawford, Thomas, *Society and the Lyric* (Edinburgh, 1979). Puts Burns's songs in the context of the popular culture of his period.

Ellis, P. Berresford and Mac a' Ghobhainn, Seumas, *The Scottish Insurrection of 1820* (London, 1970). Discusses the republican movement in Scotland and comments on the trials and transportation of Thomas Muir and Thomas Palmer.

Legman, G., *The Horn Book* (New York, 1964). A wide-ranging study of erotica with a discussion of the bawdy work of Burns.
Murison, David, *The Guid Scots Tongue* (Edinburgh, 1977). Discusses the Scots revivalist resistance to the imposition of English on Scotland.
Olson, Richard, *Scottish Philosophy and British Physics 1750-1880* (Princeton, 1975). A study of Scottish Common Sense philosophers, including Burns's friend Dugald Stewart.

FICTIONAL ACCOUNTS

Barke, James, *Immortal Memory: A Novel of the Life and Loves of Robert Burns* (5 vols, Glasgow, 1946–54). The separate novels are *The Wind that Shakes the Barley* (1946), *The Song in the Green Thorn Tree* (1947), *The Wonder of All the Gay World* (1949), *The Crest of the Broken Wave* (1953), *The Well of the Silent Harp* (1954). An epilogue, *Bonnie Jean*, about the life of Jean Armour, appeared in 1959.
Campsie, Alistair, *The Clarinda Conspiracy* (Edinburgh, 1989)
Kemp, Robert, *The Other Dear Charmer* (London, 1957). Play about Burns and Mrs McLehose.
MacDiarmid, Hugh, *At the Sign of the Thistle* (London, 1934). Contains the satirical sketch 'The Last Great Burns Discovery'.
McLellan, Robert, *Rob Mossgiel*. BBC Radio Play, broadcast 26 January 1959.

JOURNALS

The *Burns Chronicle* (established 1892), the annual of the Burns Federation, Kilmarnock, contains articles and essays on all aspects of the poet's writing and reputation.

Part VI:
Appendixes

Appendixes

APPENDIX A: PREFACE TO THE KILMARNOCK EDITION

The Preface to the Kilmarnock Edition of *Poems, Chiefly in the Scottish Dialect* – an edition of 612 copies, costing three shillings each, published by subscription, printed and issued by John Wilson on 31 July 1786 – determined the tone of the critical response to Burns. Though the poet had received a good educational grounding from John Murdoch and was well-versed in literature, he chose to project himself as a humble rustic bard (as he also appears in 'The Vision'). Disarming sophisticated critics in advance, Burns stressed his linguistic limitations, his grim circumstances 'amid the toil and fatigues of a labouring life', his artistic insecurity ('fear and trembling'), his inferiority to his Scots predecessors Ramsay and Fergusson. The book was duly received as the work of a social phenomenon. A notice in the *Edinburgh Magazine*, October 1786, cited the poet's 'untutored fancy' (CH, 64); a letter in the *Edinburgh Evening Courant*, November 1786, described the author as 'a common farmer [and] self-taught poet' (CH, 65); and, most influentially, Henry Mackenzie (*Lounger*, 9 December 1786) praised 'this Heaven-taught ploughman from his humble and unlettered station' (CH, 70). Viewed retrospectively the Preface was a promotional masterstroke, enabling a self-styled poetic primitive to be patronised by the intellectual elite of Edinburgh.

*   *   *

The following trifles are not the production of the Poet, who, with all the advantages of learned art, and perhaps amid the elegancies and idlenesses of upper life, looks down for a rural theme, with an eye to Theocrites or Virgil. To the Author of this, these and other celebrated names their countrymen are, in their original languages,

403

'A fountain shut up, and a book sealed'. Unacquainted with the necessary requisites for commencing Poet by rule, he sings the sentiments and manners, he felt and saw in himself and his rustic compeers around him, in his and their native language. Though a Rhymer from his earliest years, at least from the earliest impulses of the softer passions, it was not till very lately, that the applause, perhaps the partiality, of Friendship, wakened his vanity so far as to make him think any thing of his was worth showing; and none of the following works were ever composed with a view to the press. To amuse himself with the little creations of his own fancy, amid the toil and fatigues of a labouring life; to transcribe the various feelings, the love, the griefs, the hopes, the fears, in his own breast; to find some kind of counterpoise to the struggles of a world, always an alien scene, a task uncouth to the poetical mind; these were his motives for courting the Muses, and in these he found Poetry to be its own reward.

Now that he appears in the public character of an Author, he does it with fear and trembling. So dear is fame to the rhyming tribe, that even he, an obscure, nameless Bard, shrinks aghast, at the thought of being branded as 'An impertinent blockhead, obtruding his nonsense on the world; and because he can make a shift to jingle a few doggerel, Scotch rhymes together, looks upon himself as a Poet of no small consequence forsooth.'

It is an observation of that celebrated Poet [Shenstone], whose divine Elegies do honor to our language, our nation, and our species, that 'Humility has depressed many a genius to a hermit, but never raised one to fame.' If any Critic catches at the word genius, the Author tells him, once for all, that he certainly looks upon himself as a possest of some poetic abilities, otherwise his publishing in the manner he has done, would be a manoeuvre below the worst character, which, he hopes, his worst enemy will ever give him: but to the genius of a Ramsay, or the glorious dawnings of the poor, unfortunate Fergusson, he, with equal unaffected sincerity, declares, that, even in his highest pulse of vanity, he has not the most distant pretensions. These two justly admired Scotch Poets he has often had in his eye in the following pieces; but rather with a view to kindle at their flame, than for servile imitation.

To his Subscribers, the Author returns his most sincere thanks. Not the mercenary bow over a counter, but the heart-throbbing gratitude of the Bard, conscious how much he is indebted to Benevolence and Friendship, for gratifying him, if he deserves it, in that dearest wish of every poetic bosom – to be distinguished. He begs his readers, particularly the Learned and the Polite, who may honor him with a perusal, that they will make every allowance for Education and Circumstances of Life: but, if after a fair, candid, and impartial criticism, he shall stand convicted of Dulness and Nonsense, let him be done by, as he would in that case do by others – let him be condemned, without mercy, to contempt and oblivion.

APPENDIX B: DEDICATION TO THE NOBLEMEN OF GENTLEMEN OF THE CALEDONIAN HUNT

When Burns decided to bring out a second and enlarged edition of *Poems, Chiefly in the Scottish Dialect* he found John Wilson, the Kilmarnock printer of the first edition, indifferent to the venture so he decided on an Edinburgh production. On 7 December 1786, eight days after his first arrival in Edinburgh, Burns wrote to Gavin Hamilton, 'Through [the Earl of Glencairn's] influence it is inserted in the records of the Caledonian Hunt, that they universally, one & all, subscribe for the 2nd Edition' (CL, 66). This exclusive club of noblemen and country gentlemen subscribed for 100 copies and Burns duly dedicated the First Edinburgh Edition to them.

Proposals for the new edition were issued on 14 December 1786; 2,876 copies were subscribed for; and the volume was printed by William Smellie and published by William Creech, by subscription 'for the sole benefit of the author', on 17 April 1787. (As the edition was over-subscribed it was reset and reprinted almost immediately, the second form of the 1787 edition becoming known as the 'Stinking Burns' because of a misprinting of 'skinking' in the last stanza of 'Address to a Haggis'). The price of the First Edinburgh Edition was five shillings to subscribers, six shillings to other purchasers.

The fanciful dedication to the Caledonian Hunt is a fulsome variation on the theme announced in the Preface to the Kilmarnock Edition. Again Burns (with his 'wild, artless notes') is the poetic primitive but, since he is no longer unknown, he is more asertive: 'I was bred to the Plough, and am independent.' His attribution of heroic virtues to the Scottish gentry is at variance with many of his most powerful poems, but Burns was often ambivalent in his attitude to the aristocracy if sympathetic aristocrats were involved. The highly polished prose shows the poet trying, successfully, to seduce a responsive audience with a calculated performance

DEDICATION TO THE NOBLEMEN AND GENTLEMEN OF THE CALEDONIAN HUNT

My Lords and Gentlemen,

A Scotch Bard, proud of the name, and whose highest ambition is to sing in his Country's service, where shall he so properly look for patronage as to the illustrious names of his native Land; those who bear the honours and inherit the virtues of their Ancestors? The Poetic Genius of my Country found me, as the prophetic bard Elijah did Elisha – at the Plough; and threw her inspiring mantle over me. She bade me sing the loves, the joys, the rural scenes and rural pleasures of my natal Soil, in my native tongue: I tuned my wild, artless notes, as she inspired. – She whispered me to come to this ancient Metropolis of Caledonia, and lay my Songs under your honoured protection: I now obey her dictates.

Though much indebted to your goodness, I do not approach you, my Lords and Gentlemen, in the usual style of dedication, to thank you for past favours: that path is so hackneyed by prostituted Learning, that honest Rusticity is ashamed of it. – Nor do I present this Address with the venal soul of a servile Author, looking for a continuation of those favours: I was bred to the Plough, and am independent. I come to claim the common Scottish name with you, my illustrious Countrymen; and to tell the world that I glory in the title. – I come to congratulate my Country, that the blood of her ancient heroes still runs uncontaminated; and that, from your courage, knowledge, and public spirit, she may expect protection, wealth, and liberty. – In the last place, I come to proffer my warmest wishes to the Great Fountain of Honour, the Monarch of the Universe, for your welfare and happiness.

When you go forth to waken the Echoes, in the ancient and favourite amusement of your Forefathers, may Pleasure ever be of your party; and may Social Joy await your return! When harassed in courts or camps with the justlings of bad men and bad measures, may the honest consciousness of injured worth attend your return to your native seats; and may Domestic Happiness, with a smiling welcome, meet you at your gates! May Corruption shrink at your kindling indignant glance; and may tyranny in the Ruler, and licentiousness in the People, equally find you an inexorable foe!

I have the honour to be,
  With the sincerest gratitude and highest respect,
    MY LORDS AND GENTLEMEN
      Your most devoted humble servant,
        ROBERT BURNS

Edinburgh
April 4, 1787

APPENDIX C: THE AUTOBIOGRAPHICAL LETTER

The long Autobiographical Letter to Dr John Moore is the main source of all biographical speculation on Burns. According to the poet, describing it in a letter of 5 January 1788 to Mrs McLehose, 'it is truth, every word of it' (CL, 378). The original is in the British Library, the following text is from CL, 248–57.

Mauchline, 2nd August, 1787
Sir

For some months past I have been rambling over the country, partly on account of some little business I have to settle in various places; but of late I have been confined with some lingering complaints originating as I take it in the stomach. – To divert my spirits a little this miserable fog of Ennui, I have taken a whim to give you a history of MYSELF. – My name has made a small noise in the country; you have done me the honor to interest yourself very warmly in my behalf; and I think a faithful account of, what character of a man I am, and how I came by that character, may perhaps amuse you in an idle moment. – I will give you an honest narrative, though I know it will be at the expense of frequently being laughed at; for I assure you, Sir, I have, like Solomon whose character, excepting the trifling affair of WISDOM, I sometimes think I resemble, I have, I say, like him 'Turned my eyes to behold Madness and Folly;' [1] and like him too, frequently shaken hands with their intoxicating friendship. – In the very polite letter Miss Williams[2] did me the honor to write me, she tells me you have got a complaint in your eyes. – I pray to God that it may be removed; for considering that lady and you are my common friends, you will probably employ her to read this letter; and then goodnight to that esteem with which she was pleased to honor the Scotch Bard. – After you have perused these pages, should you think them trifling and impertinent, I only beg leave to tell you that the poor Author wrote them under some very twitching qualms of conscience, that, perhaps he was doing what he ought not to do: a predicament he has more than once been in before. –

I have not the most distant pretensions to what the pyecoated guardians of escutcheons call, A Gentlemen. – When at Edinburgh last winter, I got acquainted in the Herald's Office, and looking through that granary of Honors I there found almost every name in the kingdom; but for me,

'– My ancient but ignoble blood
Has crept thro' Scoundrels ever since the flood' – [3]

Gules, Purpure, Argent, &c. quite disowned me. – My Fathers rented land of the noble Keiths of Marshal, and had the honor to share their fate. – I do not use the word, Honor, with any reference to Political principles; loyal and disloyal I take to be merely relative terms in that ancient and formidable court known in this Country by the name of CLUB-LAW. – Those who dare welcome Ruin and shake hands with Infamy for what they sincerely believe to be the cause of their God or their King – 'Brutus and Cassius are honorable men.' [4] – I mention this circumstance because it threw my father on the world at large; where after many years' wanderings and sojournings, he pickt up a pretty large quantity of Observation and Experience, to which I am indebted for most of my little pretensions to wisdom. – I have met with few who understood 'Men, their manners and their ways' [5] equal to him; but stubborn, ungainly Integrity, and headlong, ungovernable Irrascibility are disqualifying circumstances: consequently I was born a very poor man's son. – For the first six or seven years of my life, my father was gardiner to a worthy gentleman of small estate in the neighbourhood of Ayr. – Had my father continued in that situation, I must have marched off to be one of the little underlings about a farm-house; but it was his dearest wish and prayer to have it in his power to keep his children under his own eye till they could discern between good and evil; so with the assistance of his generous Master my father ventured on a small farm in his estate. – At these years I was by no means a favorite with any body. – I was a good deal noted for a retentive memory, a stubborn, sturdy something in my disposition, and an enthusiastic, idiot – I say idiot piety, because I was then but a child. – Though I cost the schoolmaster some thrashings, I made an excellent English scholar, and against the years of ten or eleven, I was absolutely a Critic in substantives, verbs and particles. – In my infant and boyish days too, I owed much to an old Maid of my Mother's,[6] remarkable for her ignorance, credulity and superstition. – She had, I suppose, the largest collection in the country of tales and songs concerning devils, ghosts, fairies, brownies, witches, warlocks, spunkies, kelpies, elf candles, dead-lights, wraiths, apparitions, cantraips, giants, inchanted towers, dragons and other trumpery. – This cultivated the latent seeds of Poesy; but had so strong an effect on my imagination, that to this hour, in my nocturnal rambles, I sometimes keep a sharp look-out in suspicious places; and though nobody can be more sceptical in these matters than I, yet it often takes an effort of Philosophy to shake off idle terrors. – The earliest thing of Composition that I recollect taking pleasure in was, The vision of Mirza[7] and a hymn of Addison's beginning – 'How are Thy servants blest, O Lord!' I particularly remember one half-stanza which was music to my boyish ear –

'For though in dreadful whirls we hung,
High on the broken wave' –

I met these pieces in Masson's English Collection, one of my school-books. [8] – The two first books I ever read in private, and which gave me more pleasure than any two books I ever read again, were, the life of Hannibal and the history of Sir William Wallace.[9] – Hannibal gave my young ideas such a turn that I used to strut in raptures up and down after the recruiting drum and bagpipe, and wish myself tall enough to be a soldier; while the story of Wallace poured a Scotish prejudice in my veins which will boil along there till the flood-gates of life shut in eternal rest. – Polemical divinity about this time was putting the country half-mad; and I, ambitious of shining in conversation parties on sundays between sermons, funerals, &c. used in a few years more to puzzle Calvinism with so much heat and indiscretion that I raised a hue and cry of heresy against me which has not ceased to this hour. –

My vicinity to Ayr was of great advantage to me. – My social disposition, when not checked by some modification of spited pride, like our catechism definition of Infinitude, was 'without bounds or limits.' – I formed many connections with other Youngkers who possessed superior advantages; the youngling Actors who were busy with the rehearsal of PARTS in which they were shortly to appear on that STAGE where, Alas! I was destined to druge behind the SCENES. – It is not commonly at these green years that the young Noblesse and gentry have a just sense of the immense distance between them and their ragged Playfellows. – It takes a few dashes into the world to give the young Great man that proper, decent, unnoticing disregard for the poor, insignificant, stupid devils, the mechanics and peasantry around him; who perhaps were born in the same village. – My young Superiours never insulted the clouterly appearance of my ploughboy carcase, the two extremes of which were often exposed to all the inclemencies of all the seasons. – They would give me stray volumes of books; among them, even then, I could pick up some observations; and ONE, whose heart I am sure not even the MUNNY BEGUM'S scenes have tainted, helped me to a little French. – Parting with these, my young friends and benefactors, as they dropped off for the east or west Indies, was often to me a sore affliction; but I was soon called to more serious evils. – My father's generous Master died; the farm proved a ruinous bargain; and, to clench the curse, we fell into the hands of a Factor who sat for the picture I have drawn of one of my Tale of two dogs.[10] – My father was advanced in life when he married; I was the eldest of seven children; and he, worn out by early hardship, was unfit for labour. – My father's spirit was soon irritated, but not easily broken. – There was a freedom in his lease in two years more, and to weather these two years we retrenched expences. – We lived very poorly; I was a dextrous Ploughman for my years; and the next eldest to me was a brother, who could drive the plough very well and help me to thrash. – A Novel-Writer might perhaps have viewed these scenes with some satisfaction, but so did not I: My indignation yet boils at the recollection of the scoundrel tyrant's insolent, threatening epistles, which used to set us all in tears. –

This kind of life, the chearless gloom of a hermit with the unceasing moil of a galley-slave, brought me to my sixteenth year; a little before which period I first committed the sin of RHYME. – You know our country custom of coupling a man and woman together as Partners in the labors of Harvest. – In my fifteenth autumn, my Partner was a bewitching creature who just counted an autumn less.[11] – My scarcity of English denies me the power of doing her justice in that language; but you know the Scotch idiom, She was a bonie, sweet, sonsie lass. – In short, she altogether unwittingly to herself, initiated me in a certain delicious Passion, which in spite of acid Disappointment, gin-horse Prudence and bookworm Philosophy, I hold to be the first of human joys, our dearest pleasure here below. – How she caught the contagion I can't say; you medical folks talk much of infection by breathing the same air, the touch, &c. but I never expressly told her that I loved her. – Indeed I did not well know myself, why I liked so much to loiter behind with her, when returning in the evening from our labors; why the tones of her voice made my heartstrings thrill like an Eolian harp; and particularly, why my pulse beat such a furious ratann when I looked and fingered over her hand, to pick out the nettle-stings and thistles. – Among her other love-inspiring qualifications, she sung sweetly; and 'twas her favorite reel[12] to which I attempted giving an embodied vehicle in rhyme. – I was not so presumptive as to imagine that I could make verses like printed ones, composed by men who had Greek and Latin; but my girl sung a song which was said to be composed by a small country laird's son, on one of his father's maids, with whom he was in love; and I saw no reason why I might not rhyme as well as he, for excepting smearing sheep and casting peats, his father living in the moors, he had no more Scholarcraft than I had. –

Thus with me begn Love and Poesy; which at times have been my only, and till within this last twelvemonth have been my highest enjoyment. – My father struggled on till he reached the freedom in his lease, when he entered on a larger farm[13] about ten miles farther in the country. – The nature of the bargain was such as to throw a little ready money in his hand at the commencement, otherwise the affair would have been impractible. – For four years we lived comfortably here; but a lawsuit between him and his Landlord commencing, after three years tossing and whirling in the vortex of Litigation, my father was just saved from absorption in a jail by phthisical consumption, which after two years promises, kindly stept in and snatch'd him away. – 'To where the wicked cease from troubling, and where the weary be at rest.'[14] –

It is during this climacterick that my little story is most eventful. – I was, at the beginning of this period, perhaps the most ungainly,

aukward being in the parish. – No Solitaire was less acquainted
with the ways of the world. – My knowledge of ancient story was
gathered from Salmon's and Guthrie's geographical grammars;
my knowledge of modern manners, and of literature and criticism, I got from the Spectator. – These, with Pope's works, some
plays of Shakespear, Tull and Dickson on Agriculture, The Pantheon, Locke's Essay on the human understanding, Stackhouse's
history of the bible, Justice's British Gardiner's directory, Boyle's
lectures, Allan Ramsay's works, Taylor's scripture doctrine of
original sin, a select Collection of English songs, and Hervey's
meditations had been the extent of my reading.[15] – The Collection
of Songs was my vade mecum. – I pored over them, driving my
cart or walking to labor, song by song, verse by verse; carefully
noting the true tender or sublime from affectation and fustian.
– I am convinced I owe much to this for my critic-craft such
as it is. –

In my seventeenth year, to give my manners a brush, I went
to a country dancing school.[16] – My father had an unaccountable
antipathy against these meetings; and my going was, what to
this hour I repent, in absolute defiance of his commands. – My
father, as I said before, was the sport of strong passions: from
that instance of rebellion he took a kind of dislike to me, which,
I believe was one cause of that dissipation which marked my
future years. – I only say, Dissipation, comparative with the
strictness and sobriety of Presbyterean country life; for though
the will-o'-wisp meteors of thoughtless Whim were almost the
sole lights of my path, yet early ingrained Piety and Virtue
never failed to point me out the line of Innocence. – The great
misfortune of my life was, never to have AN AIM. – I had felt
early some stirrings of Ambition, but they were the blind gropings
of Homer's Cyclops round the walls of his cave: I saw my father's
situation entailed on me perpetual labor. – The only two doors by
which I could enter the fields of fortune were, the most niggardly
economy, or the little chicaning art of bargain-making; the first
is so contracted an aperture, I never could squeeze myself into
it; the last, I always hated the contamination of the threshold. –
Thus, abandoned of aim or view in life; with a strong appetite
for sociability, as well from native hilarity as from a pride of
observation and remark; a constitutional hypochondriac taint
which made me fly solitude; add to all these incentives to social
life, my reputation for bookish knowledge, a certain wild, logical

talent, and a strength of thought something like the rudiments of good sense, made me generally a welcome guest; so 'tis no great wonder that always 'where two or three were met together, there was I in the midst of them.'[17] – But far beyond all the other impulses of my heart was, un penchant á l'adorable moitiée du genre humain. – My heart was compleatly tinder, and was eternally lighted up by some Goddess or other; and like every warfare in this world, I was sometimes crowned with success, and sometimes mortified with defeat. – At the plough, scythe or reap-hook I feared no competitor, and set Want at defiance: and as I never cared farther for my labors than while I was in actual exercise, I spent the evening in the way after my own heart. – A country lad rarely carries on an amour without an assisting confident. – I possessed a curiosity, zeal and intrepid dexterity in these matters which recommended me a proper Second in duels of that kind; and I dare say, I felt as much pleasure at being in the secret of half the armours in the parish, as ever did Premier at knowing the intrigues of half the courts of Europe. –

The very goosefeather in my hand seems instinctively to know the well-worn path of my imagination, the favourite theme of my song; and is with difficulty restrained from giving you a couple of paragraphs on the amours of my Compeers, the humble Inmates of the farm-house and cottage; but the grave sons of Science, Ambition or Avarice baptize these things by the name of Follies. – To the sons and daughters of labor and poverty they are matters of the most serious nature: to them, the ardent hope, the stolen interview, the tender farewell, are the greatest and most delicious part of their enjoyments. –

Another circumstance in my life which made very considerable alterations in my mind and manners was, I spent my seventeenth[18] summer on a smuggling coast a good distance from home at a noted school,[19] to learn Mensuration, Surveying, Dialling, &c. in which I made a pretty good progress. – But I made greater progress in the knowledge of mankind. – The contraband trade was at that time very successful; scenes of swaggering riot and roaring dissipation were as yet new to me; and I was no enemy to social life. – Here, though I learned to look unconcernedly on a large tavern-bill, and mix without fear in a drunken squabble, yet I went on with a high hand in my Geometry; till the sun entered Virgo, a month which is always a carnival in my bosom, a charming Fillette[20] who lived next door to the school overset

my Trigonometry and set me off in a tangent from the sphere
of my studies. – I struggled on with my Sines and Co-sines for
a few days more; but stepping out to the garden one charming
noon, to take the sun's altitude, I met with my Angel,

> – 'Like Proserpine gathering flowers,
>   Herself a fairer flower' – 21

It was vain to think of doing any more good at school. – The
remaining week I staid, I did nothing but craze the faculties of
my soul about her, or steal out to meet with her; and the two last
nights of my stay in the country, had sleep been a mortal sin, I
was innocent. –

I returned home very considerably improved. – My reading
was enlarged with the very important addition of Thomson's
and Shenstone's works; I had seen mankind in a new phasis;
and I engaged several of my schoolfellows to keep up a literary
correspondence with me. – This last helped me much on in
composition. – I had met with a collection of letters by the Wits
of Queen Ann's reign, and I pored over them most devoutly. –
I kept copies of any of my own letters that pleased me, and a
comparison between them and the composition of most of my
correspondents flattered my vanity. – I carried this whim so far
that though I had not three farthings worth of business in the
world, yet every post brought me as many letters as if I had been
a broad, plodding son of Day-book & Ledger. –

My life flowed on much in the same tenor till my twenty third
year. – Vive l'amour et vive la bagatelle, were my sole principles
of action. – The addition of two more Authors to my library gave
me great pleasure; Sterne and Mckenzie. – Tristram Shandy and
the Man of Feeling were my bosom favorites.–Poesy was still a
darling walk for my mind, but 'twas only the humour of the
hour. – I had usually half a dozen or more pieces on hand; I
took up one or other as it suited the momentary tone of this
mind, and dismissed it as it bordered on fatigue. – My Passions
when once they were lighted up, raged like so many devils, till
they got vent in rhyme; and then conning over my verses, like a
spell, soothed all into quiet. – None of the rhymes of those days
are in print, except, Winter, a dirge, the eldest of my printed
pieces; The death of Poor Mailie, John Barleycorn, And songs
first, second and third: song second was the ebullition of that
passion which ended the forementioned school-business. –

My twenty third year was to me an important era. – Partly thro' whim, and partly that I wished to set about doing something in life, I joined with a flax-dresser in a neighbouring town, to learn his trade and carry on the business of manufacturing and retailing flax.[22] – This turned out a sadly unlucky affair. – My Partner was a scoundrel of the first water who made money by the mystery of thieving; and to finish the whole, while we were giving a welcoming carousal to the New year, our shop, by the drunken carelessness of my Partner's wife, took fire and was burnt to ashes; and left me like a true Poet, not worth sixpence. – I was oblidged to give up business; the clouds of misfortune were gathering thick round my father's head, the darkest of which was, he was visibly far gone in a consumption; and to crown all, a belle-fille[23] whom I adored and who had pledged her soul to meet me in the field of matrimony, jilted me with peculiar circumstances of mortification. – The finishing evil that brought up the rear of this infernal file was my hypochondriac complaint being irritated to such a degree, that for three months I was in diseased state of body and mind, scarcely to be envied by the hopeless wretches who have just got their mittimus, 'Depart from me, ye Cursed.'[24] –

From this adventure I learned something of a town-life. – But the principal thing which gave my mind a turn was, I formed a bosom-friendship with a young fellow, the first created being I had ever seen, but a hapless son of misfortune.[25] – He was the son of a plain mechanic; but a great Man in the neighbourhood taking him under his patronage gave him a genteel education with a view to bettering his situation in life. – The Patron dieing just as he was ready to launch forth into the world, the poor fellow in despair went to sea; where after a variety of good and bad fortune, a little before I was acquainted with him, he had been set ashore by an American Privateer on the wild coast of Connaught, stript of every thing. – I cannot quit this poor fellow's story without adding that he is at this moment Captain of a large westindiaman belonging to the Thames. –

This gentleman's mind was fraught with courage, independance, Magnanimity, and every noble, manly virtue. – I loved him, I admired him, to a degree of enthusiasm; and I strove to imitate him. – In some measure I succeeded: I had the pride before, but he taught it to flow in proper channels. – His knowledge of the world was vastly superiour to mine, and I was all attention to learn. – He was the only man I ever saw who was a greater fool than myself when WOMAN was the presiding star; but he spoke of a certain fashionable failing with levity, which hitherto I had regarded with horror. – Here his friendship did me a mischief; and the consequence was, that soon after I resumed the plough, I wrote the WELCOME inclosed.[26] – My reading was only encreased by two stray volumes of Pamela, and one of Ferdinand Count Fathom, which gave me some idea of Novels. – Rhyme, except some religious pieces which are in print, I had given up; but meeting with Fergusson's Scotch Poems,[27] I strung anew my wildly-sounding, rustic lyre with emulating vigour. – When my father died, his all went among the rapacious hell-hounds that growl in the kennel of justice; but we made a shift to scrape a little money in the family amongst us, with which, to keep us together, my brother and I took a neighbouring farm.[28] – My brother wanted my harebrained imagination as well as my social and amorous madness, but in good sense and every sober qualification he was far my superior. –

I entered on this farm with a full resolution, 'Come, go to, I will be wise!'[29] – I read farming books; I calculated crops; I attended markets; and in short, in spite of 'The devil, the world and the flesh,' I believe I would have been a wise man; but the first year from unfortunately buying in bad seed, the second from a late harvest, we lost half of both our crops; this overset all my wisdom, and I returned 'Like the dog to his vomit, and the sow that was washed to her wallowing in the mire – '.[30]

I now began to be known in the neighbourhood as a maker of rhymes.–The first of my poetic offspring that saw the light was a burlesque lamentation on a quarrel between two reverend Calvinists, both of them dramatis personae in my Holy Fair[31] – I had an idea myself that the piece had some merit; but to prevent the worst, I gave a copy of it to a friend who was very fond of these things, and told him I could not guess who was the Author of it, but that I thought it pretty clever. – With a certain side of both clergy and laity it met with a roar of applause. – Holy Willie's Prayer next made its appearance, and alarmed the kirk-Session so much that they held three several meetings to look over their holy artillery, if any of it was pointed against profane Rhymers. – Unluckily for me, my idle wanderings led me, on another side, point blank within the reach of their heaviest metal. – This is the unfortunate story alluded to in my printed poem, The Lament.[32]

– 'Twas a shocking affair, which I cannot yet bear to recollect; and had very nearly given me one or two of the principal qualifications for the place among those who have lost the chart and mistake the reckoning of Rationality. – I gave up my part of the farm to my brother, as in truth it was only nominally mine; and made what little preparation was in my power for Jamaica. – Before leaving my native country for ever, I resolved to publish my Poems.[33] – I weighed my productions as impartially as in my power; I thought they had merit; and 'twas a delicious idea that I would be called a clever fellow, even though it should never reach my ears a poor Negro-driver, or perhaps a victim to that inhospitable clime gone to the world of Spirits. – I can truly say that pauvre Inconnu as I then was, I had pretty nearly as high an idea of myself and my works as I have at this moment. – It is ever my opinion that the great, unhappy mistakes and blunders, both in a rational and religious point of view, of which we see thousands daily guilty, are owing to their ignorance, or mistaken notions of themselves. – To know myself had been all along my constant study. – I weighed myself alone, I balanced myself with others; I watched every means of information how much ground I occupied both as a Man and as a Poet: I studied assiduously Nature's DESIGN where she seem'd to have intended the various LIGHTS and SHADES in my character. – I was pretty sure my Poems would meet with some applause; but at the worst, the roar of the Atlantic would deafen the voice of Censure, and the novelty of west-Indian scenes make me forget Neglect. –

I threw off six hundred copies, of which I had got subscriptions for about three hundred and fifty. – My vanity was highly gratified by the reception I met with from the Publick; besides pocketing, all expences deducted, near twenty pounds. – This last came very seasonable, as I was about to indent myself for want of money to pay my freight. – So soon as I was master of nine guineas, the price of wafting me to the torrid zone, I bespoke a passage in the very first ship that was to sail, for

'Hungry ruin had me in the wind' – [34]

I had for some time been sculking from covert to covert under all the terrors of a Jail; as some ill-advised, ungrateful people had uncoupled the merciless legal Pack at my heels. – I had taken the last farewell of my few friends; my chest was on the road to Greenock; I had composed my last song I should ever measure in

Caledonia. – 'The gloomy night is gathering fast,' when a letter
from Dr. Blacklock to a friend of mine overthrew all my schemes
by rousing my poetic ambition.[35] – The Doctor belonged to a set
of Critics for whose applause I had not even dared to hope. – His
idea that I would meet with every encouragement for a second
edition fired me so much that away I posted to Edinburgh without
a single acquaintance in town, or a single letter of introduction in
my pocket. – The baneful Star that had so long shed its blasting
influence in my Zenith, for once made a revolution to the Nadir;
and the providential care of a good God placed me under the
patronage of one of his noblest creatures, the Earl of Glencairn:
'Oublie moi, Grand Dieu, si jamais je l'oublie!' –
    I need relate no farther. – At Edinburgh I was in a new world:
I mingled among many classes of men, but all of them new to
me; and I was all attention 'to catch the manners living as they
rise.' –[36]
    You can now, Sir, form a pretty near guess what sort of
a Wight he is whom for some time you have honored with
your correspondence. – That Fancy & Whim, keen Sensibility
and riotous Passions may still make him zig-zag in his future
path of life, is far from being improbable; but come what will, I
shall answer for him the most determinate integrity and honor;
and though his evil star should again blaze in his meridian with
tenfold more direful influence, he may reluctantly tax Friendship
with Pity but no more. –
    My most respectful Compliments to Miss Williams. – Her
elegant and friendly letter I cannot answer at present, as my
presence is requisite in Edinburgh, and I set off tomorrow. –
    If you will oblidge me so highly and do me so much honor
as now and then to drop me a letter, Please direct to me at
Mauchline, Ayrshire. –

I have the honor to be, Sir
your ever grateful humble servant
Robt Burns

APPENDIX D: GILBERT'S NARRATIVE

Gilbert Burns's informative memoir of his brother was originally written in 1797 as a letter to Mrs Dunlop, and thereafter included in various editions of Burns's works. It gives an excellent account of Burns's education and also defends him against the charge of drunkenness, perhaps for two reasons: Gilbert was writing to an easily offended lady (see her entry in 'The Burns Circle') and he was aware of malicious gossip about his brother (Robert Heron's 'Original Memoirs of the Late Robert Burns' was first published in the *Monthly Magazine and British Register*, January–June 1797). Only a year after the poet's death, Gilbert was anxious to bear witness to his brother's good character.

As most of the books cited by Gilbert are identified in the notes to the Autobiographical Letters, the endnotes are kept to a minimum in this case.

*   *   *

I have often heard my father describe the anguish of mind he felt when he parted with his elder brother Robert on the top of a hill, on the confines of their native place, each going off his several ways in search of new adventures, and scarcely knowing wither he went. My Father undertook to act as a gardener and shaped his course to Edinburgh, where he wrought hard when he could get work, passing through a variety of difficulties. Still, however, he endeavoured to spare something for the support of an aged parent, and I recollect hearing him mention his having sent a bank-note for this purpose, when money of that kind was so scarce in Kincardineshire, that they hardly knew how to employ it when it arrived.

Passing from Edinburgh into Ayrshire, he lived for two years as gardener to the laird of Fairly in Dundonald parish, and then changed his service for that of Mr Crawford of Doonside in the parish of Alloway. At length, being desirous to settle in life, he took a perpetual lease of some acres of land from Dr Campbell, physician in Ayr, with a view to cultivate it as a nursery and meal-garden. With his own hands he built a house on part of this ground, and in December 1757, married Agnes Brown, belonging to respectable connexions near Maybole in Carrick. The first fruit of the marriage was the subject of this memoir, born on 25th January 1759. The education of my brother and myself was in common, there being only twenty months between us, in respect of age. Under Mr John Murdoch we learned to read

English tolerably well, and to write a little. He taught us too the English grammar. I was too young to profit much from his lessons in grammar, but Robert made some proficiency in it, a circumstance of considerable weight in the unfolding of his genius and character; as he soon became remarkable for the fluency and correctness of his expression, and read the few books that came in his way with much pleasure and improvement; for even then he was a reader when he could get a book. Murdoch, whose library at that time had no great variety in it, lent him *The Life of Hannibal*, which was the first book he read (the school books excepted) and almost the only one he had an opportunity of reading while he was at school; for the *Life of Wallace* which he classes with it in one of his letters, he did not see for some years afterwards, when he borrowed it from the blacksmith who shod our horses.

At Whitsunday 1766 we removed to Mount Oliphant, a farm of seventy acres (between 80 and 90 English statute measure) the rent of which was to be forty pounds annually for the first six years, and afterwards forty-five pounds. My father endeavoured to sell the leasehold property in Alloway, for the purpose of stocking his farm, but at that time he was unable, and Mr Fergusson lent him a hundred pounds for that purpose. It was I think not above two years after this that Murdoch, our tutor and friend, left this part of the country, and there being no school near us, and our little services being useful on the farm, my Father undertook to teach us arithmetic in the winter evenings by candlelight, and in this way my two elder sisters got all the education they received. I remember a circumstance that happened at this time, which, though trifling in itself, is fresh on my memory, and may serve to illustrate the early character of my brother. Murdoch came to spend a night with us, and to take his leave when he was about to go into Carrick. He brought us a present and memorial of him, a small compendium of English Grammar, and the tragedy of *Titus Andronicus*, and by way of passing the evening, he began to read the play aloud. We were all attention for some time, till presently the whole party was dissolved in tears. A female in the play (I have but a confused recollection of it) had her hands chopt off, her tongue cut out, and then was insultingly desired to call for water to wash her hands. At this, in an agony of distress, we with one voice desired he would read no more. My father observed that if we would not hear it out, it would be needless to leave the play with us. Robert replied that if it was left he would burn it. My father was going to chide him for this ungrateful return to his tutor's kindness; but Murdoch interposed, declaring that he liked to see so much sensibility; and he left the *School for Love* a comedy (translated I think from the French) in its place.

Nothing could be more retired than our general manner of living at Mount Oliphant; we rarely saw any body but the members of our own family. There were no boys of our own age, or near it, in the neighbourhood. Indeed the greater part of the land in the vicinity was at that time possessed by shopkeepers, and people of that stamp, who had retired from business, or who kept their farm in the country at the same time that they followed business in the town. My father was for some time almost the only companion we had. He conversed familiarly on all subjects with us as if we had been men, and was at great pains, while we accompanied him in the labours of the farm, to lead the conversation to such subjects as might tend to increase our knowledge, or confirm our virtuous habits. He borrowed Salmon's *Geographical Grammar* for us, and endeavoured to make us acquainted with the situation and history of the different countries in the world; while, from a book-society in Ayr, he procured for us Durham's *Phisico and Astro-Theology*, and Ray's *Wisdom of God in Creation*, to give us some idea of astronomy and natural history.[1] Robert read all these books with an avidity and industry scarcely to be equalled. My Father had been a subscriber to Stackhouse's *History of the Bible*, then lately published by John Meuros in Kilmarnock: from this Robert collected a pretty competent knowledge of ancient history: for no book was so voluminous as to slacken his industry, or so antiquated as to damp his researches. A brother of my mother who had lived with us some time, and had learned some arithmetic by our winter evening's candle, went into a bookseller's shop in Ayr, to purchase *The Ready Reckoner, or Tradesman's sure Guide*, and a book to teach him to write letters. Luckily, in place of *The Complete Letter-Writer*, he got by mistake a small collection of Letters by the most Eminent Writers, with a few sensible directions for attaining an easy epistolary style. This book was to Robert of the greatest consequence. It inspired him with a strong desire to excel in letter-writing, while it furnished him with models by some of the first writers in our language.

My brother was about thirteen or fourteen, when my father,

regretting that we wrote so ill, sent us week about during a summer quarter, to the parish school of Dalrymple, which, though between two and three miles distant, was the nearest to us, that we might have an opportunity of remedying this defect. About this time a bookish acquaintance of my father's procured us a reading of two volumes of Richardson's *Pamela*, which was the first novel we read, and the only part of Richardson's works my brother was acquainted with till towards the period of his commencing author. Till that time too he remained unacquainted with Fielding, with Smollett (two volumes of *Ferdinand Count Fathom*, and two volumes of *Peregrine Pickle* excepted), with Hume, with Robertson, and almost all our authors of eminence of the later times. I recollect indeed my father borrowed a volume of English history from Mr Hamilton of Bourtree-hill's gardener. It treated of the reign of James the First, and his unfortunate son, Charles, but I do not know who was the author; all that I remember of it is something of Charles's conversation with his children. About this time [1772] Murdoch, our former teacher, after having been in different places in the country, and having taught a school some time in Dumfries, came to be the established teacher of the English language in Ayr, a circumstance of considerable consequence to us. The remembrance of my father's former friendship, and his attachment to my brother, made him do every thing in his power for our improvement. He sent us Pope's works, and some other poetry, the first that we had an opportunity of reading, excepting what is contained in *The English Collection*, and in the volume of *The Edinburgh Magazine* for 1772; excepting also *those excellent new songs* that are hawked about the country in baskets, or exposed on stalls in the streets. The summer after we had been at Dalrymple school, my father sent Robert to Ayr, to revise his English grammar, with his former teacher. He had been there only one week, when he was obliged to return, to assist at the harvest. When the harvest was over, he went back to school, where he remained two weeks; and this completes the account of his school education, excepting one summer quarter, some time afterwards, that he attended the parish school of Kirk-Oswald (where he lived with a brother of my mother's), to learn surveying.

During the two last weeks that he was with Murdoch, he himself was engaged in learning French, and he communicated the instructions he received to my brother, who, when he returned, brought home with him a French dictionary and grammar, and the *Adventures of Telemachus* in the original. In a little while, by the assistance of these books, he had acquired such a knowledge of the language, as to read and understand any French author in prose. This was considered as a sort of prodigy, and, through the medium of Murdoch, procured him the acquaintance of several lads in Ayr, who were at that time gabbling French, and the notice of some families, particularly that of Dr Malcolm, where a knowledge of French was a recommendation.

Observing the facility with which he had acquired the French language, Mr Robinson, the established writing-master in Ayr, and Mr Murdoch's particular friend, having himself acquired a considerable knowledge of the Latin language by his own industry, without ever having learnt it at school, advised Robert to make the same attempt, promising him every assistance in his power. Agreeably to this advice, he purchased *The Rudiments of the Latin Tongue*, but finding this study dry and uninteresting, it was quickly laid aside. He frequently returned to his *Rudiments* on any little chagrin or disappointment, particularly in his love affairs; but the Latin seldom predominated more than a day or two at a time, or a week at most. Observing himself the ridicule that would attach to this sort of conduct if it were known, he made two or three humorous stanzas on the subject, which I cannot now recollect, but they all ended,

'So I'll to my Latin again.'

Thus you see Mr Murdoch was a principal means of my brother's improvement. Worthy man! though foreign to my present purpose, I cannot take leave of him without tracing his future history. He continued for some years a respected and useful teacher at Ayr, till one evening that he had been overtaken in liquor, he happened to speak somewhat disrespectfully of Dr Dalrymple, the parish minister, who had not paid him that attention to which he thought himself entitled. In Ayr he might as well have spoken blasphemy. He found it proper to give up his appointment. He went to London, where he still lives, a private teacher of French. He has been a considerable time married, and keeps a shop of stationery wares.

The father of Dr Paterson, now physician at Ayr, was, I believe, a native of Aberdeenshire, and was one of the established teachers in Ayr when my father settled in the neighbourhood. He early recognised my father as a fellow native of the north of Scotland, and a certain degree of intimacy subsisted between them during Mr Paterson's life. After his death, his widow, who is a very genteel woman, and of great worth, delighted in doing what she thought her husband would have wished to have done, and assiduously kept up her attentions to all his acquaintance. She kept alive the intimacy with our family, by frequently inviting my father and mother to her house on Sundays, when she met them at church.

When she came to know my brother's passion for books, she kindly offered us the use of her husband's library, and from her we got the *Spectator, Pope's Translation of Homer*, and several other books that were of use to us. Mount Oliphant, the farm my father possessed in the parish of Ayr, is almost the very poorest soil I know of in a state of cultivation. A stronger proof of this I cannot give, than that, notwithstanding the extraordinary rise in the value of lands in Scotland, it was, after a considerable sum laid out in improving it by the proprietor, let a few years ago five pounds per annum lower than the rent paid for it by my father thirty years ago. My father, in consequence of this, soon came into difficulties, which were increased by the loss of several of his cattle by accidents and disease. To the buffettings of misfortune, we could only oppose hard labour and the most rigid economy. We lived very sparingly. For several years butcher's meat was a stranger in the house, while all the members of the family exerted themselves to the utmost of their strength, and rather beyond it, in the labours of the farm. My brother, at the age of thirteen, assisted in threshing the crop of corn, and at fifteen was the principal labourer on the farm, for we had no hired servant, male or female. The anguish of mind we felt at our tender years under these straits and difficulties was very great. To think of our father growing old (for he was now above fifty) broken down with the long continued fatigues of his life, with a wife and five other children, and in a declining state of circumstances, these reflections produced in my brothers' mind and mine sensations of the deepest distress. I doubt not but the hard labour and sorrow of this period of his life, was in a great measure the cause of that depression of spirits, with which Robert was so often afflicted through his whole life afterwards. At this time he was almost constantly afflicted in the evenings with a dull headache, which, at a future period of his life, was exchanged for a palpitation of the heart, and a threatening of fainting and suffocation in his bed, in the night time.

By a stipulation in my father's lease, he had a right to throw it up, if he thought proper, at the end of every sixth year. He attempted to fix himself in a better farm at the end of the first six years, but failing in that attempt, he continued where he was for six more years. He then took the farm of Lochlea, of 130 acres, at the rent of twenty shillings an acre, in the parish of Tarbolton, of Mr —— 2, then a merchant in Ayr, and now a merchant in Liverpool. He removed to this farm at Whitsunday 1777, and possessed it only seven years. No writing had ever been made out of the conditions of the lease; a misunderstanding took place respecting them; the subjects in dispute were submitted to arbitration, and the decision involved my father's affairs in ruin. He lived to know of this decision, but not to see any execution in consequence of it. He died on the 13th of February, 1784.

The seven years we lived in Tarbolton parish (extending from the nineteenth to the twenty-sixth of my brother's age) were not marked by much literary improvement; but, during this time, the foundation was laid of certain habits in my brother's character, which afterwards became but too prominent, and which malice and envy have taken delight to enlarge on. Though when young he was bashful and awkward in his intercourse with women, yet when he approached manhood, his attachment to their society became very strong, and he was constantly the victim of some fair enslaver. The symptoms of his passion were often such as nearly to equal those of the celebrated Sappho. I never indeed knew that he *fainted, sunk, and died away*: but the agitation of his mind and body exceeded anything of the kind I ever knew in real life. He had always a particular jealousy of people who were richer than himself, or who had more consequence in life. His love, therefore, rarely settled on persons of this description. When he selected any one out of the sovereignty of his good pleasure to whom he should pay his particular attention, she was instantly invested with a sufficient stock of charms, out of the plentiful stores of his own imagination; and there was often a great disparity between his fair captivator, and her attributes. One generally reigned paramount in his affections; but as Yorick's affections flowed out toward Madame de L—— at the remise door, while the eternal vows of Eliza were upon him, so Robert was frequently encountering other attractions, which formed so many under-plots in the drama of his love. As these connexions were governed by the strictest rules of virtue and modesty (from which he never deviated till he reached his twenty-third year), he became anxious to be in a situation to marry. This was not likely to be soon the case while he remained a farmer, as the stocking of a farm required a sum of money he had no probability of being master of for a great while. He began, therefore, to think of trying some other line of life. He and I had for several years taken land of my father for the purpose of raising flax on our own account. In the course of selling it, Robert began to think of turning flax-dresser, both as being suitable to his grand view of settling in life, and as subservient to the flax raising. He accordingly wrought at the business of a flax-dresser in Irvine for six months, but abandoned it at that period, as neither agreeing with his health nor inclination. In Irvine he had contracted some acquaintance of a freer manner of thinking and living than he had been used to, whose society prepared him for over-leaping the bounds of rigid virtue which had hitherto restrained him. Towards the end of the period under review (in his twenty-sixth year), and soon after his father's death, he was furnished with the subject of his Epistle to John Rankin. During this period also he became a freemason, which was his first introduction to the life of a boon companion. Yet, notwithstanding these circumstances, and the praise he has bestowed on Scotch drink (which seems to have misled his historians), I do not recollect, during these seven years, nor till towards the end of his commencing author, (when his growing celebrity occasioned his being often in company) to have ever seen him intoxicated; nor was he at all given to drinking. A stronger proof of the general sobriety of his conduct need not be required, than what I am about to give. During the whole of the time we lived in the farm of Lochlea with my father, he allowed my brother and me such wages for our labour as he gave to other labourers, as a part of which, every article of our clothing manufactured in the family was regularly accounted for. When my father's affairs grew near a crisis, Robert and I took the farm of Mossgiel, consisting of 118 acres, at the rent of £90 per annum (the farm on which I live at present), from Mr Gavin Hamilton, as an asylum for the family in case of the worst. It was stocked by the property and individual savings of the whole family, and was a joint concern among us. Every member of the family was allowed ordinary wages for the labour he performed on the farm. My brother's allowance and mine was seven pounds per annum each. And during the whole time this family concern lasted, which was four years, as well as during the preceding period at Lochlea, his expenses never in any one year exceeded his slender income. As I was intrusted with the keeping of the family accounts, it is not possible that there can be any fallacy in this statement in my brother's favour. His temperance and frugality were everything that could be wished.

The farm of Mossgiel lies very high, and mostly on a cold wet bottom. The first two years that we were on the farm were very frosty, and the spring was very late. Our crops in consequence were very unprofitable, and notwithstanding our utmost diligence and economy, we found ourselves obliged to give up our bargain, with the loss of a considerable part of our original stock. It was during these two years that Robert formed his connexion with Jean Armour, afterwards Mrs Burns. This connexion could no longer be concealed, about the time we came to a final determination to quit the farm. Robert durst not engage with a family in his poor unsettled state, but was anxious to shield his partner by every means in his power from the consequences of their imprudence. It was agreed therefore between them that they should make a legal acknowledgement of an irregular and private marriage, that he should go to Jamaica to push his fortune, and that she should remain with her father till it might please Providence to put the means of supporting a family in his power.

Mrs Burns was a great favourite of her father's. The intimation of a marriage was the first suggestion he received of her real situation. He was in the greatest distress, and fainted away. The marriage did not appear to him to make the matter any better. A husband in Jamaica seemed to him and to his wife little better than none, and an effectual bar to any other prospects of a settlement in life that their daughter might have. They therefore expressed a wish to her that the written papers which respected the marriage should be cancelled, and thus the marriage rendered void. In her melancholy state, she felt the deepest remorse at having brought such heavy affliction on parents that loved her so tenderly, and she submitted to their entreaties. This wish was mentioned to Robert, he felt the deepest anguish of mind. He offered to stay at home and provide for his wife and family in the best manner that his daily labours could provide for them; that being the only means in his power. Even this offer they did not approve of; for humble as Miss Armour's station was, and great though her imprudence had been, she still, in the eyes of her partial parents, might look to a better connexion than with my friendless and unhappy brother, at that time without house or hiding-place. Robert at length consented to their wishes, but his feelings on this occasion were of the most distracting nature, and the impression of sorrow was not effaced, till by a regular marriage they were indissolubly united. In the state of mind which the separation produced, he wished to leave the country as soon as possible, and agreed with Dr Douglas [3] to go out to Jamaica, as an assistant over-seer, or as I believe it is called, a book-keeper, on his estate. As he had not sufficient money to pay his passage, and the vessel in which Dr Douglas was to procure a passage for him was not expected to sail for some time, Mr Hamilton advised him to publish his poems in the meantime by subscription, as a likely way of getting a little money to provide him more liberally in necessaries for Jamaica. Agreeably to this advice, subscription bills were printed immediately, and the printing was commenced in Kilmarnock, his preparations going on at the same time for his voyage. The reception however which his poems met with in the world, and the friends they procured him, made him change his resolution of going to Jamaica, and he was advised to go to Edinburgh to publish a second edition. On his return in happier circumstances, he renewed his connexion with Mrs Burns, and rendered it permanent by an union for life.

NOTES TO APPENDIX C

1. Ecclesiastes 2:12. 'And I turned myself to behold wisdom, and madness, and folly . . . '
2. Helen Maria Williams, English writer and friend of Dr Moore. See her entry in 'The Burns Circle'.
3. Alexander Pope, *An Essay on Man*, 1V, 211.
4. Shakespeare, *Julius Caesar*, III, ii.
5. Alexander Pope, *January and May*, 1.157.
6. Betty Davidson, a familiar figure in the cottage William

Burnes built at Alloway. See her entry in 'The Burns Circle'.

7. Joseph Addison's allegory *The Vision of Mirzah* sees life as a bridge over which multitudes move.

8. Arthur Masson, *A Collection of Prose and Verse, from the Best English Authors – For the Use of Schools.*

9. The book on Hannibal, lent to Burns by Murdoch, cannot be identified. The history of Wallace was Blind Harry's *Wallace* as abridged and Anglicised by William Hamilton of Gilbertfield in his edition of 1722.

10. Provost William Fergusson of Ayr, who rented Mount Oliphant to William Burns, died on 7 November 1769 and his affairs were handled by a Factor.

11. Nelly Kilpatrick, celebrated by Burns in his first song; in his first Common Place Book; in the Autobiographical Letter; and in his poem 'To the Guildwife of Wauchope-House'. See her entry in 'The Burns Circle'.

12. Burns's lyric is matched to the tune 'I am a man unmarried'.

13. Lochlea farm, rented by William Burnes from 1777 until his death in 1784.

14. Job 3:17. 'There the wicked cease *from* troubling; and there the weary be at rest.'

15. Burns's reading list includes Thomas Salmon, *A New Geographical and Historical Grammar*; William Guthrie, *A New Geographical, Historical and Commercial Grammar*; Jethro Tull, *The Horse-Hoing Husbandry: or an Essay on the Principles of Tillage and Vegetation*; Adam Dickson, *A Treatise on Agriculture*; Andrew Tooke, *Pantheon*; John Locke, *Essay Concerning Human Understanding*; Thomas Stackhouse, *A New History of the Holy Bible*; William Derham's *Physico-Theology* and *Astro-Theology* [these two being the 'Boyle's lectures' mentioned by Burns]; John Taylor, *Scripture Doctrine of Original Sin*; James Hervey, *Meditations among the Tombs*. The collection of songs was *The Lark* (1765).

16. The country dancing school was in Tarbolton, 1777.

17. Matthew 18:20. 'For where two or three are gathered together in my name, there am I in the midst of them.'

18. 'seventeenth' deleted and 'nineteenth or twentieth' substituted in another hand.

19. Hugh Rodger's school, Kirkoswald, where Burns studied in the summer of 1775.

20. Peggy Thomson, see her entry in 'The Burns Circle'.
21. John Milton, *Paradise Lost*, IV, 11.269–70. 'where Prosperine gathering flowers/Herself a fairer Flower'.
22. Burns went to Irvine, to learn the flax trade, in the spring of 1781.
23. Alison Begbie, see her entry in 'The Burns Circle'.
24. Matthew 26:41. 'Then shall he say also unto them on the left hand, Depart from me, ye cursed, into everlasting fire, prepared for the devil and his angels.'
25. Richard Brown, see his entry in 'The Burns Circle'.
26. 'A Poet's Welcome to his Love-Begotten Daughter'. This is addressed to the poet's first illegitimate child, Elizabeth, who was born on 22 May 1785, the outcome of Burns's affair in the winter of 1783–4 with Elizabeth Paton, see her entry in 'The Burns Circle'.
27. Burns owned a copy of the Second Edition of Robert Fergusson's *Poems* (1782).
28. Mossgiel which Burns and his brother Gilbert moved into in March 1784.
29. Ecclesiastes 7:23. 'All this have I proved by wisdom: I said, I will be wise; but it *was* far from me.'
30. 2 Peter 2:22. 'The dog *is* turned to his own vomit again; and the sow that was washed to her wallowing in the mire.'
31. Rev Alexander Moodie and Rev John Russell, two Auld Licht ministers mentioned in 'The Holy Fair', are featured as the antagonists in 'The Twa Herds: or, The Holy Tulzie' – an account of their doctrinal squabble.
32. 'The Lament', included in the Kilmarnock Edition, deals with Burns's despair at his treatment following his affair with Jean Armour: on learning, in March 1786, that his daughter was pregnant by Burns, James Armour repudiated the poet and had his marriage attestation mutilated.
33. The Kilmarnock Edition.
34. Not identified.
35. Dr Blacklock's letter of 4 September 1786 was written to the Rev George Lawrie who sent it to Gavin Hamilton, who gave it to Burns.
36. Alexander Pope, *An Essay on Man*, I, l. 14. 'And catch the manners living as they rise.'

NOTES TO APPENDIX D

1. Gilbert's reference to 'Durham's *Phisico and Astro-Theology*'
    confusingly runs together two separate books by William
    Derham: *Physico-Theology* (1713) and *Astro-Theology* (1714).
    John Ray's *The Wisdom of God Manifested in the Works of the
    Creation* (1691) was frequently reprinted.
2. David McLure.
3. Dr Patrick Douglas of Garallan, see his entry in 'The Burns
    Circle'.

Glossary

The glossary gives the English equivalents of Scots words used by Burns – and other poets, such as Fergusson – in passages quoted in this Companion. Those with a specialist interest in Scots are referred to *The Scottish National Dictionary* (10 vols, Edinburgh, 1929–76) edited by William Grant and David D. Murison. Useful one-volume dictionaries are *Chambers's Scots Dictionary* (Edinburgh, 1911), compiled by Alexander Warrack; and *The Concise Scots Dictionary* (Aberdeen, 1985) edited by Mairi Robinson.

ae, one, a certain
a-fiel, in the field, outside
aiblins, perhaps
agley, askew
airn, iron
airt, direction, quarter
aith, oath
amaist, almost
ance, once
aqua-vitae, whisky, alcohol
aspar, with legs apart
aughtlins, anything, in the least
auld, old
awa, away
ay, always

ba', ball
backit, backed
backlins-comin, returning
bairn, child
bairn-time, all the offspring
   of one mother
baith, both
baggie, belly
bauckie-bird, bat
bauld, bold
baws'nt, having a white stripe
   down the face
bear, barley
beas, vermin
ben, indoors, within
besom, broom
bicker, beaker
bid, ask
bide, remain, await, stay for
bield, shelter
birkie, fellow
bizz, buzz
bizzing, dry
blastie, pest
blate, shy
blather, bladder

432

blaud, slap
blaw, blow
bleering, only half-seeing
bleezing, blazing
blether, chatter, talk foolishly
blethers, nonsense
bluid, blood
bogle, ghost, spectre, goblin
bolus, large medicinal pill
bonnock, bannock, round flat girdle-baked cake of oatmeal, barley, pease, or flour
boot, o, into the bargain, as well
bore, crevice, crack
brae, hillside
braid, broad
brats, scraps, rags
braw, fine, handsome
breeks, britches, trousers
brig, bridge
brose, oatmeal mixed with boiling water or milk, with salt and butter added
brunstane, brimstone
buirdly, stalwart, elegant
bum, hum
burdie, lady, girl (bird)
burn, brook
buskit, dressed
by-job, side-line (fornication)
byke, hive

caird, tinker
Caledon, Scotland
callan, stripling
callet, girlfriend
cankert, ill-natured
cannie, pleasant, gentle canty,
cantie, jolly, lively
cap-stane, coping stone
car, primitive wheeleless cart

carlin, old woman
cartes, cards
cauld, cold
chanter, song, part of bagpipe on which the melody is played
chap, strike
chiel, fellow
chimla lug, chimney-corner, side wall of chimney recess
chittering, shivering, trembling
clachan, village
claes, clothes
claise, clothes
clean-shankit, clean-limbed
cleg, horsefly
clink, cash
clips, shears
clishmaclavers, nonense
cloot, hoof
coof, fool
coost, cast
cootie, tub, dish
core, crowd
cosh, comfortable
coulter, ploughshare
cour, curb
couthy, sociable
cowpet, upset
craigie, craig, throat
craik, corncrake
cranreuch, hoar-frost
crap, top
creeshie, greasy, filthy
croose, cocksure
crowl, crawl
cuif, clown, fool, lout
cutty, short

daffin, fun
darg, work

daud, pelt
daur, dare
deal, divide, distribute
deil, devil
deil-haet, nothing, damn all (devil have it)
deil-mak-matter, no matter
dight, wipe, clean
dink, trim
ding, weary
divets, turfs
dochter, daughter
douce, sedate, sober
downa, cannot
doyt, stagger
drift, blown snow
drouthy, thirsty
dry-bob, masturbation
dub, puddle
dud, rag
duddie, ragged
duddies, rags
dunt, throb
durk, dirk, short Highland dagger worn in the belt
dyke, low dry-stone wall
dyvor, bankrupt

een, eyes
eldritch, unearthly, haunted

fain, content
fairin, reward
fallow, fellow
fash, bother
fause-house, conical frame of a haystack (literally, false house)
fauld, fold
faut, fault
fawsont, seemly

feat, spruce
ferlie, marvel, wonder
fidge, fidget
Fient haet, Devil have it
fiere, friend, comrade
fit, foot
flainen, flannel
flaffin, flapping
fley, terrify, frighten
fodgel, plump and good-humoured
foggage, coarse grass
forby(e), besides, as well as
forjesket, fatigued, worn out
fou, full, drunk
foughten, harassed, worn out
frae, from
fu, full
fyke, fidget

gab, mouth, chatter
gaed, went
gager, exciseman
gang, go
gangrel, vagabond
gar, make, compel
garten, garters
gash, shrewd, respectable
gate, way, road
gauger, exciseman
gear, wealth
Geordie, guinea
get, offspring, brat
ghaist, ghost
gie, give
gilly, vessel holding a gill
girdle, griddle
girn, grin, snarl
gled, buzzard, kite
gleg, quick, lively
glunch, sneer

goom, gum
gooset, gusset
gowan, daisy
gowff, golf
graff, grave
grain, groan
gree, social degree, supremacy
groat, small silver coin (four
 pence)
grun', ground, earth
gruntle, face
grushie, thriving, growing
gudeman, head of the
 household
guid-willie-waught, cup of
 kindness
guse-feathers, goose-quills
gut-scraper, fiddler

ha', hall
hae, have
haet, have it
haffet, side-lock of hair
haflins, halfway, partly
hairn, save
hairst, harvest
halland, wooden partition
haly, holy
hame, home
hap, hop
harkit, listened
hash, fool
haud, hold
hauf, half
hauffet, temple
haurl, drag
heels o'er gowdie, topsy-turvy
hizzie, wench, silly girl, whore
herryment, waste
hoddin, coarse grey homespun
 cloth of mixed black and

white wool
hog-shouther, push with the
 shoulder
hoodock, grasping
Hornie, the Devil
hotch, jerk about
houghmagandie, fornication
houlet, owl
houpe, hope
howe, hollow
hum, humbug
hurcheon, hedgehog
hurdies, buttocks

ilk, each
ilka, every
ingle, fire burning on a hearth
ingle-lowe, firelight
ither, other

jad, jade, hussy
jag-the-flae, contemptuous
 name for a tailor (lit.
 'pierce-the-fly')
jaw, dash
jowler, bulldog
jundie, jostle

kail, cabbage, broth
kain, dues
keckle, cackle
keek, peep
ken, know
kend, known
kennin, trifle
Kilbaigie, a Clackmananshire
 whisky distillery
kimmer, gossip
kin, kind
kittle, tickle
kittle, (adj) tricky, ticklish,

difficult
kiutle, caress, fondle
knaggie, knobbly
knappin-hammer, stone-
  breaking hammer
kythe, tell

lade, load
Lallans, Lowland Scots
lane, alone
langsyne, long ago
lap, leaped
lave, rest
lay, lea
leal, loyal
lear, learning
leeze . . . on, blessing
leuk, look
limmer, jade, mistress, whore
lintwhite, linnet
loof, palm
loot, let
loun, rogue, fellow
lowin, flaming
lug, ear
lunt, steam
lyart, withered, grizzled, grey

mae, more
mair, more
marled, parti-coloured
mashlum, maslin, mixed meal
maskin-pat, teapot
maukin bucks, buck hares
maun, must
meikle, big
mense, grace
messan, cur, lap-dog
monie, many
moss, bog
mottie, spotty

mou, mouth
mow, intercourse
mowe, (v) fuck
muckle, big

nae, no
naig, small horse, pony
nane, none
nappy, ale
natch, notching shears
neuk, corner
niest, next
nowte, cattle

onie, any
orra, spare
owthor, author

paitrick, partridge
pang, cram
pawkie, crafty, sly
penny-wheep, small beer
plack, small coin (4 pennies
  Scots), nothing worth
plaidie, woolen cloak
pliver, plover
pleugh-pettle, plough-scraper
plumrose, primrose
poind, seize goods and sell
  them under warrant
poortith, poverty
pou, pull
pouther, powder
puir, poor
prie, taste
propone, put forward
pussie, hare, puss (pejorative
  term for a woman)

quat, quit, leave
quean, young girl, hussy

quine, girl

raible, recite
rair, roar
ramfeezl'd, exhausted
ram-stam, reckless, headstrong
randie, riotous
rant, roister
raploch, course, homely
raucle, sturdy
raxin, elastic
ream, froth
reck, heed
rede, advice
reek, smoke
reest, rest
rief, plunder
rigg, row
rin, run
ripp, handful of unthreshed
   corn
roger, fuck
rokelay, mantle
roosty, rusty
rowte, bellow
runt, stunted cabbage stalk
ruth, pity
ryke, reach

sae, so
sair, serve
sair, (adj.) sore, hard
saft, soft, silly
sark, chemise, shift
sarkit, clothed
saugh-woodies, ropes of
   twisted sallow-withes
saul, soul
saunt, saint
saut, salt
sax, six

shangan, cleft stick
shaw, small wood in a hollow
   place
shaw, (v) show
sheugh, ditch
shool, shovel
shure, reaped
sicker, sure, secure
sin', since
sinn, sun
skaith, harm
skiegh, skittish
skirl, shriek, yell
skouth, play
skyte, lash
slee, sly
sleekit, glossy-coated
snash, abuse, insolence
sned, prune, cut off
snell, bitter
snick, latch
snoove, go steadily on
sodger, soldier
sonse, luck
sonsie, good-natured, plump
souple, supple
sow'ns, sour puddings of
   oats and water
spail, splinter
speet, skewer
spence, parlour
splore, carousal
spunk, spark, spirit
spunkie, demon
stacher, stagger
stack, stuck
staggie, colt
stang, sting
stank, pool
staumrel, stammering, silly
staw, stole

steek, stitch
steer, molest
steerin, wagging
steer stook, set of corn
 sheaves placed on end in
 two rows, against each
 other, in the field
steeve, trim
sten', leap
stent, impost, duty
stey, steep
stirk, young bullock,
stot, young bullock
stoure, battle, tumult,
storm, dust
stowlins, stealthily
stowp, cup
strang, strong
straught, straight
streight, straight
strunt, strut
strunt, liquor
studdie, anvil
Suthron, Englishmen
 (southerners)
swaird, sward
swank, agile
swatch, sample
swats, new small beer
swinge, flog
swoor, swore
syne, then

tak, take
tangs, tongs
tapetless, heedless, foolish
tap-pickle, grain at end
 of cornstalk
tapsalteerie, topsy-turvy
tarry-breeks, nickname for
 a sailor

tauld, told
tent, care
tentie, prudent
thae, those
thairm, fiddle-string
thairms, catguts
theekit, thatched
thig, beg
thole, endure, suffer
thrang, crowd, press of people
thrang, (adv.) busily, earnestly
thraw, twist, turn
threap, argue obstinately
thretten, thirteen
thrum, spin
till, to
timmer, timber, trees
tinkler, tinker
tint, lost
tippenny, twopenny beer
to-fa', falling-to, beginning (of
 night)
toop, tup
touzie, shaggy
trogger, pedlar
trow, trust
tway, two
towsing, ruffling
toy, cap
trig, smart
tulzie, quarrel, contest, brawl
twa, two
'twad, it would
twin, deprive
twissle, twist, wrench
tyke, dog
tythe, tenth

unco, odd, strange

vera, very

vittle, food

wabster, weaver
wad, wager
wad, would
wae, sad
waefu, woeful
waft, weft in a web
wale, choice, best
wame, belly, stomach
wark, work
warklum, *wark-lume*, tool, penis
warl, world
warsle, wrestle, struggle
wast, west know
wauken, waken
waukit, calloused
waukrife, wakeful
waur, worse
wawlie, handsome
wean, child
weel, well
weet, wet

westlin, westerly
whalpit, whelped
whare, where
whiles, sometimes
whitter, draught of litter
whittle, knife
whunstane, whinstone
whyles, sometimes
whittle, knife
wi, with
wimble, gimlet, *fig.* phallus
winnock, window
winsome, comely
wooer-babs, love-knots
wyliecoat, flannel vest

yestreen, last night
yett, gate
yeuk, itch
yill, ale
yill-caup, ale-cup
yird, earth
yowie, ewe-lamb

General Index

Index of Poems